Cognitive Neuroscience of Natural Language Use

When we think of everyday language use, the first things that come to mind include colloquial conversations, reading and writing emails, sending text messages or reading a book. But can we study the brain basis of language as we use it in our daily lives? As a topic of study, the cognitive neuroscience of language is far removed from these language-in-use examples. However, recent developments in research and technology have made studying the neural underpinnings of naturally occurring language much more feasible. In this book a range of international experts provide a state-of-the-art overview of current approaches to making the cognitive neuroscience of language more 'natural' and closer to language use as it occurs in real life. The chapters explore topics including discourse comprehension, the study of dialogue, literature comprehension and the insights gained from looking at natural speech in neuropsychology.

ROEL WILLEMS is a senior researcher at the Donders Institute for Brain, Cognition and Behaviour and Max Planck Institute for Psycholinguistics, Nijmegen, The Netherlands.

Cognitive Neuroscience of Natural Language Use

Edited by

Roel M. Willems

CAMBRIDGE
UNIVERSITY PRESS

CAMBRIDGE
UNIVERSITY PRESS

University Printing House, Cambridge CB2 8BS, United Kingdom

Cambridge University Press is part of the University of Cambridge.

It furthers the University's mission by disseminating knowledge in the pursuit of education, learning and research at the highest international levels of excellence.

www.cambridge.org
Information on this title: www.cambridge.org/9781107042018

First published 2015

Printed in the United Kingdom by Clays, St Ives plc

A catalogue record for this publication is available from the British Library

Library of Congress Cataloguing in Publication data
Cognitive neuroscience of natural language use / edited by Roel M. Willems.
p. ; cm.
Includes bibliographical references and index.
ISBN 978-1-107-04201-8 (hardback)
1. Biolinguistics. 2. Neurolinguistics. 3. Language and languages – Origin. 4. Natural language processing. I. Willems, Roel M., 1980– , editor. [DNLM: 1. Language. 2. Cognition – physiology. 3. Neuropsychology. P 107]
P132.C64 2014
401–dc23

2014032247

ISBN 978-1-107-04201-8 Hardback

Contents

Plates

The color plate section appears between pages 114 and 115

Figures

Contributors

CARSTEN ALLEFELD Bernstein Center for Computational Neuroscience Berlin, Charité–Universitätsmedizin Berlin, Berlin, Germany and Berlin Center of Advanced Neuroimaging, Charité–Universitätsmedizin Berlin, Berlin, Germany

SILKE ANDERS Department of Neurology, University of Lübeck, Lübeck, Germany

MICHAEL ANDRIC Center for Mind/Brain Sciences (CIMeC), University of Trento, Trento (TN), Italy

SHARON ASH Department of Neurology, Perelman School of Medicine of the University of Pennsylvania, Philadelphia, PA, USA

MARK BLOKPOEL Donders Institute for Brain, Cognition and Behaviour, Radboud University Nijmegen, Nijmegen, The Netherlands

GIOVANNA EGIDI Center for Mind/Brain Sciences (CIMeC), University of Trento, Trento (TN), Italy

MURRAY GROSSMAN Department of Neurology, Perelman School of Medicine of the University of Pennsylvania, Philadelphia, PA, USA

URI HASSON Center for Mind/Brain Sciences (CIMeC), The University of Trento, Trento (TN), Italy

JOHN-DYLAN HAYNES Berlin School of Mind and Brain, Humboldt-Universität zu Berlin, Berlin, Germany, Bernstein Center for Computational Neuroscience Berlin, Charité – Universitätsmedizin Berlin, Berlin, Germany and Berlin Center of Advanced Neuroimaging, Charité–Universitätsmedizin Berlin, Berlin, Germany

ARTHUR M. JACOBS Neurocognitive Psychology, Free University of Berlin, Germany and Dahlem Institute for Neuroimaging of Emotion (D.I.N.E.), Berlin, Germany

PIA KNOEFERLE Cognitive Interaction Technology Excellence Center (CITEC), Bielefeld University, Germany

LINE BURHOLT KRISTENSEN Department of Scandinavian Studies and Linguistics, University of Copenhagen, Copenhagen S, Denmark and Center of Functionally Integrative Neuroscience, Aarhus University Hospital, Aarhus C, Denmark

ANNA K. KUHLEN Berlin School of Mind and Brain, Humboldt-Universität zu Berlin, Berlin, Germany, Bernstein Center for Computational Neuroscience Berlin, Charité–Universitätsmedizin Berlin, Berlin, Germany and Berlin Center of Advanced Neuroimaging, Charité–Universitätsmedizin Berlin, Berlin, Germany

CHRISTOPHER A. KURBY Grand Valley State University, Allendale, MI, USA

IRIS VAN ROOIJ Donders Institute for Brain, Cognition and Behaviour, Radboud University Nijmegen, Nijmegen, The Netherlands

JEREMY I. SKIPPER Division of Psychology and Language Sciences, University College London, London, UK

STEVEN L. SMALL Department of Neurology, University of California, Irvine School of Medicine, Irvine, CA, USA

ARJEN STOLK Donders Institute for Brain, Cognition and Behaviour, Radboud University Nijmegen, Nijmegen, The Netherlands

IVAN TONI Donders Institute for Brain, Cognition and Behaviour, Radboud University Nijmegen, Nijmegen, The Netherlands

MIKKEL WALLENTIN Center of Functionally Integrative Neuroscience, Aarhus University Hospital, Aarhus C, Denmark and Center for Semiotics, Aarhus University, Aarhus C, Denmark

ROEL M. WILLEMS Donders Institute for Brain, Cognition and Behaviour, Radboud University Nijmegen, Nijmegen, The Netherlands and Max Planck Institute for Psycholinguistics, Nijmegen, The Netherlands

JEFFREY M. ZACKS Washington University, St. Louis, MO, USA

Abbreviations

AD	Alzheimer's disease
aI	anterior insula
aIPS	anterior intraparitel sulcus
Amy	amygdala
ANEW	Affective Norms for English Words
ANS	autonomic nervous system
AOS	apraxia of speech
AROM	associative read-out models
aTL	anterior temporal lobe
BA	Brodmann area
BAWL	Berlin Affective Word List
BIASLESS	Biasless Identification of Activated Sites by Linear Evaluation of Signal Similarity
BOLD	blood-oxygenation-level dependent
bvFTD	behavioral variant frontotemporal dementia
CBS	corticobasal syndrome
dACC	dorsal anterior cingulate cortex
DCM	dynamic causal modelling
DEF	definitive
DMN	default-mode network
dmPFC	dorsomedial prefrontal cortex
DoA	Dictionary of Affect
dPCC	dorsal posterior cingulate cortex
EEG	electroencephalography
ELN	extended language network
ERP	event-related potential
EST	event segmentation theory
FA	fractional anisotropy
FAS	verbal fluency test using the letters F, A, S
FFG	fusiform gyrus
fMRI	functional magnetic resonance imaging
fNIRS	functional near-infra red spectroscopy

FPC	frontopolar cortex
FTD	frontotemporal dementia
fvFTD	frontal variant frontotemporal dementia
FWE	family-wise error
FWHM	full width at half maximum
GLM	general linear model
GM	gray matter
HRV	heart rate variability
IAPS	International Affective Picture System
ICA	independent components analysis
IFG	inferior frontal gyrus
IFGOp	inferior frontal gyrus, pars opercularis
IFGOr	inferior frontal gyrus, pars orbitalis
IFGTr	inferior frontal gyrus, pars triangularis
IPL	inferior parietal lobule
ISC	inter-subject correlations
LBD	Lewy body disease
LBSD	Lewy body spectrum disorder
LH	left hemisphere
LIFG	left inferior frontal gyrus
lvPPA	primary progressive aphasia, logopenic variant
mCC	middle cingulate cortex
MEG	magnetoencephalography
MLU	mean length of utterance
MMSE	mini Mental State Examination
mPFC	medial prefrontal cortex
MR	magnetic resonance
MRI	magnetic resonance imaging
MROM	multiple read-out model
MT+	middle temporal complex
MTG	middle temporal gyrus
MVPA	multi-voxel pattern analysis
naPPA	primary progressive aphasia, non-fluent/agrammatic variant
NOLB	natural organization of language and the brain
NP	noun phrase
OLB	organization of language and the brain
OS	object–subject
OSV	object–subject–verb
OVS	object–verb–subject
PCG	precentral gyrus

PD	Parkinson's disease
PDD	Parkinson's disease with dementia
PFC	prefrontal cortex
PPA	primary progressive aphasia
PPI	psycho-physiological interactions
PRS	present tense
PSP	progressive supranuclear palsy
pSTS	poster superior temporal sulcus
REFL	reflexive
RH	right hemisphere
ROI	region of interest
RS	repetition suppression
rTMS	repetitive transcranial magnetic stimulation
SD	standard deviation
SEM	structural equation modeling
SFG	superior frontal gyrus
SII	secondary somatosensory cortex
SMA	supplementary motor area
SMG	supramarginal gyrus
SO	subject–object
SOA	stimulus onset asynchrony
SOV	subject–object–verb
SPL	superior parietal lobule
STG	superior temporal gyrus
STP	supratemporal plane
svPPA	primary progressive aphasia, semantic variant
TL	temporal lobe
ToM	Theory of Mind
TPJ	temporo-parietal junction
TS	time series
tvFTD	temporal variant frontotemporal dementia
VAR	vector autoregressive modelling
vmPFC	ventromedial prefrontal cortex
VP	verb phrase
vPMC	ventral premotor cortex
WM	white matter
wpm	words per minute

1 Cognitive neuroscience of natural language use: introduction

Roel M. Willems

The cognitive neuroscience of language investigates the neural infrastructure underlying the comprehension and production of language. When we think of language use in our daily lives, the first things that come to mind include colloquial conversations, the small chat on your way to work, reading and writing emails, sending text messages, reading a book. To the surprise of outsiders, the topic of study in the cognitive neuroscience of language is rather far removed from these language-in-use examples. There are well-founded (historical) reasons for this (see below), but the current excitement in the study of language comes from new developments that make studying the neural underpinnings of naturally occurring language much more feasible.

The chapters in this book provide a state of the art overview of current approaches to making the cognitive neuroscience of language more 'natural' in the sense of closer to language as it occurs in real life. Before giving an overview of the book's content, I will briefly introduce two strands of language research, that approaches in this book draw upon.

Two traditions of language research

Two research traditions in the study of language are important for present purposes.

(1) The controlled, simplified stimuli tradition

Research in this tradition is done in the laboratory, under controlled circumstances, presenting participants with carefully selected stimuli.

For instance, participants see single words presented on the screen and they have to decide as fast as possible whether the word is a noun or a verb. Or, participants listen to phonemes ('d' and 'b'), and the phonemes are manipulated to make the one sound more like the other. Task for the participant is to decide whether she hears a 'b' or a 'd'.

In this style of research, the researcher has tight control over experimental factors of interest, and potentially confounding factors ('nuisance variables') are taken care of. The drawback is that the setting is highly unnatural, and that the language that participants listen to is decontextualized.

This tradition dates back at least to the early days of reaction time experiments, notably the experiments in the laboratories of Wundt and Donders (e.g. Donders, 1869; see Levelt, 2012 for a historical overview). Sophistication in experimental design and analysis, and understanding of the cognitive processes underlying language, has increased enormously since then. However, the basic mode of working in this research tradition has remained the same: Careful isolation of a subprocess of language is studied under highly controlled conditions with decontextualized and simplified language stimuli.

(2) The ecological laboratory tradition

In this line of research, stimuli and situations are closer to language in real life. Research is usually done in a laboratory, but participants are much less restrained in their behaviour as in the other tradition.

For instance, pairs of participants come to the lab and they solve a problem (e.g. matching two shapes, as in a puzzle) together. One individual knows something about the problem that is important for the other one to be able to solve it. The focus of the research could be on how people adapt their gesturing or speaking to the amount of information that is shared between participants. The dependent variable in this line of research gets quantified (e.g. number of gesture elements), and often requires researcher-dependent coding ('What counts as a gesture?'). The flavour is much more towards naturalistic language use, at the expense of a loss of 'experimental control', meaning that there are more degrees of freedom for behaviour of the participant than in the other research tradition.

The first, controlled, tradition has been most popular in experimental psychology and cognitive neuroscience, and, although tremendously productive, its limits are starting to become more seriously considered. Simply put, there is a growing understanding that studying what happens when people read a single word or sentence, does not necessarily scale up to what we do when we understand natural language, say read an e-mail or talk with our neighbour.

Combining the two research traditions in studying the brain basis of language

The usual status quo is that the two research traditions are thought of as mutually exclusive. Increasing ecological validity comes at the cost of experimental control, and tightening experimental control decreases ecological validity. Hence, combining them is considered impossible. This is even more pertinent for studying the brain basis of language. Experimental constraints reduce the possibility of studying more natural language even further (e.g. participants cannot move in an MR scanner). The main starting point for this book is that there is no reason for such pessimism: recent studies have investigated natural language with cognitive neuroscience methods, and they have obtained much more encouraging results than one may expect from the standard 'impossible' reply.

This book brings together scholars who borrow from both research traditions, in order to come to a cognitive neuroscience of natural language use. The combination of research traditions is more obvious in some contributions than in others, but generally speaking there are two starting points:

First, the language investigated is 'natural language': language as it could be encountered by participants in the real world. This means contextualized, and in larger chunks than usually done (beyond word and single sentence level).

Second, experiments maintain tight experimental control, and use the tools of cognitive neuroscience in a creative manner to enable the study of naturalistic language.

However diverse the topics of the separate chapters are, together they make the case that using more naturalistic settings and stimuli is (a) possible while keeping experimental control, and (b) provides new insights into the cognitive neuroscience of language.

Why study the cognitive neuroscience of natural language use?

A commonly heard reply to pleas for cognitive neuroscience to 'go more natural' is: 'Why?' Why not stick to the syllables and single-word experiments, that we know how to do so well? What is the added value of using more natural stimuli, why make experiments unnecessarily complicated? A simplistic answer is that one should study one's topic of interest ('language') as close to real life as possible. Recent developments in data acquisition and analysis show that it is possible to stay closer to natural language, and still find interesting and interpretable results. This will not satisfy a skeptic who will reply that it is unnecessary to stay close to natural language, because one can extrapolate findings from well-controlled and simplified experiments to more natural language situations.

And here is where the better answer comes in: extrapolation from findings obtained in restrained lab settings to real life may be much less obvious than we think. In the visual (neuro)sciences, it is becoming more and more clear that some basic rules about visual perception, apply to perception in more natural settings only to a limited degree. An example case is visual search, where recent experiments show that the search rules discovered in controlled lab experiments, should be complemented by additional rules to explain visual search in more complex scenes (Wolfe, Võ, Evans & Greene, 2011). On a similar note, others have argued that the use of simplified and decontextualized stimuli has been an important hindrance in understanding the working of visual brain areas (Olshausen & Field, 2005), and studying the neural basis of visual perception with more natural and complex stimuli is currently an important topic in the visual neurosciences (e.g. Çukur, Nishimoto, Huth & Gallant, 2013; Peelen & Kastner, 2014).

This is not to say that findings obtained with controlled lab experiments, using simplified stimuli, are uninteresting. Quite the contrary, some of these findings will also apply to more natural settings, but to a more limited degree than thought by proponents of the controlled, simplified stimuli approach. As I will stress again in the concluding paragraph of this introduction, it is still too early days to appreciate whether and how studying more natural language use will change the landscape of cognitive neuroscience. But initial results are interesting and push towards a revision of some of our knowledge about language and the brain.

A final answer to the question 'Why study cognitive neuroscience of natural language?' is more obvious. Stepping up from single words and sentences allows to investigate the neural basis of for example narrative comprehension, face-to-face communication, event segmentation, etc. These are part of normal language use, but are often ignored in cognitive neuroscience because of the perceived difficulties in studying them. One message of the chapters in this book is that those difficulties can be overcome.

An issue that I have left aside so far is what counts as 'natural language' and what does not. This is done on purpose. What counts as natural language to the student of phonology will likely look like a much impoverished version of language to those with an anthropology background. What I think will not help the field forward is quarrelling about how natural the language under study has to be, or, even less productive, me providing a definition of 'natural language use'. It should be obvious from what I have written so far that natural language use refers to richer language stimuli than often used in lab experiments (less simplified), understood in richer contexts than is often the case. There will often be a tension between the degree of naturalness and the possibility of doing well-controlled and interpretable experiments. No hard rules can be given on how to strike the balance between the two, and researchers will have to decide what they find the optimal balance for themselves.

Overview of chapters

The chapters in this volume can all be read as stand alone, and are grouped thematically only loosely. Each chapter starts with a brief abstract to orient the reader, and emphasis has been put on readability to a broad readership. All chapters are a combination of overview of recent experimental work, and opinion by the authors. Speculation was not discouraged, making the chapters well suited as starting points for discussion.

In Chapter 2, **Andric** and **Small** give an overview of methods and techniques used in fMRI studies that use more natural language stimuli than is usually done. Such experiments ask for unorthodox analysis methods, and the state of the art is reviewed in this chapter. In Chapter 3, **Ash** and **Grossman** provide a coherent overview of their substantial neuropsychological (patient) work on natural speech production. Using speech elicitation methods such as narrative retellings, their work illustrates the powerful combination of exact characterization of the deficits in natural speech production and measures of neural impairments in a variety of patient populations. In Chapter 4, **Kurby** and **Zacks** describe behavioural and neural studies that give insight into how readers construct and update situation models during narrative and discourse comprehension. The study of situation models is a nice example of a question that can by definition only be asked using stimuli which go beyond the word or sentence level, and the chapter illustrates the explanatory power of cognitive neuroscience in investigating this issue. In Chapter 5, **Knoeferle** shows how studying language comprehension can be enriched by taking non-linguistic (visual) context into account. Listeners quickly use visual information when available, extending the scope of traditional research beyond the study of isolated language stimuli. In Chapter 6, **Skipper** introduces his model of the Natural Organization of Language and the Brain, a model specifically designed to understand the neural instantiation of natural language comprehension. In Chapter 7, **Jacobs** sketches a neurocognitive model of an instance of natural language in optima forma, namely the reading of literature. Drawing upon insights from literary science, as well as on findings from experimental studies, he outlines what a model of literary reading looks like, providing an important theoretical basis for future work. In Chapter 8, **Kristensen** and **Wallentin** add novel insights into the debated role of Broca's area in language production and comprehension. They focus specifically on the influence of context, an often neglected but important factor in understanding how this part of cortex adds to language, as is evidenced by their overview. In Chapter 9, **Kuhlen, Allefeld, Anders** and **Haynes** look into the growing literature on the cognitive neuroscience of dialogue. The chapter shows what has been established from studying brain signals from two people while they are in dialogue, and what remains to be done. In Chapter 10, **Stolk, Blokpoel, van Rooij** and **Toni** illustrate how studying brain activation while participants play a novel communication game, provides new insights into the neural basis of our communicative abilities. They moreover present a model for human referential communication, which – while based on studies that did not employ linguistic codes – has implications for our understanding of communication by linguistic means as well. Finally, in Chapter 11, **Hasson** and **Egidi** outline how processes at higher levels of language comprehension (e.g. discourse comprehension) can be understood in terms of more basic neural processes. They warn against misinterpretation of studies into natural language comprehension, and provide guidelines that should inform future studies of natural language comprehension.

Away from the sterile

In preparation of this chapter, I came across the following quotation, that I much sympathise with:

> that gradually, more and more scientific psychologists were willing to abandon the somewhat sterile environment of nonsense syllables and other laboratory-produced elements, for the study of objects less removed from real life. (De Groot, 1946, p. 56; transl. RW)[1]

This quote from renowned chess psychologist Adriaan de Groot's doctoral dissertation (*Thought and Choice in Chess*) voices a struggle that every student of language has to face. How close do you stay to real life when translating your topic of interest into a testable experiment? De Groot's solution was 'guided introspection', a methodology made popular by the Würzburg school in psychology (see Levelt, 2012), and one that most current psychologists would frown upon.

What I like about the original wording is the use of 'sterile': De Groot speaks about the 'sterile environment of nonsense syllables and other

[1] The original Dutch: 'dat gaandeweg steeds meer wetenschappelijke psychologen bereid bleken de ietwat steriel geworden sfeer van de zinlooze lettergrepen en andere alleen in het laboratorium te isoleeren 'elementen' te verlaten voor excursies naar minder levensvreemde gebieden' (De Groot, 1946, p. 56).

A digital copy of the English version of this lovely book (*Thought and Choice in Chess*) is freely available from the Amsterdam University Press website.

laboratory-produced elements'. Just like a surgeon who sterilizes his equipment before surgery, we have sterilized language by stripping off unwanted elements, until we end up with purely controlled language stimuli such as nonsense syllables.

The difference is that the surgeon has good reason to sterilize his equipment. After all it is not his purpose to understand what bacteria exist and how they grow, he needs to get rid of them, full stop. Students of language, on the contrary, lose something when they sterilize their material. They lose the capacity to understand language as it is in reality, dirty and complicated. It is my hope that the chapters in this book will help in re-establishing the cognitive neuroscience of language, away from the sterile.

References

Çukur, T., Nishimoto, S., Huth, A. G. & Gallant, J. L. (2013). Attention during natural vision warps semantic representation across the human brain. *Nature Neuroscience*, *16*(6), 763–770. doi:10.1038/nn.3381

De Groot, A. D. (1946). *Het denken van den schaker*. Amsterdam: Noord-Hollandse Uitgevers Maatschappij.

Donders, F. C. (1869 / 1969). On the speed of mental processes. *Acta Psychologica*, *30*, 412–431.

Levelt, W. J. M. (2012). *A History of Psycholinguistics: The Pre-Chomskyan Era*. Oxford University Press.

Olshausen, B. A. & Field, D. J. (2005). How close are we to understanding v1? *Neural Computation*, *17*(8), 1665–1699. doi:10.1162/0899766054026639

Peelen, M. V. & Kastner, S. (2014). Attention in the real world: toward understanding its neural basis. *Trends in Cognitive Sciences*. doi:10.1016/j.tics.2014.02.004

Wolfe, J. M., Võ, M. L.-H., Evans, K. K. & Greene, M. R. (2011). Visual search in scenes involves selective and nonselective pathways. *Trends in Cognitive Sciences*, *15*(2), 77–84. doi:10.1016/j.tics.2010.12.001

2 fMRI methods for studying the neurobiology of language under naturalistic conditions

Michael Andric & Steven L. Small

Abstract People ordinarily use language in complex, continuously occurring contexts. These contexts include rich and varied sources of information that can combine and exert shared influence. A common example is face-to-face conversation. When two people talk in person, there is not only spoken auditory information, but also visual information from facial and manual movements, as well as from the surrounding environment in which the conversation takes place. There may also be endogenous signals that a person experiences in context, such as memories relating prior conversations with a given speaker. In short, it is typical that a person mediates multiple multifaceted information sources when using language. By contrast, fMRI studies of the neurobiology of language often use conditions that present only features of language in isolation. In large part, this is because researchers need rigorous, reliable experimental protocols that minimize potential sources of variance ("noise") not directly relating a feature of interest. But such traditional protocols also often minimize, if not eliminate, the way people actually know and use language in their naturalistic, "everyday" experience. Thus, a fundamental challenge for researchers studying the neurobiology of language is to understand brain function as it might occur in typical experience. In this chapter, we highlight some available approaches that can address this challenge using fMRI. With specific examples, we discuss the importance of context and ways to incorporate it in understanding brain function when people process language under more naturalistic conditions.

Introduction

People ordinarily use language in rich and varied contexts, continuously mediating information from diverse sources. This includes information a person perceives in the external world, as well as from his or her own internal states and processes. Moreover, these sources typically combine in exerting shared influence. For example, when two people talk face-to-face, they might each focus on the other's vocalizations, facial and manual movements, and the meanings these convey. Understanding brain processes as they relate these features is an important area in neuroimaging research, and numerous studies have aimed experimentally to characterize the neural bases of such context effects.

However, naturalistic experience – or "everyday life" – typically presents many information sources in continuous, complex combinations. In other words, it is rare, if ever the case, that people encounter a feature of language in isolation, as they do in experimental settings. Whether or not the entire amount of contextual information is directly relevant to a particular conversation's meanings or effects, it is present nonetheless. For example, imagine a face-to-face conversation on a busy street corner, where there is ongoing audiovisual information from passersby, automobile traffic, and other diverse sources. Also present are a person's internal ongoing signals – anything from their remembering that the person with whom they are talking is known for telling lies, to the indigestion from something they just ate – that can also influence the way a person interprets what their conversational partner says. Such complex rich natural settings are not ideal for isolating a controlled variable. Yet it is these kinds of settings in which people actually know and use language on a regular basis.

Certainly, rigorous experimental protocols require controlled variables. To determine an effect for a given feature of interest, researchers typically seek to minimize influence from potentially surrounding sources of non-interest ("noise" variance). But this necessity contrasts with naturally occurring contexts, which inherently comprise diverse, dynamic, and interacting information. This contrast among settings poses a great challenge for researchers: as a researcher, how is it possible to study language and these myriad sources of information in the way people actually use and experience them, yet at the same time employ experimental methods that are reliable and valid, and that ultimately yield informative results?

Increasingly, fMRI researchers acknowledge this challenge. Recently developed fMRI protocols better address natural experience than was possible previously. Some research now incorporates stimuli and methods that give and use contextual information, i.e., information that surrounds a feature of primary interest, rather than going to great lengths to minimize it. Importantly, results from these efforts are proving informative. This is not just because these results uniquely characterize ways that the brain functions. It is also because such results characterize ways that the brain functions under experimental conditions that people recognize – that better generalize to people's actual use and experiences – than has been typical in earlier fMRI studies.

In this chapter, we outline and discuss several approaches and methods for language fMRI research that move towards maintaining rigorous and reliable experimental methods in protocols that, at least partly, resemble people's typical naturalistic language experiences. First, for perspective, we briefly highlight a number of mainstream findings in language fMRI, along with the traditional experimental designs used to acquire them. Next, we reiterate the importance of context in studying brain and language, as well as their accompanying features. We then highlight more recent studies. Our focus is on investigations that use methodological approaches that allow analysis of data acquired under stimulus conditions that resemble naturalistic, everyday situations. To convey the accessibility of these approaches, we discuss – over multiple sections of this chapter – specific examples of these methodologies. Finally, we conclude by summarizing and looking ahead to the utility of fMRI in future studies that seek to understand language function in naturalistic contexts.

Early findings and the methods they use

As a whole, fMRI characterizations of the functional anatomy of language encompass a large scope. In large part, this is because language affords many levels of processing, with many diverse questions that fMRI can help answer. For example, questions are asked about brain responses at multiple levels, from discourse, to words and sentences, to syllables and phonemes. Within just these linguistic levels, further specificity of analysis can be performed. For example, a topic of recent interest for fMRI research is whether processing action words involves responses that might be present when people perform those actions (see Pulvermuller, 2005). There is also much research focusing on brain function when people perceive actions that accompany and convey meaning with language, as with "co-speech gestures" (for review, see Andric & Small, 2012; Willems & Hagoort, 2007). Even such "higher-level" aspects as brain encodings for semantic concepts represent an active research area (see Binder *et al.*, 2009). Not only for receptive language, questions that focus on brain function when people produce language also branch into many categories and levels of analysis. Put simply, the dimensions, questions, and analyses of brain processes that can classify as "language" are broad, numerous, and multifaceted.

Interestingly, as diverse as the questions and angles from which people examine language are, to this point, the fMRI protocols and analyses researchers use are generally uniform, comprising relatively few techniques. In the following, we highlight some of the earlier questions and findings from language fMRI studies, and briefly discuss some of the common approaches researchers use to derive such findings.

Basic responses Early language fMRI studies provide an important basis for current work, giving insight into fundamental issues and properties of brain function when people process language. At the same time, since such studies were at the forefront of functional brain imaging research in language, they were frequently motivated by results from classic lesion-based studies. This includes those by Broca (1861) and Wernicke (1874/1977), from which parts of inferior frontal and lateral temporal cortex, respectively, gain standing as seemingly crucial structures for the way the brain normally implements language processes. Many early fMRI studies thus proceed from this basis, with a focus on refining and elaborating our knowledge of the functional significance and roles of these areas.

It is import to consider, however, that the classic lesion analysis (neuropsychological) approach can impart an underlying perspective, whereby a disrupted function is attributed to damage in a particular brain area. Such a perspective can suggest more of a one-to-one structure-to-function dependency than what may, in actuality, be a more comprehensive brain organization that involves a many-to-many structures-to-functions mapping. It has only been through functional neuroimaging that this latter view has been able to emerge. Yet in the early studies, a basic one-to-one assumption carries through, in which identifying a function (rather than many ongoing functions) for a particular area in a given task satisfies the explicit investigative purpose.

Because of their importance in classic language models, the inferior frontal gyrus and superior temporal gyrus (posteriorly), particularly on the left, receive a lot of attention in early language fMRI studies. For example, one early study characterizes "virtually the entire inferior frontal gyrus" as active when people hear a noun that names an animal ("turtle") and decide whether that animal is both "native to the United States" and "used by humans" (Binder *et al.*, 1997). However, these authors also describe activity in adjoining superior and middle frontal gyri, large parts of lateral and ventral temporal cortices, the angular gyrus, as well as parts of the posterior cingulate, and precuneus (Binder *et al.*, 1997). Thus, even in early fMRI findings, activity for language tasks appears widespread across the brain, implicating more than just inferior frontal or lateral temporal regions.

Certainly, one of fMRI's advantages as a research tool is its spatial resolution, allowing researchers to investigate brain function at a relatively fine scale. Results from fMRI thus also regularly differentiate responses between sub-regions of more gross designations like "inferior frontal" or "lateral temporal." Researchers regularly attribute responses from particular sub-regions. In the inferior frontal cortex, this includes pars opercularis (IFGOp), pars triangularis (IFGTr), and pars orbitalis (IFGOr). At this level of description, results often implicate anterior inferior frontal regions when people make semantic judgments. For example, researchers have been able to distinguish IFGTr activity when people determine a word's semantic basis as concrete or abstract (Friederici, Opitz, & Cramon, 2000) and IFGOr activity when people judge whether two sentences mean the same thing, despite using different words (Dapretto & Bookheimer, 1999). In contrast, when people determine a word's syntactic category (Friederici *et al.*, 2000) or judge whether two sentences that use different word order, or voice (active or passive), mean the same thing (Dapretto & Bookheimer, 1999), there is significant IFGOp activity.

Univariate activity maps In fact, many fMRI results distinguish functional brain regions by tasks and analyses that seek to disentangle what researchers frame as selective responses. The most prevalent approach in fMRI studies is to use a general linear model (GLM) and derive a univariate activity map of brain function. This approach often follows a relatively straightforward logic: to profile where brain activity in one condition is stronger than in another, a researcher subtracts responses in one condition from responses in another. Researchers then often report their findings along the lines of "Activity in condition A is greater than in condition B, in brain region X. Therefore, there is a brain effect for this condition, with region X showing sensitivity to condition A." Characterizing results in this way is at the heart of many interpretations. However, this perspective may also be limiting, if not to a degree misleading.

Using only relative differences to mark an effect between conditions can limit subsequent interpretations as relative to those conditions. That is, the strength of their explanatory power is bound by the accuracy of those conditions used in eliciting responses for a function of interest. From a more technical standpoint, consider also that fMRI signals are not linear in relation to underlying neural signals (Logothetis *et al.*, 2001) and can vary in timing, amplitude, and shape across regions and subjects (Aguirre, Zarahn, & D'Esposito, 1998; *et al.*, 2000). Thus, a linearly differentiated group effect for a brain region, on the basis of simply subtracting one condition's responses from another across the whole-brain, likely excludes more comprehensive brain function. With this in mind, it is again important to consider that typical language use entails many ongoing processes that operate on many features. People do not normally encounter isolated properties, such as individual words, phonemes, or sentence fragments. Thus, a perspective that attributes a conditional difference to a particular brain region may unfairly narrow as isolated, marginal effects what are actually more comprehensive neurobiological processes.

Co-active regions as a "network" Similarly, researchers sometimes label a set of regions that are co-active for a given stimulus as a "network," without characterizing these regions' relationships, or interdependencies. If recognizing a network, formally, to involve links or interactions between units (e.g., brain regions), such labeling can be misleading. For example, in an audiovisual speech perception task, parts of the inferior frontal, parietal, and posterior temporal cortices may all show blood-oxygen-level dependent (BOLD) activity that exceeds a researcher's chosen threshold. Indeed, these regions may each be important when people perceive speech. Yet to label such a collection of co-active regions as a "network," without qualifying an interconnecting relationship among them, muddies the interpretation and nature of their potential mutual sensitivity.

Particularly, it is important to understand whether a set of co-active regions function cohesively or if they each index different properties. For example, it may be that each region is selective to different features present in the stimulus, e.g., one region may be sensitive to visual motion from the speaker's facial movements, whereas another region's responses are to the spoken contents in speech. Alternatively, a given feature in the stimulus may evoke responses in a region that then potentiates further downstream responses in those other regions with which it commonly interacts, functioning as an interconnected circuit. Thus, labeling a co-activity profile as a "network" can imply common interconnectivity among regions for which this might not necessarily be the case.

Seed-based functional connectivity To quantify functional links between brain areas in terms of their mutual importance for a given task – or its absence, in the resting state – a popular method for fMRI researchers is a functional connectivity analysis. These analyses typically calculate whether areas, or points, in the brain share a statistical relationship. Moreover, these statistical relationships are often based on functional response covariances across different brain areas, or the correlation strength between time series' responses.

In many cases, functional connectivity analyses anchor from a "seed," i.e., a time series from a specified voxel or region. This seed is typically chosen by the researcher, based on some experimental question and previously known structure/function relationships. It is not directly measured with a scanner or recording instrument. For example, a seed might be an average time series over all voxels from a chosen region of interest, itself functionally or anatomically defined. The analysis typically proceeds to correlate that seed series with that from every other voxel or brain area, or, in a further simplified version, between other derived times series that represent other regions. After significance thresholding and clustering, the typical resulting brain map then depicts links (degrees of correlation) between the seed and other brain regions.

This type of functional connectivity approach appears to better approximate network attributes than, for example, simply labeling co-active regions a "network." But its utility is still limited in terms of characterizing comprehensive network structures. Notably, a single seed narrows this approach's potential to describe interconnectivity as it extends beyond units with direct relationships to the seed. For example, network nodes (or brain areas) that follow secondary or tertiary links (paths) from a seed would not necessarily correlate past a chosen threshold. Thus, in this case the "network" might include only those areas with similar phase dynamics to the seed.

Moving forward with context and everyday information

Having highlighted past findings and experimental approaches that lay a foundation for language fMRI research as it moves forward, we now elaborate some of these newer directions with examples. Particularly, our focus is on methods that acknowledge and allow use of more naturalistic stimuli. That is, we describe methods that better allow researchers to put participants in experimental situations that more closely approximate everyday situations, presenting multifaceted, ongoing information sources. But we begin by first providing a basis for these directions and discussing the importance of "context."

Considering context Context can be taken to mean many things. Here, we focus on context in terms of two aspects that are particularly important for language fMRI research. The first is exogenous context, which includes information sources, i.e., externally or internally originating inputs, that people perceive and interact with, and that inform everyday experience. The second is endogenous context, involving the diverse, interactive brain structures and functions that participate in comprehension, and which McIntosh (2000) refers to as a "neural context." Neural context comprises the interactive and interconnected spatio-temporal properties of neural processes as they dynamically interact and function in a many-to-many (network) relationship of brain nodes to behavioral functions.

In terms of exogenous (or environmental) context, information from the environment (broadly construed) continuously embeds people's experiences. Such experiences as they typically occur in perceptually rich, complex (everyday) scenarios, are shaped by multiple, ongoing sources of information sources (inputs). People engage these ongoing inputs and process them in dynamic ways that cohere and carry meaning.

One example that illustrates people's routine experience with multiple ongoing inputs is interpersonal conversation, particularly as it involves non-verbal features such as co-speech gestures. These gestures are hand and arm actions that people regularly produce and perceive when they communicate in spoken language (Goldin-Meadow, 2003; McNeill, 1992, 2005). For example, a person might say, "I just hurried home," while pointing their index and middle fingers down and wiggling them back and forth. In this case, the speaker's words express only so much. But the gesture says more: it conveys walking. Moreover, such conversational experiences in context also typically involve additional information and not necessarily deriving solely from immediate inputs. For example, the observer in this example might also incorporate previous knowledge that the person they are talking with planned to go to the grocery store. In this case, then, the observer understands not only that the speaker went to the store, but, by the speaker's hand gestures, that s/he walked there. People regularly convey and construe meaning in such instances, by which multiple information sources, in continuous contexts, cohere and connect.

In terms of endogenous or "neural" context, the brain works by interaction. Extensive fiber pathways course throughout the brain to connect both distant and local neural units. At multiple levels – between neurons, populations of neurons, regions – the brain's interactions modulate and influence processes in other units. Moreover, this massive interconnectivity is most likely integral for common behavioral and cognitive functions, as information interacts with dynamic consequences.

As discussed by McIntosh (2000), such neural context is integral for typical cognitive processes, which require processing of multiple, interactive information sources. These higher-level processes such as language comprehension or production have their mechanistic basis in neural interactions that enable binding and coherence of signals that are sensitive to different types of information. These neural interactions appear to involve reciprocal and semi-redundant connectivity (Tononi & Sporns, 2003) and distributed networks (Mesulam, 1990). Indeed, a topic of much recent discussion concerns exactly which potential fiber pathways might be particularly important for language (see Dick & Tremblay, 2012 for review).

At the same time, it is important to recognize that this emphasis on distributed, interactive properties does not aim to minimize the importance also of the brain's regional specializations. Rather, it warrants fuller examination, particularly considering that "regional specialization is, in part, determined by the connectivity of the area," with "functional relevance that cannot be realized unless it operates in conjunction with other parts of the brain" (McIntosh, 2000, p. 868).

It is thus important to map and try to understand those brain parts and properties that respond to particular features. Yet it is also crucial to do so with experimental contexts that, to whatever extent possible, reflect inputs of interest, as people typically process them in rich naturalistic settings.

The most commonly used methods in fMRI research often make it difficult to map response selectivity to features as people process them in context. However, some recent methods have begun to address this. In the following sections, we highlight techniques that facilitate use of more naturalistic stimulus environments, allowing researchers to examine task-dependent and resting state BOLD responses in context.

Determining responses to events in naturalistic stimuli From continuous streams of information, people recognize meaningful boundaries and events. However, the way that people mark events can vary along numerous dimensions, especially in context, with continuous information. For example, if you were to ask a basketball novice watching a game, "How'd they score?", that person might mark the event only by a ball going through a hoop. In contrast, a basketball expert could respond to the same question with details as to what play was run and player movements that unfold over multiple time courses. While both perspectives fit the event, one includes finer details while the other conveys a broader whole. Nonetheless, people mark what commonly qualifies as the same event, but by different feature sets from continuous sequences.

Conversely, people may also process the same sets of occurrences as different events. Again, in the above scenario: to the basketball expert, "the score" may involve a comprehensive set of occurrences, whereas the novice would not recognize all the constituent parts and features as coherent. Thus, there are various ways that people's perceptions of events, especially in continuous, everyday sequences operate in context.

Since people regularly understand meaningful events from continuous information, it is important to understand and characterize brain functions that implement the needed process. In the following, we discuss two approaches for fMRI research that examine people's brain responses to language phenomena in continuous naturalistic input. The first approach uses people's subjective impressions of the relevant phenomena in a post hoc analysis of the continuous input. The second approach uses an external characterization of the input stream in a data-driven analysis. Nonetheless, both allow systematic study of people's responses to events, as they process continuous, more naturalistic information.

Subjective segmentation Given that people perceive ongoing events by different features, and distinguish them from each other by event boundaries, many current methods for modeling BOLD responses to events in experimentally controlled stimuli prove difficult. This is because such methods typically use a fixed predictor model of events, which are separated clearly from one another by time periods containing little relevant information, against which a researcher can assess brain function. More naturalistic stimuli and contexts – those that include numerous, diverse, continuous information sources – make this a challenge. In the least, the more information sources a stimulus carries, the more available features there are to which a person might respond. In other words, diverse complexity in the stimuli allows that participants may vary in the ways they perceive features or factors, sometimes apart from what a researcher seeks to examine.

Zacks *et al.* (2001) use an approach for characterizing brain function for event processing that inverts this potential problem. Crucially, they point out that "event segmentation is subject to individual differences and is hard to characterize by normative criteria" (Zacks *et al.*, 2001). In typical event-related fMRI analyses, an *a priori* model of events marks the time points at which events of interest occur in the stimuli. In contrast, Zacks *et al.* (2001) constructively use the way that participants subjectively perceive event boundaries in continuous stimuli. Simply, they ask the participants to mark and segment the events. It is these individual boundaries that the authors then use to model BOLD responses. Thus, their approach incorporates participant's subjective interpretations as to what marks an "event."

Generally, Zacks *et al.*'s (2001) approach proceeds as follows. First, in the fMRI scanner, participants passively watch continuous movie clips. These clips may show a person in a naturalistic, common activity, such as doing the dishes or making the bed. Participants then view the clips twice more. In one viewing, participants mark *coarse* events in the stimuli: those "largest units that seem natural and meaningful." In the other viewing, participants mark *fine* events: the "smallest natural meaningful units" (Zacks *et al.*, 2001). Each individual's annotations then inform the subsequent analytic models that the researchers use to assess their BOLD responses. In these models, the segment boundaries anchor 35-second intervals – 17.5 seconds before the mark and 17.5 seconds after. There is thus a window around the event that inherently accommodates potential lag and heterogeneous timing in the BOLD response. In a step that is familiar to many fMRI researchers, these individual level effects then propagate to second-level statistical analyses characterizing *coarse* and *fine* boundary-effects across the participant group.

Ultimately, this approach's utility arises from the way it deals with a potentially subversive issue in typical event-related analyses: variance in people's subjective perceptions. Rather than start with a single *a priori* model of events, a model that may not accurately reflect individual differences in event perception, this approach proceeds by valuing events that participants perceive and then examines responses to them. In this way, people's subjective perceptions become integral to the analytic procedure, instead of a potentially subversive source of variability.

Another more recent method also inverts a potential problem to examine people's responses to events within naturalistic, continuous stimuli. The second approach differs from this one just described in that it does not use people's varying, subjective perceptions to inform the analytic model. In contrast, this other approach uses the varying surrounding sources of information in the stimuli to identify points in the BOLD response that show selective changes to events of interest.

Peaks and valleys in the BOLD response In a face-to-face conversation, people encounter enormous amounts of diverse, continuous ongoing and embedded information. At its minimum, this involves auditory and visual information from one speaker to another. An observer can focus on a speaker's vocalizations, but further auditory sources from the surrounding environment are typically also present. Likewise, an observer may visually perceive a speaker's face, arm, and hand movements, including eye movements and facial gestures, as these accompany what the speaker says. In addition, there is further sensory information in the surrounding environment that embeds the conversational setting. Thus, an observer must mediate ample diverse, interrelatable information sources in context.

In an fMRI experiment, Skipper *et al.* (2009) demonstrate that diverse, surrounding contextual information can be useful for determining responses to a feature or event of interest within continuous, naturalistic stimuli. Typically, in brain imaging experiments, there is an emphasis on an inverse methodology: researchers determine responses to a particular event by trying to individuate the information of interest, often isolating its presentation to participants. In contrast, the method we describe here identifies systematic fluctuations in the BOLD response by their evaluation against responses that occur outside those points of interest, to other features throughout the presentation of stimuli.

In their study, Skipper *et al.* (2009) use a "peak and valley analysis" to analyze the fMRI time series (TS) data. These "peaks" and "valleys" in the BOLD TS correspond to those points where the response changes magnitude, as it inflects higher ("peak") and lower ("valley"), from the points immediately prior to them in the TS. They use this method to assess whether there is a systematic relation between peaks and valleys in participants' BOLD TS responses and features that occur in the stimuli.

Similar to Zacks *et al.* (2001), Skipper *et al.*'s analysis is useful for analyzing responses to stimulations that unfold over continuous epochs, such as during videos that depict a person in naturally occurring activities. For example, Skipper *et al.* present participants with audiovisual videos in which a woman retells adaptations of Aesop's fables.

This peak-and-valley analysis includes the following: first, the authors preprocess the fMRI TS to remove potential noise signals, i.e., signals that might index sources of non-interest, including those that associate motion artifacts. From these "clean" TS, they split and then concatenate segments corresponding to each condition's presentation. From these clean series for each condition, they next extract TS for voxels in anatomical regions of interest that show activity above a certain level in any one of their four experimental conditions. (Note: the voxel-level significance they use here corresponds to activity found in a separate, prior analysis.) For each condition, they then average the voxel TS in each region, across participants, establishing one representative series for each region, in each condition. Skipper *et al.* then identify the peaks and valleys in each of these representative series.

To identify peaks and valleys for each region, in each condition, Skipper *et al.* (2009) calculate the second derivative of the TS to first find the peaks. They then fit gamma functions (approximating a hemodynamic function) to each peak and use their full widths at half maximum (FWHM/2) to determine whether they temporally align to a feature of interest in the stimulus (e.g., a hand gesture, a particular word type, a phonological feature). Finally, to assess whether peaks and valleys in the series differentiate by features of interest in the stimuli, they use two-by-two contingency tables. Specifically, these two-by-two contingency tables evaluate the distribution of peaks and valleys against the presence or absence of a particular feature, e.g., gesture or no gesture, at each peaks and valleys. The work of Skipper *et al.* (2009) represents an analysis based in part on a general concept and related method described by Hasson *et al.* (2008) and Hasson *et al.* (2004) (see next section).

Using this approach, Skipper *et al.* (2009) identified particular regions that differentially respond to various features, as they occur throughout the naturalistic stimulus. For example, they identify a set of cortical areas that show "tuning" to instances when the actress in their videos performs meaningful hand gestures. Importantly, these meaningful gestures are not gross features the researchers present in isolation and to which observers receive instruction to follow. Rather, they are continuously, naturally, occurring features in the stimuli to which participants' BOLD responses, in passive viewing, show systematic selectivity.

Assessing correspondence without external predictors Usually fMRI analyses evaluate brain function by whether there is a significant statistical relationship between BOLD responses and an *a priori* predictor model. Researchers often create this model by convolving a gamma-shaped function, approximating a hemodynamic response, with temporal markers that correspond to points of interest (predictors) in the stimuli. Responses that deviate from this temporal predictor model then typically either comprise part of an assumed baseline or an error term, reflecting signal of non-interest ("noise"). However, such "error" responses may not necessarily be due to error – or trivial – with respect to their potential relation to a stimulus. That is, if responses vary in ways that do not systematically align with the predictor model, this deviance could be due to factors that are nevertheless systematic and informative. Particularly, an *a priori* predictor might not fully explain the relation between a particular stimulus and profile of brain function elicited by a stimulus. This is especially relevant if the stimulus carries diverse information that requires complex processes. Furthermore, a single predictor might miss potential inter-individual variability in brain responses. Indeed, hemodynamic responses can vary, both in their shape and timing, not only for different individuals but also for different brain areas (Aguirre *et al.*, 1998; Buckner, 1998). Thus, by its very nature, an external predictor model can fail to characterize important brain effects that might not be part of the prediction, muting a researcher's potential for discovery.

Intra-subject correlations To counter some of the potential limitations of evaluating BOLD responses against *a priori* predictor models, some fMRI methods instead focus on whether responses show systematic correlation, typically within or between individual participants. An early example of this is an approach by Levin and Uftring (2001) that they name "Biasless Identification of Activated Sites by Linear Evaluation of Signal Similarity" ("BIASLESS"). This approach does not rely on assumptions about the temporal or spatial characteristics of the hemodynamic response. Instead, it works from a premise that "the time course of signal in activated voxels will not vary significantly when an entire task protocol is repeated by the same individual" (Levin & Uftring, 2001).

Thus, Levin and Uftring (2001) use BIASLESS to evaluate the hemodynamic function for its systematic reproducibility over repeated experimental runs. In a study demonstrating this approach, participants perform an identical sequence of hand-clenching motor tasks in two consecutive runs. After preprocessing the functional time series to remove trend components and spatially register the series, they compute a correlation coefficient between the two series for each voxel. Levin and Uftring then assess significance by a twofold criterion of (i) selecting correlation coefficients above a chosen threshold, that (ii) group by a contiguous volumetric cluster size. Aside from their significance criteria, however, the key principle is this: rather than evaluate BOLD responses against an external predictor model, with the potential limitations it introduces (with "bias"), this BIASLESS method evaluates BOLD responses against themselves.

In other words, a predictor model might better reflect a researcher's explicit expectations (or biases) in relation to their own experimental interests than what the responses actually are for given a stimulus. In contrast, this BIASLESS approach seeks to evaluate responses by their systematic reproducibility. This principle also similarly emerges in one of the better-known studies to examine BOLD responses to natural stimuli, which we talk about next.

Inter-subject correlations Whereas the BIASLESS method focuses on within-participant correlations, a better-known method uses correlations between participants' responses in an innovative way. This method's development proceeds from a fundamental question: "Do we all see the world in the same way?" (Hasson *et al.*, 2004). Thus, these researchers employ analyses to model BOLD responses not against an external predictor, but against other participants' responses.

Hasson *et al.* (2004) develop an fMRI analysis approach that examines to what extent different people exhibit the same brain responses during passive ("free") viewing of the same naturalistic stimuli. In a passive viewing task, the researchers show participants video clips from the classic film, *The Good, The Bad, and The Ugly*. After preprocessing to register, normalize, and smooth the fMRI data, the researchers measure inter-subject correlations (ISCs) in the following way: on a voxel-by-voxel basis, they use each participant's time series as a predictor of responses for every other participant's time series. Put another way, the researchers evaluate whether responses are systematic across repeated viewings. However, rather than repeated viewings *within* a participant, as Levin and Uftring (2001) apply, repeated viewings in this analysis are *between* participants. A subsequent transformation of ISC values to z-scores then permits the researchers to evaluate coefficients in parametric statistical analyses. In this way, the researchers are able to identify brain areas that show statistically significant synchronization across participants.

To then further evaluate whether features in the stimuli relate to synchronous responses across participants, Hasson *et al.* (2004) use a reverse correlation method. For this procedure, the researchers take the average time series from a region of interest, remove the non-specific temporal fluctuation component from that series, then temporally mark places in the series where there are peaks. Those times at which peaks occur serve as the times to which the researchers identify what was occurring in the movie. For example, their resulting findings show activation peaks in the fusiform gyrus when there is a face prominently visible in the movie, and in the postcentral gyrus when there is a hand performing a motor task.

Thus, Hasson *et al.* (2004) succeed with this method in multiple ways. In one way, they are able to replicate deep-seated findings for the fusiform gyrus, despite a majority of those findings deriving from more traditional analyses. Yet, with their result for the postcentral gyrus, Hasson *et al.* (2004) also show their approach's potential for discovery of effects not previously well recognized in the literature, or that were anticipated in their investigation. An important aspect of this result, particularly for the current topic of this chapter, is that this method is not just adequate for, but exemplified by, its use in analyzing data collected under conditions that more closely resemble those experienced in the natural world than in the laboratory.

Data-driven discovery These methods just described have the common feature that they do not rely on an external *a priori* predictor model. Instead, they derive results, largely, by assessing how responses within and between participants systematically correspond to each other. This underlying notion of "letting the data speak" by determining results from the inherent characteristics of a data set, rather than by its relation to an external predictor, carries further in other methods that categorize as "data-driven." These methods can help scientific discovery by diminishing a researcher's need (or opportunity) to intervene in the analysis pipeline with decisions that might bias findings. In effect, this also gives more room for discovery, as it can equally allow results that a researcher might not anticipate. This would be particularly applicable when a researcher has to examine responses collected under stimuli contexts that are complex, continuous, and naturalistic, i.e., for which *a priori* models may be unknown.

One prominent "data-driven" technique with use in numerous prior fMRI studies is independent component analysis (ICA). In fact, the use of ICA in fMRI is long-standing (e.g., Calhoun *et al.*, 2001; McKeown *et al.*, 1998). Yet its application in innovative ways is still developing (see Robinson & Schopf, 2013 and related articles in that special issue). Generally put, this method permits separating and identifying maximally independent sources from linearly mixed signals. As it applies in fMRI analyses, from a set of times series (e.g., a brain volume), ICA can help identify distinct temporal signals at spatially separable positions (e.g., anatomical locations, or sets of voxels). Moreover, it does not need *a priori* knowledge about those signals. This makes it well suited for cases where a researcher acquires data under conditions involving complex, multifaceted information such as those discussed in this chapter.

A study by Bartels and Zeki (2004) demonstrates the usefulness of this technique for analyzing BOLD responses to naturalistic stimuli, when the waveforms and anatomical locations of responses are unknown *a priori*. The authors' intent in using this approach was to "identify the sets of voxels belonging to each distinctly activated functional subdivision that has an inherently distinct [activity time course] and isolate them in a separate component" (Bartels & Zeki, 2004). In the study, participants while in the fMRI scanner viewed segments from a James Bond movie. During this "free-viewing" session, movie segments were shown in continuous epochs, each over the course of a few minutes. After preprocessing the fMRI data to register spatially, smooth, and temporally align the functional images, the authors applied ICA to a matrix containing the time series data at each acquisition for all voxels in the brain image. From this procedure, they were able to derive spatially distinct components, each with an associated time course.

Without explicit *a priori* knowledge of the spatial and temporal activation dynamics that would result from "free-viewing," it is up to the researchers to determine which resulting components are meaningful. To frame it another way, just as ICA can be useful for identifying components that relate to noise artifacts in fMRI data (e.g., McKeown *et al.*, 2005; Tohka *et al.*, 2008), conversely, it is important also to be able to recognize components of interest.

In this particular study, Bartels and Zeki (2004) were able to evaluate components in a systematic way by working from their predication that the stimuli would evoke similar brain responses in the same brain areas across participants. First, they screen components by their anatomical similarity, then by their temporal correspondence across participants. To determine correspondence across participants, they test components time courses both for pairwise inter-subject correlations, as well as their ranks. This latter measure is done to ensure that even components with strong correlation values need to hold at least a relative degree of anatomical relation across participants to pass screening.

Using these procedures, Bartels and Zeki (2004) characterize numerous brain areas that respond with strong correspondence across participants. Considering that "free-viewing" involved presentation of a perceptually diverse and complex stimulus without task directives, the strong inter-subject correspondence of results and functional specificity is an encouraging achievement.

Importantly, the authors also find that these procedures favorably compare against results from a more conventional approach. In a complementary analysis, they determine components for responses to circumscribed stimuli shown in a traditional block design. Instead of "free-viewing" over time spans of a couple minutes, the block design uses 30-second epochs, each presenting 6-second movie clips of different common objects in motion. To compare the numbers of components in this block design against those in "free-viewing," the authors count the average number of components that significantly correlate between each pair of subjects for comparison against the number of components found from "free-viewing." Between responses in a conventional block design and those when participants were able to freely view portions of the James Bond movie, the number of components determined in the latter was far greater than in the former. Thus, to the extent that found components reflect maximally independent signals, their far greater numbers for responses collected in "free-viewing" indicates this design elicits responses with far greater specificity. This finding leads the authors to suggest that a "more complex stimulus activated many more areas with different [activity time courses], and each in a distinct way, though consistently across subjects." Thus, with this study, Bartels and Zeki (2004) not only demonstrate a way to use complex, naturalistic stimuli, but also their findings ultimately suggest it gives an advantage over conventional approaches for mapping functional specificity in greater detail.

Summary

As neuroimaging methodologies advance, so too can the questions they permit and the depth of findings they provide. For understanding brain function when people process language, methodological development is especially crucial. Early fMRI studies investigating brain function in language processing provide a strong foundation for future work. However, these studies are built on relatively non-ecological approaches that use univariate models to isolate features in language and to associate brain effects with these features in isolation. Yet people do not use language by single features in isolation. Rather, language use by real people in the real world involves ongoing sources of information in contexts that are diverse, multifaceted, and complex.

Importantly, recent fMRI efforts are moving from profiling brain effects in isolation towards profiles that reflect responses in more naturalistic conditions. In this chapter, we have highlighted some of these developments. First, to get a sense of the underlying perspective (and its assumptions), we began by describing some early methods and results from which language fMRI research has gained footing. We then transitioned to more recent work by first outlining the importance of context. In this, we discussed context both as it concerns experimental conditions that incorporate greater surrounding information (exogenous context), as well as in terms of ways that the brain can more wholly incorporate widespread, ongoing function (endogenous or neural context).

We highlighted some of the methods that can be used to study brain responses in more naturalistic contexts. By discussing these in terms of specific examples from published works, we aimed to convey not just their applicability, but also, in simple terms, to emphasize their ease of use. We described two methods that can be used to identify responses to events in continuous, naturalistic conditions. The first of these methods ("subjective segmentation") was an approach that incorporates people's subjective perceptions in the analytic models, whereas the second ("peaks and Valleys in the BOLD response") uses the data themselves to identify points of interest. We then discussed two ways to use correlation. In basic terms, both operate by evaluating repeated responses, but one uses intra-subject responses ("intra-subject correlations"), whereas the other uses responses between-participants ("Inter-subject correlations"). Finally, we further emphasized the benefits of using data-driven approaches. We exemplified this by describing the use of ICA to analyze data acquired under naturalistic conditions. Although ICAs use in fMRI is by no means new, its application remains wholly relevant. In particular, this is the case for data analyses in which information about the response is unknown *a priori*, as when responses are to continuous, complex, "uncontrolled" (e.g., naturalistic) stimuli.

Collectively, these approaches carry some common principles to consider in future work. Notably, they largely free researchers from reliance on *a priori* information and models. Similarly, another principle we imparted here is to "let the data speak." In other words, whether it is by using response inflections to identify points of differentiation, using a response as a predictor, or separating signals in the response by their maximal independence, there is valuable information in the acquired data that can be used to systematically identify effects. Not only does this lessen potential biases that a researcher might introduce in the analysis pipeline, but it also leaves room for researchers to discover effects that they might not otherwise have been anticipating.

Finally, in a departure from conventional studies, these methods work by using complex, naturalistic information to profile brain function. This is important. In any given everyday scenario, people's language use regularly incorporates diverse information sources. Accordingly, this would also associate an array of diverse biological and cognitive processes, and not, necessarily, just those relating components of what researchers classically study as "language" (e.g., words, phonemes, sentences, discourse).

It is worth reiterating that such sources and the diverse processes they would require in natural language use are continuous. Recognizing this, we emphasized methods in this chapter that are particularly capable for analyzing BOLD data collected under continuous exposures. This offers a relative point of departure from many classic, traditional approaches in fMRI that use more circumscribed feature presentations in hopes of isolating particular responses.

Exactly what processes are necessary and sufficient, and, importantly, how the brain instantiates them in natural, everyday language use are not yet known. To present artificial information in brief, isolated exposures and devoid of continuity, as is the case with stimuli that strip away language's diverse complexity, may yield precise experimental effects. But it may not reflect an accurate profile that speaks to what is actually happening at the neurobiological level when people engage these functions in the world. Thus, it is a challenge for language fMRI studies moving forward to try to understand brain function when people use language in ways that are typical of the world rather than typical in the experimental laboratory.

References

Aguirre, G. K., Zarahn, E., & D'Esposito, M. (1998). The variability of human, BOLD hemodynamic responses. *Neuroimage*, *8*(4), 360–369.

Andric, M., & Small, S. L. (2012). Gesture's neural language. *Front Psychol*, *3*, 99. doi:10.3389/fpsyg.2012.00099

Bartels, A., & Zeki, S. (2004). The chronoarchitecture of the human brain: natural viewing conditions reveal a time-based anatomy of the brain. *Neuroimage*, *22*(1), 419–433. doi:10.1016/j.neuroimage.2004.01.007

Binder, J. R., Desai, R. H., Graves, W. W., & Conant, L. L. (2009). Where is the semantic system? A critical review and meta-analysis of 120 functional neuroimaging studies. *Cerebral Cortex*, *19*(12), 2767–2796.

Binder, J. R., Frost, J. A., Hammeke, T. A., Cox, R. W., Rao, S. M., & Prieto, T. (1997). Human brain language areas identified by functional magnetic resonance imaging. *J Neurosci*, *17*(1), 353–362.

Broca, P. (1861). Remarques sur le siège de la faculté du langage articulé; suivies d'une observation d'aphémie. *Bulletin de la Société Anatomique*, *6*, 330–357.

Buckner, R. L. (1998). Event-related fMRI and the hemodynamic response. *Hum Brain Mapp*, *6*(5–6), 373–377. doi:10.1002/(SICI)1097–0193(1998)6:5/6<373::AID-HBM8>3.0.CO;2-P [pii]

Calhoun, V. D., Adali, T., Pearlson, G. D., & Pekar, J. J. (2001). A method for making group inferences from functional MRI data using independent component analysis. *Hum Brain Mapp*, *14*(3), 140–151.

Dapretto, M., & Bookheimer, S. Y. (1999). Form and content: dissociating syntax and semantics in sentence comprehension. *Neuron, 24*(2), 427–432.

Dick, A. S., & Tremblay, P. (2012). Beyond the arcuate fasciculus: consensus and controversy in the connectional anatomy of language. *Brain, 135*(12), 3529–3550. doi:10.1093/brain/aws222

Friederici, A. D., Opitz, B., & Cramon, D. Y. v. (2000). Segregating semantic and syntactic aspects of processing in the human brain: an fMRI investigation of different word types. *Cerebral Cortex, 10*(7), 698–705.

Goldin-Meadow, S. (2003). *Hearing Gesture: How Our Hands Help Us Think.* Cambridge, Mass.: Belknap Press of Harvard University Press.

Hasson, U., Nir, Y., Levy, I., Fuhrmann, G., & Malach, R. (2004). Intersubject synchronization of cortical activity during natural vision. *Science, 303*(5664), 1634–1640.

Hasson, U., Skipper, J. I., Wilde, M. J., Nusbaum, H. C., & Small, S. L. (2008). Improving the analysis, storage and sharing of neuroimaging data using relational databases and distributed computing. *Neuroimage, 39*(2), 693–706.

Levin, D. N., & Uftring, S. J. (2001). Detecting brain activation in FMRI data without prior knowledge of mental event timing. *Neuroimage, 13*(1), 153–160. doi:10.1006/nimg.2000.0663

Logothetis, N. K., Pauls, J., Augath, M., Trinath, T., & Oeltermann, A. (2001). Neurophysiological investigation of the basis of the fMRI signal. *Nature, 412*(6843), 150–157.

McIntosh, A. R. (2000). Towards a network theory of cognition. *Neural Networks, 13*, 861–870.

McKeown, M., Hu, Y. J., & Jane Wang, Z. (2005). ICA denoising for event-related fMRI studies. *Conf Proc IEEE Eng Med Biol Soc, 1*, 157–161. doi:10.1109/IEMBS.2005.1616366

McKeown, M. J., Makeig, S., Brown, G. G., Jung, T. P., Kindermann, S. S., Bell, A. J., & Sejnowski, T. J. (1998). Analysis of fMRI data by blind separation into independent spatial components. *Hum Brain Mapp, 6*(3), 160–188.

McNeill, D. (1992). *Hand and Mind: What Gestures Reveal about Thought.* Chicago: University of Chicago Press.

McNeill, D. (2005). *Gesture and Thought.* Chicago: University of Chicago Press.

Mesulam, M.-M. (1990). Large-scale neurocognitive networks and distributed processing for attention, language, and memory. *Ann Neurol, 28*(5), 597–613.

Miezin, F. M., Maccotta, L., Ollinger, J. M., Petersen, S. E., & Buckner, R. L. (2000). Characterizing the hemodynamic response: effects of presentation rate, sampling procedure, and the possibility of ordering brain activity based on relative timing. *Neuroimage, 11*(6), 735–759.

Pulvermuller, F. (2005). Brain mechanisms linking language and action. *Nat Rev Neurosci, 6*(7), 576–582.

Robinson, S. D., & Schopf, V. (2013). ICA of fMRI studies: new approaches and cutting edge applications. *Front Hum Neurosci, 7*, 724. doi:10.3389/fnhum.2013.00724

Skipper, J. I., Goldin-Meadow, S., Nusbaum, H. C., & Small, S. L. (2009). Gestures orchestrate brain networks for language understanding. *Curr Biol, 19*, 1–7.

Tohka, J., Foerde, K., Aron, A. R., Tom, S. M., Toga, A. W., & Poldrack, R. A. (2008). Automatic independent component labeling for artifact removal in fMRI. *Neuroimage, 39*(3), 1227–1245. doi:10.1016/j.neuroimage.2007.10.013

Tononi, G., & Sporns, O. (2003). Measuring information integration. *BMC Neurosci, 4*, 31.

Wernicke, C. (1874/1977). The aphasic symptom complex (G. E. Eggert, trans.). Reprinted in *Wernicke's Works on Aphasia: A Source Book and Review* (pp. 91–144). The Hague, Netherlands: Mouton.

Willems, R. M., & Hagoort, P. (2007). Neural evidence for the interplay between language, gesture, and action: a review. *Brain and Language, 101*(3), 278–289.

Zacks, J. M., Braver, T. S., Sheridan, M. A., Donaldson, D. I., Snyder, A. Z., Ollinger, J. M., & Raichle, M. E. (2001). Human brain activity time-locked to perceptual event boundaries. *Nat Neurosci, 4*(6), 651–655.

3 Why study connected speech production?

Sharon Ash & Murray Grossman

Abstract The speech that is termed "natural speech" or "connected speech" – the speech that is spoken spontaneously and with minimal monitoring by the speaker – is the most systematic form of language production and the most representative of an individual's linguistic capabilities. It stands in contrast to speech that is elicited one word at a time, with full attention focused on the production of the word, as in confrontation naming, verbal fluency, or repetition tasks. In our work, we elicit a lengthy body of continuous speech by asking subjects to tell a story from a children's picture book. We examine the resulting speech in patients with a range of neurodegenerative diseases in an effort to differentiate among the conditions. In each case, the level of linguistic analysis is based on hypotheses about the effects on language production of the different forms of neuropathology. We also relate performance on linguistic variables to gray matter atrophy and reduced fractional anisotropy in white matter in order to illuminate the neuroanatomic substrates of natural language production. In this chapter, we discuss analyses of connected speech production with respect to speech rate, speech errors and apraxia of speech, lexicon, grammar, and discourse structure in individuals with primary progressive aphasia, frontotemporal degeneration, Alzheimer's disease, and variants of Parkinson's disease.

Why study connected speech production?

Why should we study the unmonitored, spontaneous, continuous speech production of patients with a neurological condition? Why should researchers be concerned with such unregulated, connected speech, rather than exclusively examining individual sounds, words, and perhaps sentences that are elicited in response to direct questioning? More generally, why should we study connected speech in any population? Every native speaker of a language can rightly consider him- or herself to be an expert on language, as one who speaks and understands flawlessly and without need of reflection.

However, the lack of a need to reflect on how to speak one's thoughts or how to understand others' speech does not mean that a speaker of a language knows, by introspection, what he or she actually says or comprehends. One of the present authors (SA) once interviewed a 32-year-old woman in a middle-class neighborhood of Philadelphia as part of a course in field work. SA asked her about the construction known as "positive *anymore*," the use of *anymore* in a positive sentence, such as "John smokes a lot *anymore*." This use of *anymore* is an extension of the use of *anymore* in negative sentences, such as "John doesn't smoke *anymore*." In the latter case, *anymore* expresses a contrast between the present state and a previous state: John does not smoke now, but he did in the past. This is standard usage and is found throughout the dialects of English. In a positive sentence, the effect of *anymore* is parallel in that it denotes a contrast: John smokes a lot nowadays, but he did not do so in the past. The use of positive *anymore* is widespread and almost universally understood in the U.S. Midland, a wide swath of territory from the Mid-Atlantic states, including eastern Pennsylvania, stretching west to the Mississippi River and beyond. The young woman with whom SA was speaking was nonplussed by the question, "What would it mean to say, 'John smokes a lot anymore'?" She had no idea. A few minutes later, she said something like, "Anymore I always walk. I don't like to wait for the bus," thus using that very construction, completely naturally and appropriately, in her own speech.

This is one out of innumerable demonstrations of the fallacy of testing a speaker's competence by asking "Could someone say this?" which often is translated into "Could I say this?" We cannot prejudge or effectively introspect about the language that a speaker uses fluently and effortlessly, the language that is acquired in childhood, passed from parent to child and down through the generations, creating the history of a language, complete with dialectal variants and change over time, at the levels of phonetics, phonology, morphology, lexicon, syntax, discourse, and pragmatics.

A researcher concerned with the neural substrates of language would want to know how a speaker produces language, considering all levels of analysis, as much as how a speaker can perform tasks of comprehension and retrieval, such as phoneme discrimination, naming objects and actions, or responding to a question that depends on comprehending sentences containing different types of dependent clauses. In normal speakers, natural speech production is systematic and rule-governed, but speakers are not consciously aware of most of the system or the rules. It has been reported, for instance, that an Italian aphasic was able to produce the correct form of an adjective to agree with a noun according to gender, but she was not consistently able to identify the gender of a noun when explicitly asked to do so (Scarna & Ellis, 2002). Thus language use may be better preserved than metalinguistic knowledge.

The elicitation of connected speech

In order to study language production, the researcher would want a means of eliciting speech that meets several criteria: (1) it should be engaging, both easy and pleasant to perform; (2) it should produce a continuous, free flow of speech consisting of complete sentences, without making the speaker work hard to decide how to continue from one sentence to the next; (3) the elicited speech should have a known target, so that the clinician or researcher can know what the speaker is trying to say; (4) it should provide stimuli for varied syntactic constructions; (5) it should be a novel task, one that the speaker is unlikely to have performed previously; (6) it should produce a coherent body of speech that can be analyzed at levels ranging from phonetics to discourse; (7) it should elicit a considerable volume of speech, which suggests that it should not involve time constraints.

A speech elicitation task that satisfies these requirements is the narration of a story from a picture book that has no printed words. It is important that the pictures be very clear as to their content, so that subjects performing the task will have no difficulty following the story. It is important that the story have some unexpected elements, to maintain interest and to test the subject's attention and insight. And it is important that the story be of sufficient length to elicit a speech sample that can contain a variety of lexical and syntactic forms. In our work, we investigate the neural substrates of language by studying patients with neurodegenerative diseases. We have used the children's picture book *Frog, Where Are You?*, by Mercer Mayer (1969), which satisfies these criteria quite well. The story consists of 24 scenes drawn in exquisite detail, of which only a few contain elements that sometimes are misinterpreted by patients and occasionally by healthy subjects. Those elements include a sock on the floor of the boy's room, which is sometimes misinterpreted as a bird, and bushes outside the boy's window are also sometimes seen as birds. However, these confusions apply to individual items in the pictures and do not affect the understanding of the story as it unfolds.

This speech elicitation task, henceforth known as Frog Story, has to date been administered to approximately 275 individuals in our lab over a period of about 10 years. All the narrations have been recorded digitally. About 30 of these subjects have recorded Frog Story twice, and two have recorded it three times. The narratives generally range from about 4 minutes to about 20 minutes, although they vary widely, from an actual minimum of about 1 minute to a maximum of about 25 minutes.

In addition to Frog Story, we have used the Cookie Theft scene from the Boston Diagnostic Aphasia Examination (Goodglass & Kaplan, 1972) to elicit samples of connected speech. The instructions for the Cookie Theft scene usually ask that the subject describe the picture for a fixed, limited period of time, normally 60 or 90 seconds. As a brief, timed task, this protocol elicits a limited amount of speech, so it can be transcribed and coded in much less time than a speech sample that is fifteen times longer. We have digital recordings of more than 700 Cookie Theft descriptions from more than 400 individuals. While the Cookie Theft protocol is easy to administer and easy to transcribe and code due to its brevity, it does not elicit a narrative, unlike Frog Story, so it does not provide the opportunity to examine organizational aspects of speech production. Another limitation is that it relies heavily on the subject's executive functioning, since the subject must be able to decide what is reportable in the picture in order to maintain the flow of speech without excessive prompting. If a subject is apathetic or cannot determine what to talk about in the picture for some other reason, then the speech sample may not accurately represent his or her linguistic abilities. Nonetheless, descriptions of a complex picture such as the Cookie Theft scene have a well-established place in the neuropsychological test battery for patients with language impairments.

Analysis of the speech samples begins with transcription, which is carried out using the signal-processing software Praat (1992–2014). This program was developed by two linguists in The Netherlands as a tool for phonetic analysis. ("Praat" means *talk*/ *talks*/ *is talking* in Dutch.) It is downloadable at no cost, easy to use, and quite powerful, and so it has come to be widely used by linguists and researchers in related fields. Numerous other software packages are also available for signal processing.

For purposes of analyzing samples of connected speech, we have established a set of transcription conventions. A complete description of these conventions is given elsewhere (Ash *et al.*, 2006). An important part of the transcription is parsing it into units termed "utterances." Following Hunt (1965), an utterance is defined as one independent clause and all clauses dependent on it. This provides a principled way of segmenting the discourse into meaningful units that are amenable to further analysis. For Frog Story, it respects the characteristic of narrative speech that independent clauses are stated in the temporal order in which the corresponding events occurred (Labov, 2013). The Frog Stories we have collected average around 60 utterances, with a range of 8 to 203 utterances. The Cookie Thefts we have analyzed to date average around 14 utterances, with a range of 3 to 35 utterances.

Table 3.1 summarizes the demographic and clinical characteristics of most of the subject groups for whom we have recorded Frog Stories.

Table 3.1 *Mean (SD) demographic and clinical characteristics*[1,2]

	Healthy seniors	naPPA	svPPA	lvPPA	bvFTD	AD	PD	PDD/DLB
N (m/f)	6/13	10/10	9/5	8/7	10/5	6/12	16/10	10/5
Age	66.3 (8.4)	69.7 (9.8)	64.3 (7.1)	67.1 (10.1)	64.6 (11.5)	73.4 (11.8)	69.7 (9.0)	72.1 (9.3)
Education (yr)	15.3 (2.5)	15.3 (2.5)	15.1 (3.1)	15.7 (3.0)	16.9 (3.3)	14.3 (2.1)	15.5 (3.0)	15.5 (2.9)
Disease duration (yr)	–	3.7 (2.0)	5.4 (2.5)	3.3 (1.5)	3.6 (1.5)	5.0 (2.1)	6.1 (2.8)	6.5 (1.3)
MMSE	29.1 (1.1)	24.3** (4.5)	20.0** (8.2)	21.6** (5.2)	24.9 (6.5)	21.2** (6.1)	27.6** (2.0)	20.3** (5.0)
Neuropsychological measures								
Forward digit span	7.7 (1.2) [12]	4.9** (1.7) [19]	5.1** (1.7)	4.8** (1.3)	5.7** (1.5)	6.1* (1.6)	7.1 (1.3)	5.5** (1.5) [12]
Reverse digit span	5.4 (1.5) [11]	3.2** (1.1) [19]	3.2** (1.3)	3.5** (1.6)	4.0* (1.5) [14]	4.1* (1.6)	4.9 (1.3) [20]	3.0** (0.8) [12]
Letter-guided fluency (FAS)	45 (11) [13]	15** (9) [19]	17** (10) [13]	20** (10) [14]	24** (17)	22** (18) [16]	37 (16) [21]	18** (11) [13]
Category fluency (animals)	21.7 (4.8) [15]	10.7** (5.7)	7.4** (5.4) [12]	8.9** (5.0) [14]	13.1** (5.3)	11.6** (6.7)	16.8* (6.6) [21]	6.7** (3.6) [13]
Boston naming test (% correct)	92 (10) [13]	80* (17)	42** (33) [14]	71** (24) [12]	89 (11) [13]	74[4] (24)	93 (8) [16]	82** (13) [13]
Pyramids and Palm Trees (max = 52)[3]	52 (1) [6]	48** (7) [15]	40** (11) [13]	47** (2) [12]	45** (7)	46** (6) [16]	49* (2) [8]	45** (6) [10]

1. Differs from controls, $*p < 0.05$; $**p < 0.01$
2. Number of subjects with available data is given in square brackets
3. Average score for presentation in words and pictures
4. $p = 0.0512$

Healthy seniors are recruited for comparison to the patient population, which is in general older, with at least some education after secondary school: the mean age for all subjects is 68.2 yr (SD = 9.2), and the mean years of education for all subjects is 15.4 (SD = 2.8). The patient groups that are most represented in our studies are those with primary progressive aphasia (PPA), including the nonfluent/agrammatic variant (naPPA), semantic variant (svPPA), and logopenic variant (lvPPA). We have also recruited, among others, cohorts of patients with behavioral variant frontotemporal dementia (bvFTD), Alzheimer's disease (AD), and Lewy body spectrum disorder (LBSD), which encompasses Parkinson's disease (PD), Parkinson's disease with dementia (PDD), and Lewy body disease (LBD). The last two, PDD and LBD, are grouped together, since they share common histopathology but differ in the timing of onset of symptoms of dementia relative to symptoms of a movement disorder, according to established criteria (McKeith, 2006).

The object of our studies has been twofold: (1) to distinguish among the different conditions by means of the differing linguistic presentations of the various patient groups, as an aid to diagnosis, and (2) to investigate the neural substrates of each different set of clinical symptoms. In this exposition of methodological considerations, we will address the levels of speech production that are available to analysis through the study of connected speech. A basic level of analysis is "fluency." This term is problematically vague, although it is widely used. It is often applied to semantic category fluency (as in, "Name as many animals as you can think of in one minute") (Lezak, 1983) or letter-guided fluency (as in, "Name all the words you can think of that begin with the letter *F* in one minute") (Lezak, 1983). For our purposes, "fluency" means speech rate, measured as the number of complete words spoken per minute, or simply "words per minute" (WPM). This is a measure that is relatively easy to calculate when transcription of a body of speech has been completed, if the precise total duration of the speech sample has also been recorded. A difficulty that can arise in this calculation is the occurrence of silences in the subject's speech. If a silence is due to pausing because the subject is thinking about what to say next or having difficulty continuing, that could appropriately be reflected in the calculation of the subject's speech rate. If there is a silence because the subject has run out of things to say and is not inclined to speak further without prompting, then the silence is not directly reflective of the subject's speaking rate, and the duration of such a silence, including other speakers' prompts, should be subtracted from the total duration of the speech sample. These problems are partially alleviated in the Frog Story task because the drawings form a sequence that carries the speaker from one event to the next without the need for intervention by the examiner; such is the character of narrative discourse. Still, a speaker who has difficulty initiating speech may be silent for an extended time and require prompting. In consideration of the significance of silent pauses, our transcriptions of recorded speech include the notation of pauses of 2 seconds or more, both within and between utterances.

In what follows, we will discuss research we have conducted in studying the neural substrates of natural languagc production at several levels of linguistic analysis.

Speech rate

Table 3.2 summarizes the speech production results for speech output, grammaticality, and discourse variables in our sample. The average speech rate in WPM is given for selected patient groups that we have recorded and analyzed. For some groups, the results are quite consistent. Healthy seniors speak at a rate of about 140 WPM in the Frog Story task, with little individual variation. For the patient groups, there are dramatic differences in comparison to this control group. Patients with naPPA show the most extreme limitation in their speech output, with an average WPM of about one-third that of healthy seniors. This group, and every other patient group except non-demented Parkinson's disease patients, is impaired in speech rate compared to healthy seniors at a significance level of $p < 0.005$. However, this does not mean that the durations of individual words are lengthened or that words are spoken in a choppy manner, with silences between successive words. When the durations of silences of 2.0 seconds or greater are subtracted from the speech samples, only naPPA and lvPPA patients exhibit a speech rate that is significantly reduced compared to that of healthy seniors. Indeed, one of the diagnostic criteria for lvPPA is "slowed speech" (Gorno-Tempini *et al.*, 2011), and the adjusted measure of speech rate provides quantitative confirmation of the clinical impression that these patients are impaired in producing continuous speech. Thus, in terms of gross WPM, all the patient groups have slowed speech compared to controls. For most patient groups, the slowing corresponds to frequent pausing, rather than to a lengthening of the duration of words or frequent brief pauses between words.

While slowed speech is one of the most obvious manifestations of neurological deficits, it can occur for a variety of reasons. In studies of non-fluent speech in naPPA, we have found that WPM correlated with deficits in grammatical expression, but not with speech errors or executive impairments (Ash *et al.*, 2009; Gunawardena *et al.*, 2010). In this work, WPM was significantly correlated with the total number of words, the mean length of utterance (in words), the frequency of complex structures

Table 3.2 *Mean (SD) speech output and discourse performance*[1]

	Healthy seniors	naPPA	svPPA	lvPPA	bvFTD	AD	PD	PDD/DLB
Words and sentences								
Number of words	594 (219)	411** (283)	594 (452)	794 (507)	451* (189)	603 (210)	536 (210)	434** (288)
Duration (sec)	258 (103)	489** (291)	343 (239)	620** (371)	352 (258)	379** (142)	262 (123)	430 (254)
Number of utterances	59 (18)	49 (22)	74 (52)	85 (59)	48 (17)	70 (28)	52 (25)	49* (27)
Words per minute	142 (22)	53** (24)	92** (31)	78** (24)	97** (46)	102** (32)	130 (34)	72** (38)
Adjusted words per minute[2]	150 (19)	95** (40)	142 (38)	106** (23)	135 (29)	135 (23)	156 (33)	136 (31)
Mean length of utterance (words)	10.1 (1.5)	7.9** (2.7)	7.9** (1.8)	9.5 (2.4)	9.3 (2.1)	8.8** (1.1)	10.8 (2.3)	9.3 (3.9)
Speech errors / 100 words	0.07 (0.15)	8.22** (17.32)	0.79** (1.05)	1.52** (1.33)	0.16 (0.27)	0.24 (0.34)	0.16 (0.25)	1.80** (2.39)
% Grammatically well-formed sentences	96 (4)	63** (24)	83** (10)	70** (21)	78** (25)	84** (16)	95 (6)	77** (23)
Dependent clauses / utterance	0.20 (0.11)	0.11** (0.12)	0.14 (0.09)	0.20 (0.14)	0.16 (0.11)	0.23 (0.08)	0.29 (0.20)	0.17 (0.16)
Nouns /100 words	20.0 (2.6)	21.4 (13.6)	13.3** (3.9)	16.4** (8.1)	21.0 (5.1)	16.3** (4.0)	19.7 (3.1)	19.9 (5.7)
Inflected verbs /100 words	14.2 (1.5)	13.9 (2.9)	15.6 (2.4)	13.4 (2.0)	13.6 (1.9)	14.5 (1.6)	13.5 (5.1)	13.2 (2.5)
Percent pause time[3]	5.5 (5.9)	43.1** (22.1)	31.4** (22.6)	26.3** (17.8)	31.0** (26.2)	25.1** (20.6)	16.3** (16.2)	49.0** (20.1)
Discourse								
Accurate report (max = 30)	23.5 (4.6)	11.1** (8.0)	8.9** (10.1)	8.0** (6.6)	13.3** (9.5)	11.4** (7.0)	19.0 (7.6)	7.0** (6.6)
Local connectedness (max = 30)	27.5 (2.7)	18.8** (8.4)	16.7** (8.8)	19.5** (8.7)	18.6* (10.6)	20.0** (7.7)	25.2 (5.0)	16.0** (8.6)
Search theme (max = 4)	3.95 (0.23)	2.42** (1.64)	2.08** (1.88)	2.00** (1.75)	2.10** (1.60)	1.75** (1.44)	3.15 (1.52)	1.33** (1.63)
% Subjects with Global connectedness	95	63*	38**	50**	30**	13**	72	33**

1. Differs from controls, $^{*}p < 0.05$; $^{**}p < 0.01$
2. Speech rate is adjusted by excluding time of pauses of 2.0 sec or longer
3. For pauses ≥ 2.0 sec

(dependent clauses and phrasal adjuncts (Ash *et al.*, 2009)), and the number of verbs per utterance. In svPPA, WPM was only correlated with the frequency of existential subjects (as in "*There* is a bees' nest" or "*Here* is an owl"), and in bvFTD, there were no correlations of WPM with other speech measures, but only with the executive/semantic measure of category-guided fluency. We also have found that in lvPPA, slowed speech correlated with a deficit in short-term auditory memory (forward digit span) and working memory (Ash, Weinberg, *et al.*, 2013b). In another set of studies, we examined speech impairments in LBSD (Ash, McMillan, *et al.*, 2012). While PD patients were not significantly different from healthy seniors on many features, the LBSD group as a whole was impaired in speech rate, which is in part a reflection of long pauses that occur in the patients' speech. The reduced speech rate was correlated with impaired executive functioning, grammatical comprehension, and episodic memory in this patient cohort. In addition, reduced speech rate in LBSD was correlated with speech sound errors, which are also associated with long pauses between utterances (see below).

To investigate the neural substrates of language production, we have conducted high-resolution structural MRI scans of patients. The data from these patients' scans is normalized and compared to MRI scans of a set of healthy age- and education-matched control subjects to determine the regions of cortical atrophy in the patient groups relative to controls. We perform a whole-brain analysis to identify regions of atrophy and then use those regions as an explicit mask to examine the relationship between a variable of interest, such as speech rate, and brain areas known to be significantly atrophied from the prior analysis of whole-brain gray matter (GM) atrophy. We consider only regions where measures of language performance are related to GM areas that exhibit atrophy because the correlation of test performance with a region of cortical atrophy implies that that cortical region plays a role in performance on the correlated measure. At the same time, we do not have a basis for interpreting significant associations between patients' performance and non-atrophied regions.

In many cases, we have also obtained diffusion tensor imaging data and so are able to map reduced fractional anisotropy (FA) in cortical white matter (WM) in patients relative to controls. Where there are regions of reduced FA in WM, a regression analysis similarly reveals WM regions that appear to be implicated in impaired performance. In the study of variants of FTD referred to above (Ash *et al.*, 2009), a regression of cortical volume with WPM for all three groups of FTD patients taken together was found in left inferior frontal (BA 44) and anterior superior temporal (BA 22) regions, as shown in Plate 3.1 (see color plate section).

This finding is consistent with results of a report of cortical volume related to performance on widely used language tasks (Amici *et al.*, 2007), which found a relation of fluency to inferior frontal gyrus. Other evidence suggests that left inferior frontal cortex may be invoked in syntactic processing during fluent speech production (Cooke *et al.*, 2006). The overlap of the regression of WPM with cortical volume and cortical atrophy in svPPA in left anterior superior temporal cortex is consistent with evidence that this region is important in word-level processes (Indefrey & Levelt, 2004; Scott & Wise, 2004), in comprehension of syntax (Friederici *et al.*, 2000; Friederici *et al.*, 2003), and in the construction of basic phrase structures in speech production (Hickok & Poeppel, 2007; Humphries *et al.*, 2005).

In a study that compared lvPPA to other PPA variants (Ash, Weinberg, *et al.*, 2013b), we found a correlation in lvPPA of GM atrophy with WPM bilaterally (Plate 3.2 – see color plate section) in regions involved in attention, initiation, and working memory (BA10) (Gilbert *et al.*, 2006; Ramnani & Owen, 2004) and in other left middle frontal regions (BA 8/9) related to uncertainty, attention, and working memory.

In LBSD, where reduced speech rate was correlated with executive functioning and grammatical comprehension (Ash, McMillan, *et al.*, 2012), we found that regression analyses related speech rate, grammatical difficulty, executive impairments, and lengthy between-utterance pauses to frontal atrophy. In a subset of 11 LBSD patients, we conducted separate regressions of cortical atrophy with speech rate and three measures of neuropsychological test performance. We found overlap of the regression for speech rate with that for executive functioning and pauses again in right medial frontal cortex (BA 10), as indicated above, an area reported to be associated with attention, initiation, and working memory (Gilbert *et al.*, 2006; Ramnani & Owen, 2004), shown in Plate 3.3A (see color plate section). An overlap of the regressions for speech rate and executive functioning, pauses, and grammatical impairment was found in two areas of left ventrolateral prefrontal cortex (BA 47), displayed in Plate 3.3B (see color plate section). This region bilaterally has been shown to have a role in working memory, episodic memory retrieval, and decision-making.

Speech errors and apraxia of speech

The recently published guidelines for assessing the variants of primary progressive aphasia (PPA) (Gorno-Tempini *et al.*, 2011) state that one requirement for a diagnosis of non-fluent/agrammatic primary progressive aphasia (naPPA) is that a patient either exhibit agrammatism in language production or produce "effortful, halting speech with inconsistent speech sound errors and distortions (apraxia of speech)" (p. 1009).

Apraxia of speech (AOS) is defined as a motor disorder, meaning that a patient has incomplete control of the articulators and therefore makes errors in controlling the airflow from the lungs and configuring the lips, teeth, tongue, and velum to pronounce the speech sounds that comprise well-formed segments, syllables, and words. To understand the symptoms presented by aphasic patients, it is necessary to distinguish between phonetic errors and phonemic errors. A phonetic error is the production of a sound that is not part of the inventory of sounds in the speaker's language. For example, there may be a failure of the tongue to make contact with the roof of the mouth in the articulation of a stop consonant, resulting in a fricative that does not exist in English. In the Frog Story narrations, this is often heard of the /g/ in *frog* and *dog*, which is weakened to a segment that is transcribed as [ɣ] in the International Phonetic Alphabet. In contrast, a phonemic error is the production of a speech segment that constitutes a correct realization of a sound in the speaker's language but is produced in the wrong place at the wrong time. When a speaker says *farg* for *frog*, as sometimes occurs in the Frog Story narratives, he or she is producing the wrong vowel and has also switched the positions of the vowel and the /r/, in a process known as metathesis, which is common in the history of languages. (For example, English *burn* corresponds to German *brennen*, both descended from a common West Germanic ancestor.) Thus ill-formed segments could be a manifestation not only of a motor difficulty per se, but alternatively of an impairment of motor planning or programming. A phonetic error must be caused by faulty movement of the articulators, as a consequence of either a motor disorder or a degraded system of articulatory programming, but a phonemic error implies a deficit in the process of assembling phonemes into words and does not necessarily imply a motor disorder.

In a study of speech errors in 16 naPPA patients, we found that 18% were phonetic errors, which we can ascribe to a motor impairment, and 82% were phonemic errors (Ash *et al.*, 2009). An extract of a Frog Story from an naPPA patient is given in Speech Sample 1 (see Appendix). This extract clearly illustrates the effortfulness seen in this patient group. Speech errors were not correlated with speech rate, nor with any neuropsychological measures (Ash, McMillan, et al., 2010). The only associations of speech sound errors with language production measures we have found are that the percentage of utterances that are well-formed sentences is negatively correlated with both phonetic errors and phonemic errors. In addition, phonemic errors are correlated with the frequency of editing breaks and hesitation markers (Ash, McMillan, *et al.*, 2010). We conclude that speech sound errors in naPPA arise within the linguistic system and, for the most part, are not a consequence of either a motor disorder or executive deficits. Healthy seniors, as shown in Table 3.2, rarely make speech sound errors. All of the speech errors we have identified among controls are phonemic errors; none are phonetic errors.

A caution regarding this work is that the distinction between phonetic and phonemic errors may not always be clear, and reports of the frequency of phonetic vs. phonemic disturbances vary. In some cases, authors have not distinguished between AOS and phonemic paraphasias (Knibb *et al.*, 2009; Rohrer *et al.*, 2010). Other authors may report a greater frequency of apraxia of speech than we have found (Croot *et al.*, 2012), while we more often ascribe speech sound errors to phonemic paraphasias. In other cases, the assessment of AOS may depend on an ascertainment bias. Thus, Josephs *et al.* (2006) state that reports of phonemic paraphasia in naPPA "probably . . . refer to phonetic (i.e. motor) rather than phonemic (i.e. linguistic) distortions" (p. 1386). It is also possible that there have been differences between our series and those reported from other centers; in other centers naPPA patients may have had more pronounced motor impairments related to movement disorders such as corticobasal syndrome (CBS) or progressive supranuclear palsy (PSP).

From our studies, we conclude that errors of word formation at the phonemic level are frequent in naPPA. These speech errors are somewhat systematic in that they most often involve the replacement of one phoneme by a phoneme that is similar in articulation, differing by only one distinctive feature in the majority of instances. This suggests that phonemic errors are governed by the linguistic properties of the phonologic system. Phonetic errors are relatively infrequent in naPPA, at least at the stages of mild or moderate severity of disease. When phonetic errors do occur, they may be caused by a motor planning impairment such as AOS.

Lexicon

Some patients with PPA are said to have word-finding difficulty or to use circumlocutions in speech. The most dramatic deterioration of semantics is found for patients with the semantic variant of primary progressive aphasia (svPPA). These patients stand out due to their loss of knowledge of objects, as well as their difficulty in retrieving the words for objects (Bonner *et al.*, 2010; Grossman & Ash, 2004; Hodges & Patterson, 2007). When shown a vegetable peeler in the clinic, for instance, they cannot say what it is for. They may shake it and comment on the rattling sound it makes, like a baby's toy. In the spontaneous speech of narrating the Frog

Story, this deficit is manifested by hesitation and casting about for the word for an object, as in Speech Sample 2.

In this excerpt, it is evident that the speaker is hard-pressed to come up with the names of *things*, that is, nouns, although he does not appear to be similarly impaired in his production of verbs. Many svPPA patients eventually lose so much of their word-finding capability that they become mute. Analysis of the Frog Stories confirms quantitatively that the production of nouns is impaired in svPPA, while the production of verbs is relatively spared (Ash *et al.*, 2009; Ash, Weinberg, *et al.*, 2013b). One mechanism for maintaining fluent speech despite impaired access to the lexicon is to replace specific nouns with pronouns, even when the referent is not immediately available. Another strategy that can be documented in the Frog Story transcripts is to replace specific nouns with nouns designating superordinate categories. Thus some patients with svPPA make frequent use of *thing* or *animal* in place of *frog*, *dog*, *bees*, *deer*, and other concrete nouns, as in Speech Sample 3. This excerpt illustrates both the strategies of replacing a noun with a pronoun and replacing a specific noun with a superordinate label. Cortical atrophy in svPPA is seen bilaterally in anterior temporal lobes, as shown in Plate 3.1, Panel B.

Data from the Cookie Theft recordings also illustrates the impairment of svPPA patients in the production of nouns (Ash, Evans, *et al.*, 2013). In this work, as in other studies, svPPA patients were impaired relative to controls on tests of verbal fluency (letter-guided fluency and semantically guided fluency), associative object knowledge (Pyramids and Palm Trees), and the frequency of nouns per 100 words. A correlation of cortical atrophy with noun production was found in GM regions implicated in noun production, including ventral and middle temporal regions in the left hemisphere.

Further evidence of the difficulty of lexical access in PPA is provided by the Frog Story data in the form of the occurrence of silent pauses within utterances. Silences of 2 seconds or more are marked in the transcriptions, and these silences are coded for their occurrence in relation to grammatical constituents. Examples 1 to 4 illustrate the four categories:

1. Before noun phrase: "They were behind (2.7 sec) an old trunk of a tree."
2. Within noun phrase: "They were behind an old (2.7 sec) trunk of a tree."
3. Before verb phrase: "They (2.7 sec) were behind an old trunk of a tree."
4. Within verb phrase: "They were behind an old trunk (2.7 sec) of a tree."

Patients with naPPA pause more frequently than healthy seniors in all positions within a sentence: before and within noun phrases (NP) and before and within verb phrases (VP). They also pause equally frequently in the environment of NPs and VPs. In contrast, svPPA patients pause significantly more frequently than healthy seniors only in the environment of NPs, and they also pause more frequently in the environment of NPs than they do in the environment of VPs (Ash, Adamowicz, *et al.*, 2010; Ash, Weinberg, *et al.*, 2013a). These observations provide quantitative support for other evidence of the impairments in naming, word comprehension, and degraded object knowledge that are the hallmarks of svPPA. Plate 3.4 (see color plate section) illustrates the correlation of pauses preceding and within NPs with cortical atrophy in svPPA. Extensive GM atrophy is found in left temporal regions, and a correlation of pauses with GM atrophy is seen in a left temporal region associated with confrontation naming.

Patients with a logopenic variant of primary progressive aphasia (lvPPA) are also characterized as having word-finding difficulty, but the impairment of object knowledge characteristic of svPPA is not a feature of lvPPA (Gorno-Tempini *et al.*, 2011). This patient group may be the most difficult to diagnose on the basis of speech production, since these patients do not stand out on any one linguistic feature (Ash, Weinberg, *et al.*, 2013b). Rather, their speech production is intermediate on many features. Their speech is slow, but not as slow as that of naPPA patients; they make speech errors, but less frequently than naPPA patients; and they produce fewer nouns as a proportion of total words, but not as few as svPPA patients. These patients take the longest time, on average, to narrate the Frog Story, as they tend to ramble and produce a good deal of extraneous talk while they progress slowly through the telling of the story, as illustrated in Speech Sample 4.

Alzheimer's patients also have word-finding difficulty for nouns, as shown in Table 3.2. A large proportion of the patients who present with lvPPA have underlying AD and are reclassified as such as their disease progresses. Accordingly, Table 3.2 shows that the lvPPA and AD groups are very similar on many of the measures of language production. The greatest differences are in total output (in number of words), duration of the narratives, speech rate, and speech errors. Speech errors are one of the diagnostic features of lvPPA. It is a novel, if incidental, finding from the Frog Story protocol that lvPPA patients talk more and take longer to tell the story than AD patients, but they speak at a slower rate. Recent studies of lvPPA have focused on distinguishing this variant from other variants of PPA (Ash, Evans, *et al.*, 2013; Gorno-Tempini *et al.*, 2008; Gorno-Tempini *et al.*, 2011; Mesulam *et al.*, 2012; Sajjadi *et al.*, 2012;

Wilson *et al.*, 2010), but it is also the clinician's task to distinguish lvPPA from AD.

Grammar

Grammaticality is most often assessed by testing patients' understanding of sentences. This can be done, for instance, by increasing the level of complexity, beginning with simple, subject–verb–object declarative sentences and progressing to sentences with passives, right-branching relative clauses, center-embedded relative clauses, clefts, sentences with constituents lengthened by the insertion of adjectives and prepositional phrases, and more. Such sentences typically place demands on working memory, and so it is difficult to judge whether subjects' errors are due to limitations of their linguistic capabilities or of their executive functioning. There is a need for studies that examine complexities in the linguistic system per se, such as complex verb phrases, embedded clauses, and compound tense constructions. In examining spontaneously produced speech, we can observe whether such complex constructions occur. A limitation of observational studies is that the absence of a construction does not assure that the speaker is not capable of producing or comprehending it. The patients in our studies do produce complex constructions. For instance, the svPPA patient quoted in Speech Sample 2 says, "and he started, to make some noise to see if he can find where the- the- the frog is." This sentence contains a complex main verb, with the inceptive "started (to make)." Embedded in this clause is the non-finite purposive "to see if . . . " A finite "if"-clause is embedded within that, and the free relative clause "where the frog is" is embedded within that as a complement of the verb "find." This constitutes four levels of embedding, demonstrating a high level of grammatical sophistication.

All of the patient groups in our sample except non-demented PD patients produced a significantly reduced frequency of utterances that were grammatically well-formed sentences compared to healthy seniors. The most common type of error is an utterance that is incomplete. For example, an lvPPA-FTD patient said, "A little bird in the room as well." While it is true that healthy individuals often speak such sentence fragments, especially as a qualification of something said previously, in the narrations of the Frog Story, the utterances of healthy seniors consisted of complete, well-formed sentences 96% of the time. Another common grammatical error is the absence of a determiner, that is, of *a, an, the, this*, and so on, as in "Dog fell down," spoken by another lvPPA-FTD patient.

A third fairly common type of grammatical error is non-agreement of subject and verb, as in this statement by the same lvPPA-FTD patient:

> And- and therefore (3.3 sec) they were in danger of getting stung . . . especially since the *dog were* sitting around the . . . the beehive.

An alternative form of assessment of grammaticality in speech production is to calculate the mean length of utterance in words (MLU). This is based on the premise that longer utterances are necessarily more elaborated than shorter utterances. By this metric, we find that naPPA, svPPA, and AD patients are impaired relative to healthy seniors, all having an average MLU of less than 9 words (SD = 1.0 to 2.7), compared to the healthy seniors' average of 10.1 words (SD = 1.5).

In a study of impairments of speech fluency in LBSD (Ash, McMillan, *et al.*, 2012), we found that reduced speech rate in LBSD correlated with measures of production of grammar, between-utterance pauses, and executive functioning. A composite measure of grammatical competence was constructed by summing the proportions of utterances that were well-formed sentences, utterances with complex structures, and nouns that had a determiner when a determiner was required. In the imaging analysis, we identified two cortical areas where there was significant overlap of atrophy with speech rate, between-utterance pauses, executive functioning, and grammaticality of speech production. These cortical regions are located in right medial frontal (BA 10) and left ventrolateral prefrontal (BA 47) regions, displayed in Plate 3.3, as described above.

In the study of non-fluent speech in naPPA cited above (Ash *et al.*, 2009) measures of grammatical sentence production were compromised and correlated with the main measure of interest, WPM. These measures of grammaticality include mean length of utterance, frequency of complex sentence structures, and verbs per utterance. In a related study of speech fluency in naPPA (Gunawardena *et al.*, 2010), we measured grammaticality by the percentage of complex structures in the utterances comprising the narration, and we found that this was impaired in naPPA compared to healthy seniors. In the imaging studies, we found that areas of significant cortical thinning associated with reduced grammatical complexity overlapped areas related to reduced speech rate in left inferior frontal cortex and anterior superior temporal cortex.

As noted above, lvPPA patients are intermediate among the PPA patients on several measures of impairment, and this is found for grammaticality as well as speech rate and lexical access (Ash, Weinberg, *et al.*, 2013b). All three groups of PPA patients produced utterances that were well-formed sentences at a significantly lower rate than controls. In lvPPA, there was a correlation of GM atrophy with well-formed sentences in left middle frontal regions (BA 8/9) and right insula, as shown in Plate 3.5 (see color plate section).

A similar metric of grammatical complexity in speech production is given by the proportion of dependent clauses per utterance. In a study of speech elicited by the Cookie Theft protocol, we examined the correlation of a composite measure of grammaticality with GM atrophy and WM reduced FA (Ash, Evans, *et al.*, 2013). In order to differentiate among patient populations, we constructed a composite measure of grammatical performance by averaging the *z*-scores for mean length of utterance, dependent clauses per utterance, and proportion of utterances that were well-formed sentences in the three variants of PPA. GM atrophy, reduced FA, and the regressions for grammaticality are displayed in Plate 3.6 (see color plate section). The imaging analyses reveal distinctive patterns of GM and WM disease corresponding to the overlapping grammatical impairments in the variants of PPA. In naPPA, GM atrophy is seen in the left frontal lobe, extending to right frontal and left anterior superior temporal regions, and the composite measure of grammaticality is related to left frontal and anterior superior temporal regions (Grossman *et al.*, 1996; Grossman *et al.*, 2013). In WM, grammatical production is related to an area approximating the superior longitudinal and arcuate fasciculi, a portion of the dorsal stream connecting frontal and posterior temporal regions. This network has previously been related to grammatical deficits in naPPA (Grossman *et al.*, 2013; Wilson *et al.*, 2012). In lvPPA, grammaticality was related to left inferior parietal atrophy in a large cluster extending into temporal regions, implicating short-term memory deficits in the grammatical production impairment (Gorno-Tempini *et al.*, 2004; Rogalski *et al.*, 2011; Wilson *et al.*, 2010). In svPPA, grammaticality was related to temporal and frontal areas that are important for access to the lexicon, suggesting that atrophy in these regions impairs the selection and integration of lexical items into sentence contexts.

Discourse

It is necessary to be able to form grammatical sentences with appropriate lexicon, but that is not enough for effective communication. Sentences must be organized into coherent discourse in order to be meaningful in the exchange of information and ideas between speakers. This is the level of language production which draws most heavily on executive resources. At this level, patients who are not aphasic and who can produce fully grammatical sentences with appropriate semantic content may still be seriously impaired, to the extent that they cannot easily participate in the fabric of daily life.

The difficulties of patients with executive resource limitations are most prominent at the level of discourse analysis. In order to study the discourse of the Frog Story narratives, we analyzed the story as a series of episodes, each episode consisting of a sequence of orientation, a complicating action, and a resolution, following principles established for the analysis of first-person narratives of personal experience (Labov & Waletzky, 1967). Following this model, the story was analyzed as consisting of seven episodes, with a total of 30 events. The narrations were evaluated in relation to this standard for accuracy of content, local connectedness, maintenance of the search theme, and global connectedness. Accuracy of content requires the full reporting of each event, with no contradictory content. Local connectedness is the linking of each event to the preceding event, which is accomplished by rhetorical markers such as sequencing adverbials, pronominal reference to preceding nouns, reference by definite as opposed to indefinite determiners, and statements of cause and effect. Maintenance of the theme of searching for the frog is scored from 0 to 4 by counting points accrued for mentions of the search (Reilly *et al.*, 2004). Global connectedness is a categorical variable which registers whether the speaker understands and acknowledges the point of the story, namely, that the frog found at the end is the frog that was present in the boy's room at the beginning (Ash *et al.*, 2006).

We first examined narrative competence in the variants of FTD, including naPPA, svPPA, and bvFTD. All three patient groups had slowed speech compared to controls, as has been evident in all our studies of connected speech. In addition, all three patient groups were less accurate than controls in their report of the content of the story. Most notably, the bvFTD patients exhibited profound discourse deficits, despite not being aphasic. These patients did not understand the elements of the story, as they demonstrated in many ways. One example is given in Speech Sample 5. After describing the opening scene, the speaker describes a page of the story which depicts the boy asleep in bed, with the dog curled up on the bed at his feet (lines 3–5). In the same picture, the frog is in the process of climbing out of the jar, but the speaker does not mention the frog's action, the fact that it is still in the jar. The next three lines describe the next page. It is morning, and the boy is awake on the bed, staring at the empty jar with his mouth agape in dismay. The dog is next to him, also looking at the jar in surprise. The speaker's description of these two scenes only enumerates the elements that are present in the drawings, and he does not even mention the events that have taken place. Thus the speaker fails on accuracy of content for both pages. For the first of these two pages, the speaker must state that the frog climbs out of the jar, and on the second page, he must note that the frog has disappeared. In addition to errors of accuracy in this extract, the speaker also loses a point for the search theme by failing to note that the frog is missing. Lines 3–5 of the extract also demonstrate a failure of local connectedness, since no connection is made between the scene being described and the preceding scene. The poor performance on local connectedness in bvFTD is correlated with their performance on a test of verbal fluency (FAS), consistent with the hypothesis that these patients have impaired executive functioning and that this interferes with their ability to tell a coherent story.

The bvFTD patients also performed poorly on global connectedness, the ability to make the connection between the disappearance of the frog at the beginning of the story and the frog that is found at the end. For example, one bvFTD patient describes the climax of the story, which occurs in scene 22 of the 24 scenes, as in Speech Sample 6. In this excerpt, it is clear that the speaker makes no connection between this frog and the frog that appeared at the beginning of the story. The failure rate of global connectedness in bvFTD is 70%, despite the absence of aphasia.

The imaging study of bvFTD related local connectedness to atrophy in several frontal regions of the right hemisphere, including inferior frontal (BA 45 and 47), dorsolateral prefrontal (BA 10), polar prefrontal (BA 10), and superior frontal (BA 6), as well as anterior temporal regions (BA 21 and 38) and left superior frontal cortex (BA 6). Previous studies of bvFTD patients have shown cortical atrophy in these right frontal and temporal regions, consistent with the evidence of this study for the functional significance of these brain regions for discourse (Grossman *et al.*, 2004; Rosen *et al.*, 2002; Williams *et al.*, 2005).

The only patient group with a higher rate of failure to make the connection between the frog at the beginning and the frog at the end is the AD patients, who succeed on global connectedness in only 13% of cases. It is clear from the narratives that the AD patients simply forget that there was a frog at the beginning of the story. On average, AD patients make no further mention of searching for the frog after about 60 seconds of narration, while the stories average more than 6 minutes. An example of this is given in Speech Sample 7. In line 5, the speaker acknowledges that the frog has disappeared, and in line 11, she indicates that the boy and dog are looking for the frog. However, at the end of the story, she clearly misses the point. Even though she sees that the boy is holding one of the frogs in his hand, she speaks as if the frogs found here have no precedent in the story.

We have also found that executive resources play a central role in the ability of PDD/LBD patients to organize a narrative (Ash, McMillan, *et al.*, 2012; Ash *et al.*, 2011). Patients with PD are impaired relative to healthy seniors only on the Mini Mental State Examination (MMSE) and in the amount of time taken by silent pauses in their narratives, although, of all the patient groups, they spend the least time in silent pauses. Patients with LBD and PDD, on the other hand, exhibit deficits in speech rate (not adjusted for silent pauses), speech errors, and grammaticality, although they are not impaired relative to healthy seniors on the grammaticality measures of MLU and dependent clause frequency. They appear not to have difficulty with lexical access as measured by the frequency of nouns and verbs. However, they are severely impaired on discourse measures. An example of discourse impairment is seen in Speech Sample 8. In this extract, the LBD patient is talking about the bees that are coming out of their hive. The hive is on the ground after falling from the tree where it was hanging, since the dog shook the tree by jumping up on it as he barked at the beehive. The speaker then refers to the boy, who has climbed partway up another, larger tree, and is looking in a hole in the trunk. In the third line, the focus moves from the dog and the bees to the boy, although the boy is only referred to as *that* [is ... about ... halfway up the tree]. In addition, the tree has been newly introduced into the narrative, and so it should have an indefinite determiner, i.e., "*a* tree," rather than "*the* tree." This is a failure of local connectedness.

In PDD/LBD, we find a correlation of both impaired local connectedness and impaired search theme with executive measures and reduced speech rate. Executive measures and WPM also correlate with each other (Spearman's rho = 0.69, $p < 0.01$ for the average z-score for four measures of executive functioning for the entire cohort of 32 LBSD patients). Imaging studies of a subset of LBSD patients revealed a correlation of local connectedness with atrophy in bilateral ventromedial and ventrolateral prefrontal regions and in left cingulate, putamen, and temporal cortex. These observations suggest that ventral frontal cortex may be involved in processing narrative production by contributing to the maintenance of cohesion within the narrative. This is supported by an fMRI study of healthy young adults, who showed greater bilateral ventral frontal activation in judgments of more closely related events compared to less closely related events in short scripts (Farag *et al.*, 2010). This fMRI study also included naPPA and bvFTD patients. These groups did not distinguish between more and less closely related events, and they exhibited atrophy in a region of interest that corresponded to the left ventral frontal activation seen in healthy young adults. Thus ventral frontal regions appear to be important in the processing of discourse cohesion. Another study used arterial spin labeling perfusion fMRI in healthy young adults to examine response to the Frog Story scenes. Activation was found bilaterally in ventral frontal regions for the narration of a continuous story relative to describing single, unconnected pictures (Troiani *et al.*, 2008). The involvement of right hemisphere regions not directly associated with language processing is consistent with the hypothesis that narrative organization is supported by executive resources which may be general, rather than specialized for language.

Production and comprehension: mirror images?

What is the relation between production and comprehension of language? Do these two processes depend on the same neural substrates? To respond to these questions, we compared expression and comprehension in the same set of LBSD patients (Ash, Xie, *et al.*, 2012). To measure expression, we tested search theme maintenance and local connectedness of the narratives on the Frog Story task. We assessed comprehension by measuring accuracy and latency of judgments on the ordering of events from scripts describing familiar activities, such as going fishing or making a sandwich, as a follow-up to earlier studies (Farag *et al.*, 2010; Gross *et al.*, 2013). We examined correlations of these measures with performance on neuropsychological tests of executive functioning, and also comprehension and expression of semantics and grammaticality. The measures of narrative expression and comprehension were highly correlated with each other. In addition, narrative expression and comprehension were both correlated with measures of executive functioning, implying that organization and planning resources are important in both production and comprehension. Further, narrative expression and comprehension were not correlated with semantic or grammatical production or comprehension. Finally, the imaging findings showed overlapping regions of the regressions of atrophy with measures of narrative expression, script comprehension, and executive functioning in prefrontal brain regions. These findings support the conclusion that impairments in narrative discourse organization, including both expression and comprehension, are significantly related to executive functioning deficits in LBSD, and not to language-specific capabilities.

Summary and conclusion

Speech rate, easily measured as the number of complete words spoken per minute, is a simple metric of language performance that clearly differentiates impaired speech from normal speech. Phonetic and phonological analyses are important in the transcription of all varieties of speech, in varying degrees. Virtually all speakers make errors of articulation; however, this level of analysis is more important in studying some patient groups, such as naPPA and lvPPA, and less important in the study of other groups, such as AD.

Deficits in the lexicon take many forms. Frog Story, Cookie Theft, and similar stimuli are productive in that they elicit a speech sample in which the speaker's intended meaning is known. The limitation of such stimuli is that they elicit a rather limited list of words, and most of the nouns are concrete nouns. It would be valuable to devise an interview module that would generate discussion of abstract concepts, such as political views, interpersonal issues, or decision-making problems, while still maintaining the virtue of a known target.

The study of grammatical competence in speech production produces fruitful results in every population of subjects. Almost any extended speech sample that responds to a complex stimulus will exhibit a variety of grammatical structures. If the stimulus offers the opportunity for the speaker to draw inferences about the logical progression of events, instances of cause and effect, and possibility versus reality, the speaker will have the opportunity to demonstrate the extent of his grammatical competence.

At the level of discourse analysis, a narrative – with a beginning, a middle, and an end – has a clear advantage over expository prose or conversational turn-taking. A narrative gives the speaker the opportunity to hold the floor for an extended time and provides material to enable him or her to speak continuously in a naturalistic task. The structure of narrative has been extensively studied, so a basis has been established for measuring the performance of an individual against a standard. Finally, telling a story is part of the fabric of everyday life. To improve the lives of our patients, we strive to support their ability to participate in everyday communication.

We have discussed some of the findings that have emerged from the analysis of spontaneous, connected speech in patients with a neurodegenerative disease. We have seen that the analysis of a body of speech can be productive at multiple levels of linguistic analysis and provides insight into more complex levels of language than does the elicitation of single words. A deeper understanding of the deficits inflicted by neurodegenerative conditions is a step towards differentiating among those conditions, alleviating those conditions, and gaining insight into how the human brain generates that uniquely human attribute, language.

APPENDIX: SPEECH SAMPLES

In what follows, the following transcription conventions are used:

Normal orthography is used when it is unambiguous. Where normal orthography would not accurately convey the sounds that are spoken, phonemic transcription is given between slashes, and phonetic transcription is given in square brackets.

A comma indicates a pause of 0.5 to 0.9 sec. Two dots indicate a pause of 1.0 to 1.4 sec. Three dots indicate a pause of 1.5 to 1.9 sec. A pause of 2.0 sec or more is given in parentheses, with duration given to the nearest tenth of a second. Only silences of 2.0 sec or more are indicated at the ends of utterances.

A segment that is articulated weakly or not at all is written in parentheses.

Comments and glosses are given in square brackets.

SPEECH SAMPLE 1. A 72-YEAR-OLD WOMAN WITH A 5-YEAR HISTORY OF naPPA; MMSE = 20

So they, it- there's a, child with em.. um . . . ə th- tay- take, what do you call them?, the um . . . the ek- covens, the- eh and the.. and the boy, the eh.. and this child.
And he also has his clothes not on yet.
Getting up to bed
And I'm trying to think about the one that, is in the drawer that eh . . . is in there.
Ahh, I'll see it some day.
Oh, now he must have been gone to sleep because.. um.. the p- the um, prob, crop, crab.. is trying to get out.
And he went back to bed and left all his clothes and the dog on the sh- on the ah
And in this one he got up
And he didn't see.. the eh (2.0 sec) the.. ah cof- crad, crab?
No it's not crab, but one of those little, things
And he got out of the.. the uh . . . gov, the big eh . . . eh, whatever
And this is his clothes still out.

SPEECH SAMPLE 2. A 58-YEAR-OLD MAN WITH A 6-YEAR HISTORY OF svPPA; MMSE = 28

Then.. he looked out
and he started, to make some noise to see if he can find where the- the
[Examiner: frog] the frog is. (4.0 sec)
So he's looking around to try to find where the far- frog is.
And he's looking down a hole
and in the- the hole there's a.. some kind of thing coming out of the ground
And uh . . . the.. the- the dog was looking up, where the bees were. (2.8 sec)
Well.. n the look- the dog was looking at the- at the uh . . . the (2.0 sec) [sigh] . . . [Examiner: the bees] yeah with the bees.. got him looking kind- the dog, wondering what was going on there. (2.2 sec)

The dog was gloo- looking into a tree, looking into a hole, to see if he can find where, th- the [Examiner: the frog] the frog. (2.2 sec)
Well.. when he looked in the hole (4.0 sec) the . . . that kind of (2.5 sec) [Examiner: bird] Hmm? [Examiner: a bird] y- OK but just a bird,
I know what it is, it's an owl.

SPEECH SAMPLE 3. A 69-YEAR-OLD MAN WITH A 7-YEAR HISTORY OF svPPA; MMSE = 25

And he was sleeping with two animals
and one animal woke him up (4.7 sec)
then he had his shoes or something on
another animal, the other animal got his head.. in a glass, and a bottle whatever it's called
I'm sorry
and then he fell outside with it, and broke it
and he went out and got him (2.8 sec)
then they were outside.. taking a look at the uh, weather.. him and his dog
and then the animal came up out of the ground (2.4 sec)
and the dog was after the animal
and the son went up on a uh tree, fell down off the tree because there was a.. bird that got him
and his son was running aw- his dog was running away (3.0 sec)
and the animal was still after him
and he went up on the top (4.5 sec)
and he got hit . . . by a big animal
then a big animal knocked him off (4.5 sec)
he ended up falling in the water.. with his dog
and he's telling his dog to keep quiet
and they got out
and him and his dog were on top of a.. tree branch looking at other animals (3.3 sec)
and then they were just playing with the animals.

SPEECH SAMPLE 4. A 55-YEAR-OLD WOMAN WITH A 7-YEAR HISTORY OF lvPPA; MMSE = 21

He's looking in the hole
and there's dog . . . with hole (2.7 sec) and a h- beep . . . a bee hanging down (3.5 sec)
and (4.7 sec) he doesn't like it

Eh and oh it's a (2.0 sec) um . . . a dog. (14.6 sec)
Beehive.. have tha(t)'s bees coming out and out of it, and the dog. (3.9 sec)
He's going- the little boy's going into- to the p- tree (2.7 sec)
And (9.2 sec) the do- dog is running (2.8 sec) away from the (4.2 sec) bees. [Examiner: You skipped a page] (2.5 sec)
Oh. [Examiner: The pages are really sticky today] (7.1 sec)
Eh, yeah.
Okay.. there's a hawk. [Examiner: Wait, I think you still skipped a page. Oh no.] (10.1 sec)
Oh, okay. (4.7 sec)
Little boy's əz- is uh.. t- uh (5.7 sec)
Is a owl?
and looks like a (3.3 sec) I don't know what that is. (19.4 sec)
Do he have (5.0 sec) ba- the- th- th- boy (3.1 sec) has, um . . . oh (9.0 sec) æ- anklers?
And one, on un eh and then, flip away. (4.9 sec)
And he's on the uh (2.3 sec) uh (4.3 sec) he's.. on his back. (7.2 sec)

SPEECH SAMPLE 5. AN 86-YEAR-OLD MAN WITH A 3-YEAR HISTORY OF bvFTD; MMSE = 23

The boy and the dog (2.0 sec) looking in- into a jar with a frog and this is in their bedroom. (16.5 sec)
The boy is asleep in his bed. (2.5 sec)
The frog is in a jar. (2.5 sec)
And his.. his.. his boots are on the floor, nex- next to his uh . . . next to his shirt. (10.3 sec)
Boy's in bed (2.2 sec) next to his dog (3.5 sec)
His boots are on the floor
and so are his sandals.. and an empty jar, and his shirt. (9.8 sec)
The boy's in his bedroom (3.6 sec)

SPEECH SAMPLE 6. A 33-YEAR-OLD MAN WITH A 3-YEAR HISTORY OF bvFTD; MMSE = 30

Dog- or boy's.. over log
Dog's over the log too
Um . . . they're on the log
See two frogs
See the mom and.. dad and a mom frog
And you got one, two, three, four, five.. seven little- eight little toads.
Um (2.8 sec) guess boy's going back home with dog.
(Tha)t's it.

SPEECH SAMPLE 7. AN 82-YEAR-OLD WOMAN WITH A 3-YEAR HISTORY OF AD; MMSE = 28

The little boy has a frog in th- in the, b-jar
And his- his doggy is wa- is watching with him.
And now they go to sleep,
And the frog climbs out of the jar.
And in the morning the little boy and the dog find that the frog is gone
And, the dog in some way gets out of the room with his head in the jar
And the little boy holds the dog safe.
Did I, I- I'm sorry..
Did I – [Examiner: That's OK.]
And they start looking around,
Where oh where, what happened to the frog?
[. . . 17 utterances . . .]
Only, the reindeer lets him fall down down down off of the edge of the mountain or whatever it is
And the dog does too.
He falls right in the water.
But it wasn't very deep
and there he sits in the water with the dog on his shoulders.
And then he comes along, uh comes to a log,
And he st- he puts his finger to his mouth to tell the dog to be quiet.
So they climb over the log,
And there's two frogs sitting on the other side,
Un, then, there are lots of frogs, little baby frogs
And he has one in his hand,
and he's- he's waving,
I don't know what they are.
The dog is still watching
I don't know what they are,
They look like.. gnomes or something.

SPEECH SAMPLE 8. AN 80-YEAR-OLD MAN WITH A 10-YEAR HISTORY OF LEWY BODY DISEASE; MMSE = 20

It's a (3.1 sec) it's an ug [enough?] bees, from- from the one hive, I guess. (3.7 sec)
Oh! by golly there's another one.
Uh that's t- about midway the- (2.3 sec) halfway up the tree, where the tree is- the base is broken.
And uh . . . we're probably gonna see some action there.

Hope(f)ully though nobody gets hurt.
Oh-ho yeah, there's someone
That's a- it's a hawk.. a hawk at a higher level, maybe ten feet high. (2.9 sec)
And the bee.. bees now have taken after, after the dog.
He probably wishes he hadn't disturbed them. (6.7 sec)
And our hawk friend who came early on the scene (3.5 sec) is (3.3 sec) is b- becoming active with the (4.2 sec) with the hawk and the, and the bees. (2.2 sec)

References

Amici, S., Ogar, J., Brambati, S. M., Miller, B. L., Neuhaus, J., Dronkers, N. L., & Gorno-Tempini, M. L. (2007). Performance in specific language tasks correlates with regional volume changes in progressive aphasia. *Cogn Behav Neurol, 20*(4), 203–211.

Ash, S., Adamowicz, D., McMillan, C., & Grossman, M. (2010). Sounds of silence: pauses in the speech of progressive non-fluent aphasics. Paper presented at the American Academy of Neurology, Toronto, ON.

Ash, S., Evans, E., O'Shea, J., Powers, J., Boller, A., Weinberg, D., . . . , Grossman, M. (2013). Differentiating primary progressive aphasias in a brief sample of connected speech. *Neurology, 81*, 1–8.

Ash, S., McMillan, C., Gross, R. G., Cook, P., Gunawardena, D., Morgan, B., . . . , Grossman, M. (2012). Impairments of speech fluency in Lewy body spectrum disorder. *Brain Lang, 120*(3), 290–302.

Ash, S., McMillan, C., Gross, R. G., Cook, P., Morgan, B., Boller, A., . . . , Grossman, M. (2011). The organization of narrative discourse in Lewy body spectrum disorder. *Brain Lang, 119*(1), 30–41.

Ash, S., McMillan, C., Gunawardena, D., Avants, B., Morgan, B., Khan, A., . . . , Grossman, M. (2010). Speech errors in progressive non-fluent aphasia. *Brain Lang, 113*(1), 13–20.

Ash, S., Moore, P., Antani, S., McCawley, G., Work, M., & Grossman, M. (2006). Trying to tell a tale: discourse impairments in progressive aphasia and frontotemporal dementia. *Neurology, 66*, 1405–1413.

Ash, S., Moore, P., Vesely, L., Gunawardena, D., McMillan, C., Anderson, C., . . . , Grossman, M. (2009). Non-fluent speech in frontotemporal lobar degeneration. *J Neurolinguistics, 22*, 370–383.

Ash, S., Weinberg, D., Haley, J., Boller, A., Powers, J., McMillan, C., & Grossman, M. (2013a). Silences in speech in primary progressive aphasia. Paper presented at the Society for Neuroscience, San Diego, CA.

Ash, S., Weinberg, D., Haley, J., Boller, A., Powers, J., McMillan, C. T., & Grossman, M. (2013b). Second best: non-specific speech deficits in logopenic progressive aphasia. Paper presented at the American Academy of Neurology, San Diego, CA.

Ash, S., Xie, S. X., Gross, R. G., Dreyfuss, M., Boller, A., Camp, E., . . . , Grossman, M. (2012). The organization and anatomy of narrative comprehension and expression in Lewy body spectrum disorders. *Neuropsychology*, *26*(3), 368–384.

Boersma, P., & Weenink, D. (1992–2014). Praat, v. 5.3.63. Institute of Phonetic Sciences, University of Amsterdam.

Bonner, M. F., Ash, S., & Grossman, M. (2010). The new classification of primary progressive aphasia into semantic, logopenic, or nonfluent/agrammatic variants. *Curr Neurol Neurosci Rep*, *10*(6), 484–490.

Cooke, A., Grossman, M., DeVita, C., Gonzalez-Atavales, J., Moore, P., Chen, W., . . . , Detre, J. (2006). Large-scale neural network for sentence processing. *Brain Lang*, *96*(1), 14–36. doi:10.1016/j.bandl.2005.07.072

Croot, K., Ballard, K., Leyton, C. E., & Hodges, J. R. (2012). Apraxia of speech and phonological errors in the diagnosis of nonfluent/agrammatic and logopenic variants of primary progressive aphasia. *J Speech Lang Hear Res*, *55*(5), S1562–1572.

Farag, C., Troiani, V., Bonner, M., Powers, C., Avants, B., Gee, J., & Grossman, M. (2010). Hierarchical organization of scripts: converging evidence from fMRI and frontotemporal dementia. *Cerebral Cortex*, *20*(10), 2453–2463.

Friederici, A. D., Meyer, M., & von Cramon, D. Y. (2000). Auditory language comprehension: an event-related fMRI study on the processing of syntactic and lexical information. *Brain Lang*, *74*(2), 289–300.

Friederici, A. D., Ruschemeyer, S. A., Hahne, A., & Fiebach, C. J. (2003). The role of left inferior frontal and superior temporal cortex in sentence comprehension: localizing syntactic and semantic processes. *Cerebral Cortex*, *13*, 170–177.

Gilbert, S. J., Spengler, S., Simons, J. S., Steele, J. D., Lawrie, S. M., Frith, C. D., & Burgess, P. W. (2006). Functional specialization within rostral prefrontal cortex (area 10): a meta-analysis. *J Cogn Neurosci*, *18*(6), 932–948.

Goodglass, H., & Kaplan, E. (1972). *Boston Diagnostic Aphasia Examination.*

Gorno-Tempini, M. L., Brambati, S. M., Ginex, V., Ogar, J., Dronkers, N. F., Marcone, A., . . . , Miller, B. L. (2008). The logopenic/phonological variant of primary progressive aphasia. *Neurology*, *71*(16), 1227–1234.

Gorno-Tempini, M. L., Dronkers, N. F., Rankin, K. P., Ogar, J. M., Phengrasamy, L., Rosen, H. J., . . . , Miller, B. L. (2004). Cognition and anatomy in three variants of primary progressive aphasia. *Ann Neurol*, *55*(3), 335–346.

Gorno-Tempini, M. L., Hillis, A. E., Weintraub, S., Kertesz, A., Mendez, M., Cappa, S. F., . . . , Grossman, M. (2011). Classification of primary progressive aphasia and its variants. *Neurology*, *76*(11), 1006–1014.

Gross, R. G., Camp, E., McMillan, C. T., Dreyfuss, M., Gunawardena, D., Cook, P. A., . . . , Grossman, M. (2013). Impairment of script comprehension in Lewy body spectrum disorders. *Brain Lang*, *125*(3), 330–343. doi:10.1016/j.bandl.2013.02.006

Grossman, M., & Ash, S. (2004). Primary progressive aphasia: a review. *Neurocase*, *10*, 3–18.

Grossman, M., McMillan, C., Moore, P., Ding, L., Glosser, G., Work, M., & Gee, J. C. (2004). What's in a name: voxel-based morphometric analyses of

MRI and naming difficulty in Alzheimer's disease, frontotemporal dementia, and corticobasal degeneration. *Brain, 127*, 628–649.

Grossman, M., Mickanin, J., Onishi, K., Hughes, E., D'Esposito, M., Ding, X. S., . . . , Reivich, M. (1996). Progressive nonfluent aphasia: language, cognitive and PET measures contrasted with probable Alzheimer's disease. *J Cogn Neurosci, 8*(2), 135–154.

Grossman, M., Powers, J., Ash, S., McMillan, C., Burkholder, L., Irwin, D., & Trojanowski, J. Q. (2013). Disruption of large-scale neural networks in non-fluent/agrammatic variant primary progressive aphasia associated with frontotemporal degeneration pathology. *Brain Lang, 127*(2), 106–120.

Gunawardena, D., Ash, S., McMillan, C., Avants, B., Gee, J., & Grossman, M. (2010). Why are patients with progressive nonfluent aphasia nonfluent? *Neurology, 75*(7), 588–594.

Hickok, G., & Poeppel, D. (2007). The cortical organization of speech processing. *Nat Rev Neurosci, 8*(5), 393–402.

Hodges, J. R., & Patterson, K. (2007). Semantic dementia: a unique clinicopathological syndrome. *Lancet Neurol, 6*, 1004–1014.

Humphries, C., Love, T., Swinney, D., & Hickok, G. (2005). Response of anterior temporal cortex to syntactic and prosodic manipulations during sentence processing. *Hum Brain Mapp, 26*(2), 128–138.

Hunt, K. W. (1965). *Grammatical Structures Written at Three Grade Levels*. Champaign, IL: National Council of Teachers of English.

Indefrey, P., & Levelt, W. J. M. (2004). The spatial and temporal signatures of word production components. *Cognition, 92*, 101–144.

Josephs, K. A., Duffy, J. R., Strand, E. A., Whitwell, J. L., Layton, K. F., Parisi, J. E., . . . , Petersen, R. C. (2006). Clinicopathological and imaging correlates of progressive aphasia and apraxia of speech. *Brain, 129*(6), 1385–1398.

Knibb, J. A., Woollams, A. M., Hodges, J. R., & Patterson, K. (2009). Making sense of progressive non-fluent aphasia: an analysis of conversational speech. *Brain, 132*(10), 2734–2746.

Labov, W. (2013). *The Language of Life and Death: The Transformation of Experience in Oral Narrative*. Cambridge: Cambridge University Press.

Labov, W., & Waletzky, J. (1967). Narrative analysis: oral versions of personal experience. In J. Helm (ed.), *Essays on the Verbal and Visual Arts: Proceedings of the 1966 Annual Spring Meeting of the American Ethnological Society* (pp. 12–44). Seattle, WA: University of Washington Press.

Lezak, M. (1983). *Neuropsychological Assessment*. Oxford: Oxford University Press.

Mayer, M. (1969). *Frog, Where Are You?* New York: Penguin Books.

McKeith, I. G. (2006). Consensus guidelines for the clinical and pathologic diagnosis of dementia with Lewy bodies (DLB): report of the Consortium on DLB International Workshop. *J Alzheimers Dis, 9*(3 Suppl.), 417–423.

Mesulam, M.-M., Wieneke, C., Thompson, C., Rogalski, E., & Weintraub, S. (2012). Quantitative classification of primary progressive aphasia at early and mild impairment stages. *Brain, 135*(5), 1537–1553.

Ramnani, N., & Owen, A. M. (2004). Anterior prefrontal cortex: insights into function from anatomy and neuroimaging. *Nat Rev Neurosci, 5*, 184–194.

Reilly, J., Losh, M., Bellugi, U., & Wulfeck, B. (2004). "Frog, where are you?" Narratives in children with specific language impairment, early focal brain injury, and Williams syndrome. *Brain Lang*, *88*, 229–247.

Rogalski, E., Cobia, D., Harrison, T. M., Wieneke, C., Thompson, C. K., Weintraub, S., & Mesulam, M. M. (2011). Anatomy of language impairments in primary progressive aphasia. *J Neurosci*, *31*(9), 3344–3350.

Rohrer, J. D., Rossor, M. N., & Warren, J. D. (2010). Syndromes of nonfluent primary progressive aphasia: a clinical and neurolinguistic analysis. *Neurology*, *75*(7), 603–610.

Rosen, H. J., Gorno-Tempini, M. L., Goldman, W. P., Perry, R. J., Schuff, N., Weiner, M., . . . , Miller, B. L. (2002). Patterns of brain atrophy in frontotemporal dementia and semantic dementia. *Neurology*, *58*, 198–208.

Sajjadi, S. A., Patterson, K., Arnold, R. J., Watson, P. C., & Nestor, P. J. (2012). Primary progressive aphasia: a tale of two syndromes and the rest. *Neurology*, *78*(21), 1670–1677.

Scarna, A., & Ellis, A. W. (2002). On the assessment of grammatical gender knowledge in aphasia: the danger of relying on explicit, metalinguistic tasks. *Lang cogn processes*, *17*(2), 185–201.

Scott, S. K., & Wise, R. J. (2004). The functional neuroanatomy of prelexical processing in speech perception. *Cognition*, *92*(1–2), 13–45.

Troiani, V., Fernandez-Seara, M. A., Wang, Z., Detre, J. A., Ash, S., & Grossman, M. (2008). Narrative speech production: an fMRI study using continuous arterial spin labeling. *Neuroimage*, *40*(2), 932–939.

Williams, G. B., Nestor, P. J., & Hodges, J. R. (2005). Neural correlates of semantic and behavioural deficits in frontotemporal dementia. *Neuroimage*, *24*, 1042–1051.

Wilson, S. M., Galantucci, S., Tartaglia, M. C., & Gorno-Tempini, M. L. (2012). The neural basis of syntactic deficits in primary progressive aphasia. *Brain Lang*, *122*(3), 190–198.

Wilson, S. M., Henry, M. L., Besbris, M., Ogar, J. M., Dronkers, N. F., Jarrold, W., . . . , Gorno-Tempini, M. L. (2010). Connected speech production in three variants of primary progressive aphasia. *Brain*, *133*(7), 2069–2088.

4 Situation models in naturalistic comprehension

Christopher A. Kurby & Jeffrey M. Zacks

Abstract Reading a discourse often leads to the construction of a situation model – a mental representation of the state of affairs described by the text. Situation model construction is associated with specific behavioral and neural markers. In this chapter, we consider the following questions: How does reading that involves constructing a situation model differ from other kinds of reading? Do the behavioral and neurophysiological data support a distinction between incremental updating of situation model components and global updating by abandoning an old situation model to form a new one? Do situation models represent information about sensory and motor features in analog representational formats during normal reading for comprehension? The available results indicate that specific mechanisms underlie different forms of situation model updating, that situation model-based reading is qualitatively different from reading without forming situation models, and that readers routinely deploy perceptual and motor representations to understand features of the situations described by a narrative.

Reading is a cognitive tour de force. Just guiding the eyes to focus on the right part of the text at the right time is exquisitely complex (Rayner, Raney, & Pollatsek, 1995). Readers do this effortlessly, and also recognize complex patterns to identify letters, words, and larger units of text, parse strings of words into sentences, and recognize the meanings of words and sentences. However, to us the most striking thing about what happens when people read narrative texts is that they seem to transmute black marks on paper into vivid representations of hypothetical worlds – flashing armor and clinking swords or storming skies over sinking ships (Graesser, Golding, & Long, 1991). How does a reader accomplish such a feat? In this chapter, we focus on two more specific questions about the representations that readers construct when comprehending narratives: "How does a reader build up a representation of meaningful events from a linear string of words?" and "How are perceptual and motor features of experience captured in the representations the reader constructs?" Our account builds on a larger body of research on the construction of *situation models* in language comprehension. We will start with a brief introduction to situation models. (For a more extended review, see Radvansky and Zacks (2014).)

Situation models

When people read narratives, they tend to simultaneously develop at least three types of mental representations (Kintsch, 1998; van Dijk & Kintsch, 1983). Readers can come away from a story with an unembellished memory for the exact words and syntax. This is typically called the *surface form* (Kintsch, 1998). This is the type of memory tapped when one tries to recall the exact words (usually unsuccessfully) of a line of dialog. Much research has shown that memory for the surface form is short-lived, typically decaying to a strength of zero after 4 days (Kintsch *et al.*, 1990; Kintsch, 1998; Schmalhofer & Glavanov, 1986; Zwaan & Radvansky, 1998). Readers also develop a representation of the propositions in the text, which is a structured set of relations that code the links between predicates and arguments, called the *textbase*. The textbase is likely also embellished with propositions from general knowledge (Kintsch, 1998). The textbase is more durable than the surface form (Kintsch *et al.*, 1990). Although this representation is an abstraction from the exact textual input, it is largely a representation of the text and the concepts it mentions, as its name implies. However, readers come away with much more than a memory for the words in a story and their relations to propositions. They also come away with a memory for the situation the text describes, which is abstracted from both the exact words used and from the specific propositions asserted or implied by the text (van Dijk & Kintsch, 1983; Zwaan & Radvansky, 1998). This representation is a situation model. Situation models provide a parsimonious account of a number of features of narrative comprehension: During reading, comprehenders track dimensions of the story world, including the characters, their goals, the objects with which they interact, causality, time, and space; this leads to slowing during reading when these dimensions change (Zwaan & Radvansky, 1998). Readers regularly assume information that is not stated in the text nor directly implied by specific propositions (Graesser, Singer, & Trabasso, 1994). Afterwards, they have trouble distinguishing between facts that were actually asserted by the story and facts that are consistent with the story's situation but unstated (Bransford, Barclay, & Franks, 1972). However, to make sense of such effects one needs to specify how particular features of the text are incorporated into one situation model or another one, and how successive situation models are created, updated, and possibly destroyed.

Segmentation of narrative into events

One possibility for how successive situation models are constructed is that at any given time a reader actively maintains one model that represents the current situation, and updates the model when features of the situation change (Zwaan & Radvansky, 1998). Radvansky and Zacks (2014) refer to this as the *working model*. The working model depends on recurrent neural activity, and has been proposed to be implemented in part by interactions between the prefrontal cortex and other cortical systems (Zacks *et al.*, 2007). Memory for previous events depends on synaptic changes and is associated with the hippocampus and adjacent structures in the medial temporal lobes. On this account, the distinction between *working memory* and *long-term memory* for narrative is not a matter of the delay between when one encounters material and when it is tested; instead, the critical question is whether one has updated one's working model.

How might readers update their working models? There are at least two mechanisms readers could bring to bear: *incremental* and *global* updating. In incremental updating, one component of a model is updated while the rest of the model remains intact. In global updating, a current situation model is abandoned and a new one is created from whole cloth. Incremental and global updating are not mutually exclusive; however, they are reflected to different degrees in different theories.

The event-indexing model (Magliano, Zwaan, & Graesser, 1999; Zwaan, Langston, & Graesser, 1995; Zwaan, Magliano, & Graesser, 1995; Zwaan & Radvansky, 1998) focuses on incremental updating. It proposes that situation models are organized around salient dimensions of the activity described by the text. What makes a dimension salient? This may depend on the reader's background and goals, but some dimensions are likely to be salient to most readers most of the time. Salient dimensions may include the characters and objects the story is about, temporal location, spatial location, characters' goals, and causes. When there is a shift on any salient dimension, such as when a new character enters the scene, the reader updates their working model to make their model current. This updating mechanism is incremental because only the changed information is updated, and an update on one dimension leaves the others untouched. For example, consider a scene where a child enters a kitchen and pours herself a bowl of cereal. As the child places the bowl on the counter and grabs the milk, there is a change in object contact, which gets updated in the model. However, the working model's representation of the spatial location (kitchen) and goal (to have breakfast) remain active and unaltered.

Event segmentation theory (EST) (Zacks *et al.*, 2007) focuses on global updating. It proposes a representational format similar to that proposed by the event-indexing model, with situation models that represent information about characters and objects, time, space, goals, causes, and potentially other dimensions. Event segmentation theory differs in that it proposes that the ongoing narrative is segmented into events, that the representation of the current event is maintained actively in a working model, and that at an event boundary the reader's working model is updated globally; a new working model is created based on the currently activated information and information in long-term semantic and episodic memory. The mechanism of segmentation proposed by EST is this: a reader's comprehension system continuously makes predictions about what information will be presented next in the text. These predictions are based on the current situation model (and on long-term episodic memory and knowledge). The comprehension system also monitors the quality of its predictions, comparing predicted information to what is actually presented and calculating a prediction error. When prediction error spikes, the narrative is segmented and the reader's working model is updated globally (Kurby & Zacks, 2012; Speer, Zacks, & Reynolds, 2007; Zacks, Speer, & Reynolds, 2009). Consider our example in which the child grabs milk to pour into a bowl of cereal. As the child finishes placing the bowl on the counter and turns to reach for the milk, this renders the activity a little less predictable. For example, if the text was "Jill reached for the . . .," the sentence could go on with "milk," but also could go on with "cereal," or "spoon," or "strawberries." As this example illustrates, prediction error spikes tend to occur when situational features change, and so both the event-indexing model and EST predict that updating will occur when more is changing in the situation. However, they differ in the form of the updating: the incremental updating proposed by the event indexing model affects only the information that has changed, whereas the global updating proposed by EST predicts that unchanged information is updated too. One important consequence of EST's global updating mechanism is that the information used to set up the new model has special status in working memory (Swallow, Zacks, & Abrams, 2009).

The structure-building framework (Gernsbacher, 1997) integrates both incremental and global updating. According to this theory, readers construct working models through the action of three processes: *foundation laying*, *mapping*, and *shifting*. Readers lay an initial structure for the working model using the first content encountered in the story. Onto this structure, readers map incoming information from the story. As long as the incoming story information maps on with an acceptable amount of fluency, the model grows. If mapping becomes difficult, however, such as when there is a change in the story, the reader shifts to build a brand new model. Once the shift occurs, the process starts again. The structure-building framework argues that because of the foundation-laying process, initial information at new sections – beginnings of sentences, paragraphs, episodes, etc. – has special status in the working model. It guides the mapping of new information.

In information-processing terms, the strongest dissociation between an incremental and global updating mechanism is seen in the fate of information that remains unchanged during an update. For example, suppose one were to read this passage: "Mr. Birch picked up a fishing rod, a short one with a spring in it, and started out the back door with it. The rod was rigged with a reel and a line at the end of which there was a spark plug. Mr. Birch walked out behind the house until he stood just west of the clothesline, facing the barn." The first two sentences give information about an object, the fishing rod. The third sentence changes the spatial location of the action. After this shift in location, what is the fate of information about the fishing rod? To the extent that updating is incremental, the information about this fishing rod should be unaffected because it is unchanged. However, to the extent that updating is global information about the fishing rod should be vulnerable even though it did not change. Recent studies of reading in our laboratory provide evidence that unchanged information *is* affected when readers update their situation models. However, changed information is more affected than unchanged information. This pattern of results supports the influence of both incremental and global updating on comprehension (Bailey, Kurby, Sargent, & Zacks, unpublished data; Kurby & Zacks, 2012).

Neurophysiology of situation model construction

What brain mechanisms are responsible for the construction of situation models? Some evidence is available from neuropsychological studies (Jung-Beeman, 2005); however, most of the evidence comes from neuroimaging studies, and it is on these that we will focus. One fMRI study (Friese, Rutschmann, Raabe, & Schmalhofer, 2008) adapted a behavioral paradigm developed by Schmalhofer and Glavanov (1986). In the Friese *et al.* (2008) study, participants read context sentences describing a situation and were asked to verify whether a test statement was sensible given the sentence. In one example, participants read about a passenger on a plane who was served a glass of wine when some turbulence occurred. The test statement was "wine spilled." There were four versions of the context sentences, which were written to vary the overlap between the test statement and the levels of representation of the context sentence. In the *explicit* condition, the context sentence was: "While the flight attendant served the passenger a glass of red wine turbulence caused the wine to spill." In this condition, the test statement overlapped with all three textbase representations of the sentence (the surface form, propositional, and situation). In the *paraphrase* condition, the context sentence was: "While the flight attendant served the passenger a glass of red wine turbulence caused the wine to splash." Here the test statement overlapped with propositional textbase and situation but not the surface form. In the *inference* condition, the context sentence was: "While the flight attendant served the passenger a glass of red wine turbulence occurred which was very severe." In this case, the test statement overlapped with the situation only. (Participants also verified test statements unrelated to the context sentence.) Friese *et al.* (2008) constructed a set of contrasts to separate brain activation patterns in response to each of the three levels of representation. They found that distinct brain regions increased in activity for each of these levels. Specific to situation model processing, there was an increase of left dorsomedial prefrontal cortex (dmPFC) for inference items compared to paraphrases. Regions in the right and left middle temporal lobes increased in activity for propositional comparisons. They found marginal evidence for the activation of right posterior cingulate cortex for paraphrase items compared to explicit items – surface level comparisons.

Robertson *et al.* (2000) asked which brain regions responded to the integration of sentences into a larger discourse. They had people read sets of sentences that could be integrated into a larger discourse or not, depending whether each sentence began with an indefinite ("a") or definite ("the") article. (Sentences that start with a definite article are easier to integrate into a discourse representation because definite articles signal repeated reference to a previously mentioned entity.) Compared to reading sets of indefinite-article sentences, the reading of sets of definite-article sentences was associated with an increase in activity in regions of the right superior frontal and right medial frontal cortex. (This contrast also revealed reduced activity in left inferior frontal and left anterior cingulate for definite article sentences.)

Kuperberg *et al.* (2006) investigated the neural correlates of causal inferencing during discourse comprehension. Participants read three-sentence sets that varied whether the last sentence in the set was highly causally related, intermediately related, or unrelated to the previous sentences. Participants rated the extent to which the final sentence fit. For intermediately related sentences, which require participants to draw a causal inference to understand them, there was activation of bilateral dmPFC, left lateral frontal, left inferior frontal, left parietal, and left middle temporal cortex. In a similar study, Siebörger, Ferstl, and von Cramon (2007) had participants rate the coherence of sentence pairs that varied on their strength of causal relation. Siebörger *et al.* (2007) reasoned that when participants rated the unrelated sentence pairs as somewhat coherent they were engaging in self-generated coherence-building processes. For these items, activity increased in a collection of frontal regions including the left inferior frontal, left superior frontal, left lateral orbital, and left middle frontal. Activation also was found in the parietal lobe at the angular gyrus, bilaterally, and the right intraparietal sulcus. These results converge nicely with other work on discourse processing; the dmPFC has frequently been implicated in situation model processing and maintenance (Xu *et al.*, 2005).

Indeed, the dmPFC appears to be a hub of a network that responds during reading tasks, called the extended language network (ELN) (Ferstl *et al.*, 2008). According to Ferstl *et al.* (2008), most reading experiences engage the perisylvian language areas, particularly in the left hemisphere. Outside of these areas, there is typically activation of the anterior temporal lobes, the superior temporal sulcus and inferior frontal gyrus in response to contrasts against reading single words or nonsense sentences. And, critically for the current discussion, the dmPFC and regions in the precuneus increase in activity typically when reading for coherence, sometimes revealed when readers make explicit judgments of coherence (Siebörger *et al.*, 2007). For a thorough review of the ELN see Ferstl *et al.* (2008), Ferstl (2010), and Zacks and Ferstl (2015).

Naturalistic construction of situation models

Much of the neuroimaging research to date on reading comprehension has used short artificial texts, or "textoids," that are constructed to test isolated components of comprehension (Graesser, Millis, & Zwaan, 1997). Further, most of these studies have used tasks that alter the normal reading comprehension process, such as judgments of sensibility or memory tests. Although these methodologies allow one to control surface features such as word frequency and syntax, they fail in controlling for higher-level processes, such as global coherence building and maintenance. Additionally, the use of concurrent tasks during reading may alter mechanisms engaged during reading. To what extent do the previous findings on text comprehension apply to comprehension for naturalistic materials in more naturalistic settings?

For the most part, neuroimaging studies of naturalistic discourse comprehension converge nicely with previous neuroimaging work on situation models (Ferstl, 2010). In one such study, Xu *et al.* (2005) had participants read single words, isolated sentences, and larger narratives in the scanner, one word at a time. The narratives were a selection of *Aesop's Fables*. They were coded for a number of lexical and linguistic features including word frequency, concreteness, grammatical class, and syntactic complexity. Texts were selected that matched across these sets of features. In comparison to reading single letters, all the texts (single words, single sentences, and narratives) activated perisylvian language areas. Additionally, in comparison to sentences, narratives activated regions bilaterally in the precuneus, the dmPFC, and the ventral medial prefrontal cortex (vmPFC). There was also increased activity in left middle temporal gyrus, posterior superior temporal sulcus, and lateral premotor cortex.

A critical feature of situation models is that they maintain and integrate global information about the described events. As events unfold, there are changing demands on the comprehension systems that need to be met for comprehension to be successful. Might the dmPFC be critical to such maintenance? Yarkoni, Speer, and Zacks (2008) investigated the brain systems involved in building and maintaining a working model, and the relation between regional activity and subsequent memory for the stories. They also tested for regions that showed changed dynamics as the story unfolded. In their study, participants read blocks of naturalistic narratives that were either coherent stories or scrambled stories – blocks of sentences with their order randomized. The stories were edited excerpts from a book called *One Boy's Day*, which is an observational record of a young boy's activities throughout an entire day (Barker & Wright, 1951). The stories were presented one word at a time and participants were instructed simply to read the texts for a later memory test. After each text, participants took a sentence recognition test and a four-alternative multiple-choice comprehension test. In their analyses, the authors tested for regions that changed their activation depending on story type (coherent vs. scrambled) and for regions that increased their activation over the course of each story. A number of regions showed a larger fMRI response for coherent stories than for scrambled stories, including the bilateral middle temporal gyrus, bilateral inferior frontal gyrus, left dorsal premotor cortex, and bilateral dmPFC. Further, most of these regions also increased in activity for the scrambled condition compared to baseline, suggesting that they play a role in both sentence-level and discourse-level processing. The exception was the dmPFC, which increased only during the coherent story conditions, suggesting that the dmPFC specializes in discourse-level processing only. In their analysis of temporal dynamics, they observed a set of regions in posterior parietal cortex that increased in activity at the beginning of text blocks but then decreased thereafter. These regions may be important for the initial construction of situation models, consistent with the structure-building framework. They also found a collection of frontal and temporal regions, such as right premotor cortex and anterior temporal lobe, that increased in activity as the story unfolded. This suggests these regions are important for the maintenance of situation models (see Plate 4.1 in color plate section). Additionally, the activity in a number of regions during the story condition, including the dmPFC, was positively correlated with recognition memory, and activity in the right premotor cortex, as well as left middle temporal gyrus and right cerebellum, was positively correlated with better comprehension test performance.

Further work, using naturalistic materials, has revealed the brain regions associated with the segmentation of narratives into events, perhaps similar to the so-called shifting mechanism of the structure-building framework. Speer, Zacks, and Reynolds (2007) had participants read extended excerpts (around 180 clauses long) from *One Boy's Day* (Barker & Wright, 1951), presented one word at a time, during fMRI scanning. Afterwards, participants segmented the narratives into large (coarse) and small (fine) events. Large regions in temporal-parietal cortex – bilateral precuneus, anterior temporal, and posterior superior temporal gyrus – right posterior cingulate, and right middle frontal gyrus increased in activity in a window around event boundaries. (Most regions showed larger effects for coarse than fine boundaries.) Whitney *et al.* (2009) investigated the neural correlates of processing narrative shifts. Participants passively listened to a 3581-word German novella while their brain activity was recorded with fMRI. The narrative was coded for shifts in time, space, action, and character. Compared to the effect of encountering a sentence boundary, narrative shifts (collapsed across type) elicited activity in the right precuneus, the right posterior cingulate, and the left middle cingulate cortex. Ezzyat and Davachi (2011) similarly investigated the brain response to narrative shifts, in this case temporal shifts, but also asked whether separate mechanisms contributed to the maintenance of event information vs. updating at event boundaries. Participants read extended narratives that occasionally shifted time with the phrase, "A while later" or maintained continuity with the phrase "A moment later." Compared to the sentences that maintained continuity, for the event boundaries there was an increase in activity in a large region in the right precuneus, the right ventrolateral PFC, the right dmPFC, and left superior temporal gyrus. Similarly to Yarkoni *et al.* (2008), Ezzyat and Davachi (2011) tested for regions that increased in activity over the course of each event. Those regions were bilateral ventromedial PFC, left middle temporal gyrus, and right parahippocampal cortex (see Plate 4.2 in color plate section). Further, they tested whether activity in these regions associated with event boundaries and event maintenance correlated with memory for the events. After reading each story, participants engaged a cued-recall priming paradigm to measure within-event binding. Ezzyat and Davachi (2011) found that regions which increased in activity across an event correlated with within-event binding (see Plate 4.3 in color plate section).

The above studies reveal that there is a consistent collection of brain regions that respond to the demands of situation model processing, from shifting, to construction, to maintenance (see also Ferstl (2010) for a review). A very consistent result is that the dmPFC is selectively activated under conditions in which readers construct situation models. In addition, the precuneus usually increases in activity when readers need to make inferences to establish coherence. Finally, regions including the lateral frontal cortex and regions in the temporal lobes may be important for situation model maintenance. While our review so far has discussed the processes that serve situation model processing, we are left with an important question: What is the form of representation of situation models?

Sensorimotor simulations: the form of representation of situation models

Over the last decade, embodied cognition theories have gained support from both behavioral and neuroimaging research (Barsalou, 2008). These theories argue that the brain systems important for perception and action play a critical role in the representation of knowledge (Barsalou, 2008; Gallese & Lakoff, 2005; Glenberg, 1997; Glenberg & Gallese, 2012; Zwaan, 2004). This approach has been applied to the construction of situation models, proposing that readers generate perceptual simulations of the events described in language (Zwaan, 2004). For example, in theory, when reading a sentence about a pitcher throwing a ball, the sensorimotor system important for grasping and throwing performs the neural computations needed and emulates the action, rather than engaging the body to externally conduct it (Fischer & Zwaan, 2008; Glenberg & Gallese, 2012). When reading about a visual scene, the visual system engages to mentally construct the scene from knowledge. The same logic holds for the other senses. It is likely that event models, and situation models specifically, are composed in part by sensorimotor simulations (Zwaan, 2004).

Much neuroimaging work supports the possibility that readers activate sensorimotor systems during language tasks. The majority of the studies used very short texts, sometimes single words or phrases, and at times included explicit judgment tasks. Hauk, Johnsrude, and Pulvermüller (2004) presented participants with action verbs, such as "pick," "lick," and "kick" while the participants laid in the scanner. Results showed topographically organized activity in the sensorimotor and motor cortex corresponding to the effector relevant to the action. Such results have been replicated a number of times, using slightly different tasks and dependent measures, and using action phrases instead of single words (Aziz-Zadeh *et al.*, 2006; Desai *et al.*, 2010; Tettamanti *et al.*, 2005; Willems, Hagoort, & Casasanto, 2010). For example, Willems and colleagues (2010) found that when making lexical decisions for manual verbs, right-handers activated left motor cortex more than right motor cortex, and left-handers activated right motor cortex more than left. This shows that simulations are limb-specific.

Simulation results also have been found for visual and auditory processing. Judgments about object color from verbal stimuli activate left fusiform gyrus (Simmons *et al.*, 2007), a higher-level visual area, and recall for pictures activates large areas of occipital cortex (Wheeler, Petersen, & Buckner, 2000). Making judgments about the sounds of objects (Kellenbach, Brett, & Patterson, 2001) and recall for sounds (Wheeler *et al.*, 2000) activate auditory regions such as the posterior superior temporal gyrus and middle temporal gyrus. Simulation effects have emerged also in the study of speech comprehension. Yao, Belin, and Scheepers (2011) found that the silent reading of speech activates speech-selective areas.

But how well do these results generalize to naturalistic reading? Do readers activate sensorimotor systems as a normal part of comprehending complete sentences or discourse, or do these effects require artificial stimuli and tasks? The inclusion of judgment tasks such as identifying colors or sounds is certainly not typical of most reading situations and may increase the probability that one would generate a simulation. A similar concern exists for work on motor simulation in language comprehension where participants are often asked to turn dials or push and pull levers (Fischer & Zwaan, 2008; Glenberg & Kaschak, 2002; Zwaan & Taylor, 2006).

In a notable study, Deen and McCarthy (2010) tested whether readers simulate the biological motion of characters in a story. Participants read short stories, averaging 70 words each, which described biological motion of characters, such as characters walking or moving objects, or non-biological motion. Participants read the stories for comprehension without an explicit judgment task. A biological motion localizer was used to identify biological-motion-sensitive brain regions, typically the posterior superior temporal sulcus (pSTS) (Allison, Puce, & McCarthy, 2000). Deen and McCarthy (2010) found that participants activated pSTS more for the biological motion texts than the non-biological motion ones, and that region overlapped with the regions activated by the localizer. A study by Wallentin *et al.* (2011) found that left posterior middle temporal gyrus, a region known to increase in activity for the reading of motion verbs in isolation (Kable, Lease-Spellmeyer, & Chatterjee, 2002), also increased in activity for motion verbs embedded in larger discourse.

These studies show that readers activate sensorimotor regions during comprehension, but what role do they play in situation model processing? In one possibility, these regions are engaged when the model needs to be updated. Speer *et al.* (2009) investigated the brain regions engaged when there are changes in situational dimensions in the story. Recall that according to the event-indexing model, readers track six situational dimensions – time, space, characters, goals, objects, and causes – and update their situation models when they change. Speer *et al.* (2009) conducted a theoretically driven analysis of the texts to code for points in the story where there were situational shifts. In the study, participants read extended discourses (approximately 180 clauses long), one word at a time, in the scanner. Critically, similar to Deen and McCarthy (2010), participants' only task was to read for comprehension. They did not engage in any explicit judgment tasks. They found that different brain regions responded to the different types of situational change. In some cases the areas activated for changes on a particular dimension were associated with processing that dimension in perception and action. For example, changes in character goals selectively activated a portion of prefrontal cortex which is known to play a role in the comprehension of goal directed behavior (Wood & Grafman, 2003). Changes in object interaction selectively activated left premotor cortex. The bilateral parahippocampal gyrus, important for the perceptual processing of spatial location change (Burgess, Maguire, & O'Keefe, 2002), increased in activity for spatial shifts in the story. (This region responded to other types of situation change as well.) These results suggest that when updating situation models, brain systems are engaged that are important to the type of information being updated.

Kurby and Zacks (2013) investigated whether readers activate modality-specific representations during naturalistic discourse comprehension. The study was a reanalysis of data from Speer *et al.* (2009) and Yarkoni *et al.* (2008). We asked whether readers activate visual, auditory, or somatomotor regions when encountering visual, auditory, or motor information in the story. Through norming and coding procedures, clauses were identified that elicited strong mental imagery in either the visual, auditory, or motor modality. The reading of auditory imagery clauses, such as descriptions of sounds or lines of dialog, was associated with activation in a number of regions in secondary auditory cortex, including middle temporal gyrus, and posterior superior temporal gyrus. These clauses also activated perisylvian language regions, such as the inferior frontal gyrus. The reading of motor clauses, which were descriptions of actions, activated left premotor and left secondary sensorimotor cortex. (There were no effects of reading visual imagery clauses.) These results suggest that readers activate sensorimotor simulations during the comprehension of extended discourse with the simple goal of reading to understand (see Plate 4.4 in color plate section).

Although readers generate situation models and can also generate sensorimotor simulations, it is currently unknown whether simulations are necessary for situation model construction. Strong claims have been made that simulations are necessary (Glenberg & Gallese, 2012); however, no data to date clearly support that claim. Indeed, some studies of conceptual knowledge have revealed that people do not always activate sensorimotor representations when reading about verbs (Bedny *et al.*, 2008) or making perceptual judgments about objects (Louwerse, 2011; Louwerse & Jeuniaux, 2010). We recently asked a readily testable question: Do simulations depend on situation models? In Kurby and Zacks (2013), in Study 2, we reasoned that if simulation results from forming a situation model, then disrupting the ability to form a situation model should disrupt simulation. To test this hypothesis, we reanalyzed data from Yarkoni *et al.* (2008), using the same norming and coding procedures described above to identify high-imagery clauses. Recall that in Yarkoni *et al.* (2008), participants read discourse that was either a coherent story or scrambled stories – sets of unrelated sentences. Using the regions of interest (ROIs) from Study 1 of Kurby and Zacks (2013), we replicated the imagery effects in the story condition, but none of the imagery effects replicated in the scrambled condition. Most of the imagery effects were significantly larger in the story condition than scrambled condition. These data support the possibility that sensorimotor simulations are engaged during situation model processing. And, further, simulations are not generated when the reader is unable to form a global situation model (see Figure 4.1).

However, these data do not establish that simulation is *necessary* for situation model construction. It may be that simulations provide embellishment or elaboration on situation models rather than forming the foundation of the mental model (Mahon & Caramazza, 2008). They may be downstream from situation models. There are a number of directions research needs to go to further investigate whether simulations are necessary. It will be important to test whether situation models can be constructed in the absence of simulations, as has been argued elsewhere (Zwaan, 2004). Additionally, it will be important to characterize the association between activity in situation model related regions and activity in sensorimotor regions. Are their activity correlated? Or de-phased in time? Of interest would be whether simulations occur prior to situation model operations, or the reverse, or whether they co-occur.

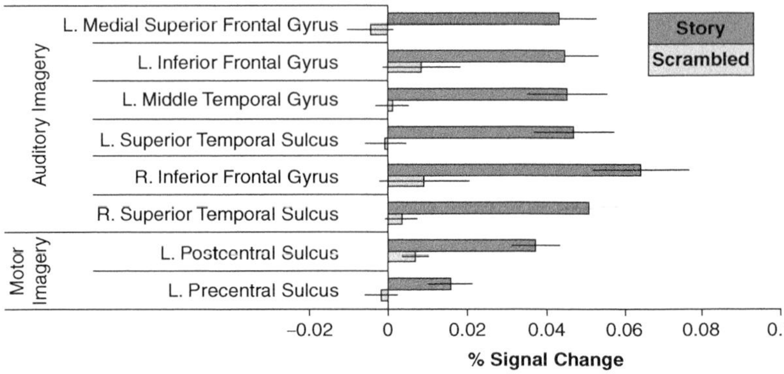

Figure 4.1 Regions that showed modality-specific imagery effects in Kurby and Zacks (2013), Study 1, increased in activity only during the reading of coherent stories (Study 2). Reproduced with permission.

Conclusion

In this chapter, we have discussed situation models in language comprehension. During comprehension, readers construct a working model that represents the current state of affairs. The working model is kept current through a combination of incremental and global updating. A diverse set of brain regions play an important role in each of these processes. Regions in posterior cortex, such as the precuneus and parietal cortex, may subserve the establishment of a new model during global updating (Ferstl, 2010; Yarkoni *et al.*, 2008). Frontal regions, with dmPFC featuring prominent, may play a large part in maintaining the working model (Ferstl *et al.*, 2008; Friese *et al.*, 2008; Xu *et al.*, 2005). Populating the model with situational features appears to engage content-specific neural systems (Speer *et al.*, 2009). Segmenting the situation to initiate global updating of the working model engages a network of temporal-parietal-occipital regions, as well as prefrontal (Speer *et al.*, 2007; Zacks *et al.*, 2001). Situational models appear to function as sensorimotor simulations of the described events, at least in part, and therefore draw on the same neural systems as are used for perception and action. Although a majority of the neuroimaging research on situation models uses short texts, and sometimes unnatural tasks, a large portion of these findings have come from studies using more naturalistic conditions. We look forward to further tests of situation model processing in discourse comprehension in reading conditions similar to everyday experiences.

References

Allison, T., Puce, A., & McCarthy, G. (2000). Social perception from visual cues: role of the STS region. *Trends in Cognitive Sciences, 4*, 267–278.

Aziz-Zadeh, L., Wilson, S., Rizzolatti, G., & Iacoboni, M. (2006). Congruent embodied representations for visually presented actions and linguistic phrases describing actions. *Current Biology, 16*, 1818–1823.

Barker, R. G., & Wright, H. S. (1951). *One Boy's Day: A Specimen Record of Behavior.* Oxford: Harper.

Barsalou, L. W. (2008). Grounded cognition. *Annual Review of Psychology, 59*, 617–645.

Bedny, M., Caramazza, A., Grossman, E., Pascual-Leone, A., & Saxe, R. (2008). Concepts are more than percepts: the case of action verbs. *Journal of Neuroscience, 28*, 11347–11353.

Bransford, J. D., Barclay, J. R., & Franks, J. J. (1972). Sentence memory: a constructive versus interpretive approach. *Cognitive Psychology, 3*(2), 193–209. doi: http://dx.doi.org/10.1016/0010-0285(72)90003-5

Burgess, N., Maguire, E. A., & O'Keefe, J. (2002). The human hippocampus and spatial and episodic memory. *Neuron, 35*(4). doi:10.1016/S0896-6273(02)00830-9

Deen, B., & McCarthy, G. (2010). Reading about the actions of others: biological motion imagery and action congruency influence brain activity. *Neuropsychologia, 48*, 1607–1615.

Desai, R. H., Binder, J. R., Conant, L. L., & Seidenberg, M. S. (2010). Activation of sensory–motor areas in sentence comprehension. *Cerebral Cortex, 20*, 468–478.

Ezzyat, Y., & Davachi, L. (2011). What constitutes an episode in episodic memory? *Psychological Science, 22*(2), 243–252. doi:http://dx.doi.org/10.1177/0956797610393742

Ferstl, E. C. (2010). Neuroimaging of text comprehension: where are we now? *Italian Journal of Linguistics, 22*(1), 61–88.

Ferstl, E. C., Neumann, J., Bogler, C., & von Cramon, D. Y. (2008). The extended language network: a meta-analysis of neuroimaging studies on text comprehension. *Human Brain Mapping, 29*, 581–593.

Fischer, M. H., & Zwaan, R. A. (2008). Embodied language: a review of the role of motor system in language comprehension. *Quarterly Journal of Experimental Psychology, 61*(6), 825–850. doi:http://dx.doi.org.ezproxy.gvsu.edu/10.1080/17470210701623605

Friese, U., Rutschmann, R., Raabe, M., & Schmalhofer, F. (2008). Neural indicators of inference processes in text comprehension: an event-related functional magnetic resonance imaging study. *Journal of Cognitive Neuroscience, 20*(11), 2110–2124. doi:http://dx.doi.org.ezproxy.gvsu.edu/10.1162/jocn.2008.20141

Gallese, V., & Lakoff, G. (2005). The brain's concepts: the role of the sensory-motor system in conceptual knowledge. *Cognitive Neuropsychology, 22*(3-4), 455–479. doi:http://dx.doi.org.ezproxy.gvsu.edu/10.1080/02643290442000310

Gernsbacher, M. A. (1997). Two decades of structure building. *Discourse Processes, 23*, 265–304.

Glenberg, A. M. (1997). What memory is for. *Behavioral and Brain Sciences, 20*, 1–55.

Glenberg, A. M., & Gallese, V. (2012). Action-based language: a theory of language acquisition, comprehension, and production. *Cortex: A Journal Devoted to the Study of the Nervous System and Behavior*, *48*(7), 905–922. doi:http://dx.doi.org.ezproxy.gvsu.edu/10.1016/j.cortex.2011.04.010

Glenberg, A. M., & Kaschak, M. P. (2002). Grounding language in action. *Psychonomic Bulletin and Review*, *9*, 558–565.

Graesser, A. C., Golding, J. M., & Long, D. L. (1991). Narrative representation and comprehension. In R. Barr, M. L. Kamil, P. Mosenthal, & P. D. Pearson (eds.), *Handbook of Reading Research*, pp. 171–205. London: Longman.

Graesser, A. C., Millis, K. K., & Zwaan, R. A. (1997). Discourse comprehension. *Annual Review of Psychology*, *48*, 163–189.

Graesser, A. C., Singer, M., & Trabasso, T. (1994). Constructing inferences during narrative text comprehension. *Psychological Review*, *101*(3), 371–395. doi:http://dx.doi.org.ezproxy.gvsu.edu/10.1037/0033-295X.101.3.371

Hauk, O., Johnsrude, I., & Pulvermüller, F. (2004). Somatotopic representation of action words in human motor and premotor cortex. *Neuron*, *41*, 301–307.

Jung-Beeman, M. (2005). Bilateral brain processes for comprehending natural language. *Trends in Cognitive Science*, *9*, 512–518.

Kable, J. W., Lease-Spellmeyer, J., & Chatterjee, A. (2002). Neural substrates of action event knowledge. *Journal of Cognitive Neuroscience*, *14*, 795–805.

Kellenbach, M. L., Brett, M., & Patterson, K. (2001). Large, colorful, or noisy? Attribute- and modality-specific activations during retrieval of perceptual attribute knowledge. *Cognitive, Affective and Behavioral Neuroscience*, *1*, 207–221.

Kintsch, W. (1998). *Comprehension: A Paradigm for Cognition*. New York: Cambridge University Press.

Kintsch, W., Welsch, D., Schmalhofer, F., & Zimny, S. (1990). Sentence memory: a theoretical analysis. *Journal of Memory and Language*, *29*(2), 133–159. doi: http://dx.doi.org.ezproxy.gvsu.edu/10.1016/0749-596X(90)90069-C

Kuperberg, G. R., Lakshmanan, B. M., Caplan, D. N., & Holcomb, P. J. (2006). Making sense of discourse: an fMRI study of causal inferencing across sentences. *NeuroImage*, *33*(1). doi:10.1016/j.neuroimage.2006.06.001

Kurby, C. A., & Zacks, J. M. (2012). Starting from scratch and building brick by brick in comprehension. *Memory and Cognition*, *40*, 812–826.

Kurby, C. A., & Zacks, J. M. (2013). The activation of modality-specific representations during discourse processing. *Brain and Language*, *126*, 338–349.

Louwerse, M. M. (2011). Symbol interdependency in symbolic and embodied cognition. *Topics in Cognitive Science*, *3*(2), 273–302. doi:http://dx.doi.org.ezproxy.gvsu.edu/10.1111/j.1756-8765.2010.01106.x

Louwerse, M. M., & Jeuniaux, P. (2010). The linguistic and embodied nature of conceptual processing. *Cognition*, *114*, 96–104.

Magliano, J. P., Zwaan, R. A., & Graesser, A. C. (1999). *The role of situational continuity in narrative understanding*. In H. van Oostendorp & S. R. Goldman (eds.), *The Construction of Mental Representations during Reading*, pp. 219–245. Mahwah, NJ: Lawrence Erlbaum Associates.

Mahon, B. Z., & Caramazza, A. (2008). A critical look at the embodied cognition hypothesis and a new proposal for grounding conceptual content. *Journal of Physiology – Paris*, *102*, 59–70.

Radvansky, G. A., & Zacks, J. M. (2014). *Event Cognition*. New York: Oxford University Press.

Rayner, K., Raney, G. E., & Pollatsek, A. (1995). Eye movements and discourse processing. In R. F. Lorch & E. J. O'Brien (eds.), *Sources of Coherence in Reading*, pp. 9–35. Hillsdale, NJ: Lawrence Erlbaum Associates.

Robertson, D. A., Gernsbacher, M. A., Guidotti, S. J., Robertson, R. R. W., Irwin, W., Mock, B. J., & Campana, M. E. (2000). Functional neuroanatomy of the cognitive process of mapping during discourse comprehension. *Psychological Science*, *11*(3), 255–260. doi:http://dx.doi.org.ezproxy.gvsu.edu/10.1111/1467-9280.00251

Schmalhofer, F., & Glavanov, D. (1986). Three components of understanding a programmer's manual: verbatim, propositional, and situational representations. *Journal of Memory and Language*, *25*(3), 279–294. doi:http://dx.doi.org.ezproxy.gvsu.edu/10.1016/0749-596X(86)90002-1

Siebörger, F. T., Ferstl, E. C., & von Cramon, D. Y. (2007). Making sense of nonsense: an fMRI study of task induced inference processes during discourse comprehension. *Brain Research*, *1166*, 77–91. doi:10.1016/j.brainres.2007.05.079

Simmons, W. K., Ramjee, V., Beauchamp, M. S., McRae, K., Martin, A., & Barsalou, L. W. (2007). A common neural substrate for perceiving and knowing about color. *Neuropsychologia*, *45*, 2802–2810.

Speer, N. K., Reynolds, J. R., Swallow, K. M., & Zacks, J. M. (2009). Reading stories activates neural representations of visual and motor experiences. *Psychological Science*, *20*, 989–999.

Speer, N. K., Zacks, J. M., & Reynolds, J. R. (2007). Human brain activity time-locked to narrative event boundaries. *Psychological Science*, *18*, 449–455.

Swallow, K. M., Zacks, J. M., & Abrams, R. A. (2009). Event boundaries in perception affect memory encoding and updating. *Journal of Experimental Psychology: General*, *138*, 236–257.

Tettamanti, M., Buccino, G., Saccuman, M. C., Gallese, V., Danna, M., Scifo, P., . . ., Perani, D. (2005). Listening to action-related sentences activates fronto-parietal motor circuits. *Journal of Cognitive Neuroscience*, *17*, 273–281.

van Dijk, T. A., & Kintsch, W. (1983). *Strategies in Discourse Comprehension*. New York: Academic Press.

Wallentin, M., Nielsen, A. H., Vuust, P., Dohn, A., Roepstorff, A., & Lund, T. E. (2011). BOLD response to motion verbs in left posterior middle temporal gyrus during story comprehension. *Brain and Language*, *119*(3), 221–225. doi:http://dx.doi.org.ezproxy.gvsu.edu/10.1016/j.bandl.2011.04.006

Wheeler, M. E., Petersen, S. E., & Buckner, R. L. (2000). Memory's echo: vivid remembering reactivates sensory-specific cortex. *Proceedings of the National Academy of Sciences USA*, *97*, 11 125–11 129.

Whitney, C., Huber, W., Klann, J., Weis, S., Krach, S., & Kircher, T. (2009). Neural correlates of narrative shifts during auditory story comprehension. *NeuroImage*, *47*(1). doi:10.1016/j.neuroimage.2009.04.037

Willems, R. M., Hagoort, P., & Casasanto, D. (2010). Body-specific representations of action verbs: neural evidence from right- and left-handers. *Psychological Science*, *21*, 67–74.

Wood, J. N., & Grafman, J. (2003). Human prefrontal cortex: processing and representational perspectives. *Nature Reviews Neuroscience*, *4*(2), 139–147. doi: http://dx.doi.org.ezproxy.gvsu.edu/10.1038/nrn1033

Xu, J., Kemeny, S., Park, G., Frattali, C., & Braun, A. (2005). Language in context: emergent features of word, sentence, and narrative comprehension. *NeuroImage*, *25*(3). doi:10.1016/j.neuroimage.2004.12.013

Yao, B., Belin, P., & Scheepers, C. (2011). Silent reading of direct versus indirect speech activates voice-selective areas in the auditory cortex. *Journal of Cognitive Neuroscience*, *23*, 3146–3152. doi:http://dx.doi.org.ezproxy.gvsu.edu/10.1162/jocn_a_00022

Yarkoni, T., Speer, N. K., & Zacks, J. M. (2008). Neural substrates of narrative comprehension and memory. *NeuroImage*, *41*, 1408–1425.

Zacks, J. M., Braver, T. S., Sheridan, M. A., Donaldson, D. I., Snyder, A. Z., Ollinger, J. M., . . ., Raichle, M. E. (2001). Human brain activity time-locked to perceptual event boundaries. *Nature Neuroscience*, *4*, 651–655.

Zacks, J. M., & Ferstl, E. C. (2015). Discourse comprehension. In G. Hickok & S. L. Small (eds.), *Neurobiology of Language*. Amsterdam: Elsevier Science Publishers.

Zacks, J. M., Speer, N. K., & Reynolds, J. R. (2009). Segmentation in reading and film comprehension. *Journal of Experimental Psychology: General*, *138*, 307–327.

Zacks, J. M., Speer, N. K., Swallow, K. M., Braver, T. S., & Reynolds, J. R. (2007). Event perception: a mind-brain perspective. *Psychological Bulletin*, *133*, 273–293.

Zwaan, R. A. (2004). The immersed experiencer: toward an embodied theory of language comprehension. In B. H. Ross (ed.), *The Psychology of Learning and Motivation*, pp. 35–62. Amsterdam: Elsevier Science Publishers.

Zwaan, R. A., Langston, M. C., & Graesser, A. C. (1995). The construction of situation models in narrative comprehension: an event-indexing model. *Psychological Science*, *6*, 292–297.

Zwaan, R. A., Magliano, J. P., & Graesser, A. C. (1995). Dimensions of situation model construction in narrative comprehension. *Journal of Experimental Psychology: Learning*, *21*(2), 386–397.

Zwaan, R. A., & Radvansky, G. A. (1998). Situation models in language comprehension and memory. *Psychological Bulletin*, *123*, 162–185.

Zwaan, R. A., & Taylor, L. J. (2006). Seeing, acting, understanding: motor resonance in language comprehension. *Journal of Experimental Psychology: General*, *135*, 1–11.

5 Language comprehension in rich non-linguistic contexts: combining eye-tracking and event-related brain potentials

Pia Knoeferle

Abstract The present chapter reviews the literature on visually situated language comprehension against the background that most theories of real-time sentence comprehension have ignored rich non-linguistic contexts. However, listeners' eye movements to objects during spoken language comprehension, as well as their event-related brain potentials (ERPs), have revealed that non-linguistic cues play an important role for real-time comprehension. In fact, referential processes are rapid and central in visually situated spoken language comprehension and even abstract words are rapidly grounded in objects through semantic associations. Similar ERP responses for non-linguistic and linguistic effects on comprehension suggest these two information sources are on a par in informing language comprehension. ERPs further revealed that non-linguistic cues affect lexical-semantic as well as compositional processes, thus further cementing the role of rich non-linguistic context in language comprehension. However, there is also considerable ambiguity in the linking between comprehension processes and each of these two measures (eye movements and ERPs). Combining eye-tracking and event-related brain potentials would improve the interpretation of individual measures and thus insights into visually situated language comprehension.

Introduction

Much of our everyday language use occurs in contextually rich settings. This is true, for instance, when we select a tram ticket to go to work and follow the instructions of a vending machine; when we read the paper; or when we buy a croissant at the corner bakery. At the vending machine, for instance, we can use verbal labels such as "day-ticket" together with depictions of zones on the city map to understand which kind of ticket we are buying and where it is valid. In the bakery, we can gesture and point to a pastry if we don't know its name, and if we see the baker select a pastry that we don't like, we can ask him to give us another one. In fact, if the baker sees us scowl when he selects one of the smaller pastries, he may well pause, reconsider, and hand us a larger one. Overall, thus, perceived actions, object-based gaze, gestures, and facial expressions constitute a rich context for, and contribute relevant information to, our everyday communication.

Language-centricity in theories of sentence comprehension While a view of comprehension as situated in a rich context seems intuitively plausible and appealing, this is not what has shaped psycholinguistic theorizing on real-time language comprehension. From the 1970s and well into the 1990s, a "language-centric" view has dominated theory formation and empirical research (e.g., Altmann & Steedman, 1988; Crocker, 1996; Forster, 1979; Frazier & Clifton, 1996; Frazier & Fodor, 1979; Gorrell, 1995; MacDonald, Pearlmutter, & Seidenberg, 1994; Mitchell *et al.*, 1995; Trueswell & Tanenhaus, 1994). Without going into too much detail, early accounts of sentence comprehension were syntax-centric and accommodated structural decisions at choice points through principles such as syntactic simplicity and the use of purely structural rules (e.g., Frazier & Fodor, 1979). However, these accounts struggled to accommodate the rapid effects of lexical–semantic information on syntactic structure building. Accordingly theorizing turned to the lexicon as an important source of grammatical knowledge (e.g., Macdonald, Pearlmutter, & Seidenberg, 1994; Trueswell & Tanenhaus, 1994) and to probabilistic information (e.g., Crocker & Brants, 2000; Mitchell *et al.*, 1995; Spivey-Knowlton & Tanenhaus, 1998). Recent approaches have accommodated comprehension by appealing to the likelihood of words in context (e.g., Hale, 2003; Levy, 2008). While the above language-centric accounts have been shaped by reading times or eye-tracking data, others have been shaped by ERP results alone. Friederici (2002), for instance, proposed a neurocognitive model comprising three serial stages in sentence processing. A related, argument-dependency model assumes three hierarchically ordered stages that allow for some parallelism (Bornkessel & Schlesewsky, 2006). By comparison with the latter two models, a neurocognitive model based on unification grammar assumes parallel competition of syntactic and lexical structures without a separate initial phrase structure stage (Hagoort, 2003).

In sum, the above accounts and frameworks have all adopted a language-centric approach to comprehension. In line with this, they contribute valuable insights into a range of semantic and syntactic processes. Crucially, however, none of them makes any predictions about how comprehension proceeds when language users can attend to and recruit all sorts of information from the immediate non-linguistic environment.

The present chapter takes the view that the latter is precisely among the situations in which we should be able to accommodate how comprehension proceeds, and how it benefits from non-linguistic relationships. Ultimately we want to model comprehension in all kinds of situations, for instance when only language is relevant, when text and pictures matter, and when speech relates (more or less) to objects and dynamically unfolding events (of which more below). This chapter reviews how the combination of continuous measures with rich non-linguistic contexts has paved the way towards examining "visually situated" language processing (i.e., language processing in situations when non-linguistic visual cues are relevant for comprehension). It further summarizes key insights into visually situated language comprehension from both eye-tracking and ERP studies. In the process, the chapter discusses issues concerning the linking hypotheses[1] in visually situated language comprehension and argues for combining these two measures to improve the interpretation of each individual measure.

Visually situated language comprehension: methodological advances and tasks The observation that language-processing models are language-centric pertains specifically to real-time comprehension. For investigating the timing of events in language comprehension, researchers have relied upon continuous recordings of either comprehenders' eye movements or their ERPs during text reading. The focus on reading and on linguistic theory arguably entailed a focus on linguistic contexts (sentences). By contrast, early research in cognitive psychology has examined language in richer contexts. One strand of research has examined picture–sentence verification (e.g., Carpenter & Just, 1976; Clark & Chase, 1972; Gough, 1965), another the nature of the mental representations underlying the processing of pictorial and linguistic stimuli (e.g., Potter *et al.*, 1986; Potter & Kroll, 1987). Further approaches have modeled comprehension as perceived or imagined events (Johnson-Laird, 1981), or examined it in a dialogue context (e.g., Garrod & Anderson, 1987).

However, among these approaches, few have influenced theorizing in the area of real-time language processing (see Pickering & Garrod, 2004 for an exception), and most have had virtually no impact on psycholinguistic accounts of incremental language comprehension. This is arguably because the early cognitive-psychology research has largely relied upon non-continuous measures. Approaches such as picture–sentence verification were indeed criticized for not reflecting the mental processes

[1] A linking hypothesis is an assumption about how patterns in the data relate to cognitive processes.

implicated in real-time language comprehension (Tanenhaus, Carroll, & Bever, 1976). This criticism was motivated by the concern that picture–sentence verification – as indexed by post-sentence response latencies – could not reveal anything about moment-by-moment language comprehension.

What seems to have been overlooked, however, is that the criticism of picture–sentence verification mostly pertained to specific measures (e.g., speeded or post-sentence verification response times) but not to the task (e.g., verification) or research issue (picture–sentence verification: see Knoeferle *et al.*, 2011b). In fact, when we employ continuous methods such as eye-tracking and ERPs to study language processing in non-linguistic visual contexts, then a range of tasks appear suitable for providing insight into the time course and nature of language processing and into the interaction of comprehension processes with information from the non-linguistic context. Among these are tasks in which participants act out instructions on objects (e.g., Tanenhaus *et al.*, 1995), listen for comprehension (e.g., Altmann & Kamide, 1999), judge sentence veracity (e.g., Guerra & Knoeferle, 2013), and verify picture–sentence congruence (e.g., Altmann & Kamide, 1999; Carminati & Knoeferle, 2013; Knoeferle *et al.*, 2011b; Vissers *et al.*, 2008; Wassenaar & Hagoort, 2007).

These methodological advances (combining visually situated language tasks with continuous measures) tie in well with the goal of modeling comprehension in rich contexts. They have paved the way for addressing long-standing psycholinguistic questions as to whether linguistic and visual processes are or aren't informationally encapsulated (Tanenhaus *et al.*, 1995; see also Fodor, 1983), and as to which extent pictures and words are processed similarly (e.g., Ganis, Kutas, & Sereno, 1996). Psycholinguists have also examined how visual context affects syntactic structuring relative to lexical biases, with the conclusion that constraint-based interactive accounts of language processing can accommodate both visual-context and lexical effects (Novick, Thompson-Schill, & Trueswell, 2008). However, these accounts, just like the above language-centric accounts, do not aim to model the *nature* of the interplay between comprehension processes (visual attention) and information from the non-linguistic visual context (see Altmann & Mirković, 2009; Crocker, Knoeferle, & Mayberry, 2010; Knoeferle & Crocker, 2006, 2007; Mayberry, Crocker, & Knoeferle, 2009).

Below I will first provide an overview of insights into visually situated language comprehension from eye-tracking data that addresses precisely this issue, and discuss the ambiguity in relating eye movements to comprehension processes. The next section introduces the possibility of complementing eye-tracking studies with ERP studies to remove ambiguity in the linking hypotheses and also discusses ERP results on the integration of rich contextual cues with language. The section addresses the interesting question of whether visual context affects comprehension in much the same way as our linguistic knowledge, and subsequently discusses ambiguity in the linking assumptions of ERPs. A final section argues that the combination of eye-tracking and ERPs can improvc the interpretation of each individual measure in visually situated language comprehension.

The interaction of language comprehension with non-linguistic cues

The time course and distribution of visual attention as cues to referential and semantic interpretation The monitoring of eye movements or ERPs during the presentation of visually situated sentences has laid the foundation for investigating how moment-by-moment language comprehension interacts with processing of (as well as visual attention in) the non-linguistic context. Results from eye-tracking studies suggest a rapid and temporally coordinated link between eye movements and language comprehension. The time course of eye movements to objects in relation to the linguistic input is crucially sensitive to referential and semantic world-language relationships, as well as to semantic and pragmatic processes. Interpretation preferences emerged in the distribution of visual attention, and between-group differences (in literacy or age) emerged in the time course and the distribution of visual attention respectively. Their sensitivity to these different factors (e.g., referential relations, pragmatic processes, or between-group differences amongst others) makes eye movements a useful measure for examining visually situated language comprehension.

In more detail, we establish reference within a few hundred milliseconds (Allopenna, Magnusson, & Tanenhaus, 1998; Tanenhaus *et al.*, 1995), a claim corroborated by the fact that listeners swiftly inspect named objects. This behavior is robust and permits researchers to gain insights into visually situated language comprehension. In the above case, looks to an object have been interpreted as reflecting that the listener is thinking about that object and has thus established reference to it. The rapid inspection of named objects also highlights that language comprehension is closely temporally coordinated with visual attention (e.g., Altmann & Kamide, 1999; Knoeferle & Crocker, 2006, 2007; Tanenhaus *et al.*, 1995). This coordination is robust even when language refers to things that were (but no longer are) in front of our eyes (Altmann,

2004), when language is abstract (Duñabeitia *et al.*, 2009), and when objects are mentioned in rapid succession (Andersson, Ferreira, & Henderson, 2011). It is also present in young infants (e.g., from around 6 months of age for basic nouns, see Bergelson & Swingley, 2012; from around 36 months of age for color adjectives, Fernald, Thorpe, & Marchman, 2010).

Importantly, changes in the time course of this temporal coordination and in the distribution of visual attention reflect differences between referential relationships (*beaker* referring to a beaker) and a less-perfect fit between an object and its name (e.g., similar-sounding or rhyme words: see Allopenna *et al.*, 1998 for a formal linking hypothesis). For *beaker*, participants inspected both the picture of a beaker and a picture of a phonological neighbor (a beetle) more often than unrelated targets from around 200 ms after word onset (e.g., see Dahan, 2010). This lasted until approximately 400 ms after which fixations to the beetle decreased. When the target word (*beaker*) rhymed with the name of another object (a speaker), then the speaker object attracted more looks from around 300 ms than phonologically unrelated objects. Thus, referents are fixated as their name unfolds and other objects are fixated to the extent that they overlap with the target in name.

It may thus be tempting to argue that a single (referential) attention mechanism serves to relate linguistic representations to representations of objects based on the goodness of the match between an object's name and potential referents. However, visual features of unmentioned objects (e.g., their color or shape) can also modulate the time course with which listeners distribute their visual attention. When participants were instructed to move a snake (depicted as stretched out) to another location, then a nearby object (a rope) depicted in a prototypical snake-shape (coiled up) was inspected less often than the snake, but more often than unrelated objects (Dahan & Tanenhaus, 2005). These eye movements occurred approximately 200–300 ms after target word onset, and thus with a similar time course as when phonological match disambiguated reference. Semantic associations between objects also affected listeners' visual attention rapidly. When listeners heard ... *he looked at the piano*, their eye gaze shifted to a piano on a higher proportion of trials than to unrelated objects, but when no piano was visible, other unnamed but semantically related objects (a trumpet) also attracted more attention than unrelated objects. With both a piano and trumpet present, listeners inspected the piano on the majority of trials, but the trumpet on a higher percentage of trials than unrelated objects (Huettig & Altmann, 2005; see also Yee & Sedivy, 2006).

Thus, more than a referential mechanism is implicated; and just as comprehenders compute a match based on referential relations, other semantic or visual features of unnamed objects also rapidly affect the distribution of visual attention. Referents are fixated as their name unfolds and non-referents are fixated to the extent that they overlap with the target in name, semantic, or visual features.

Interestingly, the time course and distribution of visual attention is also sensitive to linguistic dimensions such as the concreteness versus abstractness of a word (e.g., Duñabeitia *et al.*, 2009). Abstract nouns and scalar quantifiers such as *some* do not have clear referents and are thus useful to consider when assessing whether a referential mechanism is sufficient to accommodate visually situated language comprehension. When listeners heard a semantically associated abstract word such as Spanish "smell," they inspected the target picture (of a nose) more often and earlier (from around 200 ms after word onset) compared with their inspection of another target picture (of a baby) in response to an associated concrete word such as "crib" (from 400 ms after word onset, association strength was controlled). Such gaze differences in the inspection of the depicted nose and the baby were absent when these pictures were named, in which case participants inspected them more often than when they heard an associated word (e.g., "smell" or "crib" respectively). Thus, abstract nouns are organized primarily through semantic associations (e.g., between *smell* and the picture of a nose) while concrete nouns are organized through referential congruence (e.g., as between *nose* and the picture of a nose).

The time course of eye movements was further sensitive to the computation of scalar implicature (Huang & Snedeker, 2009). A depicted girl and a boy were each "handed" two (depicted) socks, and another girl received three balls. When the instruction was to *point to the girl that has two* . . . , participants' inspections to the girl with two socks rose from around 200 ms after the onset of *two*. By contrast, for the scalar quantifier *some*, inspections to the same girl rose only much later (around 1000 ms after the onset of *some:* Experiments 1 and 2 in Huang & Snedeker, 2009). The authors attributed the delay to the computation of scalar implicature, since gaze pattern suggested immediate interpretation of *some* when its sense disambiguated reference (this was the case when nine socks were evenly distributed among two boys and one girl: Experiment 3, Huang & Snedeker, 2009).

Overall, these results suggest a rapid and temporally coordinated link between eye movements and language comprehension. The fact that the time course of eye gaze is sensitive to referential and semantic relationships between language and the visual world, as well as to pragmatic processes and the interpretation of abstract language, makes eye movements a useful measure for examining visually situated language comprehension.

The studies discussed above have relied on temporal characteristics of the gaze record (relative delays indicate processing differences, e.g., Huang & Snedeker, 2009) and on the distribution of attention (e.g., indicating processing of referents vs. non-referents, e.g., Dahan & Tanenhaus, 2005). A few studies have also interpreted differences in the distribution of visual attention across objects as reflecting interpretation preferences. Preferential inspection pattern emerged, for instance, in a study by Knoeferle and Crocker (2006). When the verb (e.g., "spy on") in a sentence about an action between two characters was compatible with either an action performed by a non-stereotypical agent (a wizard spying) or a stereotypical agent depicted as performing a mismatching action (a detective serving food), listeners' gaze pattern revealed interpretation preferences. The listeners preferred to anticipate the agent associated with the matching action (the wizard depicted as spying) rather than the stereotypical agent (the detective). A similar preference emerged when the choice was between the target of a recently acted-upon object and another target of a future action. In this situation, listeners rapidly inspected the target of the recent action (e.g., a candelabra that had been polished) in preference to the target of a future polishing action (e.g., polishing crystal glasses, target-condition assignment was counterbalanced: Knoeferle & Crocker, 2007). The recent-event preference replicated with real-world events (Knoeferle *et al.*, 2011a) and when the within-experiment frequency of future (relative to recent) actions was increased to 75 (vs. 25) percent (Abashidze, Knoeferle, & Carminati, 2013).

In addition, eye movements have been shown to reflect qualitative differences in the interpretation between different groups of comprehenders. A comparison of skilled and less-skilled comprehenders, for instance, has revealed that these two groups can recruit verb meaning (e.g., *eat*) with the same time course for anticipating a target (e.g., a cake: Nation, Marshall, & Altmann, 2003) but differ in how often and how long they fixate that target. Less-skilled (vs. skilled) comprehenders made more but shorter fixations to the target only when the verb restricted the domain of the subsequent reference (e.g., *eat* requires edible objects while verbs such as *move* were less restrictive). These differences in fixation pattern were associated with a range of possible factors among them poor comprehenders' need to refresh memory traces, differences in general attention, or differences in inhibiting irrelevant information (from non-target pictures). Other (temporal) aspects of the eye-movement record have also been associated with qualitative differences in the interpretation (Mishra *et al.*, 2011). In a similar design as the one above, illiterates failed to anticipate the target object and only inspected it from around 300 ms after the onset of its name. By contrast, literates successfully anticipated the target object before its mention for restrictive compared with non-restrictive adjectives (e.g., a high door among other objects that did not match the adjective "high"), suggesting they but not the illiterates develop language-derived semantic expectations.

Qualitative rather than temporal differences in the distribution of visual attention emerged in the effects of facial emotion on situated language processing. When older adults inspected a happy speaker face and subsequently listened to a sentence that described a positive event, they looked at the photograph of the positive event more than when they had inspected a negative face. Younger adults, by contrast, showed such facilitation only for negative but not for positive prime faces and sentences (Carminati & Knoeferle, 2013). Visual attention and language comprehension in older compared with younger adults thus did not differ substantially concerning the time course. Rather, differences in facial valence effects on the semantic interpretation of valenced events between the two age groups emerged in preferential eye-movement responses to positive compared with negative prime faces.

In summary, the timing and distribution of visual attention across objects and events can reflect subtle differences in comprehension and the processing of different language–"world" relationships.[2] A first important point was that visual attention is closely *temporally coordinated* with language comprehension, a link that only broke down for vague or ambiguous relationships between language and the visual world (in fact, reflecting subtle differences in comprehension when reference was ambiguous). A second important point was that most attention goes to referents for concrete words whereby semantically or visually related non-referents also attract some attention. For abstract compared with concrete words, more and earlier looks land on semantically associated objects. Thus, the distribution and time course of visual attention can index the processing of *different word–object relationships*. Further, visual attention revealed *interpretation preferences*. This was evident in comprehenders' preferred reliance during comprehension on a recent action target over anticipating a future action target. Finally, eye gaze measures revealed *qualitative* differences in comprehension between groups of comprehenders.

However, we know preciously little about which linguistic, cognitive, or social factors affect which aspect of the eye-movement record. Differences

[2] For other measures and linking hypotheses, see also Altmann (2010); Arai, Van Gompel, & Scheepers (2007); Engelhardt, Ferreira, & Patsenko (2010); Scheepers & Crocker (2004).

in comprehension skill, for instance, affected the duration and frequency of eye gaze but not its time course. Age-related differences in emotion interpretation also emerged in the duration and frequency of attention rather than time course differences. By contrast, differences in literacy affected the time course of object-directed gaze.

Linking issues in eye-tracking studies: semantic versus syntactic processes All in all, there is considerable ambiguity as to which specific comprehension (sub)-processes are reflected at any given point in time by the single stream of eye movements that we record. Since the linking relies predominantly on properties of the design (minimal comparisons between individual conditions), and relative timing of the eye movements rather than on distinct fixation signatures, even minor weaknesses in the design can lead to ambiguity in linking eye movements to cognitive processes. Consider a study by Altmann and Kamide (1999) which formed the basis for the above-reviewed research on qualitative differences (e.g., Nation *et al.*, 2003). Altmann and Kamide examined eye movements to a target object (a cake) for selective verbs such as *eat* compared with non-selective verbs such as *move*. The picture showed a boy, a cake, and three (inedible) toys. The expectation was that the selectional restrictions of the verb *eat* in *The boy will eat* ... would guide the listeners' attention to the one edible object (a cake) before its mention. For the non-restrictive verb *move*, by contrast, listeners' should distribute their visual attention evenly across the four objects since all of them were moveable. Earlier eye movements to the cake for *eat* than for *move* verbs were taken to reflect the differential in verb selection restrictions. However, instead of verb selection restrictions, semantic associations between *eat* and the depicted cake could have triggered these eye movements, since the design did not control for this possibility and since we do not know whether verb selection restrictions and semantic associations are associated with distinct fixation signatures.

One solution to this problem has been to improve the design (e.g., Kamide, Altmann, & Haywood, 2003). An additional means has been to rely on complementary measures to reduce ambiguity in the linking hypothesis of a single measure (see also Willems, Özyürek, & Hagoort, 2008 and Knoeferle *et al.*, 2011a for related approaches with different measures). An example comes from a pair of studies that examined visual context effects on the disambiguation of local structural ambiguity using eye-tracking and ERPs. In the initial eye-tracking study, Knoeferle *et al.* (2005) examined the processing of German sentences with a sentence-initial structural ambiguity which was disambiguated by case marking on the determiner of a sentence-final noun phrase (e.g., *Die Prinzessin malt der*

Fechter, "The princess (object, ambiguous) paints the fencer (subject)"). Earlier disambiguation was possible if comprehenders related the verb to depicted thematic relations between the referents of the two noun phrases (the princess was depicted as washing a pirate and a fencer was depicted as painting the princess). As comprehenders heard "The princess (amb.) paints . . ." they rapidly related the verb "paints" to the action of the fencer and anticipated the fencer before it was mentioned. The visual anticipation of the fencer was interpreted as reflecting assignment of an agent role to "fencer" and of a patient role to "princess," indicating disambiguation of the syntactic and thematic role relations before linguistic disambiguation through case marking on "the" (*der*) in "the fencer" (*der Fechter* is in nominative case and is marked as the subject and agent of the sentence).

Strictly speaking, however, this gaze pattern (eye movements to the fencer before its mention) could also index an initial lexical mismatch between the action of the princess (washing) and the verb ("paints"). Upon noticing that "paints" mismatches the action of the princess, comprehenders begin to search for a matching instrument and this leads them to the action of the fencer and to increased inspection of the associated fencer. Again, since we do not know whether particular eye-movement signatures correspond to specific comprehension sub-processes such as referential matching and structural disambiguation (to the extent that such one-to-one linking exists at all), unambiguous interpretation of these fixation patterns is difficult. To reduce the ambiguity in the linking of visual attention to comprehension (or other cognitive) sub-processes, an ensuing study complemented the eye movements with another continuous measure (event-related brain potentials, of which more below).

Visually situated language comprehension: evidence from ERPs

Event-related brain potentials are a useful complementary measure since they reflect cognitive processes over time and vary both temporally and qualitatively (in their polarity) for lexical–semantic compared with compositional and syntactic processes. Lexical–semantic processes and the integration of new meaning in the semantic context have been associated with the so-called N400 effect. The effect is a negative deviation in mean amplitude ERPs approximately 400 ms after an event such as the presentation of a word or picture. The better a word fits into the preceding context, the more the mean amplitude N400s decrease (e.g., Kutas & Federmeier, 2011; Kutas & Hillyard, 1980, 1984). By contrast, syntactic revision and the processing of syntactic violations have been associated with a qualitatively distinct effect, the so-called P600 (also called syntactic positive shift: e.g., Hagoort, Brown, & Groothusen,

1993; Osterhout & Holcomb, 1992, 1993). This is a positive deviation in mean amplitude ERPs approximately 600 ms after a stimulus.[3]

Complementing eye movement studies with ERP studies can help us discard alternative interpretations of the data from an individual measure. Knoeferle *et al.* (2008) did just that with the materials from the eye-tracking study by Knoeferle *et al.* (2005), and recorded event-related brain potentials as participants inspected similar event depictions and listened to related German sentences with an initial structural and role ambiguity. When the verb related to an event depicting the referent of the first noun phrase as the patient (vs. agent), mean amplitude ERPs to the verb were more positive (P600). In an audio-only baseline condition, these mean amplitude P600 differences emerged only later, at a point in time when case marking on the determiner of the second noun phrase disambiguated towards the object–subject order. Given the comparison of the audio-visual condition with the audio-only baseline, and given the interpretation of the P600 as an index of structural revision and structural disambiguation, the depicted events likely triggered revision processes and not just a lexical–semantic mismatch and ensuing visual search for a matching action.

In this particular case, the eye-movement patterns together with the P600 suggested that the underlying processes involved the anticipation of role fillers and associated structural revision. A similar distinction between the P600 and the N400 (reflecting lexical–semantic processes) is also apparent in research on the integration of co-speech gestures (Holle *et al.*, 2012; Kelly, Kravitz, & Hopkins, 2004).

Different meaning relationships between a gesture and speech, for instance, elicited distinct N400 effects but no P600 differences (Kelly *et al.*, 2004). Comprehenders inspected a gesture that related to speech in three ways. The gesture matched speech (it underscored the verbally expressed thinness of a glass), was complementary to speech (it related to the thinness of the glass while the speech mentioned tallness of the glass), or contradicted the speech (the gesture described the shortness of a dish while a tall glass was mentioned). A fourth, speech-only / no-gesture condition served as a baseline. The condition without gestures elicited

[3] Note that the distinction between the N400 and P600s is not entirely clear-cut, as a "semantic" P600 emerged in response to what looked like semantic violations (Kolk *et al.*, 2003; Kuperberg *et al.*, 2003). Naturally, ambiguity in the linking hypotheses leads to ambiguity in understanding and modeling language comprehension processes. Interpretation problems resulting from ambiguity have also been discussed elsewhere (see Kutas, Van Petten, & Kluender, 2006 for ERPs; Tanenhaus, 2004 for eye-tracking) and one proposal for eye-movement data has been to more explicitly and formally specify one's linking hypotheses (e.g., Allopenna *et al.*, 1998; Tanenhaus, 2004).

larger broadly distributed N400 effects relative to the other three conditions. In addition, larger mean amplitude N400s emerged in the no-gesture than the other three conditions over anterior sites. Over bilateral temporal sites, ERPs to the gesture mismatches were crucially more negative than ERPs to the matches (but not to the other conditions). Follow-up analyses revealed that this difference emerged mainly over the right, but not over the left hemisphere (Kelly *et al.*, 2004; see also Wu & Coulson, 2005, 2007 for relevant results, Kelly, Creigh, & Bartolotti, 2009 on the automaticity of such integration, and Kelly & Breckinridge Church, 1998 on developmental differences).

The semantic interpretation of co-speech gestures crucially depends on the relative timing of speech and co-speech gestures. When the gestures were presented together with speech (zero milliseconds delay) or when speech was delayed by 160 ms relative to the onset of the corresponding gesture, mean amplitude N400s were larger for gesture–speech mismatches than matches. This N400 difference was absent when the gesture preceded the corresponding word by 360 ms (Habets *et al.*, 2011). In sum, variation in the N400 mean amplitudes indexed subtle differences in the semantic contribution of iconic gestures to the interpretation, and temporal coordination seems to be a key factor in the successful integration of language and non-verbal cues.

Another kind of gesture (beat gestures) can affect comprehension processes such as structural disambiguation in the face of temporary linguistic ambiguity (subject–object, SO, compared with object–subject, OS: Holle *et al.*, 2012). A verb following the ambiguous noun-phrase sequence (subject–object or object–subject) resolved the temporary ambiguity towards either the SOV (subject–object–verb) or OSV (object–subject–verb) structure. In addition to linguistic disambiguation, a video-taped speaker emphasized either none of the constituents, the first, or the second noun phrase. Control conditions showed a red dot moving along the gesture trajectory. Analyses of participants' accuracy scores on "yes/no" questions about thematic role relations revealed lower accuracy for object than subject-initial sentences.

In the ERPs, object compared with subject-initial sentences elicited an anterior negativity followed by a relative posterior positivity to the disambiguating verb in the absence of beat gestures. This relative P600 to the disambiguating verb remained virtually unchanged when a beat gesture emphasized the first noun phrase; by contrast, a beat gesture on the second, ambiguous noun phrase eliminated the P600 and only the anterior negativity remained (Experiment 1). Since the P600 difference in response to structural disambiguation at the verb was eliminated neither by an auditory pitch accent (Experiment 2) nor by the moving red dot

(Experiment 3), the authors concluded that the beat gesture affected syntactic structuring. The beat could highlight relevant information for a short period of time, which would explain the absence of gesture effects when it occurred long before disambiguation (at the first noun phrase). Alternatively, or in addition, a beat signals the sentential subject, in which case a beat on the first noun phrase is redundant since the first noun phrase is assumed to be the subject. A beat on the second of two noun phrases, by contrast, signals that the subject is in an unusual position and thus likely has a disambiguating effect.

Thus, qualitatively distinct ERP congruence effects indexed whether visual context influenced semantic interpretation (as indexed by N400 mean amplitude differences) or rather structural disambiguation (as indexed by P600 mean amplitude differences), a distinction which was useful for disambiguating alternative accounts of eye-movement results.

Linguistic versus visual context effects: same or different ERP effects? The previous section argued that complementing eye-movement studies with ERP studies can help us discard alternative interpretations of the data from an individual measure. The qualitative distinction between the N400 and the P600 was indeed used to this effect, with results suggesting rapid effects of non-linguistic cues on both semantic interpretation and syntactic disambiguation. Given that non-linguistic cues rapidly affect these comprehension processes, one might assess whether their effects on comprehension are qualitatively similar to those of linguistic cues. Finding non-linguistic cues on a par with linguistic ones would be a strong argument in favor of examining language comprehension in rich non-linguistic contexts.

Research on the semantic processing of pictures, for instance, suggests that semantic matching of pictures elicits negativities which differ at least partially from the negativities elicited by semantic interpretation in strictly linguistic contexts. One is an earlier anterior N300 difference (larger to picture–picture mismatches than matches), and the other is a later posterior negativity likened to the semantic N400 in verbal stimuli (e.g., Barrett & Rugg, 1990). The interpretation of pictures (compared with words) in sentence contexts also seems to elicit a different topography in the N400 effect (pictures: anterior; words: posterior; Ganis, Kutas, & Sereno, 1996). In addition adjectival color mismatches in the token test (object: red square; linguistic input: green square) yielded an anterior N2b component instead of a posterior N400. The N2b has been associated with mismatch detection rather than language processing (D'Arcy & Connolly, 1999; Vissers *et al.*, 2008).

By contrast, other picture–sentence congruence manipulations (e.g., noun–object: Friedrich & Friederici, 2004; verb–action: Knoeferle *et al.*, 2011b) yielded N400s akin to those in language comprehension tasks (e.g., Kutas, 1993; see also Kutas, Van Petten, & Kluender, 2006; Otten & Van Berkum, 2007; Van Berkum *et al.*, 1999), suggesting visual contexts modulated language comprehension and not other processes. Likewise, when depicted agent–action–patient events enabled structural disambiguation (Knoeferle *et al.*, 2008), the topography of P600 differences was visually indistinguishable relative to cases when structural disambiguation was enabled by case-marking on the determiner of a noun phrase. Further evidence for similarities in how linguistic compared with pictorial cues affect comprehension comes from a study by Willems, Özyürek, and Hagoort (2008). They examined the time course of the semantic integration of a word and picture with a previous sentence context. Sentences either contained no mismatch, a mismatching word, a mismatching picture, or both picture and word mismatches. In the ERPs, they observed an N400 effect which was similar for pictures and words in terms of latency, topography, and amplitude and no clear evidence for a picture-specific N300 (see also Ganis *et al.*, 1996).

Thus, for word–object mismatches, and for pictorial stimuli, ERP patterns in response to incongruence seem to be at least partially distinct compared with semantic interpretation in strictly linguistic contexts. However, for real-time sentence interpretation in rich contexts, visual context effects on both semantic and syntactic processes resembled the ERP effects observed for these processes in purely linguistic contexts (although the presence of visual information can shift the distribution of the N400). Thus, it seems that sentence comprehension draws on linguistic and non-linguistic information with the same time course and also recruits at least partially overlapping brain areas (see Willems *et al.*, 2008).

Ambiguity in linking of ERP effects to comprehension sub-processes While these experiments – by virtue of design constraints – interpreted the effects of visual context on comprehension as either semantic or syntactic, not all distinct sentence–picture relationships are dissociable by means of ERPs. Vissers *et al.* (2008), for instance, observed statistically indistinguishable P600 differences in response to two kinds of spatial mismatches (vs. matches). When participants verified depictions (□ △) against ensuing written sentences (e.g., "the triangle stands behind / in front of / below the square"), the two mismatches ("in front of / below") elicited statistically indistinguishable mean amplitude negativities and P600s relative to the matches ("behind").

Vissers *et al.* (2008) argued that the absence of a difference between distinct picture–sentence mismatches reflects a general monitoring mechanism responding to any kind of violation. If that is true, however, then it is unclear why picture–sentence incongruence processing does not always elicit a P600. When participants inspected scenes depicting an agent–action–patient event and subsequently read a related sentence in which the verb either matched or mismatched the previously inspected action, no P600 differences emerged (Knoeferle *et al.*, 2011b). Instead, mean amplitude N400s to the verb were more negative and post-sentence verification response times were longer for verb–action mismatches than matches.

Further support for the view that ERPs are sensitive to distinct picture–sentence relations comes from two studies on thematic role assignment. In one study, healthy older adults verified whether a spoken Dutch sentence (e.g., "The tall man on [*sic*] this picture pushes the young woman") accurately described a previously inspected line drawing (e.g., a man pushing a woman versus a woman pushing a man: Wassenaar & Hagoort, 2007). For active sentences, a reliably larger posterior negativity was followed by a numerically larger positivity to role relation mismatches (vs. matches) at the verb (centro-posterior from 50–450 ms; for anterior sites from about 50–300 ms), and by a broad negative shift to mismatches relative to matches in the post-verbal noun. ERPs to irreversible active and reversible passive sentences showed an early negativity, a subsequent late positivity, and a negative shift to mismatches (vs. matches). These effects were interpreted as broadly reflecting thematic role assignment with subtle differences depending on sentence type.

In another study, thematic role assignment effects were differentiated by ERPs from lexical verb–action mismatches (Knoeferle, Urbach, & Kutas, 2010, 2014). Participants read a subject–verb–object sentence (500 ms stimulus onset asynchrony (SOA) in Experiment 1), and verified post-sentence whether or not the verb and/or the thematic role relations matched a preceding picture (depicting two participants engaged in an action). Sentences either matched the picture, or mismatched in either the action or the depicted role relations, or both. These two types of mismatches (actions vs. role relations) yielded different ERP effects. Role-relation mismatch effects emerged as anterior negativities to the mismatching subject noun, and preceded action mismatch effects (centro-parietal N400s greater to the mismatching verb).

Overall, thus, more than a single mechanism is active in picture–sentence congruence processing. Distinct picture–sentence mismatches do elicit distinct ERP patterns and can distinguish lexical–semantic from compositional thematic effects. Perhaps the null effect in Vissers *et al.*

(2008) is genuine (people do not differentiate the different spatial relations online) but they do differentiate between other picture–sentence relations. Alternatively, the chosen measure (ERPs) was insensitive to the difference. Clearly, much remains to be learned about the nature of the relationship between ERPs (or eye movements) and visually situated language processing.

Summary and conclusions

The first section documented that theories providing detailed accounts of sentence processing have focused on accommodating comprehension in strictly linguistic contexts. By contrast, we ultimately want to accommodate comprehension in all sorts of situations, including those that feature a rich non-linguistic context. The remainder of the chapter proceeded to outline how methodological advances and the combination of continuous measures with visually situated tasks has facilitated research on real-time visually situated language comprehension. The second section characterized visually situated language comprehension by reviewing both eye-tracking and ERP evidence. In addition, it highlighted ambiguity in the linking assumptions where relevant.

What we can take away from this review is that referential processes are central in visually situated spoken language comprehension but that eye movements are also exquisitely sensitive to other aspects of language or the visual context. Among these aspects are the abstractness (vs. concreteness) of language, vagueness and scalar implicature, word order, and action events. When world–language relations are underspecified or when sentences are difficult, object-based eye gaze is delayed, suggesting it is sensitive to important aspects of the comprehension process. Eye movements have, in addition, revealed interpretation preferences of depicted events over, for instance, the anticipation of future events. In addition, they have been interpreted as reflecting qualitative differences in the comprehension and attention processes of illiterates and literates and between high- and low-skill comprehenders.

However, weaknesses in the design complicate the unambiguous interpretation of the gaze pattern, suggesting we must strive to improve our linking hypotheses. One way to do this, as outlined above is to complement eye-tracking studies with ERP studies to narrow the interpretation of the gaze pattern. Indeed, ERPs offer a relatively robust distinction between semantic and syntactic processes and can help us ground the interpretation of the eye-tracking data. This became clear when reviewing the effects of action events on structural disambiguation and the effects of co-speech gestures on semantic interpretation (e.g., distinct for complementary vs. mismatching gesture–sentence pairs). Distinct effects of (beat) gestures on structural disambiguation corroborated the usefulness of the N400–P600 distinction for the investigation of visually situated language comprehension. Visual and linguistic cues seemed furthermore on a par in informing sentence comprehension, as revealed by highly similar ERPs independent of whether linguistic or non-linguistic cues contributed to the interpretation and to structural disambiguation in rich contexts.

And yet, one wonders whether long-term, ERPs alone are sufficient as a window into (potentially subtle) effects of how pictorial information contributes to language comprehension. Recall that in the study by Vissers *et al.* (2008) mismatches between the spatial configuration of objects and different prepositions ("in front of" relative to "below") did not elicit a different ERP pattern. It's possible that this null effect reflects a genuine absence of differences, as argued by the authors. Imagine, however, that we presented sentences such as "The triangle stands in front of / below the square" together with the depiction of several objects, among them a triangle to the left of a square, and tracked listeners' eye movements. At "triangle," listeners would inspect the triangle, and at "stands in front of," we may expect them to anticipate the location indicated by compositional interpretation of the noun, the verb, and the preposition (to the right of the triangle: see Burigo & Knoeferle, 2011; Chambers *et al.*, 2002 for evidence of anticipatory eye movements following spatial prepositions). By contrast, for "The triangle stands below the square," listeners should anticipate the location above the triangle (since the triangle is below that location). Thus, eye-movement behavior in this kind of study would reveal a distinct distribution of visual attention for these two mismatches. This in turn could influence which other information is perceived and is available for comprehension.

Admittedly, the paradigm envisaged in this example (visual inspection of objects during spoken comprehension) differs from the one used by Vissers and colleagues (pictures followed by written sentences) and this may change the integration of language and the visual context. However, the example illustrates the potentially enriching effect of combining eye-tracking with EEG recordings (across studies and within the same experiment). This approach could constrain the interpretation of individual measures. It could also pave the way for extending current accounts of visually situated language comprehension (e.g., Knoeferle & Crocker, 2006, 2007), which have largely been shaped by eye-movement results, with a description of the functional brain correlates implicated in visually situated language processing (see Knoeferle *et al.*, 2014).

Indeed, the first step in this direction has been undertaken using a connectionist model of visually situated language comprehension (Crocker, Knoeferle, & Mayberry, 2010). The model's task is to predict thematic roles fillers in a target output representation during sentence processing. One type of sentences tested is the structurally ambiguous German SVO and OVS sentences from Knoeferle *et al.* (2005, see above). As reviewed, human participants anticipate role-fillers visually when the verb identifies the action in a depicted agent–action–patient event. The model predicted the correct role-fillers at the same point in time as comprehenders' gaze reflected the anticipation of the correct role-filler. In the ERPs, comprehenders exhibited a P600, larger to object- than subject-initial sentences time-locked to the onset of the verb and leading into the post-verbal region. In the model, effects of structural revision (through linguistic cues and depicted events) were examined through changes of hidden-layer activation from the processing step at the verb to the next word (i.e., after event-based disambiguation). These changes were larger for object-initial sentences compared to subject-initial sentences, suggesting structural revision.

In sum, such a cross-methodological venture has the potential to enrich extant models of visually situated language comprehension with measures that permit us to monitor comprehension from stimulus presentation to an overt visual response. In addition, it can enrich our understanding of how visual attention and brain responses are related to different aspects of visually situated language comprehension, thus permitting us to refine our interpretation of individual measures.

References

Abashidze, D., Knoeferle, P., & Carminati, M. N. (2013). Do comprehenders prefer to rely on recent events even when future events are more likely to be mentioned? In *Proceedings of the Conference on Architectures and Mechanisms for Language Processing*. Marseille, France.

Allopenna, P., Magnusson, J. S., & Tanenhaus, M. K. (1998). Tracking the time course of spoken word recognition using eye movements: evidence for continuous mapping models. *Journal of Memory and Language*, *38*, 419–439.

Altmann, G. T. M. (2004). Language-mediated eye-movements in the absence of a visual world: the 'blank screen paradigm'. *Cognition*, *93*, B79–B87.

Altmann, G. T. M., & Kamide, Y. (1999). Incremental interpretation at verbs: restricting the domain of subsequent reference. *Cognition*, *73*, 247–264.

Altmann, G. T. M., & Mirković, J. (2009). Incrementality and prediction in human sentence processing. *Cognitive Science*, *33*, 583–609.

Altmann, G. T. M., & Steedman, M. (1988). Interaction with context during human sentence processing. *Cognition*, *30*, 191–238.

Andersson, R., Ferreira, F., & Henderson, J. (2011). I see what you're saying: the integration of complex speech and scenes during language comprehension. *Acta Psychologica, 137*, 208–216.
Barrett, S. E., & Rugg, M.D. (1990). Event-related brain potentials and the matching of pictures. *Brain and Cognition, 14*, 201–212.
Bergelson, E., & Swingley, D. (2012). At 6–9 months, human infants know the meanings of many common nouns. *Proceedings of the National Academy of Sciences of the USA, 109*, 3253–3258.
Bornkessel, I., & Schlesewsky, M. (2006). The extended argument dependency model: a neurocognitive approach to sentence comprehension across languages. *Psychological Review, 113*, 787–821.
Burigo, M., & Knoeferle, P. (2011). Visual attention during spatial language comprehension: is a referential linking hypothesis enough? In L. Carlson, C. Hölscher, & T. Shipley (eds.), *Proceedings of the 33rd Annual Conference of the Cognitive Science Society*. Austin, TX: Cognitive Science Society.
Carminati, M. N., & Knoeferle, P. (2013). Effects of speaker emotional facial expression and listener age on incremental sentence processing. *PLoS ONE, 8*(9), e72559. doi:10.1371/journal.pone.0072559
Carpenter, P. A., & Just, M. A. (1975). Sentence comprehension: a psycholinguistic processing model of verification. *Psychological Review, 82*, 45–73.
Chambers, C. G., Tanenhaus, M.K., Eberhard, K. M., Filip, H., & Carlson, G. N. (2002). Circumscribing referential domains during real-time language comprehension. *Journal of Memory and Language, 47*, 30–49.
Clark, H. H., & Chase, W. G. (1972). On the process of comparing sentences against pictures. *Cognitive Psychology, 3*, 472–517.
Crocker, M. W. (1996). *Computational Psycholinguistics: An Interdisciplinary Approach to the Study of Language*. Dordrecht: Kluwer.
Crocker, M. W., & Brants, T. (2000). Wide coverage probabilistic sentence processing. *Journal of Psycholinguistic Research, 29*, 647–669.
Crocker, M. W., Knoeferle, P., & Mayberry, M. (2010). Situated sentence comprehension: the coordinated interplay account and a neurobehavioral model. *Brain and Language, 112*, 189–201.
Dahan, D. (2010). The time course of interpretation in speech comprehension. *Current Directions in Psychological Science, 19*, 121–126.
Dahan, D., & Tanenhaus, M. K. (2005). Looking at the rope when looking for the snake: conceptually mediated eye movements during spoken-word recognition. *Psychonomic Bulletin and Review, 12*, 453–459.
D'Arcy, R. C. N., & Connolly, J. F. (1999). An event-related brain potential study of receptive speech comprehension using a modified Token Test. *Neuropsychologia, 37*, 1477–1489.
Duñabeitia, J. A., Avilés, A., Afonso, O., Scheepers, C., & Carreiras. M. (2009). Qualitative differences in the representation of abstract versus concrete words: evidence from the visual-world paradigm. *Cognition 110*, 284–292.
Fernald, A., Thorpe, K., & Marchman, V. A. (2010). Blue car, red car: developing efficiency in online interpretation of adjective–noun phrases. *Cognitive Psychology, 60*, 190–217.
Fodor, J. (1983). *The Modularity of Mind*. Cambridge, MA: MIT Press.

Forster, K. (1979). Levels of processing and the structure of the language processor. In W. E. Cooper & E. C. T. Waler (eds.), *Sentence Processing: Psycholinguistic Studies Presented to Merrill Garrett*, pp. 27–85. Hillsdale, NJ: Lawrence Erlbaum.

Frazier, L., & Fodor, J. D. (1979). The sausage machine: a new two-stage parsing model. *Cognition*, *6*, 291–325.

Frazier, L., & Clifton, C. (1996). *Construal*. Cambridge, MA: MIT Press.

Friederici, A.D. (2002). Towards a neural basis of auditory sentence processing. *Trends in Cognitive Sciences*, *6*, 78–84.

Friedman, A., & Bourne Jr., L. E. (1976). Encoding the levels of information in pictures and words. *Journal of Experimental Psychology: General*, *105*, 169–190.

Friedrich, M., & Friederici, A. D. (2004). N400-like semantic incongruity effect in 19-month-olds: processing known words in picture contexts. *Journal of Cognitive Neuroscience*, *16*, 1465–1477.

Ganis, G., Kutas, M., & Sereno, M. I. (1996). The search for "common sense": an electrophysiological study of the comprehension of words and pictures in reading. *Journal of Cognitive Neuroscience*, *8*, 89–106.

Garrod, S., & Anderson, A. (1987). Saying what you mean in dialogue: a study in conceptual and semantic co-ordination. *Cognition*, *27*, 181–218.

Gibson, E. (1998). Linguistic complexity: locality of syntactic dependencies. *Cognition*, *68*, 1–76.

Gorrell, P. (1995). *Syntax and Parsing*. Cambridge: Cambridge University Press.

Gough, P. B. (1965). Grammatical transformations and speed of understanding. *Journal of Verbal Learning and Verbal Behavior*, *4*, 107–111.

Habets, B., Kita, S., Shao, Z., Özyürek, A., & Hagoort, P. (2011). The role of synchrony and ambiguity in speech-gesture integration during comprehension. *Journal of Cognitive Neuroscience*, *23*, 1845–54.

Hagoort, P. (2003). Interplay between syntax and semantics during sentence comprehension: ERP effects of combining syntactic and semantic violations. *Journal of Cognitive Neuroscience*, *15*, 883–899.

Hagoort, P., Brown, C. M., & Groothusen, J. (1993). The syntactic positive shift (SPS) as an ERP measure of syntactic processing. *Language and Cognitive Processes*, *8*, 439–483.

Hale, J. (2003). The information conveyed by words in sentences. *Journal of Psycholinguistic Research*, *32*, 101–122.

Holle, H., Obermeier, C., Schmidt-Kassow, M., Friederici, A. D., Ward, J., & Gunter, T. C. (2012). Gesture facilitates the syntactic analysis of speech. *Frontiers in Psychology*, *3*, 1–12.

Huang, Y. T., & Snedeker, J. (2009) Online interpretation of scalar quantifiers: insight into the semantics–pragmatics interface. *Cognitive Psychology*, *58*, 376–415.

Huettig, F., & Altmann, G. T. M. (2005). Word meaning and the control of eye fixation: semantic competitor effects and the visual world paradigm. *Cognition*, *96*, B23–32.

Johnson-Laird, P. (1981). Comprehension as the construction of mental models. *Philosophical Transactions of the Royal Society, Series B*, *295*, 353–374.

Kamide, Y., Altmann, G. T. M., & Haywood, S. (2003). The time course of prediction in incremental sentence processing: evidence from anticipatory eye-movements. *Journal of Memory and Language*, *49*, 133–156.

Kelly, S. D., & Breckinridge Church, R. (1998). A comparison between children's and adults' ability to detect conceptual information conveyed through representational gestures. *Child Development*, *69*, 85–93.

Kelly, S. D., Creigh, P., & Bartolotti, J. (2009). Integrating speech and iconic gestures in a stroop-like task: evidence for automatic processing. *Journal of Cognitive Neuroscience*, *22*, 683–694.

Kelly, S. D., Kravitz, C., & Hopkins, M. (2004). Neural correlates of bimodal speech and gesture comprehension. *Brain and Language*, *89*, 253–260.

Knoeferle, P., & Crocker, M. W. (2006). The coordinated interplay of scene, utterance, and world knowledge: evidence from eye tracking. *Cognitive Science*, *30*, 481–529.

Knoeferle, P., & Crocker, M. W. (2007). The influence of recent scene events on spoken comprehension: evidence from eye-movements. *Journal of Memory and Language*, *75*, 519–543.

Knoeferle, P., Crocker, M. W., Scheepers, C., & Pickering, M. J. (2005). The influence of the immediate visual context on incremental thematic role-assignment: evidence from eye-movements in depicted events. *Cognition*, *95*, 95–127.

Knoeferle, P., Habets, B., Crocker, M.W., & Münte, T. F. (2008). Visual scenes trigger immediate syntactic reanalysis: evidence from ERPs during situated spoken comprehension. *Cerebral Cortex*, *18*, 789–795.

Knoeferle, P., Urbach, T., & Kutas, M. (2010). Verb–action versus role relations congruence effects: evidence from ERPs in sentence–picture verification. In S. Ohlsson & R. Catrambone (eds.), *Proceedings of the 30th Annual Meeting of the Cognitive Science Society*, pp. 2446–2451. Austin, TX: Cognitive Science Society.

Knoeferle, P., Carminati, M. N., Abashidze, D., & Essig, K. (2011a). Preferential inspection of recent real-world events over future events: evidence from eye tracking during spoken sentence comprehension. *Frontiers in Psychology*, *2*, 376. doi:10.3389/fpsyg.2011.00376

Knoeferle, P., Urbach, T., & Kutas, M. (2011b). Comprehending how visual context influences incremental sentence processing: insights from ERPs and picture–sentence verification. *Psychophysiology*, *48*, 495–506.

Knoeferle, P., Urbach, T., & Kutas, M. (2014). Different mechanisms for role relations versus verb–action congruence effects: evidence from ERPs in picture–sentence verification. *Acta Psychologica*, *152*, 133–148.

Kolk, H., Chwilla, D. J., van Herten, M., & Oor, P. J. (2003). Structure and limited capacity in verbal working memory: a study with event-related potentials. *Brain and Language*, *85*, 1–36.

Kuperberg, G. R., Sitnikova, T., Caplan, D., & Holcomb, P. J. (2003). Electrophysiological distinctions in processing conceptual relationships within simple sentences. *Cognitive Brain Research*, *217*, 117–129.

Kutas, M. (1993). In the company of other words: electrophysiological evidence for single-word and sentence context effects. *Language and Cognitive Processes*, *8*, 533–572.

Kutas, M., & Federmeier, K. (2011). Thirty years and counting: finding meaning in the N400 component of the event-related brain potential (ERP). *Annual Review of Psychology*, *62*, 621–647.

Kutas, M., & Hillyard, S. A. (1980). Reading senseless sentences: brain potentials reflect semantic incongruity. *Science*, *207*, 203–205.

Kutas, M., & Hillyard, S. A. (1984). Brain potentials during reading reflect word expectancy and semantic association. *Nature, 307*, 161– 163.
Kutas, M., Van Petten, C. K., & Kluender, R. (2006). Psycholinguistics electrified II. In M. A. Gernsbacher & M. Traxler (eds.), *Handbook of Psycholinguistics*, 2nd edn, pp. 659–724. New York: Elsevier.
Levy, R. (2008). Expectation-based syntactic comprehension. *Cognition, 106*, 1126–1177.
MacDonald, M. C., Pearlmutter, N. J., & Seidenberg, M. S. (1994). The lexical nature of syntactic ambiguity resolution. *Psychological Review, 101*, 676–703.
Mayberry, M., Crocker, M. W., & Knoeferle, P. (2009). Learning to attend: a connectionist model of situated language comprehension. *Cognitive Science, 33*, 449–496.
Mishra, R. K., Singh, N., Pandey, A., & Huettig, F. (2011). Spoken language-mediated anticipatory eye-movements are modulated by reading ability: evidence from Indian low and high literates. *Journal of Eye Movement Research, 5*, 1–10.
Mitchell, D. C., Cuetos, F., Corley, M., & Brysbaert, M. (1995). Exposure-based models of human parsing: evidence for the use of coarse-grained (nonlexical) statistical records. *Journal of Psycholinguistic Research, 24*, 469–488.
Nation, K., Marshall, C., & Altmann, G. T. M. (2003). Investigating individual differences in children's real-time sentence comprehension using language-mediated eye movements. *Journal of Experimental Child Psychology, 86*, 314–329.
Novick, J., Thompson-Schill, S., & Trueswell, J. (2008). Putting lexical constraints in context into the visual-world paradigm. *Cognition, 107*, 850–903.
Osterhout, L., & Holcomb, P. J. (1992). Event-related brain potentials elicited by syntactic anomaly. *Journal of Memory and Language, 31*, 785–806.
Otten, M., & Van Berkum, J. J. A. (2007). What makes a discourse constraining? Comparing the effects of discourse message and scenario fit on the discourse-dependent N400 effect. *Brain Research, 1153*, 166–177.
Pickering, M. J., & Garrod, S. (2004). Towards a mechanistic psychology of dialogue. *Behavioral and Brain Sciences, 27*, 169–190.
Potter, M. C., & Kroll, J. F. (1987). Conceptual representation of pictures and words: reply to Clark. *Journal of Experimental Psychology: General, 116*, 310–311.
Potter, M. C., Kroll, J. F., Yachzel, B., Carpenter, E., & Sherman, J. (1986). Pictures in sentences: understanding without words. *Journal of Experimental Psychology: General, 115*, 281–294.
Spivey-Knowlton, M., & Tanenhaus, M. (1998). Syntactic ambiguity resolution in discourse: modeling the effects of referential context and lexical frequency. *Journal of Experimental Psychology: Learning, Memory, and Cognition, 24*, 1521–1543.
Tanenhaus, M.K. (2004). On-line sentence processing: past, present and, future. In M. Carreiras & C. Clifton, Jr. (eds.), *On-line Sentence Processing: ERPS, Eye Movements and Beyond*, pp. 371–392. Hove, UK: Psychology Press.
Tanenhaus, M. K., Carroll, J. M., & Bever, T. G. (1976). Sentence–picture verification models as theories of sentence comprehension: a critique of Carpenter and Just. *Psychological Review, 83*, 310–317.

Tanenhaus, M. K., Spivey-Knowlton, M. J., Eberhard, K. M., & Sedivy, J. C. (1995). Integration of visual and linguistic information in spoken language comprehension. *Science, 268,* 1632–1634.

Trueswell, J.C., & Tanenhaus, M. K. (1994). Toward a lexicalist framework for constraint-based syntactic ambiguity resolution. In C. Clifton, L. Frazier, & K. Rayner (eds.), *Perspectives on Sentence Processing,* pp. 155–179. Hillsdale, NJ: Lawrence Erlbaum.

Van Berkum, J. J. A., Hagoort, P., & Brown, C. M. (1999). Semantic integration in sentences and discourse: evidence from the N400. *Journal of Cognitive Neuroscience, 11,* 657–671.

Vissers, C., Kolk, H., Van de Meerendonk, N., & Chwilla, D. (2008). Monitoring in language perception: evidence from ERPs in a picture–sentence matching task. *Neuropsychologia, 46,* 967–982.

Wassenaar, M., & Hagoort, P. (2007). Thematic role assignment in patients with Broca's aphasia: sentence–picture matching electrified. *Neuropsychologia, 45,* 716–740.

Willems, R. M., Özyürek, A., & Hagoort, P. (2008). Seeing and hearing meaning: ERP and fMRI evidence of word versus picture integration into a sentence context. *Journal of Cognitive Neuroscience, 20,* 1235–1249.

Wu, Y. C., & Coulson, S. (2005). Meaningful gestures: electrophysiological indices of iconic gesture comprehension. *Psychophysiology, 42,* 654–667.

Wu, Y. C., & Coulson, S. (2007). How iconic gestures enhance communication: an ERP study. *Brain and Language, 101,* 234–245.

Yee, E., & Sedivy, J. (2006). Eye movements to pictures reveal transient semantic activation during spoken word recognition. *Journal of Experimental Psychology: Learning, Memory, and Cognition, 32,* 1–14.

6 The NOLB model: a model of the natural organization of language and the brain

Jeremy I. Skipper

Abstract Existing models of the organization of language and the brain (OLB) can not explain natural language comprehension. They do not account for (i) the anatomical and functional data, (ii) how we overcome language ambiguity, (iii) how networks supporting language interact with each other or other networks, (iv) the computations performed in those networks or (v) language use, including how the brain uses the contextual information available in the real-world (e.g., co-speech gestures). A model of the natural OLB (NOLB) is presented that attempts to address these shortcomings. The NOLB model is dynamic, network oriented and organized around context and not *necessarily* linguistic levels or units of analysis. Specifically, it consists of many self-organizing, distributed, simultaneously active and synchronous context networks (cnets) that cooperate and compete. These cnets are weighted by the context that is available, prior experience with that context and by other cnets. Each cnet actively uses context to predict language input. The result is to constrain language ambiguity, speed up processing and free up metabolic resources. The NOLB model can serve as a framework to generate and test hypotheses, perhaps leading to needed progress in our understanding of natural language use and the brain.

Language is my mother, my father, my husband, my brother, my sister, my whore, my mistress, my checkout girl. Language is a complimentary moist lemon-scented cleansing square or handy freshen-up wipette. Fry (1989)

Think of the tools in a tool-box: there is a hammer, pliers, a saw, a screw-driver, a ruler, a glue-pot, glue, nails and screw. The functions of words are as diverse as the functions of these objects. Wittgenstein ([1953], 2001)

There is no 'centre of Speech' in the brain . . . The entire brain, more or less, is at work in a man who uses language. James ([1890], 2011)

Introduction

As Fry and Wittgenstein allude to in the above epigraphs, language in the real world is something that we do things with, something we use for nearly everything (Clark, 1996). And yet, the study of language and the brain has predominantly focused on isolated levels of linguistic analysis (e.g., phonology, morphology, semantics or syntax) as they pertain to related units of analysis (e.g., phonemes, syllables, words, sentences or discourse). Because language is fundamentally ambiguous at each of these levels or units of analyses, listeners' comprehension of spoken language must derive from the context in which it is used. A full understanding of language and the brain, therefore, must go beyond isolated levels or units to incorporate arenas of natural language use (Clark, 1992) such as face-to-face conversation where all levels or units of linguistic analysis are available. It is only in such ecological settings that context can be found and used to reduce the problem of linguistic ambiguity. In fact, these are the very places in which language and the brain evolved, develop and typically occur and it would be surprising if the brain were not organized in such a way that it would normally make use of context. Indeed, I propose that the brain actively uses context and argue that by studying the brain with the myriad sources of context that come with language in the real world, we will arrive at a different model of the organization of language and the brain (OLB) than the one we inherited from nineteenth-century neurology.

In particular, I propose a model of the natural OLB (henceforth, NOLB) as it pertains to spoken language comprehension. This model makes sense of language use by specifying how the brain uses context to solve the putative problem of linguistic ambiguity when listening. In the model, the whole brain is involved in comprehension rather than one or a small number of static regions or networks (such as Wernicke's area). In particular, the brain self-organizes into many distributed, simultaneously active and synchronous networks that cooperate and compete with one another. These networks, rather than being organized around linguistic levels or units of analysis, are organized around the processing demands of each form of context that is available to the listener. Each network implements an active or constructive mechanism in which the form of context that is being processed in that network is used to predict the forthcoming sounds, words, phrases, etc. associated with that context.

This active mechanism obviates the need to consistently process levels or units of analysis as traditionally assumed by most models. Why would the auditory system process all of the phonemes in a word or at least process them to the same extent if the brain has already predicted that word? The constraint on the interpretation of incoming acoustic information provided by all of the active networks serves to remove or reduce ambiguity to low levels. Because context changes with use, so must the underlying networks supporting language and the brain. Given the lack of consistent processing at any one level or unit of analysis and the dynamic nature of the underlying brain regions in the NOLB, it is argued that, as William James suggested ([1890], 2011), there is no necessary centre or core to the NOLB.

Context is all Atwood (1996)

Using context

One reason our ability to comprehend language is so remarkable is the relative ease and speed with which we seem to overcome a great deal of linguistic ambiguity associated with the aforementioned levels or units of analysis. For example, speech sounds are characterized by a 'lack of invariance', i.e., a non-deterministic mapping between acoustic patterns and what we hear, most words are homonymous or polysemous, sentences are frequently semantically and/or syntactically ambiguous and they often do not convey their intended meaning directly (Skipper, 2007). How do we manage to overcome such ubiquitous ambiguity? One solution is that listeners actively use all of the context available in real-world situations to constrain the number of possible linguistic interpretations and, therefore, reduce ambiguity (Skipper *et al.*, 2006).

Though a precise definition may not be possible (Duranti and Goodwin, 1992), most definitions of context have a typical character. That is, context is said to be all the information surrounding a focal event that could play a role in determining its meaning. As this implies that context can be nearly anything, it is often easier to define context with examples. I do so here with respect to how information can serve as context along a time varying continuum from exogenous (i.e., outside the listener) to endogenous context (i.e., within the listener). Exogenous context is the physical situation of language use, including time (a sunny afternoon), place (a blue sky in a park), objects (something in the sky) and people (you and I). People include talkers, aspects of their appearance (I am not wearing my glasses) and their movements. Some of those movements serve to produce non-verbal cues that we see (mouth movements, leaning back posture, pointing skyward, a flapping co-speech gesture) and linguistic levels or units of analysis that we hear (the word 'bird').

Each of these forms of exogenous context can provide pertinent and often non-redundant information to constrain the interpretation of focal events. These focal events, once comprehended, can then become context. For example, the word 'airplane' can serve as context for interpreting a flapping co-speech gesture, which can serve as context for the word 'bird', etc. For this to work, accumulated experiences with each form of exogenous context during development needs to shape the brain through learning. These learned experiences form a unique perceptual, cognitive, linguistic and social milieu for each individual, a set of memories, knowledge, scripts, schemas, expectations, beliefs, stereotypes or associations that can be used to interpret the meaning of an event. A flapping gesture could not serve as context for the word 'bird' if we had no endogenous associations of the word 'bird' with observed flying animals.

When it has been done, research suggests that listeners use many of these exogenous and endogenous forms of context during language use, that they are usually helpful and often utilized for ambiguity resolution (Skipper, 2007; Skipper *et al.*, 2006). This suggests that we may have created more of an 'ambiguity monster' (i.e., problem) than warranted by studying isolated units or levels of analysis. Is language really that ambiguous when we have and use all of the exogenous and endogenous forms of contexts discussed above, as we do during natural language use? Indeed, if we consider all of the constraints that would be imposed, it could explain why ambiguity is rarely detrimental to comprehension in natural speech (e.g., Roland *et al.*, 2006) and why talkers do not avoid producing ambiguities that can be resolved by context (Arnold, 2004; Ferreira and Dell, 2000; Ferreira *et al.*, 2005; Haywood *et al.*, 2005). In fact the evidence suggests that, as long as context is available and informative, ambiguity in speech is a feature of language that allows for greater communicative efficiency (Piantadosi *et al.*, 2012).

How then does the brain use context? I suggest that we have very little idea because most cognitive neuroscience research has been done with isolated levels and units of linguistic analysis without much context (for some exceptions, see e.g., Bartels and Zeki, 2004; Brennan *et al.*, 2012; Cantlon and Li, 2013; Hubbard *et al.*, 2009; Lerner *et al.*, 2011 ; Malinen and Hari, 2010; Morillon *et al.*, 2010; Skipper *et al.*, 2005; Speer *et al.*, 2009; Stephens *et al.*, 2010; Wilson *et al.*, 2008). To provide support for this statement, I conducted a series of PubMed searches in 20 neuroscience journals and found that less than 1% of articles about language and the brain mention 'phonology', 'semantics' *and* 'syntax' (or variations of these words, e.g., 'syntactic') in their title or abstract whereas 85% mention only one of these levels of analysis (Figure 6.1 left). Similarly, 8% of articles mention 'sentences' or 'discourse' (with variations, e.g., 'discourse' included the word 'conversation') whereas 92% mention only 'sounds' or 'words' (again, with variations, e.g., 'sounds' included 'phonemes' and 'syllables': Figure 6.1 right). Finally, 97% of these articles do not mention 'audiovisual', 'multisensory' or 'multimodal' related terms. Collectively, these search results suggest that the neuroscience work we have done to understand the OLB is nearly bereft of any linguistic and

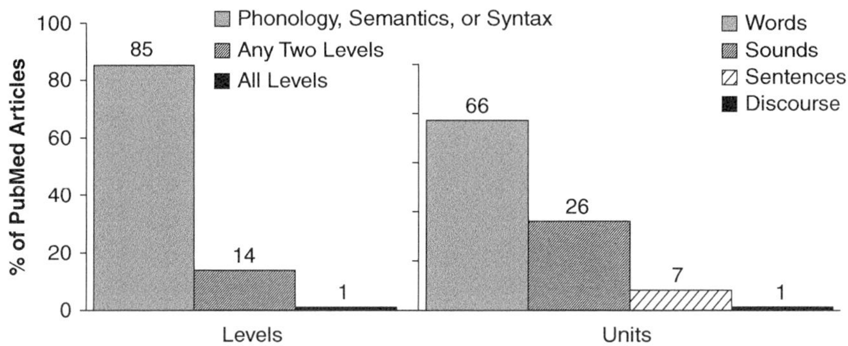

Figure 6.1 PubMed searches for terms pertaining to levels (left) and units (right) of linguistic analysis in the titles or abstracts of studies of the organization of language and the brain in 20 top neuroscience journals.

associated sensory context (and likely other non-linguistic context though searches using terms like 'pragmatics' were not done).

In what follows, I briefly review issues with both classical and contemporary models of the OLB. This should make it apparent that we need another model, one that can account for all of our linguistic levels or units of analysis as they co-occur and how the brain uses both exogenous and endogenous context. This sets the stage for the introduction of the NOLB model that I propose. It is my hope that this model will serve as a framework for future research that will bring us closer to an understanding of natural language use and how to fix the brain when disorders of language occur.

OLB models

Classical

The *Science* article 'The organization of language and the brain' (Geschwind, 1970) exemplifies the 'classical' model which mostly derives from nineteenth-century neurology. Open any textbook that discusses the OLB and you will probably find a picture that does not dramatically differ from the model presented in this article (Figure 6.2). In particular, it was proposed that all language comprehension occurred in Wernicke's area (often defined as the posterior third of the superior temporal gyrus) and speech production in Broca's areas (often defined as the pars opercularis and triangularis of the inferior frontal gyrus). Wernicke's and Broca's

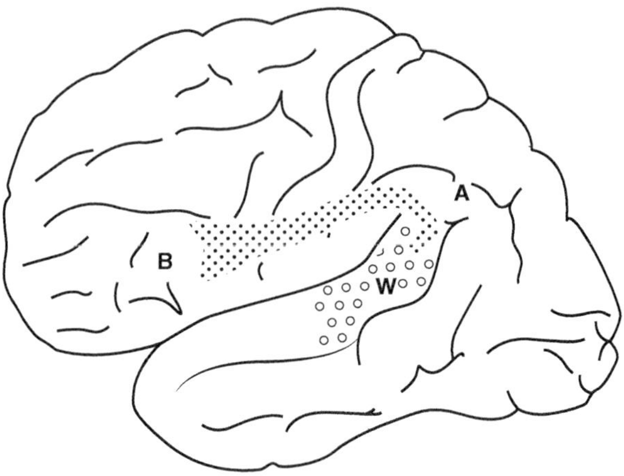

Figure 6.2 The 'classical' OLB. Reproduction of Figure 2 from 'The organization of language and the brain' (Geschwind, 1970, p. 941). 'W' is Wernicke's area (open circles), 'B' Broca's area and 'A' the connecting arcuate fasciculus axon bundle (closed circles).

areas are left-hemisphere lateralized and are connected by the arcuate fasciculus white-matter tract.

In one of the first functional magnetic resonance imaging (fMRI) studies of the OLB, Binder and colleagues said that their results indicate:

> *the need for at least some revision to this classical model. … converging sources all suggest that (1) Wernicke's area, although important for auditory processing, is not the primary location where language comprehension occurs; (2) language comprehension involves several left temporoparietal regions outside Wernicke's area, as well as the left frontal lobe; and (3) the frontal areas involved in language extend well beyond the traditional Broca's area to include much of the lateral and medial prefrontal cortex.*
> (Binder *et al.*, 1997, p. 359)

Seven years later, Poeppel and Hickock (2004, p. 5) gave a similar explanation as to why the classical OLB model was *still* problematic. It is a seriously impoverished model of language as a behaviour and the 'anatomical assertions are not true' because (I quote):

- *Broca's aphasia is not caused by damage to Broca's area*
- *Wernicke's aphasia is not caused by damage to Wernicke's area*
- [A]*spects of linguistic function … are organized bilaterally rather than unilaterally in the left hemisphere*
- *Classical speech-related regions are not anatomically or functionally homogeneous*

- [There are] *areas outside of the classical regions that are implicated in language processing* (see Poeppel and Hickok, 2004, p. 5 for supporting references)

Regarding this last point, we might ask what regions do participate in the OLB? Or, rather, what network(s) support the OLB. That is, because multiple regions are involved, we must adopt a network perspective because regions presumably need to work together to support language comprehension. We can get an idea of all the regions and networks involved by doing a meta-analysis over all existing neuroimaging studies of language, each of which typically only examines a level or unit of linguistic analysis at a time (see above, p. 00). As an example, I revisualized the results of Laird *et al.* (2011) who used independent components analysis to decompose all the data in the BrainMap database (from 1840 neuroimaging publications: 31,724 participants and 69,481 activation locations) into spatially co-occurring intrinsic connectivity network maps. They then quantified the functional specializations of each of the resulting maps by examining per-experiment contributions to each component (data are available for download at http://brainmap.org/).

Specifically, I collated the eight maps from the behavioural domain of cognition and language, speech, phonology, orthography and semantics that had a moderate or stronger correlation (i.e., >0.30) with the resulting intrinsic connectivity network maps. I did the same for the behavioural domain of cognition and memory and also found the network map with the strongest correlation with speech production (r = 0.64). By this analysis, comprehending language requires most of the brain and highly overlaps with memory and speech production (Plate 6.1, overlaps are discussed below, see colour plate section). Specifically, language comprehension related network maps collectively activated 58% of the entire surface area of the brain (much of which is not visible in Plate 6.1; note that this percentage does not take into account fMRI signal loss in temporal and frontal regions due to susceptibility artefacts). The activity in Wernicke's area alone, 'W' and open circles in Figure 6.2 and, roughly, 'W' and white outline in Plate 6.1, comprised only 2% of the surface area of the brain. That is, language comprehension activates roughly *30 times* more surface area of the brain than proposed by classical OLB models.

Contemporary

If the classical model is wrong, what are the alternatives that can explain all of language and accommodate a network perspective in which the majority of the brain is active? Unfortunately, there seems to be a general lack of model-building and almost no alternative models that meet these criteria.

Newer models that come close tend to fall under a dual-stream framework (Friederici, 2011; Hickok and Poeppel, 2007; Poeppel and Hickok, 2004; Rauschecker and Scott, 2009; Skipper *et al.*, 2006)(for a refreshing alternative see Price, 2012). This framework suggests that language can be explained by two streams emanating from auditory cortex, one for mapping sound to meaning and the other from sound to motor representations. Dual-stream models have proven useful because they explain a good deal of data and conform to existing proposals for gross processing pathways in the brain (both auditory and visual: see Skipper *et al.*, 2006). Otherwise, existing research tends to suggest relatively atheoretical explanations about activity in one region or network pertaining to one unit or level of analysis.

Issues with OLB models

Though the few contemporary models that we have are an improvement over the classical models in that they are organized around networks rather than a monolithic region for language comprehension, they have some issues that warrant a different model (at least with respect to the NOLB). The first issue is that the network perspective is not progressive enough. In current models, language processing occurs in a few networks but there are likely more networks that are more distributed than proposed (indeed, there are eight networks comprising Plate 6.2). For example, it is now fairly uncontroversial that word processing is spread out in a way that follows the organization of sensory and motor brain systems (Martin *et al.*, 1995). For example, action words referring to face, arm or leg movements differentially activate motor regions used to move those effectors (Pulvermüller, 2005). By averaging over multiple types of words not in the same word class (like action verbs), these distributed networks are being averaged out. Thus, what we probably see with neuroimaging is not the 'semantic network' (Binder *et al.*, 2009) but, rather, connectivity hubs in a distributed system (Turken *et al.*, 2011) involving as many networks as we have words and their meanings (not to mention associated words). Furthermore, these results imply that the networks supporting language are not as fixed or static as (implicitly) suggested by contemporary models. Similarly, if language comprehension requires context and the context of language comprehension is always changing, then the brain networks supporting language comprehension must also be changing. In summary, we need a model that is more consistent with general models proposing a more complex and dynamic network organization of the brain (Bressler and Menon, 2010; Bullmore and Sporns, 2009).

A second issue is that, assuming language comprehension occurs in a large set of partly independent networks, then we have no explanation of how regions or networks interact and, therefore, lack a mechanism for explaining how language comprehension occurs. The networks that have been proposed are organized around traditional levels or units of analysis. This means we have no model that explains how the brain processes information at a given level or unit of analysis in the context of other levels or units of analysis. Similarly, we have no model that explains how other cognitive processes interact with language at any given level or unit of analysis in the brain (like memory: see Plate 6.1). This has left us without a model that actually explains how language comprehension is accomplished under the assumption that comprehension, at least in the real world, is the result of the concerted effort of all these processes and their various associated networks. In summary, we need a mechanistic account of how language comprehension happens both within and across networks.

A final issue, the most important for the purposes of this proposal, is that the focus of contemporary models on language competence (i.e., the abstract knowledge of a language – isolated levels and units of analysis) means we also have no model of language performance (i.e., how we actually use language in natural settings; see Small and Nusbaum, 2004). This includes everything that goes along with language use, like how the brain uses the deluge of context it encounters. By the argument that language is ambiguous and requires context, we need a model that explains how context interacts with our linguistic levels or units and other cognitive processes in the brain and vice versa. That said, it also must be acknowledged that our networks for language might not be organized around traditional levels or units of linguistic analysis per se. There has been little attempt to confirm that these divisions are accurate or even separable. For example, there is a long-standing debate as to whether phonemes or syllables are the right unit of analysis in speech perception and a serious argument that neither has any psychological reality (Port, 2010b, 2010a). Indeed, Nusbaum and Henly (1992) demonstrated that listeners do not have a fixed size unit of analysis for recognizing speech and others have suggested that language is not separable into discrete units (e.g., Onnis and Spivey, 2012).

The NOLB model

We need an alternative model that can address the concerns enumerated in the previous section. It should explain all of language, including natural language use and should be complex enough to allow for a larger number of dynamic functional networks. The model must explain how those networks interact and explain what mechanism they implement to support language comprehension (such as how they use context). I offer a model of the NOLB that accomplishes this. Like contemporary models, this model is centred around networks, not regions per se. An organizing principle of the NOLB model is that there are many co-active networks, allowing many aspects of the natural language world to be parsed and simultancously analysed to allow language comprehension to occur efficiently. The NOLB model differs from both classical and contemporary models, however, in that what is parsed is not *necessarily* traditional linguistic levels or units of analysis (whose (neuro)psychological reality is questionable other than in descriptive terms). Rather, what is parsed are all of the exogenous and endogenous forms of context described in section 'Using context', above. That is, instead of thinking of context as noise to the brain, something to discard in experiments or something the brain must abstract away from, the many networks in the NOLB model are each 'context networks'. A context network could start with a phoneme or word as easily as it could start with a visual object, mouth movement, gesture, stereotype or expectation. Thus, the NOLB model can encompass both language competence and performance and is more dynamic than previous OLB models. What I have in mind echoes Damasio:

> *The brain not only inscribes language constituents but also provides direct and dynamic neural links between verbal representations and the representation of non-language entities or events that are signified by language ... It is that neural bond that permits the two-way, uninhibitable translation process that can automatically convert non-verbal co-activation into a verbal narrative (and vice versa), at every level of neural representation and operation.* (Damasio, 1989, p. 55)

In the NOLB model 'verbal' and 'non-verbal' are inseparable in the brain; they are continuous (Spivey, 2007). Thus, in terms of visualization of the many NOLB model context networks, I concur with Onnis and Spivey (2012) who reviewed language experiments addressing various levels or units of analysis and present:

> *a complete reorganization of how to visualize the way language works. If the various information sources in language are actually interdependent, probabilistic and continuously integrated, then ... what is needed is a single conjoined state space that combines semantic, phonetic, syntactic and other cues.* (Onnis and Spivey, 2012, p. 127)

This suggests a return to something like a 'state space semantics' proposed by Churchland in which 'the brain represents various aspects of reality by a position in a suitable state space' (Churchland, 1989,

p. 280) (see also Laakso and Cottrell, 2000). This allows NOLB model networks, given that they are context networks, to not be linguistic in any traditional sense in that the state space that describes, for example, a word can include related 'non-verbal' visual and auditory information. For example, the word 'bird' when a raven is visible can be a complex trajectory in state space that includes visual information about black feathers and expectations about ravens' intelligence (nevermore). The same word ('bird') could have a completely different state space description when a parakeet is visible (perhaps including green feathers and horrific squawking). Though this example is rather simple, actual trajectories would be through a much higher-dimensional state space (see Onnis and Spivey, 2012, for discussion). Nonetheless, given the ever-changing nature of exogenous and endogenous context during natural language use, networks in the NOLB model are always changing but can still be described.

Building on our earlier model (Skipper *et al.*, 2006), the NOLB model also differs from other models in that it is a fully active mode. Active processing models like the one I have in mind derive from Helmholtz who described visual perception as a process of 'unconscious inference' (see Hatfield, 2001). That is, visual perception is the result of forming and testing hypotheses about the inherently ambiguous information available to the retina (indeed, constructivist models are now practically the norm in vision). With respect to the NOLB model, it is proposed that each context network forms and tests hypotheses about the linguistic nature of the contextual input in a predictive manner. For example, observable context like speech-associated mouth and co-speech gesture movements can be used, in partially separable context networks, to predict the speech sounds and words associated with those movements, respectively (see Skipper *et al.*, 2006, for a more complete treatment). This constrains any ambiguity that would have been associated with those sounds and words if they had been heard in isolation.

The NOLB model also differs from earlier OLB models for a few other reasons that pertain to the active nature of the model. In addition to not requiring networks for language comprehension to revolve around traditional levels or units of analysis, the NOLB model makes no commitment to any one level or unit of analysis. This can be demonstrated with the prior example. If the gesture context network can actively predict an associated word before it occurs, the analysis of the acoustic properties of that word in terms of 'phonemes' need not occur to the same extent – if at all. Thus, following the experimental work of Nusbaum and Henly (1992) (see also Poeppel, 2003), the NOLB model implements an adaptive window of analysis that dynamically expands and contracts to any level or unit of analysis as a function of available context and the associated networks. Though this active predictive mechanism might seem neurobiologically expensive to implement, the result is both necessary (for ambiguity reduction) and ultimately metabolically less expensive because resources are conserved (as seen in the gesture example).

With that basic prelude, I turn to a more thorough explication of the NOLB model. I propose a set of six principles that account for the 'what' (neuroanatomy and neurophysiology), 'how' (neuromechanism) and 'why' (functional and neurobiological consequences) of the NOLB model. These are:

1. **What:** Comprising many self-organizing, distributed, simultaneously active and synchronous networks called context-subnetworks or cnets
2. **What:** A cnet can be fully 'reinstated' by partial activation of any one of its nodes
3. **What:** Each cnet can share nodes allowing cnets to cooperate and compete
4. **What:** The cnets are weighted by available context, prior experience and other active cnets
5. **How:** All cnets link memory and perception through an active process that uses context to predict language input
6. **Why:** Active cnet predictions constrain language ambiguity, speed up processing and free up metabolic resources

Before further describing these principles and some supporting data (see below), a very large body of existing theoretical work to which the NOLB model is indebted (but for which there is not space to review the ways in which it is indebted) must be acknowledged. Chief amongst these are the interactive constraint-based approaches to language in which context and ambiguity resolution figure prominently (e.g., Bates and MacWhinney, 1989; Cottrell and Small, 1983; MacDonald *et al.*, 1994; Marslen-Wilson, 1975; McClelland and Elman, 1986; McClelland and Rumelhart, 1981; Onnis and Spivey, 2012; Spivey, 2007). I also draw on work pertaining to network approaches to the relationship between cognition and the brain (Mesulam, 1998; Bressler and McIntosh, 2007; Bullmore and Sporns, 2009) and, more specifically, to theory about network cooperation and competition (see, e.g., Arbib, 1998; Arbib and Lee, 2008), oscillations and prediction (Arnal and Giraud, 2012; Engel *et al.*, 2001) and prediction and the brain more generally (e.g., Friston, 2005; Friston *et al.*, 2009). The NOLB model is heavily indebted to Fuster and colleagues notion of the 'cognit' (see, e.g., Fuster, 2009; Fuster and Bressler, 2012).

Principle I

Comprising many self-organizing, distributed, simultaneously active and synchronous networks called context-subnetworks or cnets

The NOLB model consists of a large-scale network (the brain) that is composed of a large array of distributed but overlapping and simultaneously active interacting subnetworks. A subnetwork is defined as a set of regions that have denser connections between them, i.e., within a subnetwork than between subnetworks. These subnetworks are called 'context-subnetworks' or simply 'cnets' (modelled after 'cognits': Fuster, 2009; Fuster and Bressler, 2012). Each cnet is a dynamically self-organizing cell assembly that organizes around and 'represents' any one form of exogenous or endogenous context. Because of the large amount of contextual information available in natural settings, there will be many cnets simultaneously active at any given time distributed across most of if not the whole brain.

Each cnet is composed of an identifiable set of distributed brain regions called nodes. The cnets can involve any number of nodes and, therefore, can be of variable size. Each node has identifiable bidirectional cortical and/or subcortical axonal connections with another node in the cnet. Activity in nodes is synchronized through these connections, allowing cnets to be characterized by specific oscillatory activity in particular frequency ranges (e.g., Beta ~13–30 Hz; Gamma ~30–100 Hz). 'Integration' need not happen in one node (the preoccupation of most studies of the neurobiology of multimodal speech perception), but can simply correspond to the activity in a bound coherently oscillating cnet. One oscillating cnet can share a node or nodes with other cnets, allowing cnets to interact. Though various cnets are simultaneously active, overlapping and interactive, they are, nonetheless partially separable. They may be separable in space, time or through their characteristic time-frequencies.

At any given moment the current linguistic state of the listener can be represented by any number of cnets, each oscillating with a high degree of coherence. For example, consider the tableau in which you and I are both staring skyward and I ask, 'Is it an airplane or a bird?' The level of description of the cnet organization associated with this scene can vary (determined by some function of the brain, experimenter, methods and neuroimaging techniques). At a relatively gross level of network description there may be visual, word, speech-associated mouth movement and co-speech gesture cnets. These might include the moving-cross-like-visual-cnet (i.e., the thing in the sky), the 'airplane'- and 'bird'-cnets, /a/- and /b/-mouth-cnets and wings-and-flapping-gesture-cnets.

Plate 6.2 (see colour plate section) visually represents this principle and should also be referred to for Principles II and III (below).

Principle II

A cnet can be fully 'reinstated' by partial activation of any one of its nodes.

The linkage or association of nodes in a cnet occurs with experience and learning through changes in synaptic weights. These changes in weights allow the spread of activity through the network to occur more easily. If the weights in a cnet are sufficiently strong, activity in one node can spread to 'reinstate' most of if not the whole network. Take the /b/-mouth-cnet in our tableau. Associations form during development between nodes involved in processing the face movements for the /b/ in 'bird' (arbitrarily called visual brain regions Va), one's own attempts to produce /b/ in 'bird' (motor brain regions Ma) and the acoustic properties of 'b' in 'bird' (auditory brain regions Aa). Thus, a /b/-mouth-cnet is composed of Va-Ma-Aa nodes. Now, if you, the listener, happen to be an ornithologist, the observed mouth movements associated with the /b/ in 'bird' in our tableau activates the visual node Va that 'reinstates' the entire Va-Ma-Aa /b/-mouth-cnet before 'b' is ever heard. This reinstatement happens because you have so much experience seeing the word 'bird' spoken (being an ornithologist) that simply seeing the /b/ face movements causes spreading activity due to the strength of associations along the entire /b/-mouth-cnet. Likewise, the strength of your semantic associations might be particularly strong such that your 'bird'-cnet might include stronger associations among certain features than those of an amateur birder. Activation of your 'bird'-cnet might involve (semantic) associations of the word 'bird' (Aa), including that they warble (Ab) and flap (Va) and have funny colours (Vb). Thus, following the /b/-mouth-cnet you might activate Aa-Ab-Va whereas a regular old bird watcher might only activate Aa.

Principle III

Each cnet can share nodes allowing cnets to cooperate and compete.

Each of the nodes in a cnet can be shared with another cnet. Therefore, activity can spread from one cnet to another, allowing cnets to form 'alliances' that are themselves more synchronized. This allows for 'cooperation' amongst cnets where each cnet can 'vote' on another by raising its level of activity through linked nodes. In our example, when I get to 'Is it an airplane ... ', your 'airplane'-cnet, due to spreading activation, also activates the 'bird'-cnet (easily demonstrated with a behavioural priming

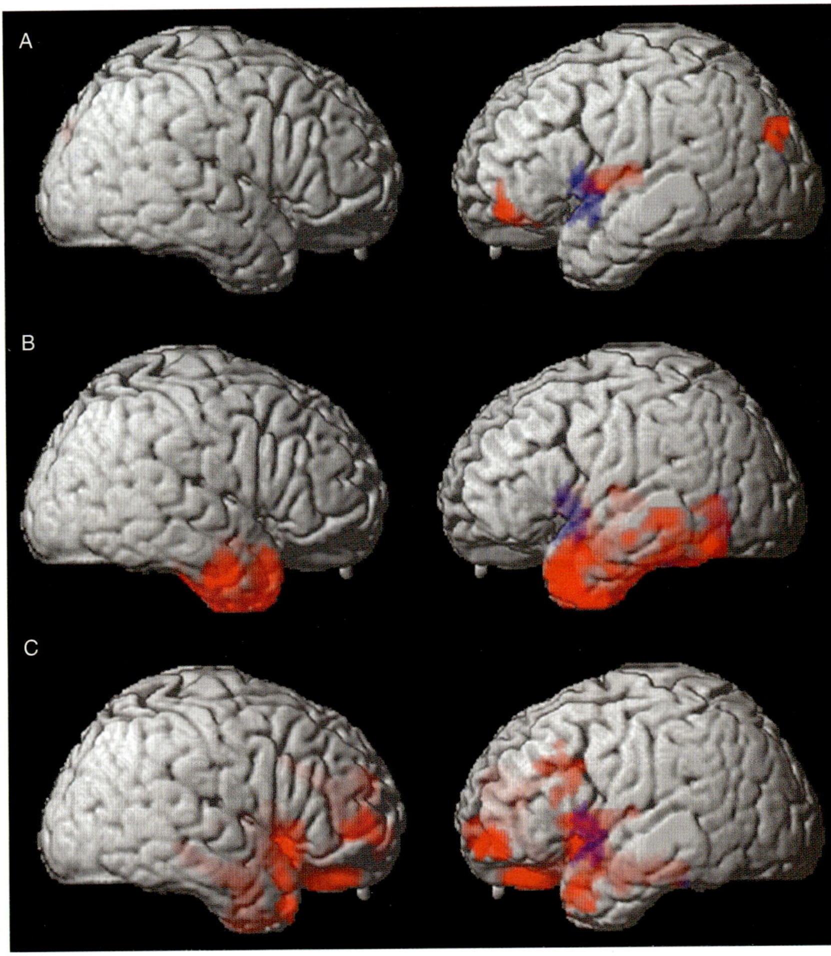

Plate 3.1 Correlations of cortical atrophy with speech rate in naPPA, svPPA, and bvFTD. Red areas indicate the anatomic distribution of significant cortical atrophy in each subgroup. The blue area indicates the region of significant correlation of speech rate and cortical volume for all FTLD patients ($N = 22$). Panel A: naPPA ($N = 6$); Panel B: svPPA ($N = 7$); Panel C: bvFTD ($N = 9$).

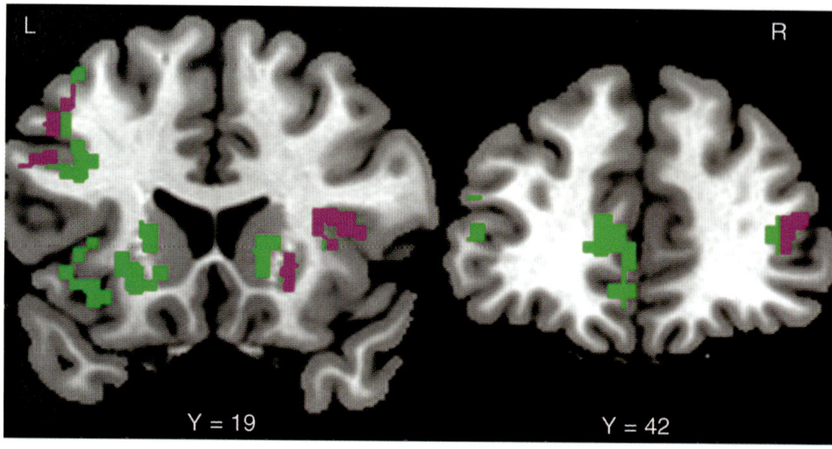

Plate 3.2 Correlation of gray matter atrophy with speech rate in lvPPA. Green areas indicate the anatomic distribution of significant cortical atrophy. Pink areas indicate regions of cortical atrophy that are correlated with words per minute.

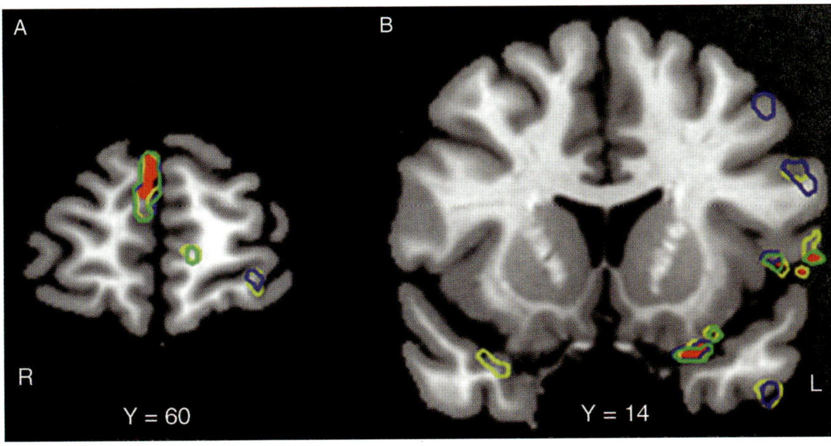

Plate 3.3 Overlap of correlations of measures of language production and neuropsychological test performance with cortical atrophy in Lewy body spectrum disorder. Red shows regions of correlation of speech rate (words per minute) with cortical atrophy; colored outlines show regions of correlation of other performance scores with cortical atrophy. Yellow = between-utterance pause time; blue = composite grammatical performance score; green = composite executive test *z*-score.

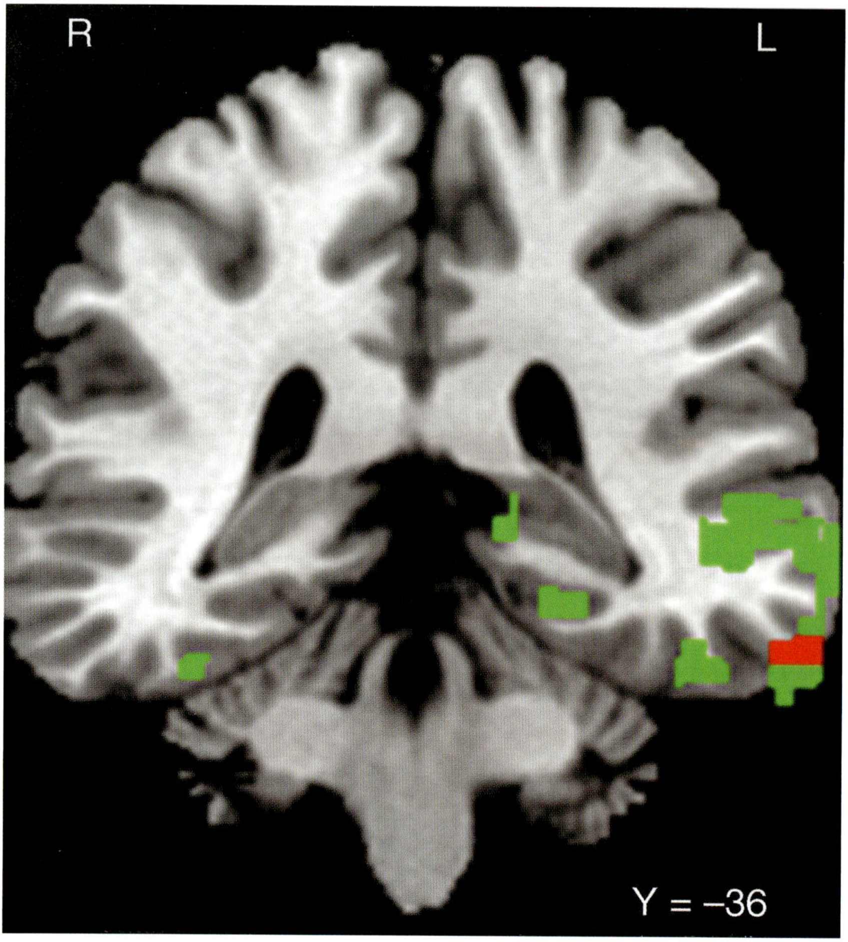

Plate 3.4 Correlation of atrophy with noun phrase pauses in svPPA. Green areas indicate the anatomic distribution of significant cortical atrophy. Red indicates a region of cortical atrophy that is correlated with noun phrase pauses.

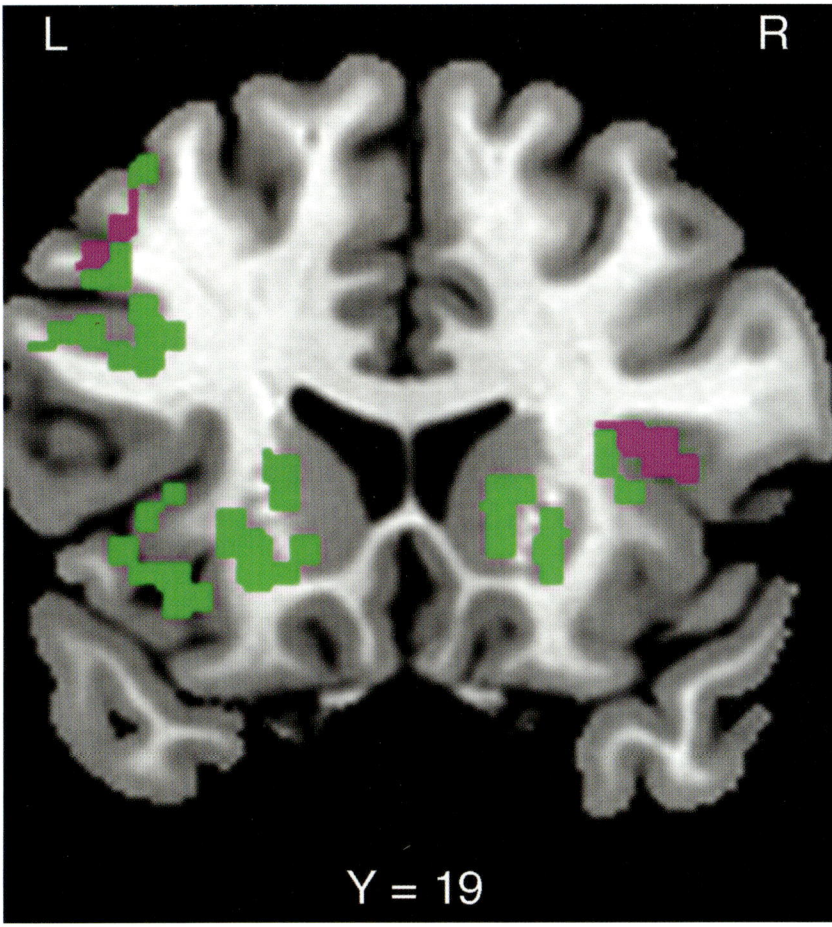

Plate 3.5 Correlation of gray matter atrophy with well-formed sentences in lvPPA. Green areas indicate the anatomic distribution of significant cortical atrophy. Pink areas indicate regions of cortical atrophy that are correlated with well-formed sentences.

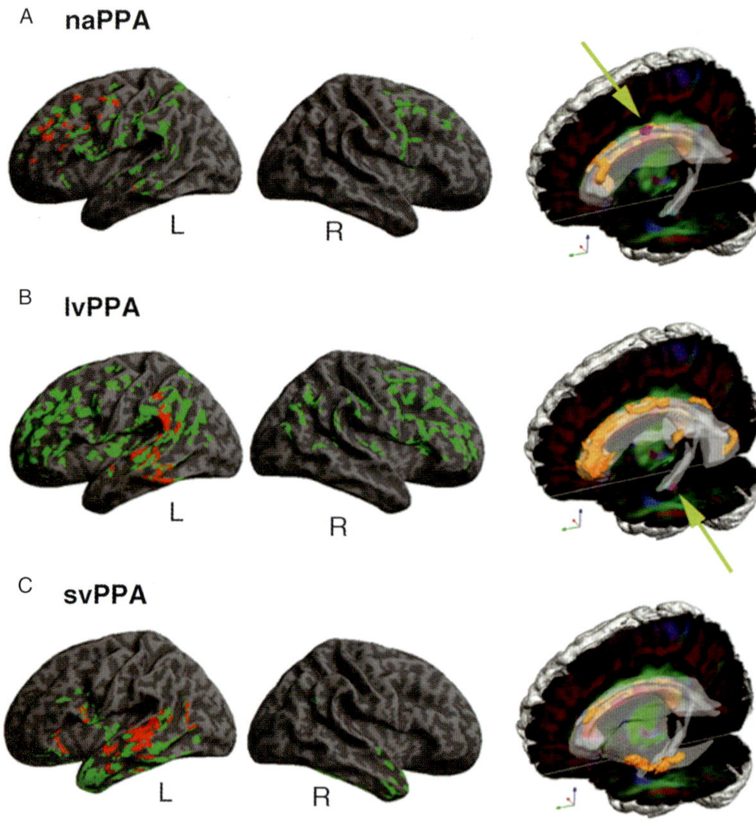

Plate 3.6 Gray matter atrophy and reduced white matter fractional anisotropy in primary progressive aphasia, and regressions relating grammaticality to neuroimaging. In the left (left hemisphere) and center (right hemisphere) columns, gray matter atrophy is shown in green ($q < 0.025$, FDR-corrected), and regressions relating grammaticality to atrophy are shown in red ($p < 0.05$). On the right, reduced white matter fractional anisotropy is shown in orange ($q < 0.01$, FDR-corrected, except svPPA $p < 0.005$ uncorrected), and regressions relating grammaticality to fractional anisotropy are shown in pink ($p < 0.01$). Yellow arrows highlight regressions in naPPA and lvPPA. Panel A: non-fluent/agrammatic PPA; Panel B: logopenic PPA; Panel C: semantic PPA.

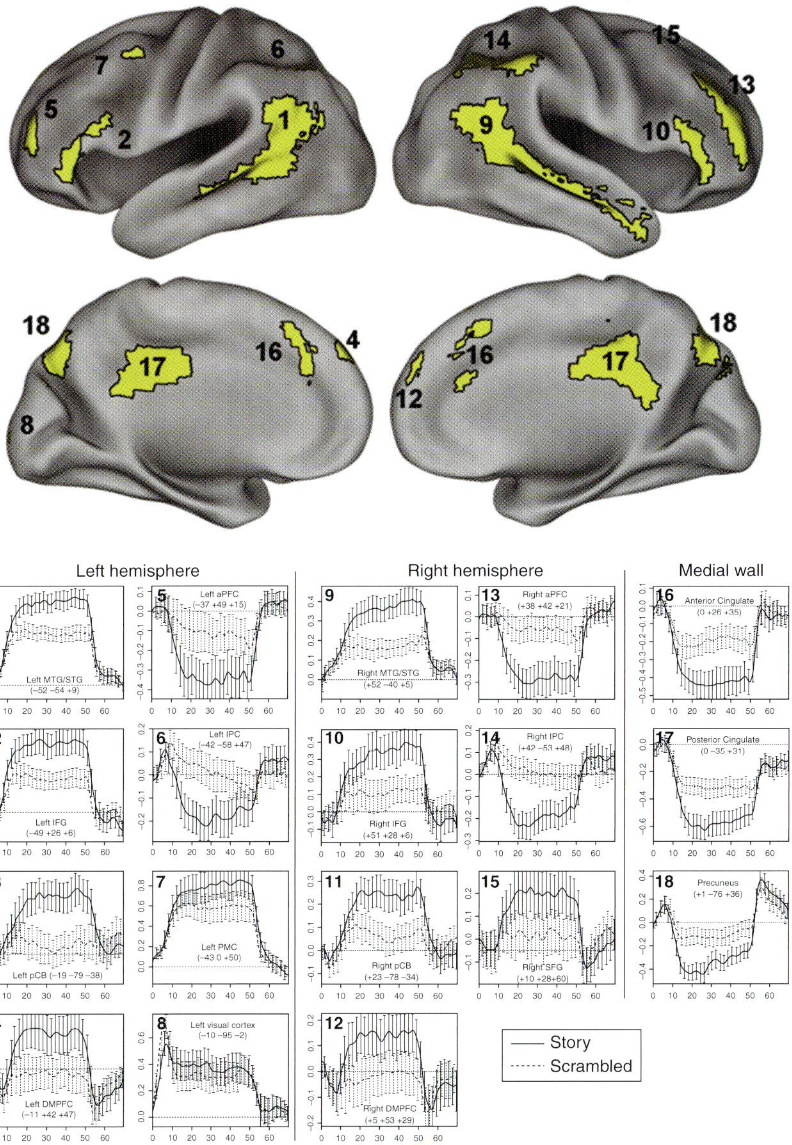

Plate 4.1 Regions that in Yarkoni *et al.* (2008) showed a significant change in activity across time by story condition, and their corresponding time courses. Reproduced with permission.

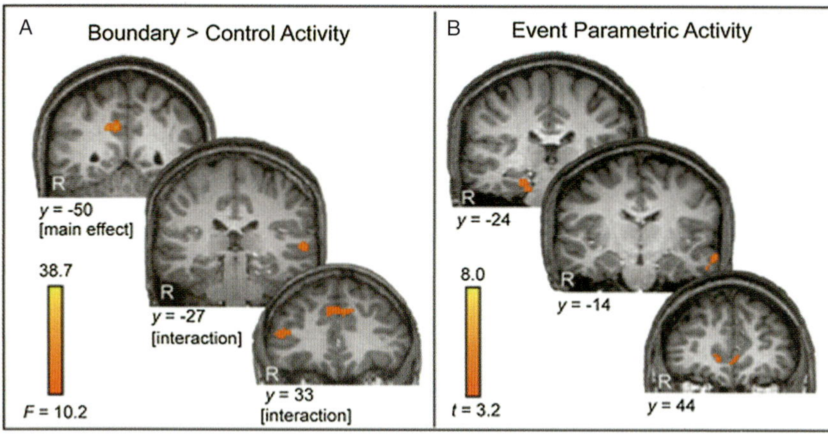

Plate 4.2 From Ezzyat and Davachi (2011). (A) Regions showing an increase in activity at event boundaries. (B) Regions showing an increase in activity as events unfolded across time. Reproduced with permission.

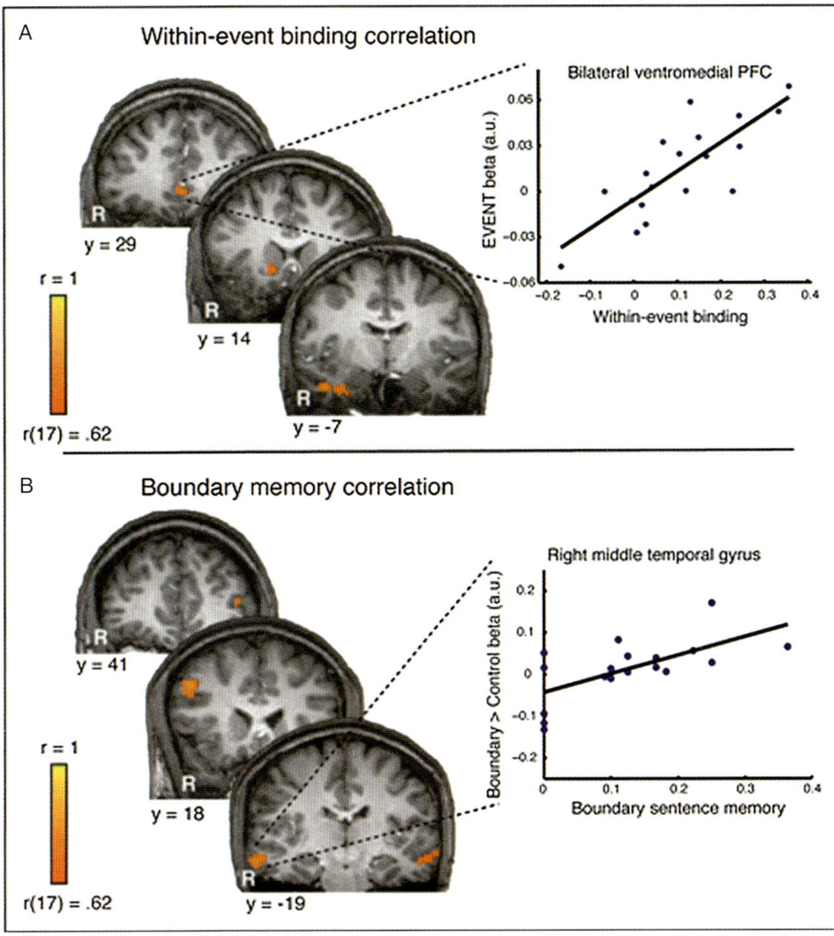

Plate 4.3 From Ezzyat and Davachi (2011). (A) Within-event binding in memory performance was correlated with three regions that increased in activity as events unfolded. (B) Memory for information in event boundaries was correlated with three regions that increased in activity at event boundaries. Reproduced with permission.

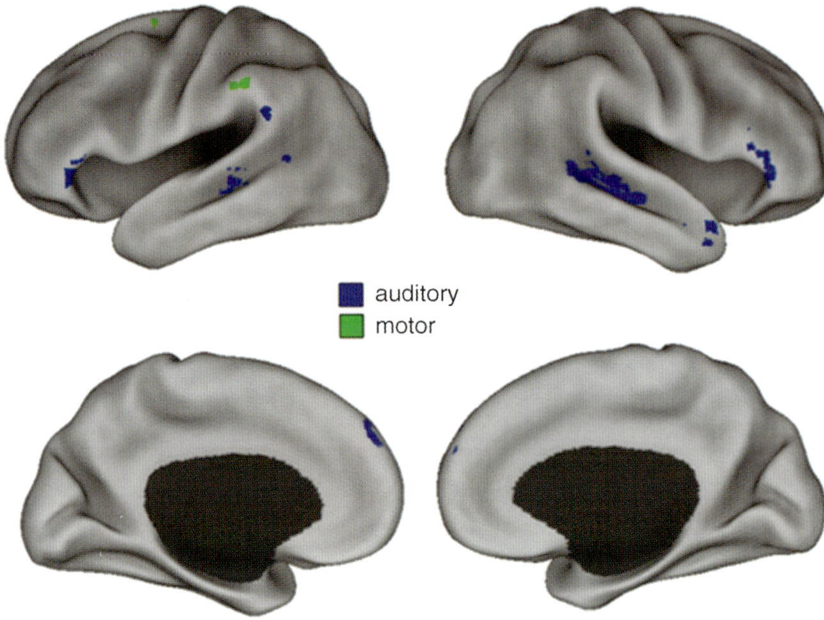

Plate 4.4 Regions showing modality-specific imagery effects in Kurby and Zacks (2013). Reproduced with permission.

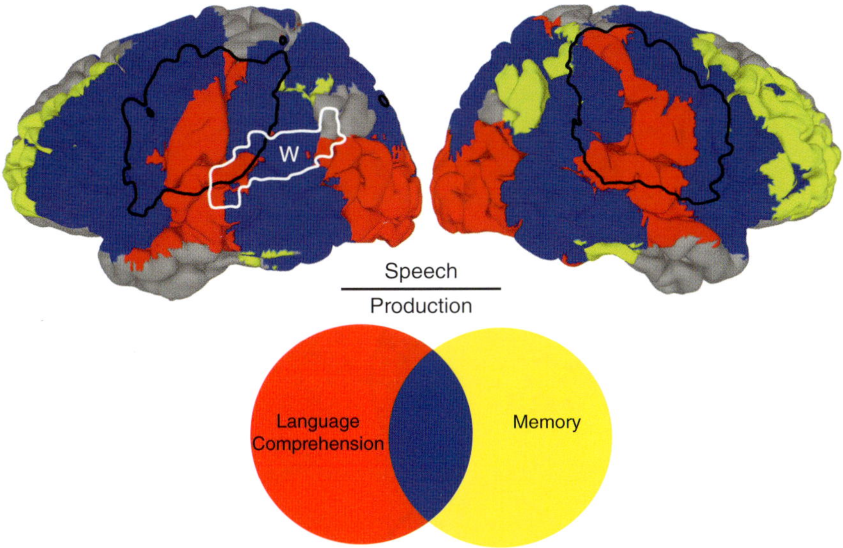

Plate 6.1 Language use is supported by most of the brain. Activity in language comprehension networks is shown across all levels and units of linguistic analysis as determined by a neuroimaging meta-analysis (Laird *et al.*, 2011). Also shown is the overlap of language comprehension networks with memory networks (blue) and a speech production network (black outline). The white outline is Wernicke's area ('W'), roughly corresponding to 'W' and open circles in Figure 6.2.

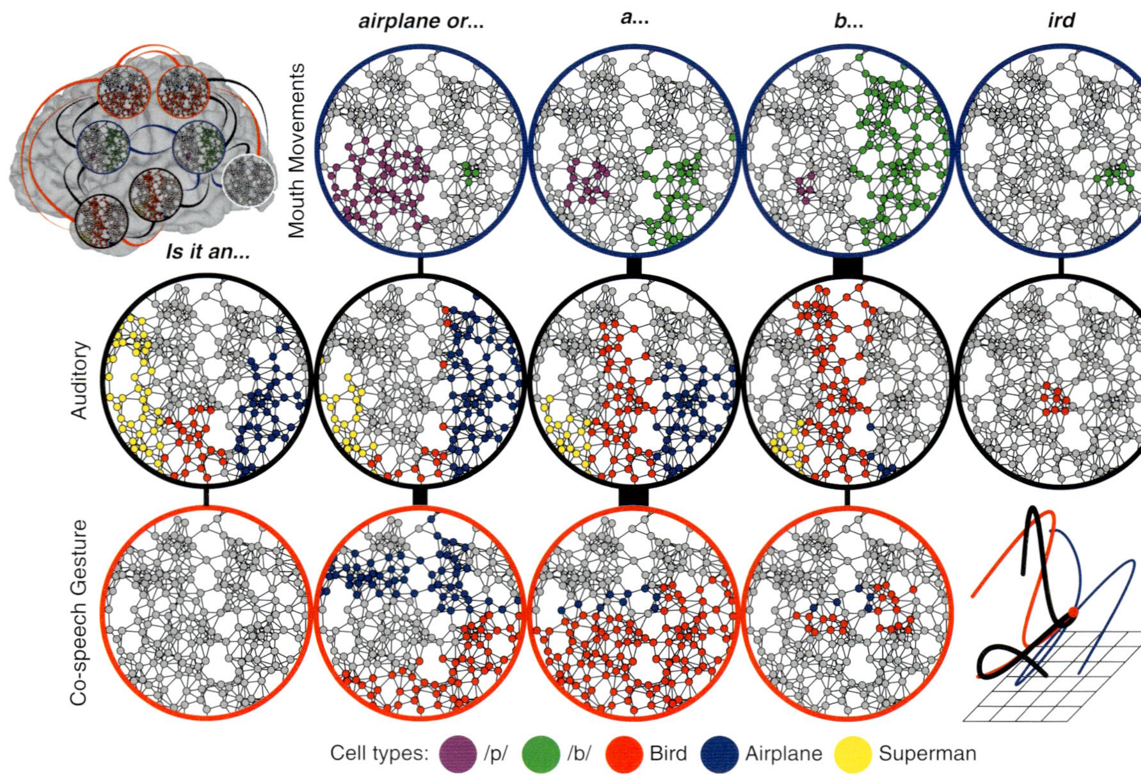
Is it an...
airplane or...
a...
b...
ird
Mouth Movements
Auditory
Co-speech Gesture
Cell types:
/p/
/b/
Bird
Airplane
Superman

Plate 6.2 Caricature of the NOLB model as applied to a listener who was looking at a moving object in the sky and who is asked 'Is it an airplane or a bird?' by a visible interlocutor. Brain (top left) shows hypothetical co-speech gesture (red), speech-associated mouth (blue), visual (white) and auditory (black) context subnetworks (cnets) that form over the duration of the sentence. Nodes in these cnets (large circles) are composed of cell assemblies and are connected by white matter tracts (bidirectional arrows). Nodes are magnified so that activity in cell assemblies can be visualized as it dynamically changes (from left to right in the figure) as a function of observable context. For example, activity in co-speech gesture nodes (red circles, bottom) increases in a cell assembly (red 'cells') for a flapping gesture observed to begin toward the end of 'airplane or'. This increases the level of activity for the 'bird' cell assembly in the auditory nodes (black circles, centre, red cells). Similarly, activity in the green /b/ cells in the observable mouth movement nodes (blue circles, top), beginning before 'b' is heard, increases the level of activity for the 'bird' cell assembly in the auditory nodes. Thus, activity in the various cnets unfolds in such a way that bird is fully active before it is heard and metabolic resources are ultimately conserved. This is an example of cooperation between cnets. The cnets also work competitively as against e.g. the 'Superman' cell assemblies whose activity is gradually suppressed. All cnets and associated cell assemblies can be visualized as sharing a high-dimensional state space, a three-dimensional version of which is shown in the bottom right for the three nodes depicted. All trajectories pass through 'bird' in this conjoined space (red circle).

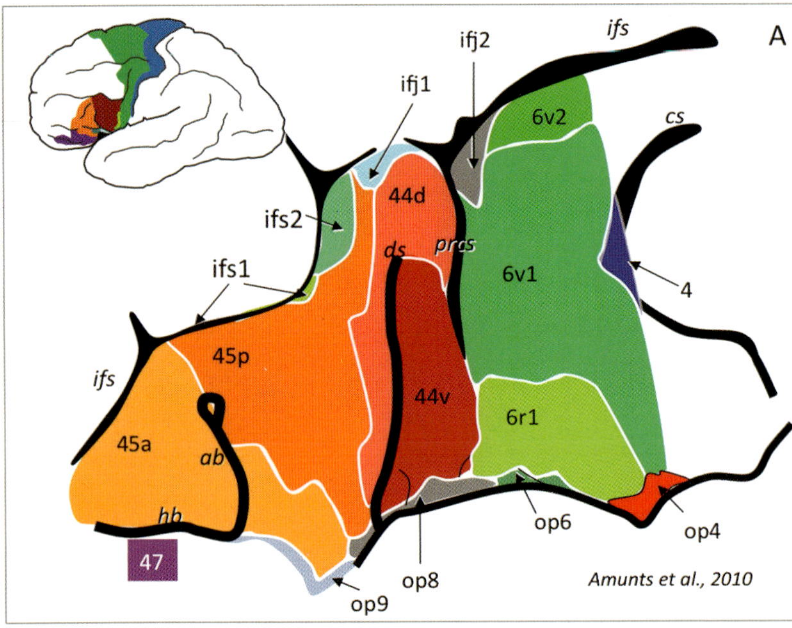

Plate 8.1 Map of Broca's region based on the distribution of receptors of neurotransmitters and modulators. BA 44 and BA 45 were found to be very similar in structure (with some subdivisions), whereas BA 47 was found to be very distinct. Reprinted with permission from the authors and from the publisher (Amunts & Zilles, 2012, figure 4).

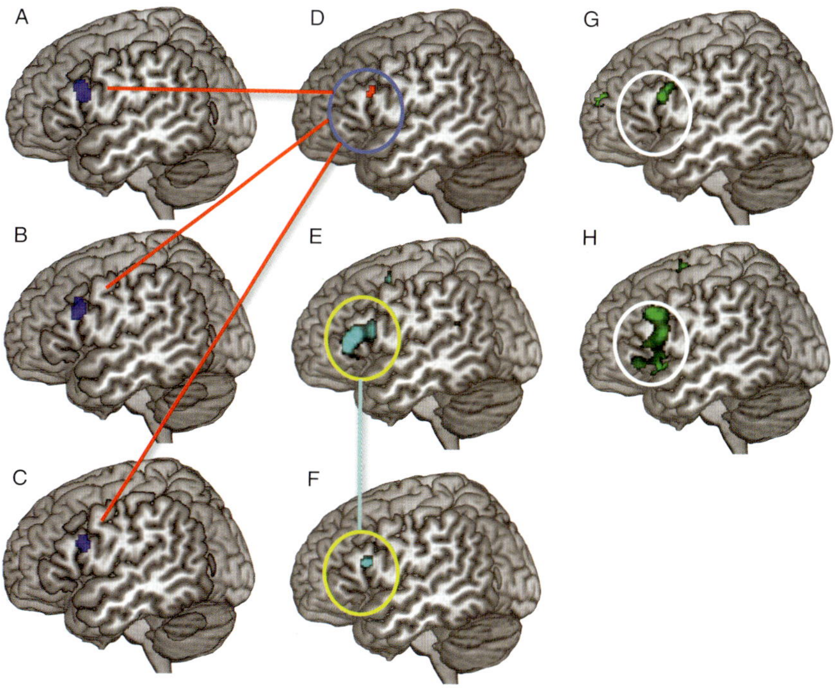

Plate 8.2 Effects in Broca's area in sentence processing. (A) Kristensen *et al.* (2014) investigated context effects on sentence processing ($p < 0.05$, FWE corrected using a Broca's area ROI). In the control task, a main effect of object-initial word order was found in BA 45 in the absence of contextual cues. (B) In the main task, an inappropriate context was found to yield greater response in BA 45, as well. (C) An interaction between word order and context was also found in the main task, suggesting that object-initial sentences are more context sensitive than subject-initial sentences. (D) An overlap for A+B+C was found in BA 45. (E + F) Single sentence data from Christensen and Wallentin (2011). Participants made comprehension judgments on single sentences. Average acceptability across participants was used as a covariate in the analysis and it was found that lower acceptability yielded higher activity in BA 45 (E). Response times were also used in the analysis and it was found that higher RT yielded greater activity in BA 45 as well (F). Display contrasts are shown for $p < 0.0001$, uncorrected, $t > 4.49$. (G) Wallentin *et al.* (2006) investigated linguistic referencing of a previously seen image. Their primary focus was the difference between spatial and non-spatial referencing, but they also found that BA 45 activity within subjects was

Caption for Plate 8.2 (cont.)

positively correlated with response time, regardless of type of reference (figure thresholded at $p < 0.0001$, uncorrected, $t > 4.7$). Broca's area activation went up whenever the participant for some reason had to spend more time on recalling the referenced context. (H) Wallentin *et al.* (2008) investigated linguistic reference to a previous sentence. Again their primary focus was between different types of reference, but based on (F) and (G) we conducted a new analysis with RT as covariate and found an identical effect (data reported here for the first time). Activity in BA 45 and BA 47 was positively correlated with trial response time (figure thresholded at $p < 0.0001$, uncorrected, $t > 4.7$, but Broca's area peaks are also significant at FDR-corrected thresholds). These effects were found to be bilateral.

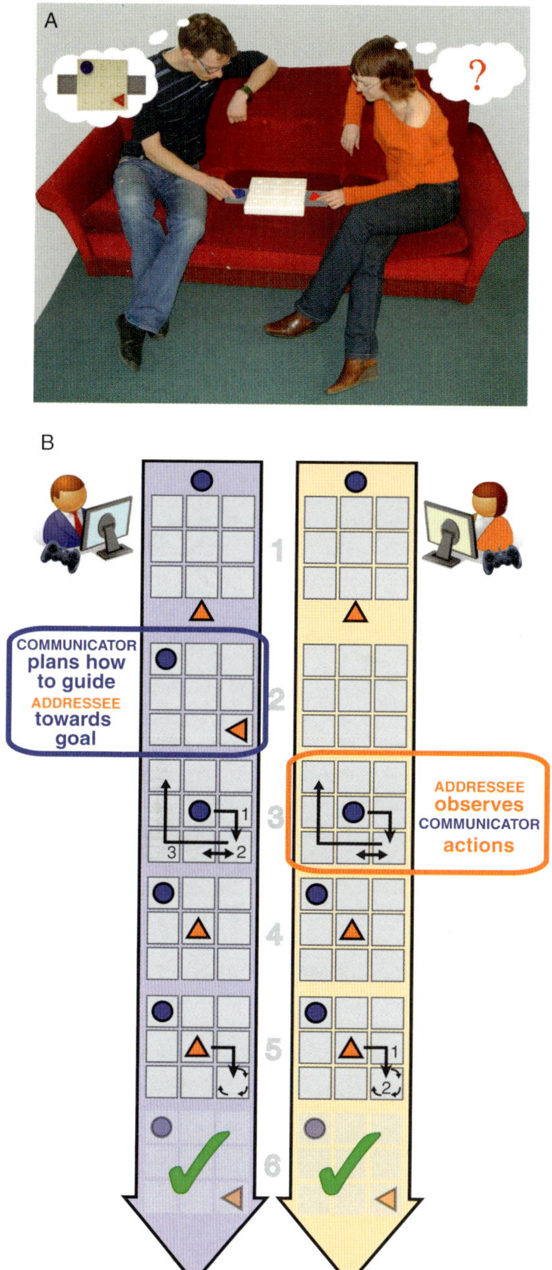

Plate 10.1 The Tacit Communication Game involves two players, a Communicator and an Addressee (left and right person respectively in the scenario depicted in panel (A), controlling geometric shape movements on a game board. Their joint task is to re-create a spatial goal configuration of two geometric shapes. The crucial manipulation is

Caption for Plate 10.1 (cont.)

that this target information is known to one of the players only – the Communicator – who then needs to convince the other player – the Addressee – to move her shape (in orange) to the desired target location and orientation. The game is tacit: the two players interact only through the visual consequences of their movements on the game board. The Communicator can thus only convey a message to the Addressee by moving his shape (in blue) knowing that she will observe those movements to decide where and how to move her shape. For experimental purposes, the game setup is computer-programmed and presented individually on two separate monitors (panel B). The players control their shape movements (horizontal and vertical translations, and 90-degree clockwise rotations) using hand-held controllers. At onset of each digitalized "trial" a shape is assigned to each player (event 1 in the same panel), followed by presentation of the goal configuration to the Communicator (event 2). During this event, he can plan as long as needed, but he has only 5 seconds to execute his movements in the next event. After pressing a start button, the Communicator's shape will appear in the center of the grid. He now can execute his actions, visible to the Addressee who needs to infer the Communicator's intentions from his movements (event 3). For instance, by first going to her target location, ostensibly "pause" to indicate the relevance of that location (number 1 action), and then "wiggle" to indicate her shape's orientation (number 2 action), and then completing his own target configuration (number 3 action). After this event, the Addressee can plan (event 4) and execute her actions (event 5) in order to complete their joint goal configuration. Finally, the same feedback on their task performance is presented to both players in the form of a green tick or a red cross (event 6). Please note that this is only one among a series of possible solutions. For instance, some participants converge on using the number of subsequent "wiggles" to mark the number of clockwise rotations that the Addressee needs to make to achieve the target orientation of her shape, while others do not use the "wiggle" but leave the triangle location along the direction to which the triangle needs to point. Reproduced with permission from Stolk, Verhagen *et al.* (2013).

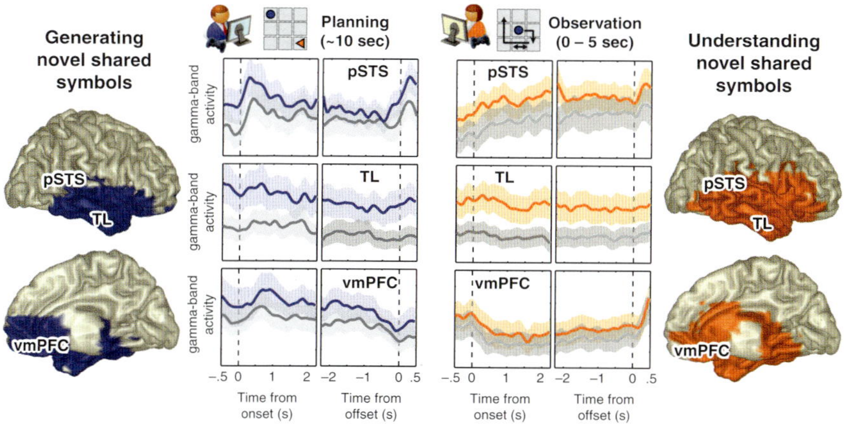

Plate 10.2 Generating (left, event 2 in Plate 10.1) and understanding (right, event 3 in Plate 10.1) novel shared symbols during live communicative interactions induced neural upregulation (of 55–85 Hz gamma-band activity) over right temporal and ventromedial brain regions. This shared tonic upregulation emerged already before the occurrence of a specific communicative problem ($t < 0$ s), but with a surprisingly matched phasic neural dynamics as non-communicative control interactions (dark and light gray traces). pSTS, posterior superior temporal sulcus; TL, temporal lobe; vmPFC, ventromedial prefrontal cortex. Reproduced with permission from Stolk, Verhagen *et al.* (2013).

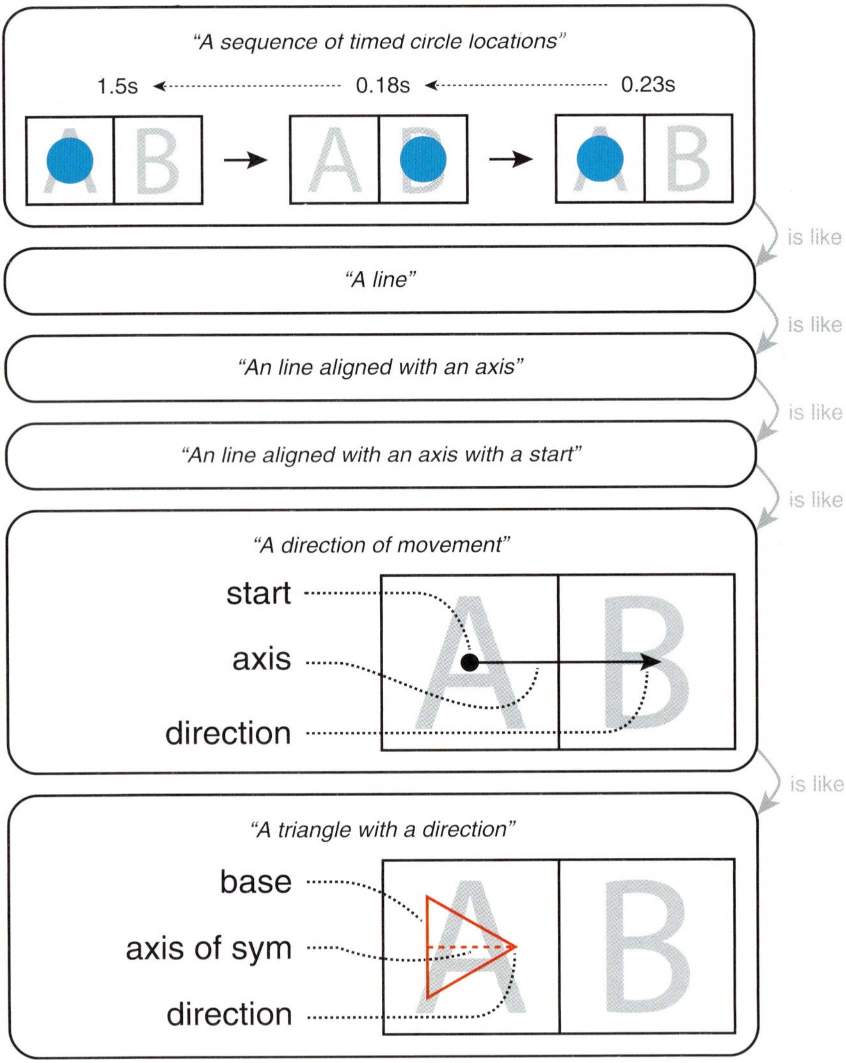

"A sequence of timed circle locations"
1.5s
0.18s
0.23s
A B
"A line"
"An line aligned with an axis"
"An line aligned with an axis with a start"
"A direction of movement"
start
axis
direction
"A triangle with a direction"
base
axis of sym
direction
is like

Plate 10.3 A sequence of analogical inferences can give rise to an inferred new meaning of a novel symbol such as the "wiggle" (here shown on two squares of a 3x3 game board used in the communication game described in Plate 10.1). Each rounded block corresponds to a conceptual structure of all objects and relations involved in that concept (e.g. "B-right_of-A" or "A-line-B"). The most cognitively salient analogy in this example is between the two bottom concepts: "A direction of movement" is like "a triangle with a direction." An analogical match between these concepts can be found which then supports the inference of meaning of the signal, i.e. the actual orientation of the triangle. The Addressee, however, has to construct this "direction of movement" concept, because she starts out with just a "sequence of timed circle locations." Augmenting this low-level representation to higher-level representations involves a sequence of smaller analogical inferences, as illustrated in this figure. Note that the final analogy is only possible with a fairly abstract and particular representation of a triangle (namely one where an equilateral triangle has a direction from base along the axis of symmetry). For a full account of meaning-mapping, one also has to explain how Addressees and Communicators construct this representation. One is able to do this by an appeal to analogical augmentation of a low-level triangle representation, similar to the augmentation of "sequence of times circle locations."

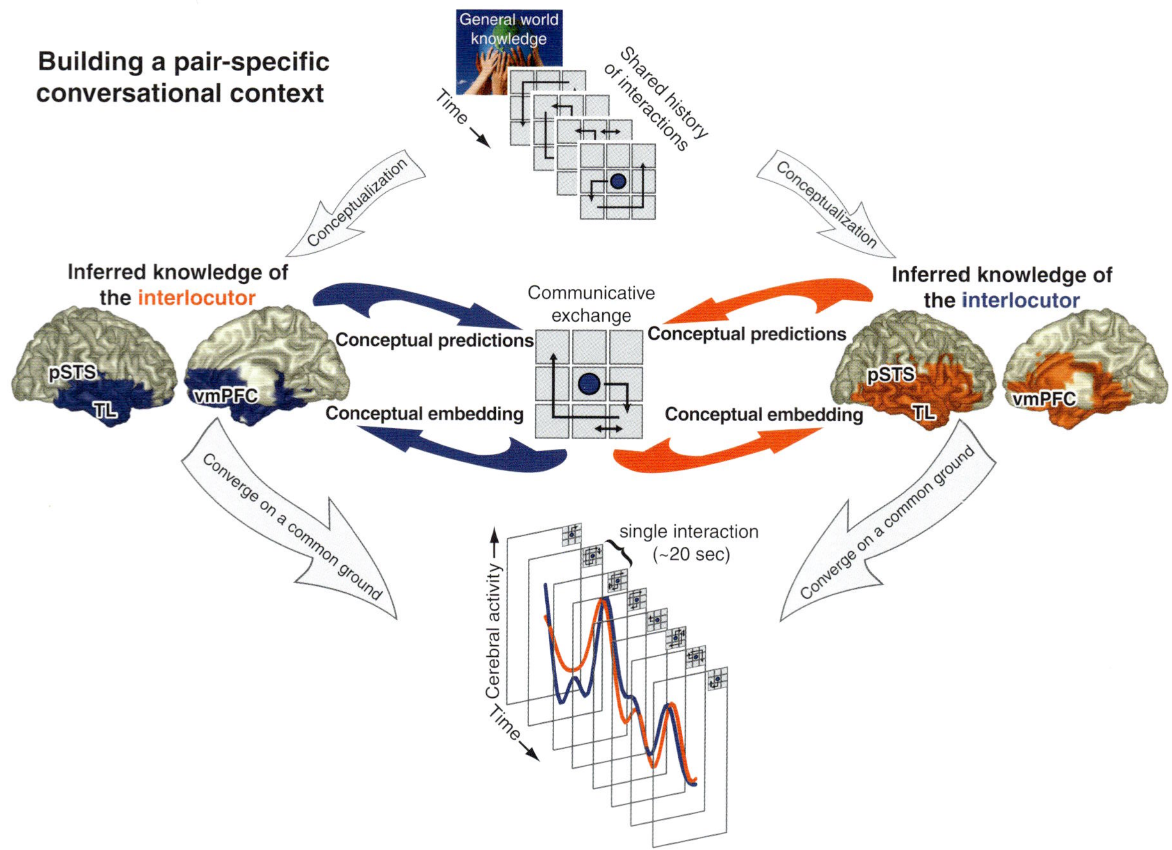

Building a pair-specific
conversational context
General world
knowledge
Time
Shared history
of interactions
Conceptualization
Conceptualization
Inferred knowledge of
the interlocutor
Inferred knowledge of
the interlocutor
Communicative
exchange
Conceptual predictions
Conceptual predictions
Conceptual embedding
Conceptual embedding
pSTS
TL
vmPFC
pSTS
TL
vmPFC
Converge on a common ground
Converge on a common ground
single interaction
(~20 sec)
Cerebral activity
Time

Plate 10.4 In human referential communication, we continuously need to disambiguate each other's behaviors by taking into account inferred knowledge and beliefs of our interlocutor, conceptual knowledge that presumably accumulates or is sharpened in our minds as we interact. In fact, when we do so, "common ground" emerges, specifically bound to the context and participants of the interaction, marked by pair-specific temporal synchronization of cerebral activity (blue and orange time courses, bottom panel), over a timescale spanning several communicative interactions. Functional imaging data, supported by observation of consequences following brain injury, highlight a fundamental role for right temporal and ventromedial prefrontal brain regions in the coordination of this conceptual knowledge. This work suggests that the right temporal lobe (TL) keeps inferred knowledge of our interlocutor aligned to the conversational context. The right posterior superior temporal sulcus (pSTS) generates predictions on stimulus material based on the shared communicative history. The ventromedial prefrontal cortex (vmPFC) guides communicative decisions on the basis of a model of inferred knowledge about the interlocutor.

Plate 11.1 The keyhole error: the world appears shaped like a keyhole when viewed through one. A view of Rome through a keyhole on the Aventine Hill. Copyright Clive Harris, photosoul.co.uk, used with permission.

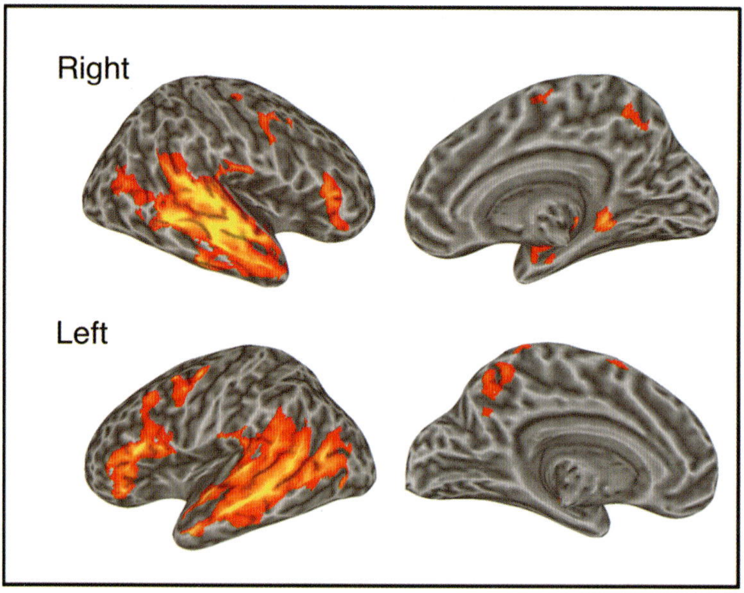

Plate 11.2 A language network? Regions where BOLD activity tracked story-related arousal in Wallentin *et al.* (2011a). We thank M. Wallentin for making available the data used to create this figure.

study). When you see my gesture begin, which will eventually describe 'bird', your flapping-gesture-cnet *also* activates your 'bird'-cnet. Thus, the activity for the 'bird'-cnet synchronizes more strongly. Therefore, when I get to 'Is it an airplane or a . . . ', when the observed mouth movement entrains the /b/-mouth-cnet, it will also vote on the 'b' in 'bird' causing even more synchrony (especially if you are an ornithologist). Conversely, 'competition' occurs. For example, presumably the 'airplane'-cnet is linked not only to the 'bird'-cnet, but also the 'superman'-cnet (perhaps from frequently hearing 'It's a Bird . . . It's a Plane . . . It's Superman'). As the 'bird'-cnet gets more and more votes the competing 'superman'-cnet that is weakly active will lose activity with evolving consensus for 'bird'-cnet.

Principle IV

The cnets are weighted by available context, prior experience and other active cnets.

The cnets are characterized by their weighting and comprehension will be dominated by the cnet with the most weight. For example, hearing 'bird' in 'Is it an airplane or a bird?' is determined by the strong weighting of the 'bird'-cnet despite the fact that the 'superman'-cnet is active. As seen under Principle I, weighting of any given cnet is determined by available context. If I am not in front of you, the /b/-mouth-cnet cannot be contributing as strongly to comprehending 'bird'. As seen under Principle II, the weighting of cnets is also determined by prior experience (as with an ornithologist who has more experience with the /b/ in 'bird'). As seen under Principle III, weighting of any given cnet is also determined by which other cnets are active. In our tableau, the 'airplane'-cnet activated the 'bird'-cnet which was lent more support by the /b/-mouth-cnet. Had we been on the phone, the /b/-mouth-cnet could not have contributed as strongly to the weighting of the 'bird'-cnet. Taken together, Principles I–III explain why cnets are dynamic and self-organizing. That is, network weights in cnets will always be changing because we use language in ever changing environments where exogenous and endogenous contexts are always changing. Thus, the word 'bird' can be supported by many different networks in different individuals depending on their prior experience (like ornithologist or not) and in the same individual depending on what other cnets are active (a function of what context is available, such as the prior use of the word 'airplane') and what the current context is (such as observable /b/ mouth movements). Finally, repeated weighting of particular nodes from cnets can lead to the formation of a new more stable cnet. Similarly, the lack of weighting can lead to cnet weight declines.

Principle V

All cnets link memory and perception through an active process that uses context to predict language input.

Memory and perception are inseparable. In the words of Fuster and Bressler (2012), '[w]e remember what we perceive and we perceive what we remember'. Indeed, I included the memory network maps from the neuroimaging meta-analysis described in section 'OLB models' above to show just how striking the overlap between memory and language is (Plate 6.1). As discussed in section 'Using context' above, the use of exogenous context requires endogenous context and vice versa. The cnets are characterized by specific re-entrant (closed-loop) oscillatory behaviour that integrates memory with perception in a predictive manner in that memory (endogenous context) is used to predict perceptual input.

In particular, each cnet initiates a backward signal that is the expected or predicted input that is propagated through the context network nodes to some lower node. The predicted input is subtracted from the actual input, representing an error signal. If the error signal is greater than zero, it means that part of the input still needs to be explained and the error signal is propagated forward through the cnet. Forward and backward propagation continues until the error signal is suppressed. A higher node that hears nothing back has 'won' and can now be used to predict the next input (or join some other context network, etc.). In our tableau, both the 'airplane'-cnet and /b/-mouth-cnet have lent weight to the 'bird'-cnet. The 'bird'-cnet initiates a backward signal that is the predicted *acoustic* input that is propagated to auditory cortex. At this point 'b' is arriving in the auditory cortex from the cochlea. The predicted 'b' in 'bird' is subtracted from the actual 'b', yielding no error signal. As there is nothing of the input left to be explained, the error signal is suppressed and auditory cortex can take on other tasks (i.e., besides processing 'bird').

The organization of cnets is not 'hierarchical' in any traditional sense because the networks are of various sizes with no clear 'top' to a cnet because the backward predictive signal could come from any level of the brain (such as from visual to auditory cortex). That said, with respect to spoken language, the speech production (motor) system likely plays a special role. Indeed, I included the speech production network maps from the neuroimaging meta-analysis described above to demonstrate the large overlap between speech production and language comprehension (Plate 6.1). This overlap is proposed to occur because most forms of context are associated with a motor program for producing the sound, word, etc. associated with that form of context (as if spoken by the listener; recall the Va-Ma-Aa nodes of the /b/-mouth-cnet). Through the backward signal from speech production regions of a cnet (or efference copy: see Skipper *et al.*, 2007a), incoming acoustic input can then be predicted (see Skipper *et al.*, 2006 for discussion).

Principle VI

Active cnet predictions constrain language ambiguity, speed up processing and free up metabolic resources.

Prediction serves several behavioural and biological functions and outcomes. Behaviourally, context and prediction together are used to constrain linguistic ambiguity. The more context there is and the more the brain can use that context (requiring experience), the stronger the resulting constraint on ambiguity. The stronger the prediction, the earlier the prediction can be confirmed (i.e., the earlier the prediction error is around zero). This has the functional effect of speeding up perception given that, for example, words can be identified earlier when compared with a purely feedforward mechanism. In addition, the stronger the prediction and earlier the prediction can be confirmed, the more free cycles become available (i.e., there are no more reverberations in a cnet). These free cycles can be used by other cnets. As such, a major advantage of prediction, other than constraining ambiguity, is that freed up metabolic resources can be used for other processes like more deeply processing language, seeking out more contextual information to do so, formulating a reply, etc.

Evidence

I turn now to the task of providing evidence for Principles I–VI. Because of space limitations, not all the evidence can be reviewed and I focus on key aspects of the principles.

Self-organization and state spaces

Principle I suggests that cnets are self-organizing around context and not traditional linguistic levels or units of analysis. There is little doubt that the brain is a self-organizing system (see e.g., Kelso, 1995; Singer, 2009). There is evidence that continuous self-organizing networks can be visualized as having levels of description corresponding to compositional structure like traditional linguistic levels or units of analysis. Specifically, robots with realistic recurrent neural networks have shown evidence for compositionality through self-organization (e.g., Tani *et al.*, 2008). More germane, similar self-organizing networks, without any (annotated) linguistic knowledge, can learn to recognize, generate and correct sentences

(Hinoshita *et al.*, 2011). By examining state spaces of the network, evidence for linguistic units of analysis can be found. Hinoshita and colleagues (2011) deduced that their model found 'words' at one timescale (including grammatical information) because the same words forming different sentences had similar trajectories in state space. Similarly, they found evidence for 'sentences' at another timescale but, notably, the correspondence between words and activations disappeared. 'Even the same words in different sentences are represented in different ways' (Hinoshita *et al.*, 2011, p. 22). It is important to keep in mind that these 'words' and 'sentences' are descriptions of the model and not really separable in the model in any traditional sense.

Subnetworks

Principle I suggests that there are *many* simultaneously active cnets. Though I suspect that few people would argue against the proposal that the brain has more than one network in operation at a time, there is not a great deal of supporting language neuroimaging data. This is likely because our existing network modelling methods (e.g., simple correlation, psycho-physiological interactions (PPI), structural equation modelling (SEM), dynamic causal modelling (DCM), vector autoregressive modelling (VAR), etc.) and the subtractive method typically used to find active regions for those models are not particularly amenable to providing evidence for multiple networks. There is, however, an increasing interest in developing a set of partitioning techniques (Hilgetag and Kaiser, 2004; Kaiser and Hilgetag, 2007; Newman, 2006; Rubinov and Sporns, 2010) to fractionate the 'scale-free' or 'small-world topology' of the brain (Bassett and Bullmore, 2006) into what have variously been called groups, clusters, modules or communities, what I have called subnetworks. Cortical thickness (Chen *et al.*, 2008) and white matter (Hagmann *et al.*, 2008) measures have revealed at least six intrinsic subnetworks and resting-state fMRI data variously show three – six subnetworks (He and Raichle, 2009; Liao *et al.*, 2011; Lord *et al.*, 2012; Tomasi and Volkow, 2012). Resting-state fMRI data also suggests that subnetworks can be decomposed into 15 or more sub-subnetworks or even sub-sub-subnetworks (Ferrarini *et al.*, 2009; Meunier *et al.*, 2010; Salvador *et al.*, 2005). Other techniques for finding subnetworks include independent components analysis (ICA) and related measures. Using ICA and resting state data, 17 (Yeo *et al.*, 2011), 23 (Beckmann *et al.*, 2005) and 26 (Varoquaux *et al.*, 2010) subnetworks have been identified.

Despite the popularity of using resting state approaches to find networks, I suspect this data dramatically underestimates the actual number of networks supporting natural stimulus driven processing. It would be quite surprising if the brain could only form 26 possible networks. Rather, Principle I states that context self-organizes regions into networks and, therefore, there are possibly as many networks as there are changing contexts. This leads to the prediction that there are far more networks during task stimulation than has been show during resting states. Indeed, we had participants watch a television game show while undergoing fMRI and found as many as 30-fold more independent component derived non-artefact subnetworks. We used speech annotations of the stimuli and our peak and valley turnpoints analysis, designed to analyse the brain under conditions of natural stimulation (see Skipper *et al.*, 2009) and found that 54 of these components were specifically tuned to speech (Skipper and Zevin, 2009). And, still, even this is likely an underestimation as the poor temporal resolution of fMRI constrains the number of dynamic time-varying networks that can be found.

Reinstatement

Principle I and II state that the brain is organized into *many* context networks (though see Bar, 2007, 2009, who discusses 'the context network') and that context can be reinstated by partial activation of any node in a cnet. Supporting these principles is a long history of behavioural research showing that we use context whether we are aware of it or not and that we store this contextual information, a requirement if it is to be reinstated. For example, memory is famously worse if participants are tested on land after studying word lists underwater compared to if they studied in and are tested underwater (Godden and Baddeley, 1975, 1980; Smith and Vela, 2001). In another example, Goldinger (1996, 1998) shows that we store seemingly irrelevant information about speech, including aspects about each individuals voice that can later affect perception.

There is also a good deal of neurobiological data demonstrating that memory is richly detailed and organized with the context in which it arrived in the brain (see Damasio, 1989). For example, Penfield quotes and describes the vivid experiences of patients upon direct stimulation of the brain who reactivate whole strips of time and has this to say:

> *One must conclude that there is, hidden away in the brain, a record of the stream of consciousness. It seems to hold the detail of that stream as laid down during each man's waking conscious hours. Contained in this record are all those things of which the individual was once aware . . . This is not a memory, as we usually use the word, although it may have some relation to it. No man can recall by voluntary effort such a wealth of detail.* (Penfield, 1958, p. 58)

More contemporary neuroscience research lends additional empirical weight to the claim that context is stored in the brain and can be 'reinstated' (Danker and Anderson, 2010). This work shows that processes engaged during encoding are later reactivated by the brain during retrieval (below the level of awareness: Johnson *et al.*, 2009) and this activation includes both uni- and cross-modal context reinstatement (Butler and James, 2011; Gottlieb *et al.*, 2010; Manning *et al.*, 2011; Skinner *et al.*, 2010). To give a language-related example, von Kriegstein *et al.* (2008) found that activity in regions involved in processing face movements is reinstated during audio-only listening if participants had previously observed that person talking and this reinstatement supports improvements in speech recognition. Similarly, read sentences can be reinstated when listening to those sentences at a later time (Briggs and Skipper, 2012; Skipper *et al.*, 2014) (see also Yoncheva *et al.*, 2009). Furthermore, the read information can be reinstated by somewhat irrelevant contextual information encoded at the time of reading (Briggs and Skipper, 2012).

Cooperation and competition

Principle III claims that cnets can share nodes so that they can cooperate and compete. This implies that nodes can be used in more than one network and, therefore, that they can have more than one function. Stated another way, nodes are 'neurally reused' (Anderson, 2010). Indeed, Anderson and Pessoa (2011) quantified the number of regions that were activated by different cognitive domains on a diversity scale ranging from 0 to 1 and found that the average value for a region was 0.70 (corresponding to 95 tasks across nine cognitive domains on average). Reused regions are not limited to 'higher-level' regions because, for example, 'action' and 'perception' regions are activated by a similar number of non-cognitive and cognitive domains (Anderson, 2010). This reuse principle is not particular to large regions (see Anderson, 2010) and even applies to individual neurons which can participate in multiple neural circuits (Niven and Chittka, 2010). Perhaps more important here, using co-activation-based network analyses, Anderson and colleagues have shown that there is a much greater average region (i.e., node) than average connection (i.e., edge) overlap for various cognitive domains (Anderson, 2008; Anderson and Penner-Wilger, 2013). That is, any given region can be part of multiple networks supporting different cognitive domains or cognitive domains are supported by different networks that might contain regions used by other domains.

What is the evidence for cooperation and competition amongst networks? There are theoretical models that propose cooperation and competition, for example, in brain development (Sirois *et al.*, 2008). Realistic computational models of cooperation and competition account for aspects of attention (Deco, 2005; Szabo *et al.*, 2004), lexical processing (Chen and Mirman, 2012) and the formation of representations of faces vs. written words (Plaut and Behrmann, 2011). There is experimental evidence for cooperation and competition at the neuronal level (Cohen *et al.*, 2010), (memory) systems level in the brain (Hartley and Burgess, 2005; Poldrack and Packard, 2003) and cooperation and competition in a dynamic and context dependent manner in large-scale brain systems (Fornito *et al.*, 2012). Using the aforementioned peak and valley turnpoints technique combined with directed network analysis and more controlled studies, we have demonstrated simultaneous activity and spatially separable context networks for processing speech-associated mouth movements and co-speech gestures (Skipper *et al.*, 2007a, 2009). Furthermore, we find these networks can differentially support the comprehension of the same sentence with each network weighed more or less as a function of the informativeness of the mouth or gesture movements (Calabrese *et al.*, 2012).

Predictions and oscillations

Principles I and V state that cnets oscillate and that each implements a strategy to use context to predict associated information in service of comprehension. There has been an explosion of theory and experimental evidence for the role of prediction in vision (Enns and Lleras, 2008; Rao and Ballard, 1999; Summerfield and Egner, 2009), memory (or vice versa: Schacter *et al.*, 2007) and the brain more generally, variously called the proactive (Bar, 2007, 2009) or predictive brain (Bubic *et al.*, 2010; Clark, 2012; Gilbert and Sigman, 2007). Consistent with the proposed NOLB model, Bubic *et al.* (2010) demonstrate that predictions can come from practically everywhere in the brain, including early unimodal sensory cortices, lateral and medial parietal and temporal regions, orbitofrontal, medial frontal and dorsolateral prefrontal cortex, premotor cortex, insula, cerebellum, basal ganglia, amygdala and thalamus.

More germane, a good amount of eye-tracking (e.g., Kamide *et al.*, 2003) and EEG (Kutas *et al.*, 2011) evidence demonstrates the predictive nature of speech perception and language comprehension. Neuroscience experiments employing methods with higher spatial resolution, as suggested by Bubic *et al.* (2010), have tended to show that prediction associated with language likely comes from multiple levels or units of analysis at multiple timescales (Arnal *et al.*, 2011; Callan *et al.*, 2010; Dikker and Pylkkänen, 2012; Gagnepain *et al.*, 2012; Rothermich and Kotz, 2013; Skipper *et al.*, 2007a; Sohoglu *et al.*, 2012; Wacongne *et al.*, 2011). That said, a great deal of this work implicates motor system involvement and at short latencies (see Callan *et al.*, 2010). For example, we have shown that the motor system is involved in predicting the acoustic patterns associated with mouth movements (Skipper *et al.*, 2005, 2007a), co-speech gestures (Seligson *et al.*, 2013; Skipper *et al.*, 2009, 2007b) and preceding discourse content (Skipper and Zevin, 2010; Skipper *et al.*, 2010).

What is the relationship between predictions and oscillations? There are many reviews collating experimental evidence for the role of neural oscillations in the assembly and ongoing activity of neural networks (e.g., Buzsáki and Draguhn, 2004) and that diverse rhythms support different aspects of cognition (Kopell *et al.*, 2010). Some suggest that higher frequencies mediate local interactions whereas slower frequencies synchronize distributed sets of nodes. For example, it has been proposed that Gamma oscillations mediate local processing and more diverse local oscillation patterns (often in Beta) mediate long-range interactions (Donner and Siegel, 2011). Wang *et al.* (2012) reviewed evidence suggesting that Gamma and Beta oscillations could pass information in opposite directions, forming a loop with Gamma and Beta bands carrying ascending and descending information respectively. Building upon this and the work of Engel *et al.* (2001), this proposal has been linked to a predictive framework in which the prediction error is propagated forward on Gamma and the prediction is propagated backward on Beta (Arnal and Giraud, 2012; Arnal et al., 2011).

Speed and metabolic savings

Consistent with Principle VI there is some evidence that prediction speeds up processing, for example, with respect to audiovisual speech (Navarra *et al.*, 2009; Stekelenburg and Vroomen, 2007; van Wassenhove *et al.*, 2005). With regard to freeing up resources, Friston (2005) has proposed that there is a relationship between repetition suppression (RS) and prediction. Indeed, both visual and auditory stimuli provide evidence that RS is, in addition to neural adaptation (Larsson and Smith, 2012), a consequence of expectations or predictions (Todorovic *et al.*, 2011). This is supported by directed functional connectivity analyses that suggest that this effect is driven in a feedback manner (Ewbank *et al.*, 2011) and that Gamma-band activity might be signalling a feedforward 'prediction error' response (Todorovic *et al.*, 2011). Using a variety of neuroimaging meta-analyses and an experiment, I have also shown that the result of predictions from various linguistic and non-verbal contexts is a dramatic freeing up of metabolic resources (Skipper, 2014). For example, target words produced *less* activity in auditory cortex when preceded by iconic co-speech gestures that visually described those words compared to those words without gestures.

Out with the old and in with the NOLB

Much more research is required. In the immediate future we need more experiments that use more than one level or unit of analysis and incorporate context. By alleviating this bias in the literature we can get a better understanding of the neurobiology of natural language use. This requires the development of more and better (multivariate) tools that allow us to parcellate imaging data into subnetworks and assign functions to those networks (Bartels and Zeki, 2004, 2005; Hasson *et al.*, 2004; Skipper *et al.*, 2009). Such methods would not only be important from a basic science perspective but also for understanding disorders that are characterized by a constellation of symptoms but that have been predominantly studied in isolation. For example, autism is characterized by impaired use of non-verbal behaviours, emotional processing and social communication but most imaging studies have focused on only one of these symptoms at a time (for example, by using static pictures of faces expressing emotions) despite their probable interdependence.

I also suggest that in the immediate future we should start investigating more natural forms of language use and more varied forms of context. Language is far more complex and interesting than a few isolated phonemes or words, unimodally presented. We use language to put together Legos and furniture, learn from lectures and news media, imagine great or horrific possible worlds in literature, make complex decisions about which wines to purchase and we use language as a social tool to meet future partners or broker world peace. For example, most of the sentences we use do not convey their meaning directly (as with 'Can you reach the salt?', Searle, 1975). And there are good reasons we say 'Would you like to see my etchings?' instead of what we actually mean (Lee *et al.*, 2010). Grice (1975) suggested that listeners must use various forms of context in comprehending such utterances. Indeed, listeners use and vary their interpretations of indirect speech acts as a function of a quite diverse array of contextual information (Ackerman, 1978; Bosco *et al.*, 2004; Clark, 1979) that goes well beyond mouth movements and gestures. Importantly, we need to start focusing on understanding the neuromechanisms underlying these complex uses of language and associated context and not simply where processing happens per se.

I think the NOLB model can act as a framework for the research that needs to be done with regard to natural language use and the brain. Unlike prior models of the OLB, the NOLB model is dynamic and network oriented, accounts for how those networks interact with each other and with other networks and is mechanistically well specified. Most importantly, it can account for complex phenomenon in language like how we use context to overcome language ambiguity during real-world language use. Having such a model allows us to form and test hypotheses about the NOLB and to make related computational models. This is an important endeavour for at least two reasons. First, arguably *every* textbook that teaches something about the OLB teaches the classical OLB, occasionally with a few caveats. Though I doubt I will see the NOLB model in every textbook, I do hope that a theoretically related model will begin to replace the classic OLB. Teaching a model that is demonstrably wrong must have some serious, negative and far-reaching consequences and it should stop.

Second, a working model of the NOLB may help us develop new and novel therapeutic interventions for language disorders, for example, aphasia following stroke. In a population-level study in Canada, aphasia had the largest negative association with health-related quality of life, larger than cancer and Alzheimer disease (Lam and Wodchis, 2010). This probably has something to do with the devastating and socially isolating effect of not being able to *use* language. Yet many therapeutic interventions necessarily evolved in some way from a combination of theories and studies of language competence (i.e., not performance or use) and the classical OLB model, itself not suited to explain language use (and perhaps this evolution is a function of our neuroscience education, see reason one above). This might help explain the relatively small effect sizes associated with improvements (when improvements are actually demonstrated) following speech and language therapy for aphasia relative to no therapy at all (Kelly *et al.*, 2010). A new language-use model might suggest novel therapies for aphasia to improve this situation (not to mention other disorders). For example, the NOLB model suggests the possibility of re-routing activity along new trajectories in a state space via preserved abilities to process some kinds of non-linguistic context.

Acknowledgements

This work was supported by NIH NICHD R00 HD060307 – 'Neurobiology of Speech Perception in Real-World Contexts' and NSF BCS-1126549 – 'MRI: Acquisition of Neuroimaging Equipment for Acquiring 4-Dimensional Brain Data from Real-World Stimuli'. Many thanks to the Rabbit-Worm, Uri Hasson, Philippa (Mom) Lauben, Sandhya Rao and Roel Willems for their helpful comments. Also, thanks to Hamilton College, the pink house and The Knob for providing homes to develop a first draft of these ideas.

References

Ackerman, Brian P. 1978. Children's understanding of speech acts in unconventional directive frames. *Child Development*, **49**, 311–318.

Anderson, Michael L. 2008. Circuit sharing and the implementation of intelligent systems. *Connection Science*, **20**(4), 239–251.

Anderson, Michael L. 2010. Neural reuse: a fundamental organizational principle of the brain. *Behavioral and Brain Sciences*, **33**(4), 245–266.

Anderson, Michael L., and Penner-Wilger, Marcie. 2013. Neural reuse in the evolution and development of the brain: evidence for developmental homology? *Developmental Psychobiology*, **55**(1), 42–51.

Anderson, Michael L., and Pessoa, Luiz. 2011. Quantifying the diversity of neural activations in individual brain regions. In: *Proceedings of the 33rd Annual Conference of the Cognitive Science Society*, pp. 2421–2426.

Arbib, Michael A. 1998. *Neural Organization: Structure, Function, and Dynamics*. Cambridge, MA: MIT Press.

Arbib, Michael A., and Lee, Jin Yong. 2008. Describing visual scenes: towards a neurolinguistics based on construction grammar. *Brain Research*, **1225**, 146–162.

Arnal, Luc H., and Giraud, Anne-Lise. 2012. Cortical oscillations and sensory predictions. *Trends in Cognitive Sciences*, **16**(7), 390–398.

Arnal, Luc H., Wyart, Valentin, and Giraud, Anne-Lise. 2011. Transitions in neural oscillations reflect prediction errors generated in audiovisual speech. *Nature Neuroscience*, **14**(6), 797–801.

Arnold, Arthur P. 2004. Sex chromosomes and brain gender. *Nature Reviews Neuroscience*, **5**(9), 701–708.

Atwood, Margaret. 1996. *The Handmaid's Tale*. London: Vintage.

Bar, Moshe. 2007. The proactive brain: using analogies and associations to generate predictions. *Trends in Cognitive Sciences*, **11**(7), 280–289.

Bar, Moshe. 2009. The proactive brain: memory for predictions. *Philosophical Transactions of the Royal Society B: Biological Sciences*, **364**(1521), 1235–1243.

Bartels, Andreas, and Zeki, Semir. 2004. The chronoarchitecture of the human brain: natural viewing conditions reveal a time-based anatomy of the brain. *NeuroImage*, **22**(1), 419–433.

Bartels, Andreas, and Zeki, Semit. 2005. The chronoarchitecture of the cerebral cortex. *Philosophical Transactions of the Royal Society B: Biological Sciences*, **360**(1456), 733–750.

Bassett, D. S., and Bullmore, E. 2006. Small-world brain networks. *The Neuroscientist*, **12**(6), 512–523.

Bates, Elizabeth, and MacWhinney, Brian. 1989. Functionalism and the competition model. In: B. MacWhinney and E. Bates (eds.), *The Crosslinguistic Study of Sentence Processing*. New York: Cambridge University Press.

Beckmann, Christian F., DeLuca, Marilena, Devlin, Joseph T., and Smith, Stephen M. 2005. Investigations into resting-state connectivity using independent component analysis. *Philosophical Transactions of the Royal Society B: Biological Sciences*, **360**(1457), 1001–1013.

Binder, Jeffrey. R., Desai, R. H., Graves, W. W., and Conant, L. L. 2009. Where is the semantic system? A critical review and meta-analysis of 120 functional neuroimaging studies. *Cerebral Cortex*, **19**(12), 2767–2796.

Binder, Jeffrey R., Frost, Julie A., Hammeke, Thomas A., Cox, Robert W., Rao, Stephen M., and Prieto, Thomas. 1997. Human brain language areas identified by functional magnetic resonance imaging. *Journal of Neuroscience*, **17**(1), 353–362.

Bosco, Francesca M., Bucciarelli, Monica, and Bara, Bruno G. 2004. The fundamental context categories in understanding communicative intention. *Journal of Pragmatics*, **36**(3), 467–488.

Brennan, Jonathan, Nir, Yuval, Hasson, Uri, Malach, Rafael, Heeger, David J., and Pylkkänen, Liina. 2012. Syntactic structure building in the anterior temporal lobe during natural story listening. *Brain and Language*, **120**(2), 163–173.

Bressler, Steven L., and McIntosh, Anthony R. 2007. The role of neural context in large-scale neurocognitive network operations. In: V. K. Jirsa and A. R. McIntosh (eds.), *Handbook of Brain Connectivity*, pp. 403–419. New York: Springer.

Bressler, Steven L., and Menon, Vinod. 2010. Large-scale brain networks in cognition: emerging methods and principles. *Trends in Cognitive Sciences*, **14**(6), 277–290.

Briggs, S. R., and Skipper, J. I. 2012. Re-visioning language and the brain: auditory language comprehension is dynamically supported by visual cortex. Paper presented at the The Fourth Annual Neurobiology of Language Conference (NLC2012), San Sebastian, Spain.

Bubic, Andreja, Von Cramon, D. Yves, and Schubotz, Ricarda I. 2010. Prediction, cognition and the brain. *Frontiers in Human Neuroscience*, **4**, 25. doi: 10.3389/fnhum.2010.00025.

Bullmore, Ed, and Sporns, Olaf. 2009. Complex brain networks: graph theoretical analysis of structural and functional systems. *Nature Reviews Neuroscience*, **10**(3), 186–198.

Butler, Andrew J., and James, Karin H. 2011. Cross-modal versus within-modal recall: differences in behavioral and brain responses. *Behavioural Brain Research*, **224**(2), 387–396.

Buzsáki, György, and Draguhn, Andreas. 2004. Neuronal oscillations in cortical networks. *Science*, **304**(5679), 1926–1929.

Calabrese, M., Kane, S., Zevin, J. D., and Skipper, J. I. 2012. Spatially separable networks for observed mouth and gesture movements during language comprehension. Paper presented at the 19th Annual Meeting of the Cognitive Neuroscience Society, Chicago, IL, USA.

Callan, Daniel, Callan, Akiko, Gamez, Mario, Sato, Masa-aki, and Kawato, Mitsuo. 2010. Premotor cortex mediates perceptual performance. *NeuroImage*, **51**(2), 844–858.

Cantlon, Jessica F., and Li, Rosa. 2013. Neural activity during natural viewing of *Sesame Street* statistically predicts test scores in early childhood. *PLoS Biology*, **11**(1), e1001462.

Chen, Qi, and Mirman, Daniel. 2012. Competition and cooperation among similar representations: toward a unified account of facilitative and inhibitory effects of lexical neighbors. *Psychological Review*, **119**(2), 417–430.

Chen, Z. J., He, Y., Rosa-Neto, P., Germann, J., and Evans, A. C. 2008. Revealing modular architecture of human brain structural networks by using cortical thickness from MRI. *Cerebral Cortex*, **18**(10), 2374–2381.

Churchland, Paul M. 1989. *A Neurocomputational Perspective: The Nature of Mind and the Structure of Science*. Cambridge, MA: MIT press.

Clark, Andy. 2012. Whatever next? Predictive brains, situated agents, and the future of cognitive science. *Behavioral and Brain Sciences*, **36**(3), 181–204.

Clark, Herbert H. 1979. Responding to indirect speech acts. *Cognitive Psychology*, **11**(4), 430–477.

Clark, Herbert H. 1992. *Arenas of Language Use*. Chicago, IL: University of Chicago Press; Center for the Study of Language and Information.

Clark, Herbert H. 1996. *Using Language*, Vol. 4. Cambridge: Cambridge University Press.

Cohen, J. Y., Crowder, E. A., Heitz, R. P., Subraveti, C. R., Thompson, K. G., Woodman, G. F., and Schall, J. D. 2010. Cooperation and competition among frontal eye field neurons during visual target selection. *Journal of Neuroscience*, **30**(9), 3227–3238.

Cottrell, Garrison W., and Small, Steven L. 1983. A connectionist scheme for modelling word sense disambiguation. *Cognition and Brain Theory*, **6**(1), 89–120.

Damasio, Antonio R. 1989. Time-locked multiregional retroactivation: a systems-level proposal for the neural substrates of recall and recognition. *Cognition*, **33**(1), 25–62.

Danker, Jared F., and Anderson, John R. 2010. The ghosts of brain states past: remembering reactivates the brain regions engaged during encoding. *Psychological Bulletin*, **136**(1), 87–102.

Deco, G. 2005. Neurodynamics of biased competition and cooperation for attention: a model with spiking neurons. *Journal of Neurophysiology*, **94**(1), 295–313.

Dikker, Suzanne, and Pylkkänen, Liina. 2012. Predicting language: MEG evidence for lexical preactivation. *Brain and Language*, **127**(1), 55–64.

Donner, Tobias H., and Siegel, Markus. 2011. A framework for local cortical oscillation patterns. *Trends in Cognitive Sciences*, **15**(5), 191–199.

Duranti, Alessandro, and Goodwin, Charles (eds.) 1992. *Rethinking Context: Language as an Interactive Phenomenon*. Cambridge: Cambridge University Press.

Engel, Andreas K., Fries, Pascal, and Singer, Wolf. 2001. Dynamic predictions: oscillations and synchrony in top–down processing. *Nature Reviews Neuroscience*, **2**(10), 704–716.

Enns, James T., and Lleras, Alejandro. 2008. What's next? New evidence for prediction in human vision. *Trends in Cognitive Sciences*, **12**(9), 327–333.

Ewbank, M. P., Lawson, R. P., Henson, R. N., Rowe, J. B., Passamonti, L., and Calder, A. J. 2011. Changes in 'top-down' connectivity underlie repetition suppression in the ventral visual pathway. *Journal of Neuroscience*, **31**(15), 5635–5642.

Ferrarini, Luca, Veer, Ilya M., Baerends, Evelinda, van Tol, Marie-José, Renken, Remco J., van der Wee, Nic J. A., Veltman, Dirk, Aleman, André, Zitman, Frans G., and Penninx, Brenda W. J. H. 2009. Hierarchical functional modularity in the resting-state human brain. *Human Brain Mapping*, **30**(7), 2220–2231.

Ferreira, Victor S., and Dell, Gary S. 2000. Effect of ambiguity and lexical availability on syntactic and lexical production. *Cognitive Psychology*, **40**(4), 296–340.

Ferreira, Victor S., Slevc, L. Robert, and Rogers, Erin S. 2005. How do speakers avoid ambiguous linguistic expressions? *Cognition*, **96**(3), 263–284.
Fornito, A., Harrison, B. J., Zalesky, A., and Simons, J. S. 2012. Competitive and cooperative dynamics of large-scale brain functional networks supporting recollection. *Proceedings of the National Academy of Sciences of the USA*, **109**(31), 12 788–12 793.
Friederici, A. D. 2011. The brain basis of language processing: from structure to function. *Physiological Reviews*, **91**(4), 1357–1392.
Friston, K. 2005. A theory of cortical responses. *Philosophical Transactions of the Royal Society B: Biological Sciences*, **360**(1456), 815–836.
Friston, Karl J., Daunizeau, Jean, and Kiebel, Stefan J. 2009. Reinforcement learning or active inference? *PLoS ONE*, **4**(7), e6421.
Fry, Stephen. 1989. *Language Conversation*. From: *A Bit of Fry & Laurie, Language Conversation*, Series 1, Programme 2.
Fuster, Joaquín M. 2009. Cortex and memory: emergence of a new paradigm. *Journal of Cognitive Neuroscience*, **21**(11), 2047–2072.
Fuster, Joaquín M., and Bressler, Steven L. 2012. Cognit activation: a mechanism enabling temporal integration in working memory. *Trends in Cognitive Sciences*, **16**(4), 207–218.
Gagnepain, Pierre, Henson, Richard N., and Davis, Matthew H. 2012. Temporal predictive codes for spoken words in auditory cortex. *Current Biology*, **22**(7), 615–621. PMID: 22425155 PMCID: PMC3405519.
Geschwind, N. 1970. The organization of language and the brain: language disorders after brain damage help in elucidating the neural basis of verbal behavior. *Science*, **170**(3961), 940–944.
Gilbert, Charles D., and Sigman, Mariano. 2007. Brain states: top-down influences in sensory processing. *Neuron*, **54**(5), 677–696.
Godden, Duncan R., and Baddeley, Alan D. 1975. Context-dependent memory in two natural environments: on land and underwater. *British Journal of Psychology*, **66**(3), 325–331.
Godden, Duncan, and Baddeley, Alan D. 1980. When does context influence recognition memory? *British Journal of Psychology*, **71**(1), 99–104.
Goldinger, Stephen D. 1996. Words and voices: episodic traces in spoken word identification and recognition memory. *Journal of Experimental Psychology: Learning, Memory, and Cognition*, **22**(5), 1166–1183.
Goldinger, Stephen D. 1998. Echoes of echoes? An episodic theory of lexical access. *Psychological review*, **105**(2), 251–279.
Gottlieb, Lauren J., Uncapher, Melina R., and Rugg, Michael D. 2010. Dissociation of the neural correlates of visual and auditory contextual encoding. *Neuropsychologia*, **48**(1), 137–144.
Grice, H. P. 1975. Logic and conversation. In: P. Cole, P. and J. Morgan (eds.), *Syntax and Semantics*, Vol. 3, *Speech Acts*. New York: Academic Press.
Hagmann, Patric, Cammoun, Leila, Gigandet, Xavier, Meuli, Reto, Honey, Christopher J., Wedeen, Van J., and Sporns, Olaf. 2008. Mapping the structural core of human cerebral cortex. *PLoS Biology*, **6**(7), e159.
Hartley, Tom, and Burgess, Neil. 2005. Complementary memory systems: competition, cooperation and compensation. *Trends in Neurosciences*, **28**(4), 169–170.

Hasson, Uri, Nir, Yuval, Levy, Ifat, Fuhrmann, Galit, and Malach, Rafael. 2004. Intersubject synchronization of cortical activity during natural vision. *Science*, **303**(5664), 1634–1640.

Hatfield, Gary. 2001. Perception as unconscious interference. In: R. Mausfield and D. Heyer (eds.), Colour Perception and the Physical World. Oxford: Oxford University Press.

Haywood, Sarah L., Pickering, Martin J., and Branigan, Holly P. 2005. Do speakers avoid ambiguities during dialogue? *Psychological Science*, **16**(5), 362–366.

He, Biyu J., and Raichle, Marcus E. 2009. The fMRI signal, slow cortical potential and consciousness. *Trends in Cognitive Sciences*, **13**(7), 302–309.

Hickok, Gregory, and Poeppel, David. 2007. The cortical organization of speech processing. *Nature Reviews Neuroscience*, **8**(May), 393–402.

Hilgetag, Claus C., and Kaiser, Marcus. 2004. Clustered organization of cortical connectivity. *Neuroinformatics*, **2**(3), 353–360.

Hinoshita, Wataru, Arie, Hiroaki, Tani, Jun, Okuno, Hiroshi G., and Ogata, Tetsuya. 2011. Emergence of hierarchical structure mirroring linguistic composition in a recurrent neural network. *Neural Networks*, **24**(4), 311–320.

Hubbard, Amy L., Wilson, Stephen M., Callan, Daniel E., and Dapretto, Mirella. 2009. Giving speech a hand: gesture modulates activity in auditory cortex during speech perception. *Human Brain Mapping*, **30**(3), 1028–1037.

James, William. 2011. *The Principles of Psychology*. Digireads.com Publishing. Original: James, W. (1890). *The Principles of Psychology* (2 vols.). New York: Henry Holt & Co.

Johnson, Jeffrey D., McDuff, Susan G. R., Rugg, Michael D., and Norman, Kenneth A. 2009. Recollection, familiarity, and cortical reinstatement: a multivoxel pattern analysis. *Neuron*, **63**(5), 697–708.

Kaiser, Marcus, and Hilgetag, Claus C. 2007. Development of multi-cluster cortical networks by time windows for spatial growth. *Neurocomputing*, **70**(10), 1829–1832.

Kamide, Yuki, Altmann, Gerry T. M., and Haywood, Sarah L. 2003. The time-course of prediction in incremental sentence processing: evidence from anticipatory eye movements. *Journal of Memory and Language*, **49**(1), 133–156.

Kelly, Helen, Brady, Marian C., and Enderby, Pam. 2010. Speech and language therapy for aphasia following stroke. *Cochrane Database Systematic Reviews*, **5**.

Kelso, J.A. Scott. 1995. *Dynamic Patterns: The Self-Organization of Brain and Behavior*. Cambridge, MA: MIT Press.

Kopell, Nancy, Kramer, Mark A., Malerba, Paola, and Whittington, Miles A. 2010. Are different rhythms good for different functions? *Frontiers in Human Neuroscience*, **4**, 187. doi: 10.3389/fnhum.2010.00187.

Kutas, Marta, DeLong, Katherine A., and Smith, Nathaniel J. 2011. A look around at what lies ahead: prediction and predictability in language processing. In M. Bar (ed.), *Predictions in the Brain: Using our Past to Generate a Future*. Oxford: Oxford University Press.

Laakso, Aarre, and Cottrell, Garrison. 2000. Content and cluster analysis: assessing representational similarity in neural systems. *Philosophical Psychology*, **13**(1), 47–76.

Laird, Angela R., Fox, P. Mickle, Eickhoff, Simon B., Turner, Jessica A., Ray, Kimberly L., McKay, D. Reese, Glahn, David C., Beckmann, Christian F., Smith, Stephen M., and Fox, Peter T. 2011. Behavioral interpretations of intrinsic connectivity networks. *Journal of Cognitive Neuroscience*, **23**(12), 4022–4037.

Lam, Jonathan M. C., and Wodchis, Walter P. 2010. The relationship of 60 disease diagnoses and 15 conditions to preference-based health-related quality of life in Ontario hospital-based long-term care residents. *Medical Care*, **48**(4), 380–387.

Larsson, J., and Smith, A. T. 2012. fMRI repetition suppression: neuronal adaptation or stimulus expectation? *Cerebral Cortex*, **22**(3), 567–576.

Lee, Jaime, Fowler, Robert, Rodney, Daniel, Cherney, Leora, and Small, Steven L. 2010. IMITATE: an intensive computer-based treatment for aphasia based on action observation and imitation. *Aphasiology*, **24**(4), 449–465.

Lerner, Y., Honey, C. J., Silbert, L. J., and Hasson, U. 2011. Topographic mapping of a hierarchy of temporal receptive windows using a narrated story. *Journal of Neuroscience*, **31**(8), 2906–2915.

Liao, Wei, Ding, Jurong, Marinazzo, Daniele, Xu, Qiang, Wang, Zhengge, Yuan, Cuiping, Zhang, Zhiqiang, Lu, Guangming, and Chen, Huafu. 2011. Small-world directed networks in the human brain: multivariate Granger causality analysis of resting-state fMRI. *NeuroImage*, **54**(4), 2683–2694.

Lord, Anton, Horn, Dorothea, Breakspear, Michael, and Walter, Martin. 2012. Changes in community structure of resting state functional connectivity in unipolar depression. *PLoS ONE*, **7**(8), e41282.

MacDonald, Maryellen C., Pearlmutter, Neal J., and Seidenberg, Mark S. 1994. The lexical nature of syntactic ambiguity resolution. *Psychological Review*, **101**(4), 676.

Malinen, Sanna, and Hari, Riitta. 2010. *Comprehension of Audiovisual Speech: Databased Sorting of Independent Components of fMRI Activity*. Technical report, Aalto University School of Science and Technology, Espoo.

Manning, J. R., Polyn, S. M., Baltuch, G. H., Litt, B., and Kahana, M. J. 2011. Oscillatory patterns in temporal lobe reveal context reinstatement during memory search. *Proceedings of the National Academy of Sciences of the USA*, **108**(31), 12 893–12 897.

Marslen-Wilson, William D. 1975. Sentence perception as an interactive parallel process. *Science*, **189**(4198), 226–228.

Martin, Alex, Haxby, James V., Lalonde, Francois M., Wiggs, Cheri L., and Ungerleider, Leslie G. 1995. Discrete cortical regions associated with knowledge of color and knowledge of action. *Science*, **270**(5233), 102–105.

McClelland, James L., and Elman, Jeffrey L. 1986. The TRACE model of speech perception. *Cognitive Psychology*, **18**(1), 1–86.

McClelland, James L., and Rumelhart, David E. 1981. An interactive activation model of context effects in letter perception: I. An account of basic findings. *Psychological Review*, **88**(5), 375–407.

Mesulam, M.-Marsel. 1998. From sensation to cognition. *Brain*, **121**(6), 1013–1052.

Meunier, David, Lambiotte, Renaud, and Bullmore, Edward T. 2010. Modular and hierarchically modular organization of brain networks. *Frontiers in Neuroscience*, **4**. doi: 10.3389/fnins.2010.00200.

Morillon, B., Lehongre, K., Frackowiak, R. S. J., Ducorps, A., Kleinschmidt, A., Poeppel, D., and Giraud, A.-L. 2010. Neurophysiological origin of human brain asymmetry for speech and language. *Proceedings of the National Academy of Sciences of the USA*, **107**(43), 18 688–18 693.

Navarra, Jordi, Hartcher-O'Brien, Jessica, Piazza, Elise, and Spence, Charles. 2009. Adaptation to audiovisual asynchrony modulates the speeded detection of sound. *Proceedings of the National Academy of Sciences of the USA*, **106**(23), 9169–9173.

Newman, Mark E.J. 2006. Modularity and community structure in networks. *Proceedings of the National Academy of Sciences of the USA*, **103**(23), 8577–8582.

Niven, Jeremy E., and Chittka, Lars. 2010. Reuse of identified neurons in multiple neural circuits. *Behavioral and Brain Sciences*, **33**(04), 285.

Nusbaum, N. S., and Henly, Anne S. 1992. Listening to speech through an adaptive window of analysis. In: M. E. H. Schouten (ed.), *The Auditory Processing of Speech: From Sounds to Words*. Berlin: Walter de Gruyter.

Onnis, Luca, and Spivey, Michael J. 2012. Toward a new scientific visualization for the language sciences. *Information*, **3**(1), 124–150.

Penfield, Wilder. 1958. Some mechanisms of consciousness discovered during electrical stimulation of the brain. *Proceedings of the National Academy of Sciences of the USA*, **44**(2), 51–66.

Piantadosi, Steven T., Tily, Harry, and Gibson, Edward. 2012. The communicative function of ambiguity in language. *Cognition*, **122**(3), 280–291.

Plaut, David C., and Behrmann, Marlene. 2011. Complementary neural representations for faces and words: a computational exploration. *Cognitive Neuropsychology*, **28**(3–4), 251–275.

Poeppel, David. 2003. The analysis of speech in different temporal integration windows: cerebral lateralization as 'asymmetric sampling in time'. *Speech Communication*, **41**(1), 245–255.

Poeppel, David, and Hickok, Gregory. 2004. Towards a new functional anatomy of language. *Cognition*, **92**(1–2), 1–12.

Poldrack, Russell A., and Packard, Mark G. 2003. Competition among multiple memory systems: converging evidence from animal and human brain studies. *Neuropsychologia*, **41**(3), 245–251.

Port, Robert F. 2010a. Language as a social institution: why phonemes and words do not live in the brain. *Ecological Psychology*, **22**(4), 304–326.

Port, Robert F. 2010b. Rich memory and distributed phonology. *Language Sciences*, **32**(1), 43–55.

Price, Cathy J. 2012. A review and synthesis of the first 20 years of PET and fMRI studies of heard speech, spoken language and reading. *NeuroImage*, **62**(2), 816–847.

Pulvermüller, Friedemann. 2005. Brain mechanisms linking language and action. *Nature Reviews Neuroscience*, **6**(7), 576–582.

Rao, Rajesh P. N., and Ballard, Dana H. 1999. Predictive coding in the visual cortex: a functional interpretation of some extra-classical receptive-field effects. *Nature Neuroscience*, **2**(1), 79–87.

Rauschecker, Josef P., and Scott, Sophie K. 2009. Maps and streams in the auditory cortex: nonhuman primates illuminate human speech processing. *Nature Neuroscience*, **12**(6), 718–724.

Roland, Douglas, Elman, Jeffrey L., and Ferreira, Victor S. 2006. Why is that? Structural prediction and ambiguity resolution in a very large corpus of English sentences. *Cognition*, **98**(3), 245–272.
Rothermich, Kathrin, and Kotz, Sonja A. 2013. Predictions in speech comprehension: fMRI evidence on the meter–semantic interface. *NeuroImage*, **70**(2), 89–100.
Rubinov, Mikail, and Sporns, Olaf. 2010. Complex network measures of brain connectivity: uses and interpretations. *NeuroImage*, **52**(3), 1059–1069.
Salvador, Raymond, Suckling, John, Coleman, Martin R., Pickard, John D., Menon, David, and Bullmore, E. D. 2005. Neurophysiological architecture of functional magnetic resonance images of human brain. *Cerebral Cortex*, **15**(9), 1332–1342.
Schacter, Daniel L., Addis, Donna Rose, and Buckner, Randy L. 2007. Remembering the past to imagine the future: the prospective brain. *Nature Reviews Neuroscience*, **8**(9), 657–661.
Searle, John R. 1975. Indirect speech acts. In: P. Cole and J. Morgan(eds.), *Syntax and Semantics,* Vol. 3, *Speech Acts*. New York: Academic Press.
Seligson, E., Calabrese, M., Azdair, J., and Skipper, J. I. 2013. Languages' transmogrifier: the role of motor cortex in processing observed iconic co-speech gestures. *Paper presented at the 19th Annual Meeting of the Organization for Human Brain Mapping*, Seattle, WA.
Singer, Wolf. 2009. The brain, a complex self-organizing system. *European Review*, **17**(2), 321–329.
Sirois, Sylvain, Spratling, Michael, Thomas, Michael S. C., Westermann, Gert, Mareschal, Denis, and Johnson, Mark H. 2008. Precis of neuroconstructivism: how the brain constructs cognition. *Behavioral and Brain Sciences*, **31**(03), 321–331.
Skinner, Erin I., Grady, Cheryl L., and Fernandes, Myra A. 2010. Reactivation of context-specific brain regions during retrieval. *Neuropsychologia*, **48**(1), 156–164.
Skipper, J. I. 2007. Lending a helping hand to hearing: brain mechanisms for processing speech-associated movements. Ph.D. thesis, University of Chicago.
Skipper, J. I. 2014. Echoes of the spoken past: how auditory cortex hears context during speech perception. *Philosophical Transactions of the Royal Society B: Biological Sciences*, **369**, 203–207.
Skipper, J. I., and Zevin, J. D. 2009. The neurobiology of communication in natural settings. Paper presented at the 1st Annual Neurobiology of Language Conference (NLC2009), Chicago, IL.
Skipper, J. I., and Zevin, J. D. 2010. How the brain predicts forthcoming words during sentence listening. Paper presented at the 17th Annual Meeting of the Cognitive Neuroscience Society, Montreal, Quebec, Canada.
Skipper, J. I., Nusbaum, H. C., and Small, S. L. 2005. Listening to talking faces: motor cortical activation during speech perception. *NeuroImage*, **25**(1), 76–89.
Skipper, J. I., Nusbaum, H. C., and Small, S. L. 2006. Lending a helping hand to hearing: another motor theory of speech perception. In: M. A. Arbib (ed.), *Action to Language via the Mirror Neuron System*. Cambridge: Cambridge University Press.
Skipper, J. I., van Wassenhove, V., Nusbaum, H. C., and Small, S. L. 2007a. Hearing lips and seeing voices: how cortical areas supporting speech production mediate audiovisual speech perception. *Cerebral Cortex*, **17**(10), 2387–2399.

Skipper, J. I., Goldin-Meadow, S., Nusbaum, H. C., and Small, S. L. 2007b. Speech-associated gestures, Broca's area, and the human mirror system. *Brain and Language*, **101**(3), 260–277.

Skipper, J. I., Goldin-Meadow, Susan, Nusbaum, Howard C., and Small, Steven L. 2009. Gestures orchestrate brain networks for language understanding. *Current Biology*, **19**(8), 661–667.

Skipper, J. I., Datta, H., and Zevin, J. D. 2010. When your brain stops listening: predicted discourse content causes the response in auditory cortex to decay. *Paper presented at the 16th Annual Meeting of the Organization for Human Brain Mapping*, Barcelona, Spain.

Skipper, J. I., Arenson, A., Cosgrove, C., and Hannon, J. 2014. Putting the text in neural context: short-term experiential reorganization of language and the brain. *Paper presented at the 20th Annual Meeting of the Organization for Human Brain Mapping*, Hamburg, Germany.

Small, Steven L., and Nusbaum, Howard C. 2004. On the neurobiological investigation of language understanding in context. *Brain and Language*, **89**(2), 300–311.

Smith, Steven M., and Vela, Edward. 2001. Environmental context-dependent memory: a review and meta-analysis. *Psychonomic Bulletin and Review*, **8**(2), 203–220.

Sohoglu, E., Peelle, J. E., Carlyon, R. P., and Davis, M. H. 2012. Predictive top-down integration of prior knowledge during speech perception. *Journal of Neuroscience*, **32**(25), 8443–8453.

Speer, Nicole K., Reynolds, Jeremy R., Swallow, Khena M., and Zacks, Jeffrey M. 2009. Reading stories activates neural representations of visual and motor experiences. *Psychological Science*, **20**(8), 989–999.

Spivey, Michael. 2007. *The Continuity of Mind*. New York: Oxford University Press.

Stekelenburg, Jeroen J., and Vroomen, Jean. 2007. Neural correlates of multisensory integration of ecologically valid audiovisual events. *Journal of Cognitive Neuroscience*, **19**(12), 1964–1973.

Stephens, G. J., Silbert, L. J., and Hasson, U. 2010. Speaker–listener neural coupling underlies successful communication. *Proceedings of the National Academy of Sciences of the USA*, **107**(32), 14 425–14 430.

Summerfield, Christopher, and Egner, Tobias. 2009. Expectation (and attention) in visual cognition. *Trends in Cognitive Sciences*, **13**(9), 403–409.

Szabo, Miruna, Almeida, Rita, Deco, Gustavo, and Stetter, Martin. 2004. Cooperation and biased competition model can explain attentional filtering in the prefrontal cortex. *European Journal of Neuroscience*, **19**(7), 1969–1977.

Tani, Jun, Nishimoto, Ryunosuke, and Paine, Rainer W. 2008. Achieving 'organic compositionality' through self-organization: reviews on brain-inspired robotics experiments. *Neural Networks*, **21**(4), 584–603.

Todorovic, A., van Ede, F., Maris, E., and de Lange, F. P. 2011. Prior expectation mediates neural adaptation to repeated sounds in the auditory cortex: an MEG study. *Journal of Neuroscience*, **31**(25), 9118–9123.

Tomasi, D., and Volkow, N. D. 2012. Resting functional connectivity of language networks: characterization and reproducibility. *Molecular Psychiatry*, **17**(8), 841–854.

Turken, U., and Dronkers, Nina F. 2011. The neural architecture of the language comprehension network: converging evidence from lesion and connectivity analyses. *Frontiers in System Neuroscience*, **5**. doi: 10.3389/fnsys.2011.00001.

van Wassenhove, V., Grant, K. W., and Poeppel, D. 2005. Visual speech speeds up the neural processing of auditory speech. *Proceedings of the National Academy of Sciences of the USA*, **102**(4), 1181–1186.

Varoquaux, G., Sadaghiani, S., Pinel, P., Kleinschmidt, A., Poline, J.B., and Thirion, B. 2010. A group model for stable multi-subject ICA on fMRI datasets. *NeuroImage*, **51**(1), 288–299.

von Kriegstein, Katharina, Dogan, Özgür, Grüter, Martina, Giraud, Anne-Lise, Kell, Christian A., Grüter, Thomas, Kleinschmidt, Andreas, and Kiebel, Stefan J. 2008. Simulation of talking faces in the human brain improves auditory speech recognition. *Proceedings of the National Academy of Sciences of the USA*, **105**(18), 6747–6752.

Wacongne, C., Labyt, E., van Wassenhove, V., Bekinschtein, T., Naccache, L., and Dehaene, S. 2011. Evidence for a hierarchy of predictions and prediction errors in human cortex. *Proceedings of the National Academy of Sciences of the USA*, **108**(51), 20 754–20 759.

Wang, Xiao-Dong, Gu, Feng, He, Kang, Chen, Ling-Hui, and Chen, Lin. 2012. Preattentive extraction of abstract auditory rules in speech sound stream: a mismatch negativity study using lexical tones. *PLoS ONE*, 7(1), e30027.

Wilson, S. M., Molnar-Szakacs, I., and Iacoboni, M. 2008. Beyond superior temporal cortex: intersubject correlations in narrative speech comprehension. *Cerebral Cortex*, **18**(1), 230–242.

Wittgenstein, Ludwig. [1953], 2001. *Philosophical Investigations*, 50th Anniversary Commemorative Edition. New York: Wiley-Blackwell.

Yeo, B. T., Krienen, F. M., Sepulcre, J., Sabuncu, M. R., Lashkari, D., Hollinshead, M., Roffman, J. L., Smoller, J. W., Zollei, L., Polimeni, J. R., Fischl, B., Liu, H., and Buckner, R. L. 2011. The organization of the human cerebral cortex estimated by intrinsic functional connectivity. *Journal of Neurophysiology*, **106**(3), 1125–1165.

Yoncheva, Y. N., Zevin, J. D., Maurer, U., and McCandliss, B. D. 2009. Auditory selective attention to speech modulates activity in the visual word form area. *Cerebral Cortex*, **20**(3), 622–632.

7 Towards a neurocognitive poetics model of literary reading

Arthur M. Jacobs

Abstract A neurocognitive poetics model of literary reading is presented in the light of experimental data and ideas from neuroscience, rhetoric, poetics, and aesthetics which should facilitate a more realistic and natural approach towards a special use of language, i.e. the reading of fiction and poetry.

Introduction

Although reading is both an unnatural, non-innate, and highly artificial activity of the mind-brain, it occupies a very significant part in the daily life of many people, presumably because its adaptive value is considerable: we read (or listen to people reading to us) to inform ourselves for optimizing decisions and actions, to learn about existing or fictive worlds stimulating our motivation, imagination, and career, and, last but not least, to be distracted from reality, to entertain us: to be amused, pleased, or emotionally and aesthetically moved. Thus, although reading is perhaps not the prototype of natural language use, it acts as a gateway to "natural" processes of language use (Kringelbach, Vuust, & Geake, 2008), and any book about this issue should include a chapter on literary reading for the sake of completeness and its ontogenetic rather than phylogenetic importance. After all, to many of us reading counts among "the most natural," i.e., most frequently used, activities we can think of.

The cognitive neuroscience of reading, much as experimental reading research ever since the days of McKeen Cattell in Wundt's laboratory, has shed a lot of light on the information processing going on while people move their eyes about 3–5 times per second across printed symbols they often took years to learn. What remains much more in the shade, however, are the affective and aesthetic processes that without doubt constitute a significant part of the reading act (Iser, 1976; Miall & Kuiken, 1994). The present chapter is an attempt to fill the cognition-emotion gap with respect to literary reading, i.e. a process, by which readers understand a text as a function – not only of basic information processing principles – but also according to their subjective impressions, emotional or (self-)reflective responses, and aesthetic preferences, which strongly depend on context and personality factors (Bleich, 1978; Jacobs, 2011; Kutas, 2006). The added value of this enterprise is hoped to be a more natural and ecologically valid, i.e., realistic and complete, picture of one of the most complex and (un)natural activities of the human mind-brain.

In the following, after some remarks on evolution and reading, I start with a discussion on "hot" vs. "cold" reading research. This is followed by an overview of our work developping and testing the Berlin Affective Word List (BAWL) as our basic tool for "hot" reading research, a discussion of the "emotion potential" of verbal materials, and a comment on the issue of literal vs. figurative language. I then introduce the neuro-cognitive poetics model of literary reading with special paragraphs on the simulation hypothesis of reading fictional material and the role of background and foreground. Backgrounding effects are then discussed in relation to the processes of immersion, suspense, and empathy, followed by an examination of foregrounding effects in relation to aesthetic processes and a summary of the empirical results informing the model.

Evolution, reading, and the *spheric fragrance* of words Although evolution has hardly had time to develop reading-specific structures in the brain, given that script-related reading activities do not seem to have started much longer than about 6000 years ago, modern neurocognitive studies of reading show reading-specific brain activity which occupies large parts of the brain (Price, 2012). Moreover, reading is a good example for how brain functions can be recycled (Anderson, 2010; Dehaene, 2005) and shaped by culture (Cornelissen, Hansen, Kringelbach, & Pugh, 2009). Although it is standard wisdom that words, both spoken or printed, can elicit even very strong emotions (e.g., insults, love poems, or death letters), the question how such presumably purely symbolic, artificial stimuli manage to do this at the level of the underlying brain functions has attracted only scarce scientific research (Citron, 2012). In spite of this, the frameworks of embodied emotion (Niedenthal, 2007) and neural reuse (Anderson, 2010; Ponz, Montant, Liegeois-Chauvel, Silva, Braun, Jacobs, & Ziegler, 2013) offer a straightforward answer to this question which was anticipated by Bühler's (1934) pioneering book on language: when heard or read, words evoke embodied memories of the thoughts, feelings, or actions associated with the things/events (and their contexts) they describe, thus activating partially the same neural networks as the corresponding "natural" events (see Willems & Casasanto, 2011). Bühler (1934) conceptualized this idea in terms of the *Sphärengeruch* (spheric fragrance) of words, according to which words have a substance, and the actions they serve – speaking, reading, thinking, feeling – are themselves substance-controlled. He gives the example of the word *Radieschen* (garden radish) which can evoke red and/or white color impressions, crackling sounds, or earthy smells and spicy tastes in the minds of the readers and "transport" them either into a garden or to a dinner table which create an entirely different "sphere" as, say, the ocean. As noted by Koerner (1984) and Schrott and Jacobs (2011) it is a pity that Bühler's early ideas – apart from his often-cited organon model – were not explicitly received and acknowledged in modern psycholinguistics, reading research, or cognitive neuroscience. Nevertheless their reinvention in theories of symbol grounding, embodied cognition, and neural reuse can explain why evolutionary young cultural objects like words are perhaps more "natural" than linguistic theory might assume, and can evoke both basic emotions and evaluative, aesthetic feelings, as is reported in many recent papers from my lab and others (Altmann *et al.*, 2012a,b; Bohrn *et al.*, 2012a, b, 2013; Briesemeister *et al.*, 2011a,b, 2014; Kuchinke *et al.*, 2005; Ponz *et al.*, 2013).

"Cold" vs. "hot" experimental reading research Neurocognitive studies of reading traditionally deal with text materials which are simple, short, and usually not part of artful literature or lyrics. Standards of experimentation constrain reading researchers to use materials which scholars from the humanities would not consider to be representative of "natural (written) language use." Extant models of word recognition, reading and eye-movement control, or text processing lack any reference to or treatment of emotional or aesthetic processes (e.g., Grainger & Jacobs, 1996; Just & Carpenter, 1980; Kintsch, 1988): much like the whole of cognitive psychology before the "emotional turn" they focus on cold cognition and remain silent with regard to hot affective processes. On the other hand, there is a rich literature on emotional and aesthetic factors in reading published by scholars from the humanities and/or psychology in journals and books featuring poetics (e.g., Bortolussi & Dixon, 2003; Brewer & Lichtenstein, 1982; Kneepkens & Zwaan, 1994; Iser, 1976; Mar *et al.*, 2011; Miall & Kuiken, 1994; 2002; Oatley, 1994). This literature basically was ignored by mainstream psychological reading research, perhaps also because the majority of these studies use empirical but not standard experimental designs or methods, and text materials which are considered to be too rich and complex to fulfill major criteria of such designs. Following our book on brain and poetry (Schrott & Jacobs, 2011), the present chapter also represents an attempt at changing this unsatisfactory state of affairs in the service of a more natural and representative approach to reading (see also Mar *et al.*, 2011).

To be able to study "hot" reading, it is crucial to have appropriate conceptual and methodological tools characterizing the emotional value of single words. The next section provides an overview of our efforts in this respect.

The Berlin Affective Word List (BAWL) as a basic tool for "hot" (ecologically more valid) experimental reading research

Our non-innate reading skill relies on two basic processes: automatic word recognition and eye-movement control. Only effortless mastering of these activities allows cognitive and affective processes which create meaning from text symbols involving morphosyntactic, semantic, or pragmatic information. Leaving aside eye-movement control processes in this chapter, I first focus on affective and aesthetic processes associated with single word recognition, because whoever wants to understand how larger text segments can induce such processes must start with those basic units at which all relevant processes and representations in language use come together: words (Miller, 1993). Of course, sub- and supralexical processes also play a role for emotional responses to literature, but we will deal with those later. As an aside, if the reader of these lines may wonder to what extent single words can induce aesthetic processes, she or he is invited to read the wonderful book by Limbach, *Das schönste deutsche Wort* ("The most beautiful German word," Limbach, 2006), which, for instance, provides impressive examples for the fact that even 9-year-old children can find beauty in single words and can also convincingly argue why (Schrott & Jacobs, 2011).

So, can we experimentally demonstrate that single words can induce affects, feelings, non-aesthetic vs. aesthetic emotions, or moods? Of course, any answer to this question depends on one's accepted definition of these highly debated terms (Kagan, 2010). Empirically, however, the answer is quite straightforward: as the pioneers of standardized experimental emotion induction materials, i.e., the International Affective Picture System (IAPS: Lang *et al.*, 2005) and its verbal twin the Affective Norms for English Words (ANEW: Bradley & Lang, 1999) have shown, English single words offer a nice distribution along the subjectively rated dimensions emotional valence (pleasure) and arousal (activation) and these subjective measures of affect can be cross-validated at the peripheral physiological and brain-electrical levels all suggesting that words evoke similar affective responses as faces or objects.

To provide a basic tool for researchers interested in affective reading processes in the German language, we have developed the BAWL over the last ten years and cross-validated it at the three relevant levels of psychological processes: the experiential (e.g., subjective ratings, self-reports: Vo *et al.*, 2006, 2009), the behavioral (e.g., response times, oculo- and pupillometric responses: Briesemeister *et al.*, 2011a,b; Vo *et al.*, 2006, 2008), and the neuronal, using both brain-electrical and fMRI methods (Conrad *et al.*, 2011; Hofmann *et al.*, 2009; Kuchinke *et al.*, 2005). In contrast to the ANEW which relies on a dimensional theory of emotion such as those of Wundt, Lang, or Russell, there is also a version of the BAWL that is compatible with discrete emotion theories, such as Darwin's or Ekman's (Briesemeister *et al.*, 2011a). Moreover there exists a multilingual version of the BAWL containing more than 6000 words allowing comparisons between German, Spanish, English, and French (Conrad *et al.*, 2011). Among other things, the BAWL can be used to estimate the *emotion potential* of single words or supralexical units.

Frege's Axiom and the emotion potential of verbal material The emotion potential of texts is a theoretical notion used in cognitive linguistics but still waiting for a proper operationalization and empirical justification, as far as I can tell (Schwarz-Friesel, 2007). A more natural and ecologically valid investigation of literary reading, however, has to face this notion, since many kinds of texts including political speeches, novels, poems, or song lyrics are believed to possess emotion potential. As will be discussed later, another reason is the role a reader's emotional involvement may play for immersive processes (absorption, transportation, flow: Appel & Richter, 2010) which any literature fan can subjectively describe, but which so far have not been the object of much experimental reading research (Schrott & Jacobs, 2011). To address this issue pragmatically, I make two assumptions. First, in its simplest form, the emotion potential of single words can be approximated by a compound variable containing the emotional valence and arousal values, as documented in databases such as BAWL, ANEW, or Whissell *et al.*'s (1986) Dictionary of Affect (DoA). Whether a third or more dimensions need to be added is an empirical question (Briesemeister *et al.*, 2011a, 2014). Second, the emotion potential of supralexical units is a function of the emotion potential of the words constituting this unit. To what extent word order and context factors come into play is also an empirical question.

The first hypothesis seems well grounded in theoretical and empirical work by Osgood (1969) and by research using the BAWL, ANEW, or DoA assuming that (i) words carry two types of meaning, a denotative/descriptive one, and a connotative/emotional one; and (ii) that while the denotative meaning is complex/high-dimensional, the emotional meaning can be quantified in terms of two or three straightforward dimensions (i.e., valence and arousal, or evaluation and activity). By using the notion emotion potential rather than emotional meaning I want to facilitate the links to the cognitive-linguistics literature (Schwarz-Friesel, 2007) and distinguish it from Osgood's notion neglecting contributions of a word's denotative aspects to the emotion potential, thus leaving open the possibility that denotative features also enter into the equation that ultimately predicts the affective and aesthetic impact of words (e.g., effects of semantic neighborhoods, figurativity, or novelty: Bohrn *et al.*, 2012a; Forgacs *et al.*, 2012).

The second assumption can be derived from the logico-philosophical tradition since Frege, according to which the literal meaning of a sentence is considered to be determined by the meanings of its parts and their syntactical combination in a sentence. This axiom has the consequence that the literal meaning of a sentence is a context free notion. Although literary reading is at least as much about figurative as about literal meaning and surely context plays a role, the point I want to make here is the following: If one wants to predict the emotion potential of supralexical units such as phrases, verses, sentences, or text segments, it seems natural to start with the emotion potential of the individual words constituting the larger unit. As suggested by Bestgen (1994) or Whissell (1994) whole passages may well be quantified in terms of the emotional or connotative meaning of their component words. Whissell validated this approach by "demonstrating that a combination of stylometric measures with emotional measures provides an improved method of text description which comes closer to representing the complexity of critical commentaries that describe authors' styles than do techniques which do not quantify emotion." Although theoretically the emotion potential of a phrase or text segment composed of only negative words could still be positive as a whole depending on its degree of figurativity and on context variables, the second hypothesis can well serve as a null model (or null hypothesis) against which any alternative model claiming higher plausibility must demonstrate its superiority in descriptive and/or explanatory adequacy while respecting Occam's razor (see Jacobs & Grainger, 1994).

Preliminary evidence for these two assumptions comes from an unpublished study from my lab by M. Lehne investigating the suspense induced by E. T. A. Hoffmann's black romantic story, *The Sandman*. As shown in Figure 7.1a, the span (max–min) of the average arousal of the story, as estimated by the arousal values of the individual words (predicted by the BAWL) making up the 65 text segments accounts for 25% of the variance

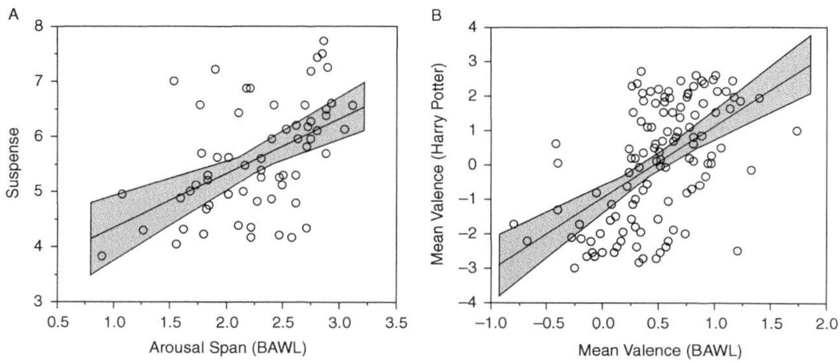

Figure 7.1 (a) Correlation between Arousal span (max–min, as estimated by the BAWL) and rated Suspense for 65 segments of the story *The Sandman*; $r^2 = 0.25$, $p < 0.0001$.

(b) Correlation between mean Emotional Valence (as estimated by the BAWL) and rated Valence for 120 excerpts from Harry Potter books (in German); $r^2 = 0.28$, $p < 0.0001$.

in suspense (rated by subjects for each text segment[1]). Further evidence is provided by data from a study by Chun-Ting Hsu (Hsu, Conrad, & Jacobs, 2014; Hsu, Jacobs, & Conrad, 2014), in which subjects read sections from Harry Potter books in either their native language or their second language. The mean BAWL valence of the 120 paragraphs (based on the individual words appearing in the texts) accounted for about 30% of the variance in the emotional valence of these paragraphs as rated by the subjects (see Figure 7.1b).

In sum, a more natural, realistic approach to literary reading should include – in addition to structural descriptions of the text's basic linguistic and back- and foregrounding features – the notion and measurement of the emotion potential, which, as a first approximation, can be estimated on the basis of the emotion potential of the individual words by use of tools like the BAWL, ANEW, or DoA. This lexical estimation of the emotion potential of words and texts can be augmented by sublexical estimates based on a recent automatized tool called EmophoN (Aryani, Conrad, & Jacobs, 2013).

Literal versus figurative language processing Besides the affective–connotative aspects discussed above, the richness and creativity in figurative language is another characteristic of literary texts and poems

[1] Since only about 30% of the words in Hoffmann's story from the eighteenthth century occur in the BAWL comprising about 6000 rated items, this value potentially underestimates the actual correlation.

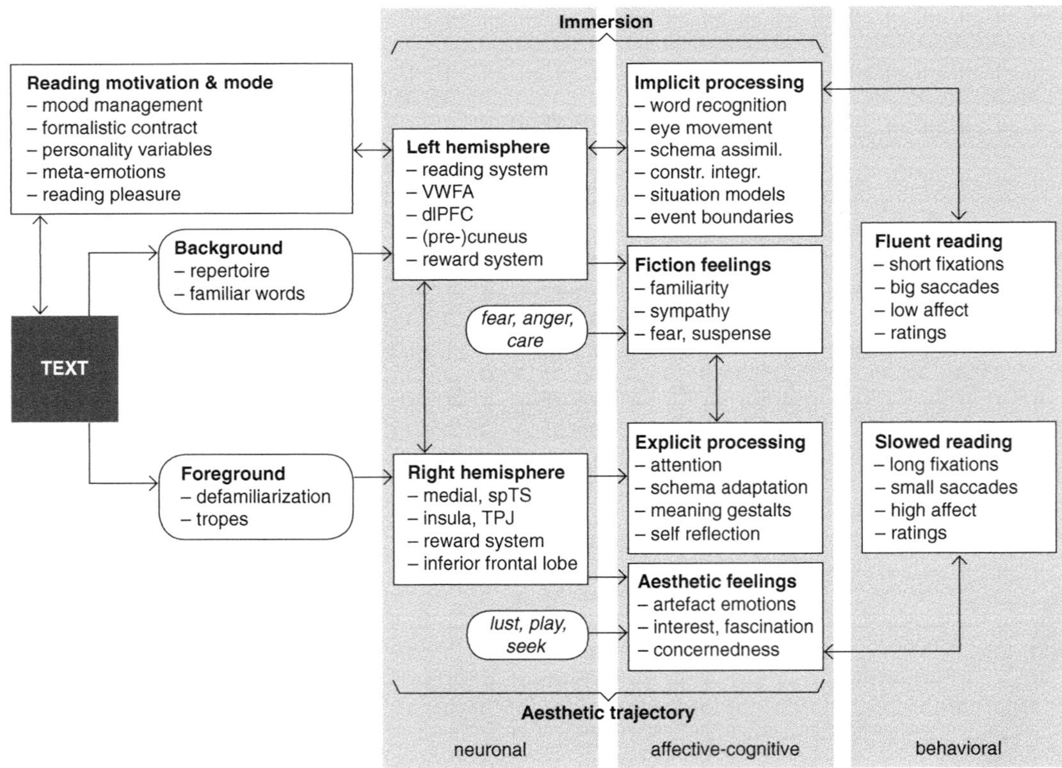

Figure 7.2 Simplified version of the neurocognitive model of literary reading (Jacobs, 2011). The model hypothesizes a dual-route processing of texts with poetic features: a fast, automatic route for (implicit) processing texts which mainly consist of "background" elements informing the reader about the "facts" of a story; and a slower route for (explicit) processing of foregrounded text elements. The fast route is hypothesized to facilitate immersive processes (transportation, absorption) through effortless word recognition, sentence comprehension, activation of familiar situation-models, and the experiencing of non-aesthetic, narrative, or fiction emotions, such as sympathy, suspense, or "vicarious" fear and hope. The slow route is assumed to be operational in aesthetic processes supported by explicit schema adaptation, artefact emotions, and the ancient neuronal play, seek, and lust systems.

which any realistic model of literary reading must tackle. Although there is a vast (neuro-)psychological literature on metaphor, idiom, or irony processing (for review, see Thoma & Daum, 2006; cf. also Bohrn *et al.*, 2012b), the question whether there exists a difference in kind or only in degree between literal and figurative meaning seems still as much open (Coulson, 2006) as the question to what extent figurative meaning processing necessarily involves right-hemisphere (RH) networks for coarse semantic coding, as postulated by Giora (1997) or Jung-Beeman (2005; but see Bohrn *et al.*, 2012b). With regard to the model discussed in the following section, the issue will be treated as one which still needs a lot of empirical work before it can be decided.

Neurocognitive poetics or the attempt to bring together form analysis, process models, and neurocognitive experiments

In our book *Brain and Poetry* (Schrott & Jacobs, 2011) we try to bridge the gap between the rich structural descriptions of literature from both poetics and linguistics, as elegantly exemplified in Roman Jakobson's analysis of three poems by Hölderlin, Klee, and Brecht (Jakobson, 1979) and reception-aesthetic theories of reader response (Iser, 1976) on the one hand, and psychological process models and neurocognitive experiments from mainstream reading research on the other hand. Ideally, a neurocognitive model of (more natural) literary reading should link (neuro-)psychological hypotheses about neuronal, cognitive, affective, and behavioral processes with assumptions from linguistics and poetics in a way allowing predictions about which text elements evoke which cognitive or aesthetic processes, and describe these processes in a way that makes them measurable and testable. In contrast to mainstream neurocognitive models it should go beyond "cold" information-processing aspects by including emotional, immersive, and aesthetic processes, as well as experiential aspects of concern or self-reflective states of mind which are characteristic of reading texts with poetic features. In the following I present a simplified model based on the more complex original published in our book and discuss recent empirical findings testing basic assumptions of the model.

The neurocognitive poetics model of literary reading

The model sketched in Figure 7.2 belongs to the family of "verbal" (i.e., prequantitative) dual-process or dual-route models, which is popular in cognitive psychology. According to the classification of word-recognition models by Jacobs and Grainger (1994), in contrast to mathematical or algorithmic models such "boxological" models attract the expression of creative ideas, when the database is still too sparse to reasonably constrain more formal models. It also attracts the organization of results coming from a broad variety of tasks, as evidenced by extant comprehensive models. In the present model, the hypothetical boxes are not to be understood as mutually exclusive, static categories, but overlapping, non-linear dynamic subsystems which ultimately have to be simulated in the form of artificial neural networks, such as those we have developed for single word recognition (Conrad *et al.*, 2009, 2010; Grainger & Jacobs, 1996; Hofmann *et al.*, 2011). However, such systems cannot easily be represented graphically, hence this simplified boxological chart here as a broad orientation help. Strongly simplifying, the model focuses on "on-line" aspects of literary reading, restricting itself to the microstructure of texts: short moments of reading sentences or passages which last from seconds to minutes and lie within the capacity of working memory. Other meso- or macroscopic aspects like the internal structure of a poem or the link between different episodes of a novel which concern reading activities of several hours or days are left aside. I will now discuss several parts of the model in turn, and describe relevant available empirical findings.

Reading motivation, perspective, and mode Reading can be understood as motivated, goal-directed behavior. Readers' intentions can be numerous and of different quality (e.g., information seeking, curiosity, decision help, reviewing, typographical error finding, pleasure, mood management, etc.) and they determine which piece of text is chosen (e.g., genre decision) and how it is processed (e.g., slow letter-by-letter scrutinizing vs. quick scan). Reading offers countless learning opportunities for simulating the social world and thus fosters the understanding of social information and the development of emotional competencies (Mar & Oatley, 2008). Mainstream psychological models of reading (Just & Carpenter, 1980) do not consider this important aspect preceding – and influencing – the actual reading activity, but a model of literary reading must deal with it, since literary genres and text types (e.g., fairy tales, short stories, crime stories, novels, poetry, etc.) act on what Miall and Kuiken (1998) have termed the "formalist contract," according to which "A reader taking up a literary text thus makes several related commitments that guide the act of reading."

The decision for or against a certain text type or genre is already influenced by motivational–emotional processes which have hardly been the object of experimental studies. Anecdotical evidence suggests that people sometimes are not "in the mood" for, say, reading poetry, whereas at other times they explicitly choose a specific poem to cheer up or solace themselves or someone else. One theoretical approach to such processes is Zillmann's (1988) mood-management theory postulating that unconscious motivations control the experience-dependent selection of media. However, the selection of literary texts is likely to be based on a more complex nexus of motivations, emotions, and cognitions than the hedonic theory of Zillmann claims. According to a recent media-psychological model by Bartsch *et al.* (2008) meta-emotions, metacognitions, and emotion regulation processes like interest, evaluation, or the personality variable dependent taste for tragic entertainment play a decisive role in this complex. Both models, Zillmann's and Bartsch's, however, still await sufficient empirical tests. However, there is good evidence for genre-specific effects on reading behavior (Carminati *et al.*, 2006; Hanauer, 1997; Zwaan, 1994). To summarize, in the model I assume that competent readers use their experience, knowledge, and motivation to make genre-specific text choices and accordingly take a reading perspective which co-determines their reading mode/behavior.

The simulation hypothesis of literary (fiction) reading A recent neurocognitive study from our lab (Altmann *et al.*, 2012b) on the issue of how genre (paratextual) information shapes the reading process shows that it makes a big difference in the mind–brain of readers if they are told (believe) that a text is *fact* vs. *fiction*. In the subjects who read short narratives with the information "This is factual" a hemodynamic activation pattern suggesting an action-based reconstruction of the events depicted in a story was obtained. This process seems to be past-oriented and leads to shorter response times at the behavioral level. In contrast, the brain activation patterns of subjects reading in a "fiction mode" seem to reflect a constructive simulation of what might have happened. This is in line with studies on imagination of possible past or future events. Focusing on fiction here, reading stories on the assumption that they refer to fictional events such as those narrated in a novel, a short story, or a crime story selectively engaged an activation pattern comprising the dorsal anterior cingulate cortex (dACC), the right lateral frontopolar cortex (FPC/dlPFC), and left precuneus, which are part of the fronto-parietal control network (Smallwood *et al.*, 2012) as well as the right inferior parietal lobule (IPL) and dorsal posterior cingulate cortex (dPCC), which are related to the default mode network (Raichle *et al.*, 2001). The lateral frontopolar region has been associated with the simulation of past and future events when compared to the recall of reality-based episodic memories (Addis *et al.*, 2009). This and other fMRI data from a psychophysiological interaction (PPI) analysis suggest that literary (i.e., fiction) reading (i) involves a process of constructive content simulation, and (ii) invites mind-wandering and thinking about what might have happened or could happen. Such simulation processes require perspective-taking and relational inferences (Raposo *et al.*, 2010) which make a co-activation of theory of mind (ToM) (perspective-taking) and affective empathy related areas (medial prefontal cortex (mPFC), dPCC, precuneus, anterior temporal Lobe (aTL)) likely. Taken together, the results for reading stories in a fictional mode are in accordance with the simulation hypothesis (Mar & Oatley, 2008), suggesting a constructive simulation of what might have happened when the events depicted in a text are believed to be fictious. They also support Oatley and Olsen's notion (2010) that factual works relate to the cooperation and alignment of individuals in the real world, whereas fictional works follow primarily the task of imagination and simulation.

Meaning gestalts and the role of background and foreground Once a genre choice has been made and the reader starts to move the eyes across the words, the main goal of the reading act is meaning construction, just as in general language use where the standard expectation is one of meaning constancy. Much as partners in a communicative act, readers have a need for meaning and they strive for meaning construction while reading. According to Iser (1976) a text offers *meaning gestalts* (often in the form of ambiguous figures) which the reader can resolve or "close" (more or less well) on the basis of the text's potential and individual capabilities. Literary meaning gestalts are open (to many different "closures" or interpretations) by definition. Like perceptual gestalts, ambiguous figures, or visual illusions they can trigger feelings of tension or even suspense (often preconscious) which ask for a solution according to the principle of a "good gestalt".

What are the text features that control this stimulating activity of meaning construction? A vast literature on this issue exists produced by formalists and structuralists (e.g., Shklovskij, Spitzer, Mukarovsky, Jakobson), reception-aesthetic and linguistic works on poetics and hermeneutics (e.g., Gadamer, Jauss, Iser, Bierwisch, Klein) and, of course, essays and empirical reports on cognitive poetics (e.g., Iser, Tsur, Miall, Kuiken, van Peer, Hakemulder). Whereas most of this literature deals with the notion of foregrounding (i.e., defamiliarization or alienation effects evoked by stylistic devices such as metaphor, ellipse, or oxymoron: van Peer & Hakemulder, 2006), relatively little has been said about backgrounding, i.e., the elements of a text that create a feeling of familiarity in the reader. Following Iser (1976) and van Holt and

Groeben (2005) the model postulates that any literary text contains both back- and foreground elements and a sometimes tense relation between them inspired by the gestalt-psychological notion of figure-ground. This tension is created by the fact that the background of a text "includes the repertoire of familiar literary patterns and recurrent literary themes and allusions to familiar social and historical contexts which, however, inevitably conflict with certain textual elements that defamiliarise what the reader thought he recognised, leading to a distrust of the expectations aroused and a reconsideration of seemingly straightforward discrepancies that are unwilling to accomodate themselves to these patterns."[2]

Thus, background elements include those conventions that are necessary for situation-model building (i.e., familiar schemata or scripts), and perhaps all that structuralists have termed "extratextual reality." Iser calls it the *primary code* of a text which provides the necessary ground for the creation of a *secondary code*, the deciphering of which brings about the aesthetic pleasure often characteristic of literary reading. Without this background, the foregrounding features aiming at defamiliarization would not work. Of course, texts differ with regards to their mixture of back- and foreground elements, as can easily be seen when comparing, say, a novel by Stephen King with one by James Joyce. And it is also safe to say that not each accumulation of foregrounding devices such as rhyme, metaphor, or ellipse necessarily produces foregrounding effects. What produces either back- or foregrounding effects is, after all, an empirical question. The model simply presents a conceptual help in that it sets a framework within which to predict and interpret such effects.

The central hypothesis distinguishes background effects from foreground effects at all three levels of description. In its simplest, extreme (i.e., categorical) version, the model postulates that background elements are implicitly processed mainly by the left hemisphere (LH) reading network, evoke non-aesthetic (fiction) feelings, and are characterized by fluent reading (e.g., high words per minute (wpm) rates) and low affect ratings (Miall & Kuiken, 1994). In turn, foreground elements are explicitly processed involving more RH networks, produce aesthetic feelings, a slower reading rate, and higher affect ratings. Background reading is hypothesized to facilitate immersive processes (transportation, absorption), while foreground reading can produce aesthetic feelings. As a starting point this extreme, black-and-white version has the merit of being easily falsified allowing revisions while the few but increasing neurocognitive studies on literary reading publish their results.

[2] Cited from: Richard L. W. Clarke: www.rlwclarke.net; LITS3303 Notes 10B.

Background(ing) effects

At the neuronal level, the effortless functioning of the strongly lateralized LH reading system described in numerous neuroscientific studies (see Price, 2012, for reviews) provides the conditions for more complex processes of inference, interpretation, and comprehension which involve RH networks (Bohrn *et al.*, 2012b; Ferstl *et al.*, 2008; Wolf, 2007). Other brain areas important for background reading and the creation of a coherent representation of a story seem to be the anterior temporal lobe (aTL) which has been associated with proposition building, the posterior cingulate cortex (PCC), the ventral precuneus, and the dorsomedial prefrontal cortex (dmPFC) and right temporal pole (rTP) which serve the ToM or *protagonist perspective network*, the former as a monitor (i.e., an executive processor activating throughout the processing of a narrative), the latter as a simulator (i.e., a processor whose role may be to actively generate expectations of events based on an understanding of the intentions of the protagonist: Mason & Just, 2009). Of course, cognitive neuroscience is only beginning to understand the complex connectivities between brain regions and networks involved in reading and the model's hypotheses therefore still are pretty speculative.

At the cognitive level, the model's upper route describes mainly implicit word and text processing, as specified by numerous cognitive models of word recognition, eye-movement control, or situation model-building and text comprehension (e.g., Gerrig, 1998; Graesser, 1981; Kintsch, 1988; Zwaan, 1993), some of which exist in a computational form and might be implemented in a future version of this model, such as the SWIFT model of eye-movement control (Engbert *et al.*, 2005) or the multiple read-out (MROM) and associative mutliple read-out (AROM) models of word recognition (Grainger & Jacobs, 1996; Hofmann *et al.*, 2011). Apart from the assumption of multidimensional situation model-building, the model also hypothesizes that readers create "event gestalts" similar to the event structure perception proposed by Speer *et al.* (2007). This research suggests that a story is segmented into events and that this process is a spontaneous part of reading which depends on neuronal responses to changes in narrative situations (e.g., PCC and precuneus).

At the affective level, background elements go together with a *feeling of familiarity* accompanying the recognition of known items. This is assumed to be of positive valence and low to middle arousal. Following Cupchik (1994) I assume that background elements are processed in a configurational mode evoking non-aesthetic, bodily feelings of harmony or stability, and autobiographical emotions related to memories about events similar to those read about (e.g., fear, joy). Some authors speak of narrative emotions or fiction feelings, like sympathy or empathy for narrative figures, and resonance with the "mood" of a scene (Kneepkens & Zwaan, 1994; Lüdtke, Meyer-Sickendieck, & Jacobs, 2014).

Immersion and suspense The model postulates that the fast route facilitates immersive processes which have been described under various names, potentially addressing different facets of the same basic phenomenon (e.g., transportation, absorption, flow), by researchers as Csikszentmihalyi, Gerrig, Tan, Hakemulder, and others. Although the phenomenon of "getting lost" in a book (Nell, 1988) and forgetting about the world around oneself is familiar to almost any ardent reader, experimental reading research has largely ignored it, as has cognitive neuroscience, too. In order to stimulate neurocognitive research on this highly interesting phenomenon Schrott and Jacobs (2011) speculated that it is related to two neuronal processes: symbol grounding and neuronal recycling or reuse.

Moreover, in accordance with media-psychological studies (Appel *et al.*, 2002; Jennett *et al.*, 2008) the model assumes that immersion is related to suspense. At the text level (of stories), a suspense discourse organization involves an initiating event or situation, i.e., an event which could lead to significant consequences (either good or bad) for one of the characters in the narrative. According to Brewer and Lichtenstein's (1982) structural-affect theory of stories the event structure must also contain the outcome of the initiating event, allowing to resolve the reader's suspense. In the model, I tentatively assume that the core affect systems FEAR, ANGER, or CARE, as decribed in Panksepp (1998) are involved in this suspense-building process, e.g., when a reader experiences suspense through vicarious fear, because a protagonist is in danger (especially when this danger is only known to the reader). Although immersion and suspense can be measured at both the subjective (through questionnaires), and more objective behavioral levels (task completion time, eye movements), at present, as far as I can tell, there are no neuroimaging results speaking directly to the issue of immersion in literary reading contexts.

However, data from two empirical studies in our lab shed some light on the model's assumptions. A first study by M. Lehne examined the development of subjective suspense in readers of E. T. A. Hoffmann's black-romantic story, *The Sandman*. Subjects read the story, divided into 65 passages of controlled length, and then rated them on a variety of dimensions. Using a subset of the suspense and immersion-related scales for assessing reading experience by Appel *et al.* (2002), Lehne found a high correlation between subjective ratings of suspense and immersion ($r = 0.96$). Not surprisingly immersion was also highly correlated with the rated amount of action going on in the story parts (r = 0.95). Thus, as hypothesized in the model, fiction feelings supported by action-rich scenes seem to correlate with immersive processes. A second study investigated the mood induction potential of classic and modernist German poems (Lüdtke *et al.*, 2014). Although, at first glance, it might seem a bold hypothesis to look for immersive processes when subjects read poems of a few verses, subjective reports on perhaps the most famous Italian poem by Quasimodo ("ed e' subito sera") suggest that people can have feelings of immersion reading these short three lines. This tempted Lüdtke *et al.* (2014) to propose that readers' resonance with mood or atmosphere of a scene, mediated by situation model-building, could be an indicator of immersive processes specific for poetry reception, a hypothesis supported by rating data.

Immersion, identification, and (affective) empathy Besides feelings of familiarity, tension, or suspense, the identification of the reader with the protagonist or other characters of a novel is assumed to facilitate immersive processes. There is a vast literature on various kinds of identification processes in media reception (e.g., Cohen, 2001; Konijn & Hoorn, 2005), but with regard to literary reading the route taken by Appel *et al.* (2002) in their scale for reading experience is perhaps the most promising. They adopt an elaborated reception-aesthetic concept (Jauss, 1982) which is not limited to the perspective-taking aspect of identification often highlighted in cognitive and social psychology studies and allows to integrate aspects of reception experience as those described by Zillmann (1991), i.e., empathy. Here I focus on the role of empathy when reading short stories.

Although there is also an abundant neuroscientifc literature on empathy in general (for review, see Walter, 2012), there is little on neurocognitive processes underlying empathy and sympathy in literary reading. In a recent study from my lab, we therefore tested the *fiction feeling hypothesis* integrated in the model, according to which narratives with emotional contents invite readers to be more empathic with the protagonists and thus engage the affective mentalizing networks of the brain more likely than stories with neutral valence (Altmann *et al.*, 2012b). Walter (2012) proposes a distinction between cognitive ToM, cognitive empathy, and affective empathy associated with distinct brain areas: cognitive ToM (temporo-parietal junction (TPJ), superior temporal sulcus (STS), dmPFC, posteromedial cortex (PMC)), cognitive empathy (vmPFC), and affective empathy (anterior insula (aI)), middle cingulate cortex (mCC), amygdala (Amy), secondary somatosensory cortex (SII), inferior frontal gyrus (IFG)). This allows to tentatively distinguish between sympathic and cognitive vs. affective empathic responses to a story's characters. Walter further assumes that affective empathy is composed of six "essential" features: affective behavior, affective experience, affective isomorphy, perspective-taking, self–other distinction, and other orientation, whereas the feature "prosocial motivation" is neither necessary, nor sufficient for it. Affective empathy thus shares only three features with cognitive empathy, but five with sympathy. However, since Walter's proposal so far is qualitative, providing no feature weights, it is hard to say whether this means that sympathy and affective empathy necessarily overlap more than affective empathy and cognitive empathy (Jacobs, 2012). In any case, the results of a PPI analysis from Altmann *et al.* (2012a) revealed a stronger engagement of affective empathy and ToM-related brain areas with increasingly negative story valence. While these results support the fiction feeling hypothesis of the model, the study did not directly measure immersive processes (but see Hsu *et al.*, 2014a) and we thus can only assume with Green and Brock (2000) that as well-crafted canonical stories, i.e., where the intentions and emotions of the characters often changed as they were confronted with several "plights" (Bruner, 1986), our negative stories immersed readers more than the neutral ones in which the characters could act upon their goals without major disturbances.

Foreground(ing) effects

At the affective-cognitive level, the model integrates standard assumptions on foregrounding effects, as developed in Miall and Kuiken's (1994) ground-breaking paper. It also highlights the aesthetic trajectory hypothesis of Fitch *et al.* (2009) according to which aesthetic experiences follow a three-phasic dynamics of (i) implicit recognition of familiar elements, (ii) surprise, ambiguity, and tension elicited by unfamiliar (i.e., foregrounded) elements, and (iii) resolution of the created tension. Note, however, that according to Iser (1976), there is a constant oscillation, integral to the aesthetic experience in reading, between illusion-formation and revision, frustration, and surprise. The *sine qua non* of the aesthetic experience is the non-achievement of a final reading. Thus, in the model I assume the third phase of the aesthetic trajectory is never really completed, but always open to new interpretations and reflections.

At the neuronal level, the pioneering studies by Kutas and Hillyard (1984) provided the first evidence for brain-electrical effects of semantic deviations which are one possibility of foregrounding. In a more recent neuroimaging study from my lab, Bohrn *et al.* (2012a) used proverbs as a well-controllable means to study the effects of foregrounding or defamiliarization, achieved through "the novelty of an unusual linguistic variation" (Miall & Kuiken, 1994, p. 391), thus giving some part of the text "special prominence" (van Peer & Hakemulder, 2006). The stimulus material allowed to achieve this variation in both a creative, artistic, meaning-changing, and an uncreative, meaning-maintaining manner, thus offering the possibility of studying affective–aesthetic effects, as decribed by the model's lower, slow route. In sum, the results demonstrated that defamiliarization is an effective way of guiding attention, but that the degree of affective involvement elicited by foregrounding depends on the type of defamiliarization: enhanced activation in affect-related regions (orbito-frontal cortex, medPFC) was found only if defamiliarization altered the content of the original proverb. Defamiliarization on the level of wording was associated with attention processes and error monitoring. Although proverb variants evoked activation in affect-related regions, familiar proverbs received the highest beauty ratings.

In what is perhaps the first neurocognitive study on aesthetic judgments of verbal material, Bohrn *et al.* (2013) identified clusters in which blood-oxygen-level dependent (BOLD) activity was correlated with individual post-scan beauty ratings of the proverbs used in the previous study. In accord with a central tenet of the model, the results indicated that some spontaneous aesthetic evaluation takes place during reading, even if not required by the task. Positive correlations were found in the ventral striatum and in mPFC, likely reflecting the rewarding nature of sentences that are aesthetically pleasing. In contrast, negative correlations were observed in the classic left frontotemporal reading network. Midline structures and bilateral temporo-parietal regions correlated positively with familiarity, suggesting a shift from the task network towards the default network with increasing familiarity. Most important with respect to the model's assumptions at the neuronal level (i.e., the lateralization hypothesis) is the fact that although the study by Bohrn *et al.* (2012a) found RH involvement in foregrounding conditions, there was no hint for a RH dominance in processing figurative language, at least not with this special stimuli. In order to assess the generalizability of these data, Bohrn *et al.* (2012b) ran a meta-analysis on 23 neuroimaging studies investigating figurative language processing (i.e., metaphors, idioms, irony) and, again, found no clear evidence for the lateralization hypothesis implemented in the model.

In another recent study from my lab we investigated the neural correlates of literal and figurative language processing with well-controlled stimuli (noun–noun compounds) allowing to disentangle the contributions of figurativity (metaphoricity) and semantic relatedness which was quantified computationally (Forgacs *et al.*, 2012). The results revealed a surprising effect: the BOLD signal in the left IFG increased gradually with semantic processing demand which was minimal for conventional, familiar literal expressions like "Alarmsignal" (alarm signal), followed by conventional metaphors like "Stuhlbein" (chair-leg), requiring the selection and suppression of certain semantic features to construct figurative meaning; then came novel literal expressions like "Stahlhemd" (steel-shirt), where a new meaning has to be constructed from the two constituents, and finally by novel metaphors like "Gelddurst" (money-thirst), requiring the construction and closing of a new meaning-gestalt (Glickson & Goodblatt, 1993; Jacobs, 2011). Together with the finding that novel metaphors also yielded the longest response times, these data support the model's assumption of a slower, more demanding processing of foregrounded, creative, figurative material. On the other hand, as the studies by Bohrn *et al.* (2012a,b) showed, they do not really support the lateralization assumption integrated in the model.

In sum, while they support basic model assumptions, these neurocognitive studies from my lab also invite certain revisions of the original model (Jacobs, 2011), in particular the lateralization assumption, and, to some extent, also the hypothesis that immersive and aesthetic processes exclude or inhibit each other. Many more studies using more natural text materials and tasks than mainstream cognitive reading research are necessary before the model outlined here can become less speculative or descriptive and more explanatory. Such a model surely would be an exciting new thing at the horizon for studying more natural language processing.

Natural language processing and reading are best viewed as resulting from the works of complex non-linear dynamical mind–brain systems that do much more than cold information processing. Words can please or make us freeze, texts can make us laugh or cry, so we need methods and models allowing us to gain a more complete and ecologically valid picture of the text/mind–brain interactions that underlie such natural effects. Therefore, experimental reading research and cognitive neuroscience should reconsider the under-complex stimuli, unrealistic tasks, and under-determined models most often used in studying language processing and reading and replace them by more ecologically valid ones.

References

Addis, D. R., Pan, L., Vu, M.-A., Laiser, N., & Schacter, D. L. (2009). Constructive episodic simulation of the future and the past: distinct subsystems of a core brain network mediate imagining and remembering. *Neuropsychologia*, 47(11), 2222–2238.

Altmann, U., Bohrn, I. C., Lubrich, O., Menninghaus, W., & Jacobs, A. M. (2012a). The power of emotional valence: from cognitive to affective processes in reading. *Frontiers in Human Neuroscience* 01/2012; 6:192. doi:10.3389/fnhum.2012.00192.

Altmann, U., Bohrn, I. C., Lubrich, O., Menninghaus, W., & Jacobs, A. M. (2012b). Fact versus fiction: how paratextual information shapes our reading processes. *Social Cognitive and Affective Neuroscience*. 09/12.

Anderson, M. L. (2010). Neural reuse: a fundamental organizational principle of the brain. *Behavioral Brain Sciences*, 33, 245–266; discussion 266–313.

Appel, M., Koch, E., Schreier, M., & Groeben, N. (2002). Aspekte des Leseerlebens. Skalenentwicklung [Aspects of the reading experience: scale development]. *Zeitschrift für Medienpsychologie*, 14, 149–154.

Appel, M., & Richter, T. (2010). Transportation and need for affect in narrative persuasion: a mediated moderation model. *Media Psychology*, 13(2), 101–135.

Aryani, A., Conrad, A. M., & Jacobs, A. M. (2013). Extracting salient sublexical units from written texts: 'Emophon', a corpus-based approach to phonological iconicity. *Frontiers in Psychology*, 4, 654. doi: 10.3389/fpsyg.2013.00654.

Bartsch, A., Vorderer, P., Mangold, R., & Viehoff, R. (2008). Appraisal of emotions in media use: toward a process model of meta-emotions and emotion regulation. *Media Psychology*, 11, 7–27.

Bestgen, Y. (1994). Can emotional valence in stories be determined from words? *Cognition and Emotion*, 8(1), 21–36. doi:10.1080/02699939408408926.

Bleich, D. (1978). *Subjective Criticism*. Baltimore, MD: Johns Hopkins University Press.

Bohrn, I. C., Altmann, U., Lubrich, O., Menninghaus, W., & Jacobs, A. M. (2012a). Old proverbs in new skins: an FMRI study on defamiliarization. *Frontiers in Psychology*, 3, 204.

Bohrn, I. C., Altmann, U., & Jacobs, A. M. (2012b). Looking at the brains behind figurative language: a quantitative meta-analysis of neuroimaging studies on metaphor, idiom, and irony processing. *Neuropsychologia*, 50, 2669–2683.

Bohrn, I. C., Altmann, U., Lubrich, O., Menninghaus, W., & Jacobs, A. M. (2013). When we like what we know: a parametric fMRI analysis of beauty and familiarity. *Brain and Language*, 124, 1–8. doi:10.1016/j.bandl.2012.10.003.

Bortolussi, M., & Dixon, P. (2003). *Psychonarratology: Foundations for the Empirical Study of Literary Response*. Cambridge: Cambridge University Press.

Bradley, M. M., & Lang, P. J. (1999). *Affective Norms for English Words (ANEW): Stimuli Instruction and Affective Ratings*, Technical Report No. C-1. Gainesville, FL: University of Florida, Center for Research in Psychophysiology.

Brewer, W. F., & Lichtenstein, E. H. (1982). Stories are to entertain: a structural-affect theory of stories. *Journal of Pragmatics*, 6, 473–486.

Briesemeister, B. B., Kuchinke, L., & Jacobs, A. M. (2011a). Discrete Emotion Norms for Nouns: Berlin Affective Word List (DENN-BAWL). *Behavior Research Methods*, 43(2), 441–448. doi:10.3758/s13428–011-0059-y

Briesemeister, B. B., Kuchinke, L., & Jacobs, A. M. (2011b). Discrete emotion effects on lexical decision response times. *PLoS ONE*, 6(8), e23743. doi:10.1371/journal.pone.0023743.

Briesemeister, B. B., Kuchinke, L., & Jacobs, A. M. (2014). Emotion word recognition: discrete information effects first, continuous later? *Brain Research*, 1564, 62–71.

Bruner, J. (1986). *Actual Minds, Possible Worlds*. Cambridge, MA: Harvard University Press.

Bühler, K. (1934). *Sprachtheorie*. Stuttgart: G. Fischer.

Carminati, M. N., Stabler, J., Roberts, A. M., & Fischer, M. H., (2006). Readers' responses to sub-genre and rhyme scheme in poetry. *Poetics*, 34, 204–218.

Citron, F. M. (2012). Neural correlates of written emotion word processing: a review of recent electrophysiological and hemodynamic neuroimaging studies. *Brain and Language*, 122, 211–226.

Cohen, J. (2001). Defining identification: a theoretical look at the identification of audiences with media characters. *Mass Communication and Society*, 4(3), 245–264.

Conrad, M., Carreiras, M., Tamm, S., & Jacobs, A. M. (2009). Syllables and bigrams: orthograpic redundancy and syllabic units affect visual word recognition at different processing levels. *Journal of Experimental Psychology: Human Perception and Performance*, 35(2), 461–479.

Conrad, M., Tamm, S., Carreiras, M., & Jacobs, A. M. (2010). Simulating syllable frequency effects within an interactive activation framework. *European Journal of Cognitive Psychology*, 22(5), 861–893.

Conrad, M., Recio, G., & Jacobs, A. M. (2011). The time course of emotion effects in first and second language processing: across cultural ERP study with German–Spanish bilinguals. *Frontiers in Language Sciences*, December, Vol. 2, Article 351, 1–16.

Cornelissen, P. L., Hansen, P. C., Kringelbach, M. L., & Pugh, K. (2009). *The Neural Basis of Reading*. Oxford: Oxford University Press.

Coulson, S. (2006). Constructing meaning. *Metaphor and Symbol*, 21, 245–266.

Cupchik, G. C. (1994). Emotion in aesthetics: reactive and reflective models. *Poetics*, 23, 177–188.

Dehaene, S. (2005). Evolution of human cortical circuits for reading and arithmetic: the "neuronal recycling" hypothesis. In *From Monkey Brain to Human Brain*, eds. S. Dehaene, J. R. Duhamel, M. D. Hauser, & G. Rizzolatti. Cambridge, MA: MIT Press, pp. 133–157.

Engbert, R., Nuthmann, A., Richter, E., & Kliegl, R. (2005). SWIFT: a dynamical model of saccade generation during reading. *Psychological Review*, 112, 777–813.

Ferstl, E.C., Neumann, J., Bogler, C., & von Cramon, D.Y. (2008). The extended language network: a meta-analysis of neuroimaging studies on text comprehension. *Human Brain Mapping*, 29(5), 581–593.

Fitch, W. T., Graevenitz, A. V., & Nicolas, E. (2009). Bio-aesthetics and the aesthetic trajectory: a dynamic cognitive and cultural perspective. In *Neuroaesthetics*, eds. M. Skov & O. Vartanian. Amityville, NY: Baywood, pp. 59–102.

Forgacs, B., Bohrn, I. C., Baudewig, J., Hofmann, M. J., Pleh, C., & Jacobs, A. M. (2012). Neural correlates of combinatorial semantic processing of literal and figurative noun–noun compound words. *NeuroImage*, 63, 1432–1442.

Gerrig, R. (1998). *Experiencing Narrative Worlds: On the Psychological Activities of Reading*. New Haven, CT: Yale University Press.

Giora, R. (1997). Understanding figurative and literal language: the graded salience hypothesis. *Cognitive Linguistics*, 8, 183–206.

Glicksohn, J., & Goodblatt, C. (1993). Metaphor and gestalt: interaction theory revisited. *Poetics Today*, 14, 83–97.

Graesser, A. C. (1981). *Prose Comprehension beyond The Word*. New York: Springer.
Grainger, J., & Jacobs, A.M. (1996). Orthographic processing in visual word recognition: a multiple read-out model. *Psychological Review*, 103, 518–565.
Green, M. C., & Brock, T. C. (2000). The role of transportation in the persuasiveness of public narratives. *Journal of Personality and Social Psychology*, 79, 701–721.
Hanauer, D. (1997). Poetic text processing. *Journal of Literary Semantics*, 26(3), 157–172.
Hofmann, M. J., Kuchinke, L., Tamm, S., Vo, M. L., & Jacobs, A. M. (2009). Affective processing within 1/10th of a second: high arousal is necessary for early facilitative processing of negative but not positive words. *Cognitive Affective Behavioral Neuroscience*, 9, 389–397.
Hofmann, M. J., Kuchinke, L., Biemann, C., Tamm, S., & Jacobs, A. M. (2011). Remembering words in context as predicted by an Associative Read-Out Model. *Frontiers in Psychology*, 252, 1–11.
Hsu, C.T., Conrad, M., & Jacobs, A. M. (2014a). Fiction feelings in Harry Potter: haemodynamic response in the mid-cingulate cortex correlates with immersive reading experience. *NeuroReport*, *10*. doi: 10.1097/WNR.0000000000000272.
Hsu, C.T., Jacobs, A.M., & Conrad, M. (2014b). Can Harry Potter still put a spell on us in a second language? An fMRI study on reading emotion-laden literature in late bilinguals. *Cortex* (in press.) doi:10.1016/d.cortex.2014.og.002.
Iser, W. (1976). *Der Akt des Lesens: Theorie ästhetischer Wirkung*. Munich: Fink Verlag.
Jacobs, A. M. (2011). Neurokognitive Poetik: Elemente eines Modells literarischen Lesens (Neurocognitive poetics: elements of a model of literary reading). In *Gehirn und Gedicht: Wie wir unsere Wirklichkeiten konstruieren*, eds. R. Schrott & A. M. Jacobs. Munich: Carl Hanser Verlag, pp. 492–520.
Jacobs, A. M. (2012). Comment on Walter's "Social cognitive neuroscience of empathy: concepts, circuits, and genes." *Emotion Review*, 4, 20–21.
Jacobs, A. M., & Grainger, J. (1994). Models of visual word recognition: sampling the state of the art. *Journal of Experimental Psychology: Human Perception and Performance*, 20(6), 1311–1334.
Jakobson, R. (1979). *Hölderlin, Klee, Brecht: Zur Wortkunst dreier Gedichte*. Frankfurt: Suhrkamp.
Jauss, H. R. (1982). *Ästhetische Erfahrung und literarische Hermeneutik*. Frankfurt: Suhrkamp.
Jennett, C., Cox, A. L., Cairns, P., Dhoparee, S., Epps, A., Tijs, T., & Walton, A. (2008). Measuring and defining the experience of immersion in games. *International Journal of Human-Computer Studies*, 66, 641–661.
Jung-Beeman, M. (2005). Bilateral brain processes for comprehending natural language. *Trends in Cognitive Sciences*, 9, 512–518.
Just, M. A., & Carpenter, P. A. (1980). A theory of reading: from eye fixation to comprehension. *Psychological Review*, 87, 329–354.
Kagan, J. (2010). Once more into the breach. *Emotion Review*, 2, 91–99.
Kintsch, W. (1988). The use of knowledge in discourse processing: a construction-integration model. *Psychological Review*, 95, 163–182.
Kneepkens, L. J., & Zwaan, R. A. (1994). Emotion and cognition in literary understanding. *Poetics*, 23, 125–138.
Koerner, K. (1984). Karl Bühler's theory of language and Ferdinand de Saussure's *Cours*, *Lingua*, 62(1–2), 3–24.

Konijn, E. A., & Hoorn, J. F. (2005). Some like it bad: testing a model on perceiving and experiencing fictional characters. *Media Psychology*, 7, 107–144.
Kringelbach, M. L., Vuust, P., & Geake, J. (2008). The pleasure of reading. *Interdisciplinary Science Reviews*, 33, 321–335.
Kuchinke, L., Jacobs, A. M., Grubich, C., Võ, M. L.-H., Conrad, M., & Herrmann, M. (2005). Incidental effects of emotional valence in single word processing: an fMRI study. *NeuroImage*, 28(4), 1022–1032.
Kutas, M. (2006). One lesson learned: frame language processing – literal and figurative – as a human brain function. *Metaphor and Symbol*, 21, 285–325.
Kutas, M., & Hillyard, S. A. (1984). Brain potentials during reading reflect word expectancy and semantic association. *Nature*, 307, 161–163.
Lang, P. J., Bradley, M. M., & Cuthbert, B. N. (2005). *International Affective Picture System (IAPS): Affective rating of measures and instruction manual*, Technical Report No. A-6. Gainesville, FL: University of Florida.
Limbach, J. (2006). *Das schönste deutsche Wort*. Freiburg: Verlag Herder.
Lüdtke, J., Meyer-Sickendieck, B., & Jacobs, A. M. (2014). Immersing in the stillness of an early morning: testing the mood empathy hypothesis of poetry reception. *Psychology of Aesthetics, Creativity, and the Arts*, 8(3), 363–377.
Mar, R. A., & Oatley, K. (2008). The function of fiction is the abstraction and simulation of social experience. *Perspectives on Psychological Science*, 3, 173–192.
Mar, R. A., Oatley, K., Djikic, M., & Mullin, J. (2011). Emotion and narrative fiction: interactive influences before, during, and after reading. *Cognition and Emotion*, 25(5), 818–833. doi:10.1080/02699931.2010.515151.
Mason, R. A., & Just, M. A. (2009). The role of the theory-of-mind cortical network in the comprehension of narratives. *Language and Linguistics Compass*, 3, 157–174.
Miall, D. S., & Kuiken, D. (1994). Foregrounding, defamiliarization, and affect: response to literary stories. *Poetics*, 22, 389–407.
Miall, D. S., & Kuiken, D. (1998). The form of reading: empirical studies of literariness. *Poetics*, 25, 327–341.
Miall, D. S., & Kuiken, D. (2002). A feeling for fiction: becoming what we behold. *Poetics*, 30, 221–241.
Miller, G. A. (1993). *Wörter: Streifzüge durch die Psycholinguistik*. Frankfurt: Zweitausendeins.
Nell, V. (1988). *Lost in a Book: The Psychology of Reading for Pleasure*. New Haven, CT: Yale University Press.
Niedenthal, P. M. (2007). Embodying emotion. *Science*, 316, 1002–1005.
Oatley, K. (1994). A taxonomy of the emotions of literary response and a theory of identification in fictional narrative. *Poetics*, 23, 53–74.
Oatley, K., & Olson, D. (2010). Cues to the imagination in memoir, science, and fiction. *Review of General Psychology*, 14(1), 56–64.
Osgood, C. E. (1969). On the why's and wherefore's of E, P, and *A*. *Journal of Personality and Social Psychology*, 12, 194–199.
Panksepp, J. (1998). *Affective Neuroscience: The Foundations of Human and Animal Emotions*. New York: Oxford University Press.

Ponz, A., Montant, M., Liegeois-Chauvel, C., Silva, C., Braun, M., Jacobs, A. M., & Ziegler, J. C. (2013). Emotion processing in words: a test of the neural re-use hypothesis using surface and intracranial EEG. *Social Cognitive and Affective Neuroscience*, 9, 619–627.

Price, C. J. (2012). A review and synthesis of the first 20 years of PET and fMRI studies of heard speech, spoken language and reading. *NeuroImage*, 62, 816–847.

Raichle, M. E., MacLeod, A. M., Snyder, A. Z., Powers, W. J., Gusnard, D. A., & Shulman, G. L. (2001). A default mode of brain function. *Proceedings of the National Academy of Sciences of the United States of America*, 98(2), 676–682.

Raposo, A., Vicens, L., Clithero, J. A., Dobbins, I. G., & Huettel, S. A. (2010). Contributions of frontopolar cortex to judgments about self, others and relations. *Social Cognitive and Affective Neuroscience*, 6(3), 260–269.

Schwarz-Friesel, M. (2007). *Sprache und Emotion (Language and Emotion)*. Tübingen: Francke.

Schrott, R., & Jacobs, A. M. (2011). *Gehirn und Gedicht: Wie wir unsere Wirklichkeiten konstruieren (Brain and Poetry: How We Construct Our Realities)*. Munich: Hanser.

Smallwood, J., Brown, K., Baird, B., & Schooler, J. W. (2012). Cooperation between the default mode network and the frontal-parietal network in the production of an internal train of thought. *Brain Research*, 1428, 60–70.

Speer, N. K., Reynolds, J. R., & Zacks, J. M. (2007). Human brain activity time-locked to narrative event boundaries. *Psychological Science*, 18, 449–455.

Thoma, P., & Daum, I. (2006). Neurocognitive mechanisms of figurative language processing: evidence from clinical dysfunctions. *Neuroscience and Biobehavioral Reviews*, 30, 1182–1205.

Van Holt, N., & Groeben, N. (2005). Das Konzept des Foregrounding in der modernen Textverarbeitungspsychologie. *Journal für Psychologie*, 13, 311–332.

Van Peer, W., & Hakemulder, J. (2006). Foregrounding. In *Encyclopedia of Language and Linguistics*, ed. K. Brown. Oxford: Elsevier.

Vo, M. L.-H., Jacobs, A. M., & Conrad, M. (2006). Crossvalidating the Berlin Affective Word List (BAWL). *Behavior Research Methods*, 38, 606–609.

Vo, M. L.-H., Jacobs, A. M., Kuchinke, L., Hofmann, M., Conrad, M., Schacht, A., & Hutzler, F. (2008). The coupling of emotion and cognition in the eye: introducing the pupil old/new effect. *Psychophysiology*, 45(1),130–140.

Vo, M. L.-H., Conrad, M., Kuchinke, L., Urton, K., Hofmann, M.J., & Jacobs, A. M. (2009). The Berlin Affective Word List Reloaded (BAWL-R). *Behavior Research Methods*, 41, 534–539.

Walter, H. (2012). Social cognitive neuroscience of empathy: concepts, circuits, and genes. *Emotion Review*, 4, 9–17.

Whissell, C. (1994). A computer program for the objective analysis of style and emotional connotations of prose: Hemingway, Galsworthy, and Faulkner compared. *Perceptual and Motor Skills*, 79, 815–824.

Whissell, C., Fournier, M., Pelland, R., Weir, D., & Makarec, K. (1986). A dictionary of affect in language: IV. Reliability, validity, and applications. *Perceptual and Motor Skills*, 62, 875–888.

Willems, R. M., & Casasanto, D. (2011). Flexibility in embodied language understanding. *Frontiers in Psychology*, 2, 116. doi:10.3389/fpsyg.2011.00116.

Wolf, M. (2007). *Proust and the Squid:The Story and Science of the Reading Brain*. New York: Icon Books.

Zillmann, D. (1988). Mood management through communication choices. *American Behavioral Scientist*, 31, 327–340.

Zillmann, D. (1991). Empathy effect from bearing witness to the emotions of others. In J. Bryant & D. Zillmann (eds.), *Responding to the Screen: Reception and Reaction Processes* (pp. 135–166). Hillsdale, NJ: Lawrence Erlbaum.

Zwaan, R. A. (1993). *Aspects of Literary Comprehension: A Cognitive Approach*. Amsterdam: Benjamins.

Zwaan, R. A. (1994). Effect of genre expectations on text comprehension. *Journal of Experimental Psychology: Learning, Memory, and Cognition*, 20(4), 920–933.

8 Putting Broca's region into context: fMRI evidence for a role in predictive language processing

Line Burholt Kristensen & Mikkel Wallentin

Abstract Broca's region is known to play a key role in speech production as well as in the processing of language input. Still, the exact function (or functions) of Broca's region remains highly disputed. Within the generativist framework it has been argued that part of Broca's region is dedicated to syntactical analysis. Others, however, have related Broca's region activity to more domain-general processes, e.g. working memory load and argument hierarchy demands. We here present results that show how contextual cues completely alter the effects of syntax in behaviour and in Broca's region, and suggest that activation in this area reflects general linguistic processing costs or prediction error. We review the fMRI literature in the light of this theory.

Introduction: the controversy over Broca's region

In 1861 Paul Broca presented the brain of one of his patients to the anthropological society in Paris. Before his death, this patient had displayed a severe speech deficit, being unable to say more than a single word, 'Tan', while apparently maintaining many of his other mental faculties (Broca, 1861). Broca found that the patient had a large lesion in the brain's left inferior frontal gyrus (LIFG). Since then, this area, now often referred to as Broca's region, has been considered a key speech/language brain region. With the advent of cell-staining techniques, Korbinian Brodmann (Brodmann, 1909) found that the LIFG, based on the cytoarchitecture, could be subdivided into distinct regions: Brodmann areas 44, 45 and 47 (BA 44/45/47). The subregions are depicted in Plate 8.1 (see colour plate section). Agrammatical speech was already early considered to be a specific symptom in aphasiology (e.g. Kussmaul, 1877), and it has subsequently been argued that Broca's region plays a significant role in the processing of syntax, both in comprehension and production of language (Friedmann, 2006; Grodzinsky & Santi, 2008).

The exact definition of Broca's region and its subregions has been the subject of later controversy. Usually, BA 44 and BA 45 are considered the core regions. Some definitions of the region include neighbouring areas such as BA 47 and part of BA 6 (Hagoort, 2005), though receptorarchitectonic studies indicate that BA 47 is distinct from BA 44/45 (see Amunts & Zilles, 2006, 2012 for a discussion). Leaving aside these definitorial concerns, we will here be primarily concerned with the function of BA 44/45.

The association between BA 44/45 and syntactic processing is recognized by most neurolinguistic theories, and the function of Broca's region is rarely defined without reference to sentence processing studies. It is, however, an intensely debated question how the relation between syntactic processing and Broca's region should be modelled (Friederici *et al.*, 2003; Grodzinsky & Santi, 2008; Hagoort, 2005). The question is highly controversial because it stirs up two basic and long-standing oppositions within theoretical linguistics. Linguists both disagree on the definition of *syntax* and *syntactic processing*, and on the relation between language and other cognitive functions.

The generativist transformation-based flank (Ben-Shacharr *et al.*, 2004; Grodzinsky, 2000; Grodzinsky & Santi, 2008) subscribes to the idea that 'language is a distinct, modularly organized neurological entity' (Grodzinsky, 2000:1). This idea takes its point of departure in Chomsky's (1965) distinction between different kinds of innate language components, e.g. a phonological component, a semantic component and a syntactic component. The generativist paradigm sees Broca's region as a highly specialized separate linguistic module dealing with the transformational component, a subcomponent of the syntactic component (Grodzinsky, 2000).

Functionalist–cognitivist paradigms within linguistics (e.g. Dik, 1997; Engberg-Pedersen *et al.*, 1996; Van Valin & LaPolla, 1997), on the other hand, see linguistic structure (including syntactic structures) as shaped by cognition and usage, i.e. by the way we communicate. Functionalist approaches do not see syntactic processes as self-contained, but as dependent on domain-general cognitive processes, e.g. working memory and prediction (Chater & Manning, 2006). Broca's region thereby becomes not the seat of an isolated syntactic module, but of some (possibly domain-general) function that happens to serve a central function in language and communication (Kaan & Swaab, 2002).

In short, the bone of contention is whether syntactic structure is independent or functionally motivated, and whether linguistic processes are based on self-contained modules or imply high-level non-linguistic cognitive functions. When defining the relation between syntactic processing and Broca's region, both of these questions must be dealt with.

The discussions of Broca's region have been fuelled with results from a variety of studies: from early lesion studies (Wernicke, 1874) via studies involving symptom/lesion mapping (Caplan *et al.*, 2007a, 2007b; Christiansen *et al.*, 2010; Dronkers *et al.*, 2004; Friedmann, 2006), behavioral studies (Christensen *et al.*, 2013) and computational models of language processing (Levy, 2008; Spivey & Tanenhaus, 1998) to ERP studies (Bornkessel *et al.*, 2003; Friederici *et al.*, 1993; Hagoort *et al.*, 2003; Hahne & Friederici, 1999) and neuroimaging studies (Ben-Shachar *et al.*, 2004; Bornkessel *et al.*, 2005; Christensen & Wallentin, 2011; Christensen *et al.*, 2013; Fiebach & Schubotz, 2006; Fiebach *et al.*, 2005; Grewe *et al.*, 2005; Hagoort *et al.*, 2004; Kim *et al.*, 2009; Makuuchi *et al.*, 2013; Wallentin *et al.*, 2006). However, while the generativist and the functionalist approaches are mutually exclusive in theory, their predictions of single sentence processing, as we shall demonstrate here, often point in the same direction. For a more differentiated description of the function of Broca's region, we therefore suggest including more factors from natural-language processing, by examining the role of contextual factors within a predictive coding framework (Chater & Manning, 2006; Clark, 2013; Friston, 2010).

Syntactic processing: different theories with similar predictions

Syntactic processing is often examined by contrasting subject-before-object (SO) structures with object-before-subject (OS) structures. A generativist framework sees the SO structure as basic, e.g. *Mary hit Peter*. The OS structure *Peter, Mary hit* is seen as a transformation of the SO version and therefore as syntactically more complex (Radford, 2004). The generativist association between transformational (sub)processes and Broca's area seems to correspond with empirical findings from a number of language experiments. In accordance with the generativist idea that transformation increases processing demands, OS clauses are, in a number of languages, more difficult to read (Finnish: Hyönä & Hujanen, 1997; Japanese: Miyamoto & Takahashi, 2004) and understand (German: Haupt *et al.*, 2008) than SO ones. In accordance with the generativist association between Broca's region and the transformational component, a number of studies have shown more activity in Broca's region for the processing of OS clauses compared to SO ones (Hebrew: Ben-Shachar *et al.*, 2004; Japanese: Kim *et al.*, 2009).

Functionalists may also consider OS structures as more complex than SO structures, but they explain the complexity differently. The movement explanation is viewed with scepticism, and the allegation of a transformational component is seen as redundant – accounts that focus on domain-general cognitive processing demands are preferred. A functionalist approach is in line with a number of different explanations to the increased processing demands for OS structures, including the working memory account, the unification model, the argument hierarchy account, and the prediction error account. According to the working-memory explanation, OS clauses increase working-memory demands as the object cannot be immediately integrated into the sentence structure and must therefore be maintained in working memory (Caplan & Waters, 1999; Fiebach *et al.*, 2005). According to the unification model, the complexity lies in an increased unification load, i.e. the phonological, morphological or syntactical constituents of the sentence are difficult to unify (Hagoort, 2005). The argument hierarchy account sees the semantic relations between the subject and object constituent as the key to the processing difficulties – processing demands are low when the agent appears before the patient (following the alleged order of the argument hierarchy), but in OS clauses the order is usually reversed, increasing argument hierarchy demands (Bornkessel *et al.*, 2005). Finally, the prediction error account proposes that OS clauses are less predictable to the recipient than SO clauses, e.g. because OS clauses are less frequent. The low frequency of OS clauses therefore should evoke a prediction error due to the difference between the expected input and the input that occurred (Kristensen *et al.*, 2014b).

In short, the generativist explanations see the correlation between activity in Broca's area and processing of OS clauses as due to transformational demands, i.e. restricted to linguistic components. The functionalist explanations refer to theories of communicatively grounded or general cognitive demands, e.g. increased working-memory demands, increased unification demands, increased argument hierarchy demands or prediction error.

While these explanations are theoretically different, the results that they predict are often hard to tell apart. According to all explanations, SO clauses are easiest to process – they involve no transformations, working-memory demands and unification demands are low, the argument hierarchy is rarely violated, and they are more frequent than OS clauses and thereby more predictable. This allows generativists to claim that neural activity in Broca's region correlates with demands on the transformational component, while at the same time functionalists can argue that it correlates with domain-general demands. The problem thus is that the difference between SO and OS clauses cannot be reduced to a difference in word order. SO clauses and OS clauses also differ when it comes to argument hierarchy demands, assumed working-memory demands and a number of frequency measures (see e.g. Grewe *et al.*, 2005 for a discussion). While the clustering of sentence-internal factors makes it difficult to manipulate them separately, context manipulations offer a window for testing the hypotheses of transformation-based and usage-based explanations. To examine whether Broca's region is the neural basis of a syntactic language-internal component or of domain-general processes (or of both: Federenko *et al.*, 2012), we will argue that it is fruitful to go beyond traditional single-sentence processing and examine sentence processing when it is contextually embedded.

Syntactic processing in context: different theories with different predictions

When examining sentence processing in context, we can make a clearer distinction between the predictions of generativist transformation-based theories and the various kinds of functionalist predictions. According to a transformation-based theory, the activity in Broca's region should be stable across different kinds of context, as transformations are not context-dependent. According to a functionalist approach, linguistic structure is not self-contained, and the increase in activation of Broca's area for OS clauses may well reflect non-linguistic context-dependent factors. When seeing linguistic structure as affected by communicative practices, it makes sense that context has an effect on the processing of word order, as it has on other aspects of linguistic processing (coherence in question–answer pairs: Caplan & Dapretto, 2001; coherence between sentences: Kuperberg *et al.*, 2006; coherence between title and paragraph: St George *et al.*, 1999). The predictions are therefore different: according to functionalist theories, context may affect activation of Broca's region, and according to generativist theories, it should not.

Two experiments on the effect of discourse context on syntactic processing

The effect of context on syntactic processing is seen in two recent studies of sentence processing in Danish (Kristensen *et al.*, 2013, 2014). Danish is well suited for examining word-order processing, as both objects and subjects can occur in the first position of Danish clauses. Danish is a V2 language (like e.g. German and Swedish), meaning that the finite verb occurs in the second position of the clause, while a variety of constituent types can occur in first position. The following two examples show that both subjects and objects can occur in the first position:

(1) Danish SO sentence:
Hun *elsker* ham
she love.PRS him
'She loves him'

(2) Danish OS sentence:
Ham *elsker* hun
him love.PRS she
'Him, she loves'

Both sentences occur in Danish, though OS sentences are less frequent (Boeg Thomsen & Kristensen, in press; Kristensen, 2013) and limited to certain contexts (Hansen & Heltoft, 2011; Harder & Poulsen, 2001). Examples (1) and (2) are disambiguated due to case-marked pronouns. However, not all transitive declarative sentences in Danish contain case-marked pronouns. Some sentences are therefore ambiguous with respect to the distribution of syntactical roles:

(3) *Susan elsker Peter*
Susan love.PRS Peter
'Susan loves Peter' or 'Susan, Peter loves'

The above ambiguous example can either be interpreted as subject-initial (with *Susan* as the subject) or as object-initial (with *Susan* as the object). While ambiguous clauses do occur in Danish, transitive clauses are typically disambiguated by means of case-marked pronouns (Boeg Thomsen & Kristensen, in press; Kristensen, 2013), as in examples (1) and (2), by the position of non-finite verbs and (to some extent) of sentential adverbs as well as semantics, e.g. verb argument restrictions or violation of argument-hierarchy (see below for examples). Besides these cues, contextual cues are a further means of disambiguation. While both object and subject can occur in first position in Danish, an object is only licensed in first position if it has a special pragmatic status, e.g. if the object is the most topic-worthy constituent in the sentence (Kristensen, 2013). One way of establishing a referent as topic-worthy is to explicitly contrast it with other elements of a set. In the first of the two sentences below, Ringo is contrasted to the remaining members of The Beatles. In the second sentence, Ringo is thus highly topic-worthy, and the object is licensed in first position.

(4) *Susan elsker The Beatles, undtagen Ringo. Ringo hader hun.*
Susan love.PRS The Beatles, except Ringo. Ringo hate.PRS she
'Susan loves The Beatles, except Ringo. Ringo, she hates'

The licensing of subjects in first position is less restricted. Subjects can occur in first position even if they are part of an all-focus sentence where all the constituents contain new information, e.g. if the sentence occurs out of context. According to these regulations, SO clauses have a processing advantage over OS clauses when the sentence occurs out of a discourse context.

Context appropriateness affects comprehension

In a reading study, Kristensen *et al.* (2014a) examined whether Danish OS sentences were more easily understood when they occurred in a supportive discourse context, in this case a discourse context that contrasted the referent of the fronted object with other members of a set (as in example (4)). By registering the responses to simple comprehension questions, the study compared the comprehension accuracy rates for unambiguous SO and OS main clauses presented in context. Half of the sentences were shown in a supportive discourse context, the other half was shown in an unsupportive context. The sentences did not contain case-marked pronouns, but were disambiguated by means of the varying positions of non-finite verbs and sentential adverbs. An example of a supportive discourse context for an OS target is given in (5), and the target is given in (6):

(5) *Denne historie handler om Anne. Peter brød sig ikke om de andre piger.*
This story deal.PRS about Anne. Peter liked 3.REFL not about the other girls
'This story is about Anne. Peter did not like the other girls.'

(6) *Anne ville Peter dog invitere til festen.*
Anne would Peter however invite to party.DEF
'Anne, however, Peter would invite to the party'

The supportive context in (5) presents both the subject and the object of the target sentence and establishes a set of alternatives to the contrasted element (*Anne* vs. *the other girls*). While the supportive context for *object*-initial target clauses supports a contrastive reading of the *object*, the supportive context for *subject*-initial target clauses (not shown here, but see example (9)) supports a contrastive reading of the *subject*.

The study examined processing differences between these two kinds of constituent order with or without supportive context. As expected, Kristensen *et al.* (2013) found greater overall processing difficulties for OS sentences: responses to comprehension questions were slower for OS sentences than for SO sentences, and responses were more frequently incorrect. However, the study also showed a significant improvement of comprehension when OS sentences occurred in supportive discourse context. In a supportive discourse context, the improvement in response accuracy and response time was more pronounced for OS sentences than for their SO counterparts (Fig. 8.1).

Context appropriateness affects Broca's region

Based on this interaction between context supportiveness and word order for comprehension in the reading time experiment, Kristensen *et al.*

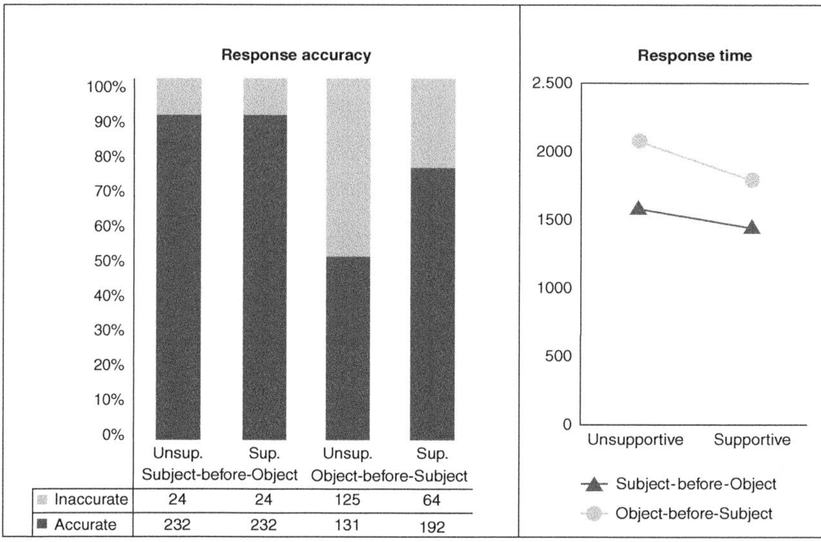

Figure 8.1 Response accuracy and response time from reading study. In a reading study, Kristensen *et al.* (2014a) found that context supportiveness interacted with word order both for comprehension accuracy and for response time. Object-initial clauses were found to be more context-sensitive than subject-initial ones, as context had a larger facilitating effect on the comprehension of object-initial clauses.

(2014b) carried out a neuroimaging experiment in order to investigate whether context supportiveness would affect Broca's region. This study (which will be described in further detail below) found an interaction between context and word order in the activity of BA 44/45 (see Plate 8.2C in colour plate section).

Stimuli for the neuroimaging experiment were auditory and consisted of a control task and a main task. The control task compared the processing of OS and SO clauses *out of context*, i.e. each sentence was presented in isolation. The main task of the neuroimaging experiment studied the processing patterns *in context* using stimuli similar to the behavioural experiment of Kristensen *et al.* (2014a). The main differences between the designs were that stimulus sentences in the neuroimaging experiment were spoken rather than written, that the target sentences involved case-marked pronouns (similar to the sentences in (1) and (2)) instead of proper nouns and that the context manipulation was slightly different. The supportive discourse context still aimed at contrasting the first constituent of the target clause with a set, as seen in the sequence consisting of (7) followed by (8):

(7) *Peter overså alle butikstyvene – undtagen Anne.*
Peter overlooked all shoplifters.DEF – except Anne
'Peter overlooked all the shoplifters – except Anne.'

(8) *Hende bemærkede han.*
Her noticed he
'Her, he noticed'

The unsupportive context to an OS clause supported the interpretation that the subject of the target, rather than the object, was contrasted with a set of alternatives, e.g. the combination of the context in (9) followed by the target in (8) is pragmatically inappropriate.

(9) *Alle overså Anne og hendes bror – undtagen Peter.*
Everybody overlooked Anne and her brother – except Peter
'Everybody overlooked Anne and her brother – except Peter.'

The context in (9) contrasts Peter with a set of people (*alle* = everybody) that overlook Anne and her brother. Anne is part of a group consisting of Anne and her brother, but Peter is singled out as a contrasted constituent. When the context in (9) precedes the target sentence in (8), the subject constituent of the target (*han*, referring to Peter) is the most topic-worthy constituent, and thereby expected to appear in first position. The object (*hende*) is lower-ranking. Compared to the subject (*han*), the object is less likely to be interpreted as involving a contrast or as involving linkage. In this inappropriate context, the object is therefore dispreferred in first position. Similarly, an SO target sentence such as (10) would be preferred after (9), but dispreferred after (7), making the design a balanced factorial design:

(10) *Han bemærkede hende.*
he noticed her
'He noticed her'

Focusing on Broca's area in an ROI analysis, the results of the control task (without context) and the main task (with an appropriate vs. inappropriate context) were analysed. The control task showed increased activation in the left BA 45 for OS sentences compared to SO sentences. However, the main task showed an effect of context appropriateness – for appropriate combinations of discourse context and target word order, such as the sequences (7) + (8) and (9) + (10), the BA 44/45 showed decreased activation compared to inappropriate combinations like (7) + (10) and (9) + (8). The study also found an interaction between context supportiveness and word order in BA 44/45: a supportive context had a larger effect on the processing of OS sentences than on SO sentences, i.e. a supportive context led to a larger decrease in activation in BA 44/45 for

OS sentences than for SO sentences. This indicates that these parts of the IFG are not restricted to syntactic processing functions, but modulated by several types of language-related expectations (see Plate 8.2A, B, C, D in colour plate section).

Predictive coding: an alternative functional interpretation

The effects of discourse context supportiveness thus challenge an understanding of Broca's region function as being attributed to transformations alone. Neither can the effects be solely attributed to increased working-memory demands or to increased argument hierarchy demands. As intraclausal factors were kept stable in the target sentences of Kristensen *et al.* (2014b), the function of Broca's region in this study cannot be attributed to intraclausal factors such as differences between the subject and the object when it comes to e.g. animacy, given new status or plausibility of agenthood. If these findings are to be reconciled, the activity observed has to originate in a more abstract function. A part of the functional linguistic paradigm involves the modelling of language processing with probabilistic means (Clark, 2013; Levy, 2008). This predictive coding paradigm entails that the brain extracts statistically stable features from the environment and uses those to predict upcoming stimuli in a hierarchical fashion, i.e. at different levels of abstraction (Friston, 2010). If the predicted input, e.g. a predicted phoneme within a word or a predicted word within a sentence, differs from the actual occurring input, then a prediction error signal is generated. This prediction error causes the predictions to change, both at the current level and further up the predictive hierarchy of abstractions (Chater & Manning, 2006). Ultimately, the predictions will be different the next time the person encounters a similar situation. We suggest interpreting the activity of Broca's region as an indicator of prediction error in the linguistic domain. When the recipient fails to predict the argument order of an upcoming clause, a surprisal effect (Clark, 2013; Levy, 2008) occurs, i.e. the less predictable the sentence, the greater the surprisal, and the more fMRI activation in Broca's region.

When it comes to the word order of upcoming linguistic input, there are a number of possible sources for making predictions about the input, e.g. combinations of speaker characteristics (van Berkum *et al.*, 2005), the frequency of the structure both in the ongoing discourse (local frequency, i.e. priming: Pickering & Ferreira, 2008) and in earlier discourse (global frequency), verb restrictions, perceptual cues and the semantics and pragmatics of the context. OS clauses are, as mentioned earlier, relatively infrequent in Danish, and they can therefore be seen as generally less predictable than SO clauses. If Danish language users base their predictions of an upcoming sentence on global frequency (in combination with other previously mentioned sources), they will likely expect sentences to be subject-initial rather than object-initial. However, under specific contextual circumstances, such as those presented above, pragmatics may influence the predictability, and the odds for an OS clause increase drastically. Our findings thus seem to be consistent with an interpretation of Broca's region activity, as indexing a sort of linguistic prediction error. In the following we will review the fMRI literature on Broca's region activation in the light of this hypothesis.

Broca's area and frequency

Frequencies of linguistic input have a strong effect on performance and brain signal. As for global frequency, word frequency effects are found even at the single word level, such as in lexical decision tasks when research participants are asked to classify letter strings as words or as non-words (Allen *et al.*, 2005; Balling & Baayen, 2012; Forster & Chambers, 1973; Grainger, 1990; Whaley, 1978). Low-frequency words take longer to categorize as words than high-frequency words. In fMRI-studies of lexical decision tasks, low frequency alone was enough to yield an increased Broca's region activation (Fiebach *et al.*, 2002; Kronbichler *et al.*, 2004).

While global frequency of structure on its own is unlikely to explain all processing differences between OS and SO clauses (Ferreira, 2003), it is possible to reinterpret a large portion of reading-time studies on syntactical manipulations (e.g. Kaiser & Trueswell, 2004) along these lines, i.e. the higher the global frequency of a structure, the shorter the reading time.

Frequencies can also be relevant at shorter timescales. It has been known for a long time that Broca's region activation decreases for word-generation tasks if the task is repeated (Raichle *et al.*, 1994), and even a very rare word order will be less surprising if it is repeated within a short time span. This effect is called structural priming (Bock & Griffin, 2000). In neuroimaging studies, structural priming effects have been found to occur in Broca's region (along with left middle temporal regions), i.e. the activation decreases when a particular linguistic structure is repeated (BA 44/6: Menenti *et al.*, 2011; BA 44/45: Weber & Indefrey, 2009).

Broca's area and within-sentence contextual effects

Another way of looking at predictability is via contextual bindings that make certain words and readings more expected than others within a particular sentence. For words with multiple meanings (e.g. *bank*), one word meaning may be dominant in relation to the other and thus the predicted reading in absence of a disambiguating context. Zempleni and co-workers (2007) studied this in Dutch with fMRI. When a sentence ended with a word that prompted for the subordinate interpretation of the sentence-initial ambiguous word, Broca's region activity was increased, compared to a sentence that ended with a word prompting for the dominant reading. This is in effect a study of different levels of 'cloze probability' (Taylor, 1953) for a given word in a sentence, i.e. the probability with which a reader will continue a given sentence with a given word. In (11) *cow* will have high cloze probability whereas *goat* or *bank account* will have lower cloze probabilities.

(11) *The farmer milked his . . .*

Similar to the semantic-ambiguity resolution study, Obleser and Kotz (2010) found that Broca's region activation was negatively correlated with cloze probability, again suggesting that Broca's region activation relates to linguistic predictability. Similarly, Broca's region activation has also been found to go down as participants adapt to novel metaphors (Cardillo *et al.*, 2012).

Predictability and acceptability may also be related. Highly predictable sentences are those that we most readily accept as meaningful, whereas less predictable are those where a greater proportion of listeners have difficulties understanding or processing the sentence. Christensen and Wallentin (2011) investigated this in an experiment where participants both read and heard sentences that could be either semantically incongruent or not. They used the so-called locative alternation constructions:

(12) *He throws snow on the door.*

(13) **He throws the door with snow.*

(14) **He blocks rocks on the road.*

(15) *He blocks the road with rocks.*

One construction only works with verbs that focus on the process, e.g. *throw*. The other only works with verbs that focus on the result, e.g. *block*. Participants judged whether a sentence made sense or not. The study design contained a syntactic manipulation as well (sentences (13) and (15) are thought to be more complex than (12) and (14)). Both the syntactically more complex sentences and the semantically incongruent sentences yielded a greater Broca's region response with peaks in the exact same region. This suggests that a failure to integrate constituents within a sentence increases Broca's region activity. Further, when the authors looked at the effect of acceptability, they found a second order relationship between the response time of the acceptability question and the number of participants who had rated a particular sentence as comprehensible. Both the strongly incomprehensible (i.e. (13) and (14)) and the clearly comprehensible sentences ((12) and (15)) yielded a fairly short response time, whereas sentences that received mixed responses (e.g. one sentence contained the Danish word *træ* which means both 'wood' and 'tree'; however, only 'wood' made sense within the context), took longest to evaluate, on average. While this is not exactly surprising given the Zempleni study presented above, the authors also found that Broca's region was linearly correlated with response time for the individual sentences, i.e. more ambiguous sentences were accompanied by greater response in Broca's region (see Plate 8.2), again suggesting that lower expectancy leads to greater Broca's region responses.

Predictions can also apply to the number of constituents in a sentence, e.g. if a transitive verb is presented, a direct object will be expected. If this expectation is not met, e.g. due to an intervening prepositional phrase between the verb and the object, then a prediction error will be produced. Fiebach *et al.* (2005) investigated this type of prediction in a neuroimaging experiment. Participants read the German versions of (16) and (17):

(16) *He asks himself who called the doctor after the accident.*

(17) *He asks himself who after the accident called the doctor.*

Meaning integration requires that both the verb, the subject and the object have been introduced. In (16), the subject, verb and object occur in succession, while in (17) there is an intervening constituent (*after the accident*) before the verb and the object. The sentence in (17) can thus be seen as putting more strain on expectations and working memory than (16). Indeed, Fiebach and co-workers found that sentences like (17) yielded greater activation of Broca's region than sentences like (16). Interestingly, it made no difference whether the relative pronoun (in English *who*) was subject or object of the embedded clause, i.e. the processing of the German version of (18) did not yield a greater activation than (16), again suggesting that predictability rather than transformations per se cause Broca's region activity to increase.

(18) *He asks himself who the doctor called after the accident.*

Working memory and language

Fiebach and colleagues (2005) attribute the observed effect to increased working memory demand. However, we will entertain the hypothesis that working memory can in fact also be described within a predictive framework. A few recent attempts at linking the working memory literature (e.g. Baddeley, 1986, 2003; Wallentin *et al.*, 2011a) with the recent probabilistic approaches to cognition (Tenenbaum *et al.*, 2011) have been made (Brady & Tenenbaum, 2013; Orhan & Jacobs, 2013). Until now, this literature has primarily focused on visual working memory. Standard work on working memory assumes a 'slot model' under which the individual has a certain number of 'slots' into which memory can be stored, e.g. the number of digits recalled in a digit-span task. This model, however, cannot account for the great variability in participants' ability to chunk and store different patterns of stimuli (e.g. the numbers 3-3-3 are easier to remember than 3-8-4) and thus expand working-memory capacity. A key feature of the predictive models thus is that they take into account perceptual grouping between retained items and some sort of higher-order summary of the stimuli that the perceiver tries to maintain. When trying to remember real-world scenes, people encode a visual and a semantic gist of what they experience. A sentence might be thought of as a prototypical unit for such a summary. In a predictive framework, this working-memory summary can be seen as affecting predictions of incoming input, including linguistic input. So, when a scene is described in a way that is incompatible with the working-memory summary, a prediction error is produced and further processing is needed in order to reach a response. We find that this idea is supported by previous neuroimaging studies of linguistic reference to a previously seen image and linguistic reference to a previously read sentence.

Linguistic reference to a previously seen image

Wallentin and co-workers investigated working memory for visual scenes using linguistic references (Wallentin *et al.*, 2006, 2008a). Participants were shown an image with three referents, a man, a woman and an object. After the image was removed, participants were asked to recall both spatial and non-spatial aspects of the image. The recall questions were presented using simple linguistic cues, e.g. *Was he in front of her?* or *Was he older than her?* The only change across trials was the personal pronouns (*he/she/it*) used to refer to individual aspects of the image, i.e. the syntax was identical across trials, and the semantics was more or less confined to referential markers. However, similar to Christensen & Wallentin (2011), Broca's region activation was linearly correlated with response time across trials, suggesting that when no easy match is found between a linguistic cue and memory content, additional processing is necessary, and this processing involves Broca's region (see Plate 8.2G). Importantly, the working-memory load (number of remembered items) was constant across all trials. This finding is therefore consistent with an interpretation that a mismatch between maintained working-memory content and incoming linguistic cue causes a prediction error and hence increased Broca's region activation.

Linguistic reference to a previously read sentence

In a follow-up study, Wallentin and co-workers investigated linguistic reference to a previously encountered sentence, i.e. again focusing on reference across the sentence boundary (Wallentin *et al.*, 2008b). The participants read sentences about a man and a woman, and their relative spatial and nonspatial relations (e.g. the Danish version of *With their backs to each other stand an elderly man and a young red-haired girl*). Subsequently the participants were probed for these internal relations with questions like *Was he facing her?* or *Was he older than her?* The authors replicated their findings of a distinct dorsal network for spatial references, but does the experiment also yield insights with respect to Broca's region? A reanalysis of the neuroimaging data (not reported in Wallentin *et al.*, 2008b) using response time as a covariate shows a statistically significant effect in Broca's region (with a peak in BA 45; see Plate 8.2H). The effect, reported here for the first time, indicates that whenever a mismatch occurs between working-memory content and a question, either due to a degradation of the working memory or due to the question not matching the content, a prediction error is generated causing additional processing.

Discussion and future avenues

We have illustrated the importance of including elements of natural-language processing in neuroimaging designs, specifically the importance of monitoring predictability and of including a discourse context when examining syntactic processing patterns. Kristensen *et al.* (2014a) showed that discourse context supportiveness affected comprehension of Danish object-initial clauses, while Kristensen *et al.* (2014b) similarly showed that it altered word order effects in BA 44/45 of Broca's region. Based on these results, we argue that the role of Broca's region can be reinterpreted within a predictive coding framework, i.e. activity increases when there is a discrepancy between the predicted input and the input that occurred. The results of other sentence-processing studies point in the same direction: when the recipient experiences sentence processing difficulties (as indicated by increased question response times), the activity in BA 44/45 increases (Christensen & Wallentin, 2011; Wallentin *et al.*, 2006, 2008a).

As neuroimaging studies have a poor temporal resolution, the time course of discourse effects in Broca's region is not clear. We suggest that a supportive discourse context facilitates the prediction of upcoming input, and thereby decreases the prediction error. An alternative explanation would be that a supportive discourse context facilitates the *reanalysis* of the target sentence, i.e. the context facilitation does not exert its effect in Broca's region until after initial processing of the sentence. Still, we find that the prediction approach is advantageous for a number of reasons:

The prediction approach fits results from time-course studies In a reading experiment with Finnish main clauses, Kaiser & Trueswell (2004) found an interaction between discourse context and word order – while a suitable discourse context did not eliminate the difference in reading time between SO and OS clauses, a suitable discourse context had a larger facilitating effect on reading times for OS clauses than for SO clauses. A similar interaction effect between discourse context and word order was found for the processing of Dutch OS and SO relative clauses (Mak *et al.*, 2008). In both reading experiments, the effects of context are more likely to be prediction-based effects than reanalysis affects, as the effects occurred online.

Likewise, context is known to influence language-related ERP effects, such as the N400 effect and the P600 effect (Federmeier, 2007; van Berkum, 2010). Still, the association between the influence of context on reading time, on ERP effects and on Broca's region needs to be further investigated.

The prediction approach can unify existing sentence processing theories As we have argued by reinterpreting the results of previous sentence processing studies, a predictive coding framework can unify and integrate theories of both working memory demands, argument hierarchy demands, structural priming and unification.

The prediction approach is not specific to language The predictive coding framework is in line with previous linguistic as well as non-linguistic research on the functioning of the brain (Friston, 2010; Tenenbaum *et al.*, 2011). The prediction-based approach thus has the advantage of explaining language processing in terms of principles shared with other kinds of processing, e.g. predictions of visual non-linguistic input (Bar, 2004, 2007). Furthermore, as the prediction approach describes linguistic and non-linguistic processes on the basis of the same principles, the approach can take into account the influences of e.g. visual input or emotional valence on linguistic processing (van Berkum, 2010).

We have argued that the function of Broca's area is not restricted to syntactic processing as such. This broader perspective does, however, not entail that the role of Broca's region is interpreted as all-encompassing and as covering predictions of all sorts.

The extent and limitations to this predictive system and Broca's regions role in it remains to be studied. We have tentatively talked about a linguistic predictive system, which may or may not function in relative isolation from other cognitive operations. But if we accept that Broca's region has a role in linguistic prediction error monitoring, is its role then confined to language or does it go beyond that, to communicative situations broadly defined, or does it apply to all unpredicted events? Judging from the priming literature, there does seem to be a limitation to what Broca's region responds to. In a number of priming experiments, the combinations of linguistic primes and targets affected Broca's region, whereas priming effects for non-linguistic primes and targets did not affect Broca's region (priming of environmental sounds: Bergerbest *et al.*, 2004; priming pictures of nonsence objects: Vuilleumier *et al.*, 2002). The difference in location of non-linguistic priming effects thus suggests that the prediction error effect in Broca's region is linguistically grounded. Whether it goes beyond the two-sentence range, discussed hitherto, is a question for future research to explore.

References

Allen, P. A., Lien, M. C., Smith, A. F., Grabbe, J., & Murphy, M. D. (2005). Evidence for an activation locus of the word-frequency effect in lexical decision. *Journal of Experimental Psychology: Human Perception and Performance*, *31*, 713–721.

Amunts, K., & Zilles, K. (2006). A multimodal analysis of structure and function in Broca's region. In Y. Grodzinsky & K. Amunts (eds.), *Broca's Region* (pp. 17–30). Oxford: Oxford University Press.

Amunts, K., & Zilles, K. (2012). Architecture and organizational principles of Broca's region. *Trends in Cognitive Sciences*, *16*, 418–426.

Baddeley, A. D. (1986). *Working Memory*. Oxford: Oxford University Press.

Baddeley, A. D. (2003). Working memory and language: an overview. *Journal of Communication Disorders*, *36*, 189–208.

Balling, L. W., & Baayen, R. H. (2012). Probability and surprisal in uditory comprehension of morphologically complex words. *Cognition*, *125*, 80–106.

Bar, M. (2004). Visual objects in context. *Nature Reviews Neuroscience*, *5*, 617–629.

Bar, M. (2007). The proactive brain: using analogies and associations to generate predictions. *Trends in Cognitive Sciences*, *11*, 280–289.

Ben-Shachar, M., Palti, D., & Grodzinsky, Y. (2004). Neural correlates of syntactic movement: converging evidence from two fMRI experiments. *NeuroImage*, *21*, 1320–1336.

Bergerbest, D., Ghahremani, D. G., & Gabrieli, J. D. E. (2004). Neural correlates of auditory repetition priming: reduced fMRI activation in the auditory cortex. *Journal of Cognitive Neuroscience*, *16*, 966–977.

Bock, K., & Griffin, Z. M. (2000). The persistence of structural priming: transient activation or implicit learning? *Journal of Experimental Psychology: General*, *129*, 177–192.

Boeg Thomsen, D., & Kristensen, L. B. (in press). Context needed: semantic role assignment in Danish children and adults. *Acta Linguistic Hafniensa*, *46*(2).
Bornkessel, I., Schlesewsky, M., & Friederici, A. D. (2003). Eliciting thematic reanalysis effects: the role of syntax-independent information during parsing. *Language and Cognitive Processes*, *18*, 269–298.
Bornkessel, I., Zysset, S., Friederici, A. D., von Cramon, D. Y., & Schlesewsky, M. (2005). Who did what to whom? The neural basis of argument hierarchies during language comprehension. *NeuroImage*, *26*, 221–233.
Brady, T. F., & Tenenbaum, J. B. (2013). A probabilistic model of visual working memory: incorporating higher-order regularities into working memory capacity estimates. *Psychological Review*, *120*, 85–109.
Broca, P. (1861). Remarques sur le siège de la faculté du langage articulé; suivies d'une observation d'aphémie. *Bulletin de la Société Anatomique de Paris*, *6*, 330–357.
Brodmann, K. (1909). *Vergleichende Lokalisationslehre der Grosshirnrinde in ihren Prinzipien dargestellt auf Grund des Zellenbaues*. Leipzig: Barth.
Caplan, D., & Waters, G. S. (1999). Verbal working memory and sentence comprehension. *Behavioral and Brain Sciences*, *22*, 77–94.
Caplan, D., Waters, G., Dede, G., Michaud, J., & Reddy, A. (2007a). A study of syntactic processing in aphasia I: behavioral (psycholinguistic) aspects. *Brain and Language*, *101*, 103–150.
Caplan, D., Waters, G., Kennedy, D., Alpert, N., Makris, N., DeDe, G., Michaud, J., & Reddy, A. (2007b). A study of syntactic processing in aphasia II: Neurological aspects. *Brain and Language*, *101*, 151–177.
Caplan, R., & Dapretto, M. (2001). Making sense during conversation: an fMRI study. *NeuroReport*, *12*, 3625–3632.
Cardillo, E. R., Watson, C. E., Schmidt, G. L., Kranjec, A., & Chatterjee, A. (2012). From novel to familiar: tuning the brain for metaphors. *NeuroImage*, *59*, 3212–3221.
Chater, N., & Manning, C. (2006). Probabilistic models of language processing and acquisition. *Trends in Cognitive Sciences*, *10*, 335–344.
Chomsky, N. (1965). *Aspects of the Theory of Syntax*. Cambridge, MA: MIT Press.
Christensen, K. R., & Wallentin, M. (2011). The locative alternation: distinguishing linguistic processing cost from error signals in Broca's region. *NeuroImage*, *56*, 1622–1631.
Christensen, K. R., Kizach, J., & Nyvad, A. (2013). Escape from the island: grammaticality and (reduced) acceptability of wh-island violations in Danish. *Journal of Psycholinguistic Research*, *42*, 51–70.
Christensen, K. R., Kizach, J., & Nyvad, A. M. (2013). The processing of syntactic islands: an fMRI study. *Journal of Neurolinguistics*, *26*, 239–251.
Christiansen, M. H., Louise Kelly, M., Shillcock, R. C., & Greenfield, K. (2010). Impaired artificial grammar learning in agrammatism. *Cognition*, *116*, 382–393.
Clark, A. (2013). Whatever next? Predictive brains, situated agents, and the future of cognitive science. *Behavioral and Brain Sciences*, *36*, 181–204.
Dik, S. (1997). *The Theory of Functional Grammar*. Berlin: Mouton de Gruyter.
Dronkers, N. F., Wilkins, D. P., Van Valin, R. D., Redfern, B. B., & Jaeger, J. J. (2004). Lesion analysis of the brain areas involved in language comprehension. *Cognition*, *92*, 145–177.

Engberg-Pedersen, E., Fortescue, M., Harder, P., Heltoft, L., & Jakobsen, L. F. (1996). *Content, Expression and Structure: Studies in Danish Functional Grammar*. Amsterdam: Benjamins.

Federenko, E., Duncan, J., & Kanwisher, N. (2012). Language-selective and domain-general regions lie side by side within Broca's area. *Current Biology*, *22*, 2059–2062.

Federmeier, K. D. (2007). Thinking ahead: the role and roots of prediction in language comprehension. *Psychophysiology*, *44*, 491–505.

Ferreira, F. (2003). The misinterpretation of noncanonical sentences. *Cognitive Psychology*, *47*, 164–203.

Fiebach, C. J., Friederici, A. D., Müller, K., & Von Cramon, D. Y. (2002). fMRI evidence for dual routes to the mental lexicon in visual word recognition. *Journal of Cognitive Neuroscience*, *14*, 11–23.

Fiebach, C. J., & Schubotz, R. I. (2006). Dynamic anticipatory processing of hierarchical sequential events: a common role for Broca's area and ventral premotor cortex across domains? *Cortex*, *42*, 499–502.

Fiebach, C. J., Schlesewsky, M., Lohmann, G., von Cramon, D. Y., & Friederici, A. D. (2005). Revisiting the role of Broca's area in sentence processing: syntactic integration versus syntactic working memory. *Human Brain Mapping*, *24*, 79–91.

Forster, K. I., & Chambers, S. M. (1973). Lexical access and naming time. *Journal of Verbal Learning and Verbal Behavior*, *12*, 627–635.

Friederici, A. D., Pfeifer, E., & Hahne, A. (1993). Event-related brain potentials during natural speech processing: effects of semantic, morphological and syntactic violations. *Brain Research Cognitive Brain Research*, *1*, 183–192.

Friederici, A. D., Rüschemeyer, S.-A., Hahne, A., & Fiebach, C. J. (2003). The role of left inferior frontal and superior temporal cortex in sentence comprehension: localizing syntactic and semantic processes. *Cerebral Cortex*, *13*, 170–177.

Friedmann, N. (2006). Speech production in Broca's agrammatic aphasia: syntactic tree pruning. In Y. Grodzinsky & K. Amunts (eds.), *Broca's Region* (pp. 63–81). Oxford: Oxford University Press.

Friston, K. (2010). The free-energy principle: a unified brain theory? *Nature Reviews Neuroscience*, *11*, 127–138.

Grainger, J. (1990). Word frequency and neighborhood frequency effects in lexical decision and naming. *Journal of Memory and Language*, *29*, 228–244.

Grewe, T., Bornkessel, I., Zysset, S., Wiese, R., von Cramon, D. Y., & Schlesewsky, M. (2005). The emergence of the unmarked: a new perspective on the language-specific function of Broca's area. *Human Brain Mapping*, *26*, 178–190.

Grodzinsky, Y. (2000). The neurology of syntax: language use without Broca's area. *Behavioral and Brain Sciences*, *23*, 1–21.

Grodzinsky, Y., & Santi, A. (2008). The battle for Broca's region. *Trends in Cognitive Sciences*, *12*, 474–480.

Hagoort, P. (2005). On Broca, brain, and binding: a new framework. *Trends in Cognitive Sciences*, *9*, 416–423.

Hagoort, P., Wassenaar, M., & Brown, C. M. (2003). Syntax-related ERP-effects in Dutch. *Brain Research Cognitive Brain Research*, *16*, 38–50.

Hagoort, P., Hald, L., Bastiaansen, M., & Petersson, K. M. (2004). Integration of word meaning and world knowledge in language comprehension. *Science, 304*, 438–441.

Hahne, A., & Friederici, A. D. (1999). Electrophysiological evidence for two steps in syntactic analysis: early automatic and late controlled processes. *Journal of Cognitive Neuroscience, 11*, 194–205.

Hansen, E., & Heltoft, L. (2011). *Grammatik over det Danske Sprog*. Odense: Syddansk Universitetsforlag.

Harder, P., & Poulsen, S. (2001). Editing for speaking: first position, foregrounding and object fronting in Danish and English. In E. Engberg-Pedersen & P. Harder (eds.), *Ikonicitet og Struktur* (pp. 1–22). Copenhagen Netværk for Funktionel Lingvistik, Engelsk Insititut.

Haupt, F. S., Schlesewsky, M., Roehm, D., Friederici, A. D., & Bornkessel-Schlesewsky, I. (2008). The status of subject-object reanalyses in the language comprehension architecture. *Journal of Memory and Language, 59*, 54–96.

Hyönä, J., & Hujanen, H. (1997). Effect of word order and case marking on sentence processing in Finnish: an eye fixation analysis. *Quarterly Journal of Experimental Psychology, 50A*, 841–858.

Kaiser, E., & Trueswell, J. C. (2004). The role of discourse context in the processing of a flexible word-order language. *Cognition, 94*, 113–147.

Kim, J., Koizumi, M., Ikuta, N., Fukumitsu, Y., Kimura, N., Iwata, K., Watanabe, J., Yokoyama, S., Sato, S., Horie, K., & Kawashima, R. (2009). Scrambling effects on the processing of Japanese sentences: an fMRI study. *Journal of Neurolinguistics, 22*, 151–166.

Kristensen, L. B. (2013). *Context, You Need: Experimental Approaches to Information Structure Processing*. Copenhagen: University of Copenhagen.

Kristensen, L. B., Engberg-Pedersen, E., & Poulsen, M. (2014a). Context improves comprehension of fronted objects. *Journal of Psycholinguistic Research, 43*, 125–140.

Kristensen, L. B., Engberg-Pedersen, E., & Wallentin, M. (2014b). Context influences word order predictions in Broca's region. *Journal of Cognitive Neuroscience* 07/2014. doi: 10.1162/jocn_a_00681.

Kronbichler, M., Hutzler, F., Wimmer, H., Mair, A., Staffen, W., & Ladurner, G. (2004). The visual word form area and the frequency with which words are encountered: evidence from a parametric fMRI study. *NeuroImage, 21*, 946–953.

Kuperberg, G. R., Lakshmanan, B. M., Caplan, D. N., & Holcomb, P. J. (2006). Making sense of discourse: an fMRI study of causal inferencing across sentences. *NeuroImage, 33*, 343–361.

Kussmaul, A. (1877). Disturbances of speech. In H. von Ziemssen (ed.), *Cyclopedia of the Practice of Medicine*. New York: William Wood.

Kaan, E., & Swaab, T. Y. (2002). The brain circuitry of syntactic comprehension. *Trends in Cognitive Sciences, 6*, 350–356.

Levy, R. (2008). Expectation-based syntactic comprehension. *Cognition, 106*, 1126–1177.

Mak, W., Vonk, W., & Schriefers, H. (2008). Discourse structure and relative clause processing. *Memory and Cognition, 36*, 170–181.

Makuuchi, M., Grodzinsky, Y., Amunts, K., Santi, A., & Friederici, A. D. (2013). Processing noncanonical sentences in Broca's region: reflections of movement distance and type. *Cerebral Cortex*, *23*, 694–702.

Menenti, L., Gierhan, S. M. E., Segaert, K., & Hagoort, P. (2011). Shared language: overlap and segregation of the neuronal infrastructure for speaking and listening revealed by functional MRI. *Psychological Science*, *22*, 1173–1182.

Miyamoto, E., & Takahashi, S. (2004). Filler-gap dependencies in the processing of scrambling in Japanese. *Language and Linguistics*, *5*, 53–166.

Obleser, J., & Kotz, S. A. (2010). Expectancy constraints in degraded speech modulate the language comprehension network. *Cerebral Cortex*, *20*, 633–640.

Orhan, A. E., & Jacobs, R. A. (2013). A probabilistic clustering theory of the organization of visual short-term memory. *Psychological Review*, *120*, 297–328.

Pickering, M. J., & Ferreira, V. S. (2008). Structural priming: a critical review. *Psychological Bulletin*, *134*, 427–459.

Radford, A. (2004). *Minimalist Syntax*. Cambridge: Cambridge University Press.

Raichle, M. E., Fiez, J. A., Videen, T. O., MacLeod, A. M., Pardo, J. V., Fox, P. T., & Petersen, S. E. (1994). Practice-related changes in human brain functional anatomy during nonmotor learning. *Cerebral Cortex*, *4*, 8–26.

Spivey, M. J., & Tanenhaus, M. K. (1998). Syntactic ambiguity resolution in discourse: modeling the effects of referential context and lexical frequency. *Journal of Experimental Psychology: Learning, Memory and Cognition*, *24*, 1521–1543.

St George, M., Kutas, M., Martinez, A., & Sereno, M. I. (1999). Semantic integration in reading: engagement of the right hemisphere during discourse processing. *Brain*, *122*, 1317–1325.

Taylor, W. L. (1953). 'Cloze procedure': a new tool for measuring readability. *Journalism Quarterly*, *30*, 415–433.

Tenenbaum, J. B., Kemp, C., Griffiths, T. L., & Goodman, N. D. (2011). How to grow a mind: statistics, structure, and abstraction. *Science*, *331*, 1279–1285.

van Berkum, J. J. A. (2010). The brain is a prediction machine that cares about good and bad: any implication for neuropragmatics? *Italian Journal of Linguistics*, *22*, 181–208.

van Berkum, J. J. A., Brown, C. M., Zwiserlood, P., Koojiman, V., & Hagoort, P. (2005). Anticipating upcoming words in discourse: evidence from ERPs and reading times. *Journal of Experimental Psychology: Learning, Memory and Cognition*, *31*, 443–467.

Van Valin, R. D., & LaPolla, R. J. (1997). *Syntax: Structure, Meaning and Function*. Cambridge: Cambridge University Press.

Vuilleumier, P., Henson, R. N., Driver, J., & Dolan, R. J. (2002). Multiple levels of visual object constancy revealed by event-related fMRI of repetition priming. *Nature Neuroscience*, *5*, 491–499.

Wallentin, M., Roepstorff, A., Glover, R., & Burgess, N. (2006). Parallel memory systems for talking about location and age in precuneus, caudate and Broca's region. *NeuroImage*, *32*, 1850–1864.

Wallentin, M., Roepstorff, A., & Burgess, N. (2008a). Frontal eye fields involved in shifting frame of reference within working memory for scenes. *Neuropsychologia*, *46*, 399–408.

Wallentin, M., Weed, E., Østergaard, L., Mouridsen, K., & Roepstorff, A. (2008b). Accessing the mental space: spatial working memory processes for language and vision overlap in precuneus. *Human Brain Mapping*, *29*, 524–532.
Wallentin, M., Kristensen, L. B., Olsen, J. H., & Nielsen, A. H. (2011a). Eye movement suppression interferes with construction of object-centered spatial reference frames in working memory. *Brain and Cognition*, *77*, 432–437.
Wallentin, M., Nielsen, A. H., Vuust, P., Dohn, A., Roepstorff, A., & Lund, T. E. (2011b). Amygdala and heart rate variability responses from listening to emotionally intense parts of a story. *NeuroImage*, *58*, 963–973.
Weber, K., & Indefrey, P. (2009). Syntactic priming in German-English bilinguals during sentence comprehension. *NeuroImage*, *46*, 1164–1172.
Wernicke, C. (1874). *Der aphasische Symptomencomplex*. Breslau: Cohen & Weigart.
Whaley, C. P. (1978). Word–nonword classification time. *Journal of Verbal Learning and Verbal Behavior*, *17*, 143–154.
Zempleni, M.-Z., Renken, R., Hoeks, J. C. J., Hoogduin, J. M., & Stowe, L. A. (2007). Semantic ambiguity processing in sentence context: evidence from event-related fMRI. *NeuroImage*, *3*, 1270–1279.

9 Towards a multi-brain perspective on communication in dialogue

Anna K. Kuhlen, Carsten Allefeld, Silke Anders, & John-Dylan Haynes

Abstract In conversation, speakers and listeners coordinate both their behavior and their mental states. Multi-brain studies, which record and relate to each other the neural activity of two or more brains, can provide insights into a coordination of neural states between communicating individuals. In this chapter we review recent multi-brain studies using functional magnetic resonance imaging (fMRI) or electroencephalography (EEG) to investigate verbal and non-verbal communication. We summarize common findings with respect to spatial and temporal aspects of inter-brain coordination. We then critically discuss challenges arising from studying dialogue in ecologically valid, yet experimentally controlled neuroscientific settings. We conclude by providing an outlook of how technical and methodological advances may enable future multi-brain studies to better address these challenges.

Introduction

Dialogue is a joint activity. Like other types of social interaction it requires coordination between two (or more) people. Being in dialogue is therefore not only an individual process: Conversational partners create meaning *together* (e.g., Clark, 1992, 1996, 1997; Goodwin, 1981; Krauss, 1987; Sacks, Schegloff, & Jefferson, 1974; Schober & Brennan, 2003). In the ensuing process of interpersonal communication, conversational partners coordinate and shape each other's behavior and mental states (e.g., Clark, 1996; Tanenhaus & Brown-Schmidt, 2008; Schober & Brennan, 2003).

Cognitive neuroscience however tends to focus on the mind and brain of the single individual (for discussion see e.g., Hari & Kujala, 2009; Hasson *et al.*, 2012; Pfeiffer *et al.*, 2013; Przyrembel *et al.*, 2013; Schilbach *et al.*, 2013). The majority of studies on the neurocognitive mechanisms underlying dialogue are conducted in single-brain settings. For example, individual participants produce or comprehend speech in isolation of a conversational context (for discussion Brennan, Galati, & Kuhlen, 2010; Menenti *et al.*, 2012; Stephens *et al.*, 2012), interpret other people's mental states based on written stories about fictional characters (e.g., Fletcher *et al.*, 1995; Saxe & Kanwisher, 2003), or interact with partners who are fictitious or whose brain activity is not recorded (for discussion see Ochsner, 2004).

More recently, it has been recognized that in order to gain a complete account of the neural basis of interpersonal communication, investigating the isolated brain might not be enough. Instead, it may be necessary to go beyond the individual, and investigate how multiple brains communicate and coordinate with each other. This means that both communicating partners' brain activity needs to be recorded, and related to each other (for discussion see Hari *et al.*, 2013; Konvalinka & Roepstorff, 2012).

In recent years, neuroscientific investigations have begun to illuminate the neural mechanisms supporting different types of social interactions from a multi-brain perspective. These studies record and relate to each other the neural activity of multiple individuals. Such multi-brain approaches provide a promising strategy for studying the neural mechanisms underlying communication in dialogue. In this chapter we review neuroscientific studies that aim to investigate verbal or non-verbal communication in dialogue, or dialogue-like settings, from a multi-brain perspective. The strengths and weaknesses of these approaches underscore the many challenges that need to be overcome when studying communication at a multi-brain level. We begin by highlighting what makes dialogue special, and worthwhile investigating.

Communication in dialogue: coordinating two minds and brains

Dialogue is different from monologue (for a complete discussion, see e.g., Bavelas & Chovil, 2000, 2006; Clark, 1996; Goodwin, 1981; Levinson, 1983; Linell, 2005; Pickering & Garrod, 2004; Schober & Brennan, 2003). One central characteristic of communication in dialogue is the presence of a conversational partner. In order to communicate successfully, conversational partners need to reach a shared understanding of what they are communicating about. Dialogue thus requires an intricate level of coordination between conversational partners (for discussion see e.g., Brennan, Galati, & Kuhlen, 2010).

This can mean that conversational partners become more similar to each other in their behavior during the course of the communication (for recent review see Branigan *et al.*, 2010): For example, conversational partners converge in their choice of words (e.g., Brennan & Clark, 1996; Garrod & Anderson, 1987) and syntactic structures (e.g., Branigan, Pickering, & Cleland, 2000; Levelt & Kelter, 1982), in their use of speech-accompanying gestures (e.g., De Fornel, 1992; Mol *et al.*, 2012), and in their style of speaking (Giles, Coupland, & Coupland, 1991; Prado, 2006). Such a convergence of behavior has been associated with mutual understanding (Richardson & Dale, 2005; Richardson, Dale, & Kirkham, 2007) and a convergence of mental states (e.g., Clark & Brennan, 1991; Pickering & Garrod, 2004).

Little is known about the convergence of neural states during communication. Such a convergence could arise from the exchange of information between brains and result in a spatial and temporal coordination across the brains of communicating individuals (e.g., Anders *et al.*, 2011; Stephens *et al.*, 2010). In order to capture such inter-brain coordination recent studies have begun to measure and relate to each other the neural activity of multiple individuals involved in interpersonal communication.

Multi-brain neuroscience: recording and relating the neural activity of multiple brains

In recent years, methodological advances have made it possible to study the brains of multiple interacting individuals (e.g., Hari & Kujala, 2009; Konvalinka & Roepstorff, 2012). Some studies within this framework employ so-called "hyperscanning" settings (Montague *et al.*, 2002), in which the brain activity of multiple individuals is recorded simultaneously during real-time interaction. Other studies record consecutively the brain activity of individuals during an offline, one-way exchange by recording the behavior produced by one person and then replaying it to another person who responds to it. Both approaches have the goal of relating the brain activity of multiple individuals to each other. These studies have primarily used functional magnetic resonance imaging (fMRI) and electroencephalography (EEG) to investigate individuals in social interaction. For example, two interacting individuals' brain activity was recorded while they were jointly making economic decisions (King-Casas *et al.*, 2005; Montague *et al.*, 2002), coordinating their eye gaze (Saito *et al.*, 2010), tapping their fingers in synchrony (Tognoli *et al.*, 2007), jointly playing guitar (Lindenberger *et al.*, 2009; Sänger, Müller, & Lindenberger, 2012), saxophone (Babiloni *et al.*, 2012), or a game of cards (Astolfi *et al.*, 2010). The findings of these studies were related to different aspects of social interaction, such as decision-making in a social context, joint attention, joint motor coordination, or competitive and cooperative encounters. They demonstrate that it is possible to record and relate to each other the neural activity of multiple interacting individuals in a meaningful way. Yet only few studies have investigated dialogue.

In the following we will review studies that investigate multiple individuals communicating verbally or non-verbally. We will first turn to a pioneering single-brain study that sets the stage for a multi-brain approach to communication by comparing brain activity associated with different conversational roles. We will then discuss several fMRI and EEG studies that investigate coordination of neural activity between communication partners from a multi-brain perspective, relating the brain activity of interacting individuals to each other. Finally, we discuss common themes and findings arising from these studies.

Single-brain studies of communication

In a single-brain fMRI study, Noordzij *et al.* (2009) scanned individuals communicating in a non-verbal communication game, which was mediated through a computer. Using entirely graphical means, participants needed to invent communicative signals to agree with their partner on the location of two tokens on a grid. Set in a live interaction, the brain of one player was scanned, while the other player was outside of the scanner. Some of the trials recorded the neural activation associated with composing a communicative message, other trials recorded the neural activation associated with understanding the partner's communicative message.

By limiting participants in their communicative moves, this paradigm was able to retain control over the ensuing interaction. Moreover, it was possible to generate control trials in which players made moves identical to communicative trials, but without communicative intention (in these trials the tokens' target locations were known to both players, making communication superfluous).

Comparing communicative with non-communicative trials, results indicate that the same brain area, the posterior part of the superior temporal sulcus (pSTS) of the right hemisphere, was activated when planning a communicative action and when recognizing its communicative intent. The authors propose that when producing a communicative message, players use their own "intention recognition system" for predicting how their partners will come to recognize communicative intention (see also Levinson, 2006).

Multi-brain studies of communication

The first study to investigate non-verbal communication from a multi-brain perspective was a study by Schippers *et al.* (2010). In this study, pairs of participants were asked to communicate through their hand gestures while playing a game of charades: one participant pantomimed a word, the other participant tried to guess the word. The participant who was currently in the scanner alternated between pantomiming while being recorded on video, and guessing the other participant's pantomimes which had been recorded previously. The authors used Granger causality, a statistical method to infer whether a time series (e.g., the brain activity of one person) predicts another (e.g., the brain activity of another person) (see e.g., Seth, 2007), to model the process of coordination between the brain of the person interpreting the gesture and the brain of the person gesturing. Areas in the pantomimer's brain, commonly associated with the so-called human mirror neuron system (parietal regions, dorsal and ventral premotor cortex), triggered activation in spatially corresponding areas in the brain of the person interpreting the pantomimes. This supports the idea that the mirror neuron system is active both during execution and observation of movement, possibly facilitating interpersonal communication and an understanding of the other person's goals (Gallese & Goldman, 1998). In addition, the pantomimer's brain activity in motor areas predicted the guessing person's brain activity in the ventromedial prefrontal cortex (vmPFC), an area often associated with "mentalizing," thinking about other people's intentions and beliefs (Amodio & Frith, 2006). The authors propose that observers comprehend pantomimes by both simulating their partners' motor movements and mentalizing about their communicative intent. In this sense, the two conversational partners' brains "resonate" with each other during communication.

Also in a non-verbal setting, a study by Anders *et al.* (2011) investigated two individuals communicating with each other via facial expressions. In this fMRI study, participants were assigned to either the role of the "sender," or the role of the "perceiver." The sender was asked to submerge herself into a given emotion (e.g., by imagining a situation that would evoke this emotion) and to facially express her feelings. The sender's facial expression was videotaped during scanning and subsequently shown to the perceiver when he was scanned. The perceiver was left completely uninformed about the sender's task and was simply asked to try to feel with the sender. Using pattern analysis (Haynes & Rees, 2006), the authors then identified brain regions in which the sender's current emotional state was encoded similarly in the brain of the sender and the brain of the perceiver. Identified brain areas of this "shared neural network" were distributed across temporal, parietal, insular, and frontal brain regions. Notably, neural signals in the brain of the perceiver were delayed relative to the corresponding neural signals in the brain of the sender by up to 8 seconds, suggesting that it takes some time to develop a full understanding of the non-verbal message.

The first study employing a multi-brain setting to investigate communication based on spoken language is an fMRI study by Stephens and colleagues (2010). This study compared the brain activity of an individual telling a story to the brain activity of individuals listening to this story. To reduce artifacts associated with speaking in the scanner, the speaker was trained to minimize head movements while telling an unrehearsed story from her life while being scanned. The audio recording of this story was then played to listeners who were also being scanned. Similar to the reviewed studies on non-verbal communication, the brain activity of listeners coordinated with the brain activity of the speaker in spatially corresponding areas. Between-brain correlations were observed in low-level auditory areas, areas related to speech comprehension (e.g., Wernicke's area) and to speech production (e.g., Broca's area) as well as areas related to mentalizing (e.g., precuneus, mPFC), suggesting a coordination process on different levels of processing. Temporally, the activity of most (but not all) areas within the listeners' brains lagged behind the speaker's brain by up to 3 seconds.

The degree of neural coordination was associated with listeners' understanding of the story: their performance in a comprehension questionnaire administered after hearing the story correlated with the degree of temporal correlation between the speaker's and the listeners' brain activity. Along similar lines, speaker's and listeners' brain activity was not correlated when the story was told in a language foreign to the listeners. The authors conclude that, during successful communication, information is transferred between the two communicating brains by coupling brain activity associated with speaking and listening.

Besides fMRI, electroencephalography (EEG) has been used to capture coordination of neural activity between communicating individuals. In comparison to fMRI, EEG is at an advantage to capture the temporal dimension of interpersonal coordination. In addition, recording neural activity with EEG is less obtrusive and has the potential for studying communication in more naturalistic settings. Nevertheless, EEG has only most recently been used to investigate communication from a multi-brain perspective.

An early study by Dumas *et al.* (2010) aimed to investigate coordination of brain activity during non-verbal communication. In this study the brain activity of two individuals was recorded simultaneously while they interacted via a live video-conference. They were instructed to move their hands in "meaningless" gestures. Comparing episodes in which participants moved their hands in synchrony with episodes in which they moved asynchronously, the authors identify a distributed network of brain areas that coordinated across interacting partners in several oscillatory frequency bands. Similar to Schippers *et al.* (2010), the authors interpret coordination in spatially corresponding areas reported for the alpha-mu band of the right centroparietal electrodes to be related to the mirror neuron system. A non-corresponding coordination, involving different electrode locations across the two communicating individuals, was found in the higher-frequency bands. This coordination of activity between non-corresponding electrodes was interpreted to arise from differential social roles in the interaction (being an imitator or a follower).

Another EEG study used a multi-brain setting to investigate spoken communication (Kuhlen, Allefeld, & Haynes, 2012). Following a similar protocol as introduced by Stephens *et al.*, speakers' EEG was recorded while they were narrating stories. Audio-visual recordings of these narrations were then played back to a group of listeners, whose brain activity was also recorded. The experimental design ascertained that a possible coordination between speakers and listeners was indeed due to processing the communicative content: recordings of two speakers, one male and one female, were superimposed so that listeners were presented with two different narrations at the same time. One group of listeners was instructed to attend to the female speaker, the other group of listeners was instructed to attend to the male speaker. Through this manipulation the stimulus videos presented to both groups of listeners were perceptually identical; what varied was which narration listeners attended to.

Relating the brain activity of both groups of listeners to each other, results showed that the EEG of listeners attending to the same narration was more similar to each other than to the EEG of listeners presented with the same video, but attending to the other narration. More importantly, the EEG of listeners was correlated with the EEG of the attended speakers. This coordination between speakers and listeners was not restricted to spatially corresponding brain areas: Speaker–listener coordination was associated with electrodes located in the right frontal areas in speakers and medial frontal areas in listeners.

Similar to previous fMRI studies (Anders *et al.*, 2011; Schippers *et al.*, 2010; Stephens *et al.*, 2010) the coordination between speakers and listeners was temporally delayed: The correlation between the speakers' EEG and listeners' EEG peaked at 12.5 seconds, indicating that listeners' neural activity lagged behind speakers' neural activity. This time delay is interpreted to correspond to the processing of larger semantic units within the story, suggesting that during story comprehension listeners coordinate with speakers a global understanding of the story content, possibly at the level of situation models (van Dijk and Kintsch, 1983; Zwaan and Radvansky, 1998; also called "mental model," Johnson-Laird, 1983).

Communicating brains: summary of basic findings The multi-brain studies on verbal and non-verbal communication reviewed so far have revealed the following basic findings: (1) The neural activity of two individuals coordinates during communication. (2) This inter-brain coordination involves spatially corresponding as well as non-corresponding brain areas, and (3) is not necessarily instantaneous: neural activity in one brain may precede or follow the other brain. In the following we will discuss each of these points in turn.

Finding 1: Neural states coordinate during communication Using different experimental protocols and analysis approaches, studies consistently report that during communication neural activation patterns coordinate across communicating individuals: neural activity associated with planning a communicative action overlaps with neural activity associated with interpreting its intent (Noordzij *et al.*, 2009); neural activity recorded in a person producing a verbal utterance coordinates with neural activity recorded in a person listening to this utterance (Kuhlen, Allefeld, & Haynes, 2012; Stephens *et al.*, 2010); and neural activity of a person producing a certain facial or gestural display coordinates with neural activity of the person interpreting or imitating this display (Anders *et al.*, 2011; Dumas *et al.*, 2010; Schippers *et al.*, 2010). This inter-individual neural coordination has been interpreted to relate to identifying a situation as communicative (Noordzij *et al.*, 2009), attending to the communicative message (Kuhlen, Allefeld, & Haynes, 2012), understanding the communicative message (Schippers *et al.*, 2010; Stephens *et al.*, 2010), empathizing with the communication partner's emotional state (Anders *et al.*, 2011), or synchronizing behavior (Dumas *et al.*, 2010).

Brain areas reported to coordinate between individuals are widely distributed across the cortex and are in part unique to the particular study, presumably due to specific task demands. But there are also some commonalities: Many studies report inter-brain correlations involving areas associated with mentalizing about a partner, such as the medial prefrontal cortex (Kuhlen, Allefeld, & Haynes, 2012; Schippers *et al.*, 2010; Stephens *et al.*, 2010), as well as somato-motor areas (Anders *et al.*, 2011; Dumas *et al.*, 2010; Schippers *et al.*, 2010). This supports the central function that has been assigned to both the mentalizing and mirror neuron systems in understanding other people's mental states, actions, and goals (see e.g., Frith & Frith, 2012; van Overwalle & Baetens, 2009). These findings demonstrate that neural coordination during communication can be observed in neural networks that span across multiple communicating individuals' brains. In this way, the brain activity of one individual shapes the brain activity of another individual during communication.

Finding 2: Neural activity coordinates across corresponding and non-corresponding brain regions Several studies report an activation of spatially corresponding brain areas in individuals producing a communicative message and those interpreting this message. A co-activation of similar neural structures across individuals may be based on a co-activation of similar linguistic representations (Hasson *et al.*, 2012; Menenti, Pickering, & Garrod, 2012; Stephens *et al.*, 2010). Such parity between speaking and listening has also been proposed by theories of dialogue based on behavioral studies (see e.g., Calvert *et al.*, 1997; Liberman & Whalen, 2000; MacKay, 1987; Mattingly & Liberman, 1986; Pickering & Garrod, 2004). Along similar lines, the computational processes for recognizing communicative intention have been proposed to overlap with those for planning communicative action (Noordzij *et al.*, 2009). A co-activation of similar brain areas has also been interpreted to support theories that see sensorimotor or somatosensory simulations, as supported through the putative mirror neuron system, as instrumental to communication (Anders *et a*l., 2011; Dumas et al., 2010; Schippers *et al.*, 2010). Common to these interpretations is the assumption of a more general cognitive principle, which assumes a coupling between processes of perception and processes of action (e.g., Hommel *et al.*, 2001).

However, interpersonal coordination of neural activity is not necessarily limited to activity in spatially corresponding brain regions. Coordination is any type of functional ordering among interacting components (Bressler & Kelso, 2001). Yet many analysis approaches chosen for studies on inter-brain coordination only account for coordination between spatially corresponding brain regions because they are (explicitly or implicitly) based on models of the coordination process that only include relations between corresponding areas. Studies that have used different analysis approaches report coordination also of non-corresponding areas (Dumas *et al.*, 2010; Kuhlen, Allefeld, & Haynes, 2012; Schippers *et al.*, 2010). This indicates that not only identical but also complementary cognitive processes underlie successful communication.

Finding 3: Neural activity in one brain may precede or follow the other brain Among the most interesting findings emerging from multi-brain studies of communication are those concerning the temporal relationship between the brain activity of the person producing a communicative message ("speaker") and the brain activity of the person comprehending a communicative message ("listener"). Many of the studies reviewed report that neural activity in listeners was delayed with respect to the corresponding neural activity in speakers (Anders *et al.*, 2011; Kuhlen, Allefeld, & Haynes, 2012; Schippers *et al.*, 2010; Stephens *et al.*, 2010). Note that even in the fMRI studies this delay is not related to the hemodynamic response, which is itself delayed with respect to the neural activity. Instead, delays have been interpreted as representing a processing cost of deciphering the communicative message (Stephens *et al.*, 2010), or an emotional "tuning in" between communicating individuals (Anders *et al.*, 2011). The different time scales at which speakers and listeners coordinate have also been interpreted to reflect informational units of different sizes (Kuhlen, Allefeld, & Haynes, 2012). According to this view, coordination between brains occurs on several different timescales, which build upon each other. Shorter timescales enable a rapid progression of the dialogue, longer timescales enable information to accumulate over the course of an exchange. Interestingly, one study reported that, in some brain areas, the neural activity in listeners' brains precedes the activity in the speaker's brain (Stephens *et al.*, 2010). Such a coordination pattern is consistent with the proposal that listeners exploit the conversational context to make predictions about what their conversational partner is about to say (e.g., van Berkum *et al.*, 2005).

In summary, multi-brain studies of communication have illuminated brain processes that underlie coordination of individual processing during communication. Extending the individual-focused approach of previous neurolinguistic studies, multi-brain studies have developed a framework that allows investigating how neural activity coordinates across communicating individuals. Inter-brain coordination can provide a basis for processes underlying communication in dialogue, such as an alignment of conversational partners at different levels of linguistic representation, the understanding of the other's inner world, and the anticipation of other's actions. Recording the neural activity of both speaker and listener can advance investigations of the temporal and spatial dimensions of interpersonal communication, and opens up exciting possibilities for developing a neural account of dialogue.

Challenges and outlook

Existing studies are likely to be just the beginning of neuroscientific studies investigating communication by measuring the brain activity of multiple interacting individuals. While in many ways the reviewed studies embrace the complexity of natural dialogue, there are many other crucial characteristics of dialogue that they do not account for. We identify (at least) three big challenges faced by multi-brain studies on communication in dialogue: (1) retaining the interactive nature of dialogue as well as the complexity of the communicative act, (2) accounting for the environment in which spontaneous communication is embedded, and (3) recording an artifact-free neural signal during communication. In the following we will discuss these challenges and provide an outlook on directions this field may pursue in the future.

Challenge 1: Retaining the interactive nature of dialogue as well as the complexity of the communicative acts Naturally occurring dialogue is interactive: conversational partners rapidly alternate between speaking and listening. In fact, even in rather monologue-like settings, such as listening to stories, listeners actively contribute to the conversation by giving verbal and non-verbal feedback (Bavelas, Coates, & Johnson, 2000; Kuhlen & Brennan, 2010; Krauss, 1987). In this way, conversational partners collaborate in creating meaning, and shape each other's behavior and thoughts online (e.g., Schober & Brennan, 2003). The ensuing dynamics of interactive dialogue are difficult to capture within a simple sender-receiver framework.

The typical cognitive experiment, though, seeks control by carefully designed stimuli and repeated observation of multiple subjects' response to these stimuli. This allows researchers to aggregate data obtained from different trials and subjects, and to be confident that the conclusions drawn relate to one specifically induced type of cognitive process. In an interactive setting, subjects' responses are not, or only partially, driven by experimenter-designed stimulus material. Instead subjects follow their own endogenous dynamics and mutually influence each other. The unfolding communicative process is difficult to control and to manipulate experimentally. This lack of control leads to a high degree of heterogeneity between different experimental trials and subjects, which complicates or precludes aggregation of data, and the possibility for detecting a systematic trend or pattern.

One approach for gaining experimental control over interactive dialogue is allowing subjects to communicate only through a limited set of communicative acts: subjects' behavior is restricted either by instruction or by mediating communication through a restricted medium, e.g., a computer system. This way, participants are not enabled to make full use of natural language, but have to adapt their communicative intent to the possibilities offered, for example, a specified set of gestures (Dumas *et al.*, 2010), or the movement of a mouse cursor on a screen (Noordzij *et al.*, 2009). The drawback is that the more the experimenter succeeds in limiting the domain of possible communicative processes, the less naturalistic the communication becomes. Even if some forms of such restricted communication may be similar to situations of everyday life, this experimental approach still moves the observed behavior away from the phenomenon of interest.

An alternative way to control the complexity of naturalistic communication is to restrain its interactivity. Studies taking this approach have separated episodes of producing a communicative message from episodes of comprehending the communicative message. By pre-recording a speaker's communicative message, statistical homogeneity can be retained by presenting exact replications of this message to multiple listeners. In this case, the communicative setting as well as the information conveyed between participants can be more complex and relatively unconstrained. Examples of this approach are the studies of Stephens *et al.* (2010) and Kuhlen, Allefeld, & Haynes (2012), which both pre-recorded verbal, spontaneously narrated stories of several minutes' length. This approach enables investigating communication that resembles the rich, contextualized, and multi-layered information structure of naturally occurring dialogue.

One important challenge for future multi-brain studies of communication will be transferring existing protocols into a setting that accounts for the simultaneous, interactive nature of natural dialogue, while at the same time allowing for rich and less constrained behavior. While ecological validity may not be an important goal for every type of research (see e.g., Banaji & Crowder, 1989; Mook, 1983), there is a trend towards investigating neural processes under real-life conditions (Hasson & Honey, 2013; Schilbach *et al.*, 2013). Overly simplified experimental settings come with risks when investigating complex phenomena such as dialogue (Bavelas, 2005; Kuhlen & Brennan, 2013). Investigating naturalistic, less constrained behavior may lead to results that refine or modify existing theories, and can also reveal phenomena that have gone unnoticed under highly controlled experimental conditions.

Behavioral studies of dialogue have developed successful strategies for investigating naturalistic dialogue under tightly controlled experimental settings (for discussion, see e.g., Ito & Speer, 2006; Kuhlen & Brennan, 2013; Schober & Brennan, 2003; Tanenhaus & Brown-Schmidt, 2008). Studies in this tradition tend to investigate task-directed communication. For example, in the "tangram task" (e.g., Clark & Schober, 1992; Clark & Wilkes-Gibbs, 1986) speakers describe to listeners a finite set of objects. In the "map task" (e.g., Anderson *et al.*, 1991) speakers instruct listeners how to follow a route on a map. The boundaries of such interactive tasks limit subjects' behavior, while still allowing them to use language spontaneously and naturalistically. Through carefully designed stimulus material and instructions, subjects can be led into a more predictable and controllable form of dialogue. Future neurolinguistic studies may benefit from bridging these existing experimental protocols to suit neuroscientific investigations.

Challenge 2: Accounting for the environment in which spontaneous communication is embedded Experimental scenarios in which subjects move around freely and coordinate in a complex physical environment are particularly challenging to achieve in a neuroscientific setting.

Particularly fMRI studies are heavily constrained in this regard due to the limited space, and the immobile, horizontal position of the subjects inside the scanner. Studies using EEG place fewer physical constraints on the subject, but still the hard-wired amplifier and the sensitivity to movement of the electrode cables restrain how freely the subject can move around. A promising development are studies exploring the use of mobile EEG sets that allow recording brain activity while subjects can navigate rather freely in space (e.g., Gramann *et al.*, 2010).

Beyond EEG and fMRI, other neural recording tools may be suitable for investigating dialogue among freely moving subjects: For example, a recent functional near-infrared spectroscopy (fNIRS) study investigated how individuals observe and execute complex everyday tasks, such as setting a table (Koehler *et al.*, 2012). This recording technique could be used for recording two individuals in face-to-face dialogue (see Suda *et al.*, 2010 for a single-brain fNIRS study on dialogue; and Cui *et al.*, 2012, for a dual-brain fNIRS study on competing or collaborating in video games).

Virtual reality devices may also provide interesting opportunities for navigating in a natural environment while engaged in a social interaction (for single-brain approaches, see e.g., Bailenson *et al.*, 2003; Schilbach *et al.*, 2006; Slater *et al.*, 2006).

Challenge 3: Recording an artifact-free neural signal during communication The small number of neuroscientific investigations on verbal communication point to the considerable challenge of recording neural activity while subjects are speaking (for discussion see Ganushchak *et al.*, 2011). In fMRI, even rather small head movements lead to a misalignment of sequentially acquired images. This problem is exacerbated by the small high-frequency movements induced by speaking. While slower movements can largely be compensated by image-realignment algorithms, faster, speech-related movements may severely degrade the quality of fMRI data because they induce artifacts within images that are not corrected by the standard algorithms (for discussion see Munhall, 2001).

In EEG, facial movements such as facial expressions or speaking pose a problem because muscle tension itself produces electric fields that appear as high-amplitude broadband noise in the recording. Since its frequency range (from about 15 Hz upwards) has significant overlap with cognitively relevant frequency bands of the EEG, muscle artifacts can conceal or distort the neuro-electric effects of interest.

Encouraging procedures for addressing these problems are being developed and evaluated for both recording modalities (for EEG see e.g., McMenamin *et al.*, 2010, 2011; Winkler *et al.*, 2011; for fMRI see e.g., Birn, Cox, & Bendettini, 2004).

Summary

By measuring and relating to each other the brain activity of multiple communicating individuals, multi-brain studies have made advancements in understanding and studying the neural processes underlying verbal and non-verbal communication. Multi-brain studies have broadened our understanding of the neural underpinnings of communication by showing how neural activity is spatially and temporally coordinated across multiple individuals. Methodologically, multi-brain studies have opened a window into studying the neural activity of multiple communicating individuals in complex, naturalistic encounters. Building upon these advances, future studies within this framework are destined to shed further light on the neural architecture supporting interactive dialogue.

References

Anders, S., Heinzle, J., Weiskopf, N., Ethofer, T., & Haynes, J. D. (2011). Flow of affective information between communicating brains. *NeuroImage*, *54*, 439–446.

Anderson, A. H., Bader, M., Boyle, E., Bard, E. G., Doherty, G., Garrod, S., Isard, S. D., Kowtko, J., MacAllister, J., Miller, J., Sotillo, C., Thompson, H. S., & Weinert, R. (1991). The H.C.R.C. Map Task Corpus. *Language and Speech*, *34*, 351–366.

Amodio, D. M., & Frith, C. D. (2006). Meetings of minds: the medial frontal cortex and social cognition. *Nature Reviews Neuroscience*, *7*, 268–277.

Astolfi, L., Toppi, J., de Vico Fallani, F., Vecchiato, G., Salinari, S., Mattia, D., Cincotti, F., & Babiloni, F. (2010). Neuroelectrical hyperscanning measures simultaneous brain activity in humans. *Brain Topography*, *23*, 243–256.

Babiloni, C., Buffo, P., Vecchio F., Marzano, N., Del Percio, C., Spada, D., Rossi, S., Bruni, I., Rossini, P. N., & Perani, D. (2012). Brains "in concert": Frontal oscillatory alpha rhythms and empathy in professional musicians. *NeuroImage*, *60*, 105–116.

Bailenson, J. N., Blascovich, J., Beall, A. C., & Loomis, J. M. (2003). Interpersonal distance in immersive virtual environments. *Personality and Social Psychology Bulletin*, *29*, 819–833.

Banaji, M. R., & Crowder, R. G. (1989). The bankruptcy of everyday memory. *American Psychologist*, *44*, 1185–1193.

Bavelas, J. B. (2005). The two solitudes: reconciling social psychology and language and social interaction. In K. L. Fitch & R. E. Sanders (eds.), *Handbook of Language and Social Interaction* (pp. 179–200). Mahwah, NJ: Lawrence Erlbaum.

Bavelas, J. B., & Chovil, N. (2000). Visible acts of meaning: an integrated message model of language use in face-to-face dialogue. *Journal of Language and Social Psychology*, *19*, 163–194.

Bavelas, J. B., & Chovil, N. (2006). Hand gestures and facial displays as part of language use in face-to-face dialogue. In V. Manusov & M. Patterson (eds.),

Handbook of Nonverbal Communication (pp. 97–115). Thousand Oaks, CA: Sage.
Bavelas, J. B., Coates, L., & Johnson, T. (2000). Listeners as co-narrators. *Journal of Personality and Social Psychology*, *79*, 941–952.
Birn, R. M., Cox, R. W., & Bendettini, P. A. (2004). Experimental designs and processing strategies for fMRI studies involving overt verbal responses. *NeuroImage*, *23*, 1046–1058.
Branigan, H. P., Pickering, M. J., & Cleland, A. A. (2000). Syntactic co-ordination in dialogue. *Cognition*, *75*, B13–B25.
Branigan, H. P., Pickering, M. J., Pearson, J., & McLean, J. F. (2010). Linguistic alignment between humans and computers. *Journal of Pragmatics*, *42*, 2355–2368.
Brennan, S. E., & Clark, H. H. (1996). Conceptual pacts and lexical choice in conversation. *Journal of Experimental Psychology: Learning, Memory, and Cognition*, *22*, 482–1493.
Brennan, S. E., Galati, A., & Kuhlen, A. K. (2010). Two minds, one dialog: coordinating speaking and understanding. In B. Ross (ed.), *The Psychology of Learning and Motivation* (Vol. *53*, pp. 301–344). Burlington, MA: Academic Press.
Bressler, S. L., & Kelso, J. A. S. (2001). Cortical coordination dynamics and cognition. *Trends in Cognitive Sciences*, *5*, 26–36.
Calvert, G. A., Bullmore, E. T., Brammer, M. J., Campbell, R., Williams, S. C. R., McGuire, P. K., Woodruff, P. W. R., Iversen, S. D., & David, A. S. (1997). Activation of auditory cortex during silent lipreading. *Science*, *276* (5312), 593–596.
Clark, H. H. (1992). *Arenas of Language Use*. Chicago, IL: University of Chicago Press.
Clark, H. H. (1996). *Using Language*. Cambridge: Cambridge University Press.
Clark, H. H. (1997). Dogmas of understanding. *Discourse Processes*, *23*, 567–598.
Clark, H. H., & Schober, M. F. (1992). Understanding by addressees and over-hearers. In H. H. Clark (ed.), *Arenas of Language Use* (pp. 176–197). Chicago, IL: University of Chicago Press.
Clark, H. H., & Wilkes-Gibbs, D. (1986). Referring as a collaborative process. *Cognition*, *22*, 1–39.
Cui, X., Bryant, D. M., & Reiss, A. L. (2012). NIRS-based hyperscanning reveals increased interpersonal coherence in superior frontal cortex during coopera-tion. *NeuroImage*, *59*, 2430–2437.
De Fornel, M. (1992). The return gesture: some remarks on context, inference, and iconic gesture. In P. Auer & A. di Luzio (eds.), *The Contextualization of Language* (pp. 159–175). Amsterdam: Benjamins.
Dumas, G., Nadel, J., Soussignan, R., Martinerie, J., & Garnero, L. (2010). Inter-brain synchronization during social interaction. *PloS ONE*, *5*(8), e12166. doi:10.1371/journal.pone.0012166.
Fletcher, P. C., Happé, F., Frith, U., Baker, S. C., Dolan, R. J., Frackowiak, R. S. J., & Frith, C. D. (1995). Other minds in the brain: a functional imaging study of "theory of mind" in story comprehension. *Cognition*, *57*, 109–128.
Frith, C. D., & Frith, U. (2012). Mechanisms of social cognition. *Annual Review of Psychology*, *63*, 287–313.

Ganushchak, L. Y., Christoffels, I., & Schiller, N. (2011). The use of electro-encephalography (EEG) in language production research: a review. *Frontiers in Psychology, 2*, 208. doi: 10.3389/fpsyg.2011.00208.

Garrod, S., & Anderson, A. (1987). Saying what you mean in dialog: a study in conceptual and semantic co-ordination. *Cognition, 27*, 181–218.

Goodwin, C. (1981). *Conversational Organization: Interaction between Speakers and Hearers*. New York: Academic Press.

Gallese, V., & Goldman, A. (1998). Mirror neurons and the simulation theory of mind-reading. *Trends in Cognitive Sciences, 2*, 493–501.

Giles, H., Coupland, N., & Coupland, J. (1991). Accommodation theory: communication, context, and consequence. In H. Giles, J. Coupland, & N. Coupland (eds.), *Contexts of Accommodation: Developments in Applied Sociolinguistics* (pp. 1–68). Cambridge: Cambridge University Press.

Gramann, K., Gwin, J. T., Bigdely-Shamlo, N., Ferris, D. P., & Makeig, S. (2010). Visual evoked responses during standing and walking. *Frontiers in Human Neuroscience, 4*, 202. doi: 10.3389/fnhum.2010.00202.

Hasson, U., & Honey, C. J. (2013). Future trends in neuroimaging: neural processes as expressed within real-life contexts. *NeuroImage, 62*, 1272–1278.

Hasson, U., Ghazanfar, A. A., Garrod, S., & Keysers, C. (2012). Brain-to-brain coupling: a mechanism for creating and sharing a social world. *Trends in Cognitive Sciences, 16*, 114–121.

Hari, R., & Kujala, M. V. (2009). Brain basis of human social interaction: from concepts to brain imaging. *Physiological Reviews, 89*, 453–479.

Hari, R., Himberg, T., Nummenmaa, L., Hämäläinen, M., & Parkkonen, L. (2013). Synchrony of brains and bodies during implicit interpersonal interaction. *Trends in Cognitive Sciences, 17*, 105–106.

Haynes, J. D., & Rees, G. (2006). Decoding mental states from brain activity in humans. *Nature Reviews Neuroscience, 7*, 523–534.

Hommel, B., Müsseler, J., Aschersleben, G., & Prinz, W. (2001). The theory of event coding (TEC): a framework for perception and action planning. *Behavioral and Brain Sciences, 24*, 849–937.

Ito, K., & Speer, S. R. (2006). Using interactive tasks to elicit natural dialogue. In P. Augurzky & D. Lenertova (eds.), *Methods in Empirical Prosody Research* (pp. 229–257). Berlin: Mouton de Gruyter.

Johnson-Laird, P. N. (1983). *Mental Models*. Cambridge, MA: Harvard University Press.

King-Casas, B., Tomlin, D., Anen, C., Camerer, C. F., Quarty, S. R., & Montague, P. R. (2005). Getting to know you: reputation and trust in a two-person economic exchange. *Science, 308*(5718), 78–83. doi: 10.1126/science.1108062.

Koehler, S., Egetemeir, J., Stenneken, P., Koch, S. P., Pauli, P., Fallgatter, A. J., & Herrmann, M. J. (2012). The human execution/observation matching system investigated with a complex everyday task: a functional near-infrared spectroscopy (fNIRS) study. *Neuroscience Letters, 508*, 73–77.

Konvalinka, I., & Roepstorff, A. (2012). The two-brain approach: how can mutually interacting brains teach us something about social interaction? *Frontiers in Human Neuroscience, 6*, 215. doi: 10.3389/fnhum.2012.00215.

Krauss, R. M. (1987). The role of the listener: addressee influences on message formulation. *Journal of Language and Social Psychology, 6*, 81–97.
Kuhlen, A. K., & Brennan, S. E. (2010). Anticipating distracted addressees: how speakers' expectations and addressees' feedback influence storytelling. *Discourse Processes, 47*, 567–587.
Kuhlen, A. K., & Brennan, S. E. (2013). Language in dialogue: when confederates might be hazardous to your data. *Psychonomic Bulletin and Review, 20*, 54–72. doi: 10.3758/s13423-012-0341-8.
Kuhlen, A. K.,* Allefeld, C.,* & Haynes, J. D. (2012). Content-specific coordination of listeners' to speakers' EEG during communication. *Frontiers in Human Neuroscience, 6*, 266. doi: 10.3389/fnhum.2012.00266. * equal contribution
Levelt, W. J. M., & Kelter, S. (1982). Surface form and memory in question answering. *Cognitive Psychology, 14*, 78–106.
Levinson, S. C. (1983). *Pragmatics*. Cambridge: Cambridge University Press.
Levinson, S. C. (2006). On the human "interactional engine". In N. J. Enfield & S. C. Levinson (eds.), *Roots of Human Sociality: Culture, Cognition, and Interaction* (pp. 39–69). Oxford: Berg.
Liberman, A. M., & Whalen, D. H. (2000). On the relation of speech to language. *Trends in Cognitive Sciences, 4*, 187–196.
Lindenberger, U., Li, S. C., Gruber, W., & Müller, V. (2009). Brains swinging in concert: cortical phase synchronization while playing guitar. *BMC Neuroscience, 10*, 22. doi: 10.1186/1471-2202-10-22.
Linell, P. (2005). *The Written Language Bias in Linguistics: Its Nature, Origins and Transformations*. London: Routledge.
Mattingly, I. G., & Liberman, A. M. (1986). Specialized perceiving systems for speech and other biologically significant sounds. In G. M. Edelman, W. E. Gall, & W. M. Cowan (eds.), *Functions of the Auditory System* (pp. 775–793). New York: Wiley.
MacKay, D. (1987). *The Organization of Perception and Action*. New York: Springer.
Menenti, L., Pickering, M. J., & Garrod, S. C. (2012). Toward a neural basis of interactive alignment in conversation. *Frontiers in Human Neuroscience, 6*, 185. doi:10.3389/fnhum.2012.00185.
McMenamin, B. W., Shackman, A. J., Maxwell, J. S., Bachhuber, D. R. W., Koppenhaver, A. M., Greischar, L. L., *et al.* (2010). Validation of ICA-based myogenic artifact correction for scalp and source-localized EEG. *NeuroImage, 49*, 2416–2432.
McMenamin, B. W., Shackman, A. J., Greischar, L. L., & Davidson, R. J. (2011). Electromyogenic artifacts and electroencephalographic inferences revisited. *NeuroImage, 54*, 4–9.
Mol, L., Krahmer, E., Maes, A., & Swerts, M. (2012). Adaptation in gesture: converging hand or converging minds? *Journal of Memory and Language, 66*, 249–264.
Montague, P. R., Berns, G. S., Cohen, J. D., McClure, S. M., Pagnoni, G., Dhamala, M., Wiest, M. C., Karpov, I., King, R. D., Apple, N., & Fisher, R. E. (2002). Hyperscanning: simultaneous fMRI during linked social interactions. *NeuroImage, 16*, 1159–1164.

Mook, D. G. (1983). In defense of external invalidity. *American Psychologist, 38*, 379–387.

Munhall, K. G. (2001). Functional imaging during speech production. *Acta Psychologica, 107*, 95–117.

Noordzij, M. L., Newman-Norlund, S. E., de Ruiter, J. P., Hagoort, P., Levinson, S. C., & Toni, I. (2009). Brain mechanisms underlying human communication. *Frontiers in Human Neuroscience, 3*, 1–13.

Ochsner, K. N. (2004). Current directions in social cognitive neuroscience. *Current Opinion in Neurobiology, 14*, 254–258.

Pfeiffer, U. J., Timmermans, B., Vogeley, K., Frith, C. D., & Schilbach, L. (2013). Towards a neuroscience of social interaction. *Frontiers in Human Neuroscience, 7*, 22. doi: 10.3389/fnhum.2013.00022.

Pickering, M. J., & Garrod, S. (2004). Toward a mechanistic psychology of dialogue. *Behavioral and Brain Sciences, 27*, 169–226.

Przyrembel, M., Smallwood, J., Pauen, M., & Singer, T. (2013). Illuminating the dark matter of social neuroscience: considering the problem of social interaction from philosophical, psychological, and neuroscientific perspectives. *Frontiers in Human Neuroscience, 6*, 190. doi: 10.3389/fnhum.2012.00190.

Pardo, J. S. (2006). On phonetic convergence during conversational interaction. *Journal of the Acoustical Society of America, 119*, 2382–2393.

Richardson, D. C., & Dale, R. (2005). Looking to understand: the coupling between speakers' and listeners' eye movements and its relationship to discourse comprehension. *Cognitive Science, 29*, 1045–1060.

Richardson, D. C., Dale, R., & Kirkham, N. Z. (2007). The art of conversation is coordination: common ground and the coupling of eye movements during dialogue. *Psychological Science, 18*, 407–413.

Saxe, R., & Kanwisher, N. (2003). People thinking about thinking people: the role of the temporo-parietal junction in "theory of mind." *NeuroImage, 19*, 1835–1842.

Sacks, H., Schegloff, E. A., & Jefferson, G. (1974). A simplest systematics for the organization of turn-taking for conversation. *Language, 59*, 696–735.

Sänger, J., Müller, V., & Lindenberger, U. (2012). Intra- and interbrain synchronization and network properties when playing guitar in duets. *Frontiers in Human Neuroscience, 6*, 312. doi: 10.3389/fnhum.2012.00312.

Saito, D. N., Tanabe, H. C., Izuma, K., Hayashi, M. J., Morito, Y., Komeda, H., Uchiyama, H., Kosaka, H., Okazawa, H., Fujibayashi, Y., & Sadato, N. (2010). "Stay tuned": inter-individual synchronization during mutual gaze and joint attention. *Frontiers in Integrative Neuroscience, 3*, 127. doi: 10.3389/fnint.2010.00127.

Schilbach, L., Wohlschlaeger, A. M., Kraemer, N. C., Newen, A., Shah, N. J., Fink, G. R., & Vogeley, K. (2006). Being with virtual others: neural correlates of social interaction. *Neuropsychologia, 44*, 718–730.

Schilbach, L., Timmermans, B., Reddy, V., Costall, A., Bente, G., Schlicht, T., & Vogeley, K. (2013). Toward a second-person neuroscience. *Behavioral and Brain Sciences, 36*, 393–414.

Schippers, M. B., Roebroeck, A., Renken, R., Nanetti, L., & Keysers, C. (2010). Mapping the information flow from one brain to another during gestural communication. *Proceedings of the National Academy of Sciences of the USA, 107,* 9388–9393.

Schober, M. F., & Brennan, S. E. (2003). Processes of interactive spoken discourse: The role of the partner. In A. C. Graesser, M. A. Gernsbacher, & S. R. Goldman (eds.), *Handbook of Discourse Processes* (pp. 123–164). Hillsdale, NJ: Lawrence Erlbaum.

Seth, A. (2007). Granger causality. *Scholarpedia, 2,* 1667. doi: 10.4249/scholarpedia.1667.

Slater, M., Antlye, A., Davison, A., Swapp, D., Guger, C., Barker, C., Pistrang, N., & Sanchez-Vives, M.V. (2006). A virtual reprise of the Stanley Milgram obedience experiments. *PLoS ONE 1,* e39.

Stephens, G. J., Silbert, L. J., & Hasson, U. (2010). Speaker–listener neural coupling underlies successful communication. *Proceedings of the National Academy of Sciences of the USA, 107,* 14 425–14 430.

Suda, M., Takei, Y., Aoyama, Y., Narita, K., Sato, T., Fukuda, M., & Mikuni, M. (2010). Fronto- polar activation during face-to-face conversation: an in situ study using near- infrared spectroscopy. *Neuropsychologia, 48,* 441–447.

Tanenhaus, M. K., & Brown-Schmidt, S. (2008). Language processing in the natural world. In B. C. M. Moore, L. K. Tyler, & W. D. Marslen-Wilson (eds.), *The Perception of Speech: From Sound to Meaning. Philosophical Transactions of the Royal Society, Series B: Biological Sciences, 363,* 1105–1122.

Tognoli, E., Lagarde, J., DeGuzman, G. C., & Kelso, J. A. S. (2007). The phi complex as a neuromarker of human social coordination. *Proceedings of the National Acadeny of Sciences of the USA, 104,* 8190–8195.

van Berkum, J. J. A., Brown, C. M., Zwitserlood, P., Kooijman, V., & Hagoort, P. (2005). Anticipating upcoming words in discourse: evidence from ERPs and reading times. *Journal of Experimental Psychology: Learning, Memory, and Cognition, 31,* 443–467.

van Dijk, T. A., & Kintsch, W. (1983). *Strategies in Discourse Comprehension.* New York: Academic Press.

van Overwalle, F., & Baetens, K. (2009). Understanding others' actions and goals by mirror and mentalizing systems: a meta-analysis. *NeuroImage, 48,* 564–584.

Winkler, I., Haufe, S., & Tangermann, M. (2011). Automatic classification of artifactual ICA-components for artifact removal in EEG signals. *Behavioral and Brain Functions, 7,* 30. doi: 10.1186/1744-9081-7-30.

Zwaan, R. A., & Radvansky, G. A. (1998). Situation models in language comprehension and memory. *Psychological Bulletin, 123,* 162–185.

10 On the generation of shared symbols

Arjen Stolk, Mark Blokpoel, Iris van Rooij, & Ivan Toni

Abstract Despite the multiple semantic ambiguities present in every utterance during natural language use, people are remarkably efficient in establishing mutual understanding. This chapter illustrates how the study of human communication in novel settings provides a window into the mechanisms supporting the human competence to rapidly generate and understand novel shared symbols, capturing the joint construction of meaning across interacting agents. In this chapter, we discuss empirical findings and computational hypotheses generated in the context of an experimentally controlled non-verbal interactive task that throw light on these fundamental properties of human referential communication. The neural evidence reviewed here points to mechanisms shared across interlocutors of a communicative interaction. Those neural mechanisms implement predictions based on presumed knowledge and beliefs of the communicative partner. Computationally, the generation of novel meaningful symbolic representations might rely on cross-domain analogical mappings. Those mappings provide a mechanism for systematically augmenting individual pre-existing representations, adjusting them to the current conversational context.

The communicative use of language

Referential communication is a complex and anomalous instance of biological social interactions (Dawkins & Krebs, 1978; Owings & Morton, 1998). Referential communication is anomalous because it relies on context-dependent behaviors designed to influence the mental state of specific addressees, rather than on stable traits designed by natural selection to reliably influence bystanders (Danchin *et al.*, 2004). Referential communication is complex because each of its behavioral vehicles can carry multiple meanings, and a given meaning can be conveyed by a variety of behaviors. A great deal of effort has been spent in understanding features and rules of the system most frequently used by humans for achieving referential communication, i.e. language (Chomsky, 1995; de Saussure, 1910–1911; Jackendoff, 2002). Although those efforts have undoubtedly improved our understanding of the cognitive structures intrinsic to the language faculty (Hauser,

Chomsky, & Fitch, 2002), considerably less emphasis has been given to defining the cognitive processes that support the communicative use of language (Clark, 1996; Levinson, 2006; Schilbach *et al.*, 2013; Wittgenstein, 1953/2001). This chapter steps into this gap by focusing on our ability to share the meaning of a *novel* symbol, independently from the conventions and additional complexities introduced by linguistic processing (de Ruiter *et al.*, 2010; Galantucci & Garrod, 2011). Although it is often assumed that pre-existing symbols can be shared across interlocutors by simply coding and decoding them, using those symbols requires a computational mechanism powerful enough to mutually negotiate them across communicators (Levinson, 2006). Studying the generation of novel shared symbols provides a *privileged window* into this mechanism: given that novel symbols lack a pre-existing shared representation, jointly establishing their meaning relies on *converging on a common ground of knowledge and beliefs across communicators*, even more so than the meaning of already known words and gestures. As elaborated in the next section, existing accounts cannot explain the exceptional flexibility of human referential communication (when compared to other forms of animal communication), which may underlie our ability to share meanings and create language in the first place (Levinson, 2006). This chapter elaborates on the mechanisms supporting this human faculty, addressing the question of how communicators can design and interpret effective communicative acts. Starting from the premise that the generation of shared symbols depends on inferred knowledge and beliefs of a communicative partner, i.e. conceptual knowledge that accumulates and is adjusted in our minds as we interact, we reason that these mechanisms should be shared by the interlocutors of the communicative exchange and involve conceptual predictions based on a dynamic conversational context. We introduce an interactive experimental platform that induces the generation of shared symbols, and we then discuss empirical findings and computational hypotheses on properties of human referential communication that appear relevant for understanding natural language use.

Existing accounts of human communication

In the late 1940s, communication was formalized by Claude Shannon as an instance of signal transmission (Shannon, 1948). In Shannon's framework, agents can communicate as long as they have the same set of predefined coding-decoding rules. However, that framework does not explain how agents can negotiate those rules. Natural selection can drive organisms towards shared coding-decoding rules across multiple generations (Danchin *et al.*, 2004), but this account does not explain how humans can rapidly disambiguate situations lacking predefined coding–decoding rules. This is not an exceptional situation. In fact, we achieve this feat during most daily conversations, when learning a language as infants, or when communicating with others in the absence of a common idiom (Levinson, 2006; Noordzij *et al.*, 2010). Even words used during natural dialogue do not contain fixed meanings – they may provide us with clues to a communicative meaning – but are coordinated through an interactive process by which people in dialogue seek and provide evidence that they understand one another (Brennan, Galati, & Kuhlen, 2010; Hofstadter & Sander, 2013). For instance, when a customer asks a bartender "Could you prepare a Margarita?", the bartender is not likely to pause wondering why the customer is questioning his skills, and the customer would not be puzzled by a logically unrelated answer like "Happy Hour starts in five minutes."

Studies on natural dialogue and recent reports in controlled experimental situations (de Ruiter *et al.*, 2010; Galantucci, 2005; Scott-Phillips, Kirby, & Ritchie, 2009) have shown that humans quickly develop new symbols when they need to, for instance novel shapes on a digitizing pad to communicate to another agent a location within a digital environment (Galantucci, 2005). However, it remains to be explained how those new symbols can be generated in the absence of an *a priori* common code. Computer simulations, using reinforcement-learning algorithms, have shown that communication systems can arise without the presence of common knowledge (Barr, 2004; Kirby & Hurford, 2002; Puglisi, Baronchelli, & Loreto, 2008; Steels, 2003). For instance, two computer agents can share novel symbols by virtue of guesses and explicit performance feedback (Steels, 2003). However, establishing these arbitrary signal–meaning mappings required many thousands of pair-wise interactions. Accordingly, general-purpose learning algorithms like temporal difference (Behrens, Hunt, & Rushworth, 2009) or Hebbian learning (Keysers & Perrett, 2004) do not seem suitable to explain the human ability to quickly grasp a meaning or to design an action that can be understood from scratch (de Ruiter *et al.*, 2010) since those learning algorithms require many trials to converge on statistically relevant features. Other scholars have suggested that human referential communication relies on cognitive modules that are involved only when communication requires it, e.g. when having to "repair" a misunderstanding (Horton & Keysar, 1996; Keysar & Horton, 1998) or when a certain representation is primed (automatically) by the utterance of an interlocutor (Garrod & Pickering, 2004). Further simplifications of this approach have led other scholars to suggest that actions can convey communicative meanings "without any cognitive mediation," by virtue of an automatic sensorimotor mechanism ("mirroring") that link the mental representation of an observed action to the representation of an executed action, and the latter to its outcome

(Rizzolatti & Craighero, 2004). However, those accounts leave unspecified how humans can effectively repair, prime, or "mirror" a communicative action when required, and they remain silent on how we organize our behavior for conveying intentions. Automatic priming, reinforcement learning, or sensorimotor associations might be instrumental in finessing a solution once a communicative action has been drafted, but they do not seem suitable to explain how we can rapidly converge on a shared understanding of a novel symbol. Those symbols, being novel, do not have well-defined priors (Fodor, 2000; Levinson, 2006; Sperber & Wilson, 2001) and dedicated neuronal circuits for unpacking their references (Giese & Poggio, 2003; Peelen, Fei-Fei, & Kastner, 2009).

Accordingly, the generation of shared symbols requires a mechanism that allows us to rapidly converge on a shared meaning, constraining a potentially infinite cognitive search space of mappings between symbols and their possible interpretations (or meanings). We suggest that this mechanism should be shared by interlocutors of the communicative exchange and, in order to alter an interlocutor's mental state in a predictable manner, should involve predictions based on presumed knowledge and beliefs of that specific interlocutor, conceptual knowledge that needs to be continuously updated and sharpened according to the shared history of the interaction (Brennan *et al.*, 2010; Clark, 1996). This account is closely linked to accounts of human social abilities based on the theory-of-mind framework (Frith & Frith, 2006; Premack & Woodruff, 1978). In this framework, the assumption is that behavior is the observable product of mental states, and making inferences about these mental states ("mentalizing": Frith & Frith, 2012) requires knowledge of their content and relationship with behavioral responses (Nichols & Stich, 2003). This concept-based account of our mentalizing abilities has been linked with cerebral structures that are distinct from the sensorimotor system, and include the superior temporal sulcus, the temporo-parietal junction, the temporal poles, and the medial prefrontal cortex (Amodio & Frith, 2006; Frith & Frith, 1999, 2006; Grezes, Frith, & Passingham, 2004; Walter *et al.*, 2004). Unfortunately, the majority of imaging studies investigating theory-of-mind have been conducted in non-interactive settings. In those settings, participants read or view story scenarios that trigger reasoning about the mental state of story characters (Saxe *et al.*, 2004). To date, the specific functions of the so-called "theory-of-mind network" remain unknown. Furthermore, the theory-of-mind framework is theoretically heterogeneous (Carruthers, 1996; Leslie, Friedman, & German, 2004; Nichols & Stich, 2003) and it remains to be seen whether and how theory-of-mind mechanisms play a role in genuine social interaction (Schilbach *et al.*, 2013).

Novel shared symbols as a privileged window into communicative interactions

The central tenet of this chapter is that the study of the generation of shared symbols provides a privileged view into the mechanisms of human communication, capturing the joint construction of meaning across interacting agents, contingent on the interaction dynamics. Unveiling the fundamental properties of human referential communication requires experimental procedures that capture these principles of human interaction, rather than the use of conventional linguistic representations. One way to address this issue is to generate experimental situations in which people need to communicate independently from the speech and gestures that are often used as behavioral vehicles for those mental representations. Novel symbols, like new words and gestures, are tokens that may represent and be used to convey ideas and beliefs while their meaning becomes shared between interlocutors. Studying how people generate shared novel symbols (technically known as "experimental semiotics": Galantucci & Garrod, 2011) therefore may provide a window into the mechanisms supporting the human competence to rapidly generate and understand communicative actions.

An experimental platform suitable for studying human communicative interaction requires that it is simple enough to be abstracted in computational models and neurophysiological experiments. Yet, it needs to be sufficiently flexible to capture non-trivial aspects of human communication. Several human communicative games have been developed and studied (Camerer, 2003; Feiler & Camerer, 2010; Galantucci, 2005; Scott-Phillips *et al.*, 2009; Selten & Warglien, 2007), with the Tacit Communication Game (de Ruiter *et al.*, 2010) being one of the few that has been studied from both a computational and neuroscientific perspective (Blokpoel *et al.*, 2011; Noordzij *et al.*, 2009; Stolk, Verhagen *et al.*, 2013). In this communication game, interlocutors do not have access to pre-existing conventions (e.g. a common language, body emblems, facial expressions) that may provide clues to the meaning of a symbol. The only available communicative vehicle consists of geometric shape movements, controlled by and visible to both players on a game board. This novel medium enforces the participant pairs to mutually negotiate novel symbols over the course of the task, effectively creating a new communication system. Consequently, the same symbol can be used by different communicative pairs to negotiate different meanings. The same symbol can even be used to convey different meanings by the same pair at different points in time, and vice versa (for examples see movies in Stolk, Verhagen *et al.*, 2013). These observations emphasize how, in this task, a symbol acquires meaning, in part, by virtue of the history of the communicative interactions within a given pair.

The goal of the communication game is for pairs of participants – labeled as a "Communicator" and an "Addressee" throughout this chapter – to jointly re-create a spatial configuration of two geometric shapes shown only to the Communicator (see the thought cloud in Plate 10.1A, and event 2 in Plate 10.1B – in color plate section). This requires the Communicator to use the movements of his shape (in blue, event 3 in Plate 10.1B) to indicate to the Addressee how she should configure her shape (in orange). There are no *a priori* correct solutions to this communicative task, nor exists a limited set of options from which the Communicator can choose. The Addressee cannot solve the communicative task by reproducing the movements of the Communicator's shape. Rather, she needs to disambiguate communicative and instrumental components of the Communicator's movements, and find some relationship between the shape movements, i.e. the symbol, and their meaning. Success in this game thus relies on the Communicator designing a symbol that can be understood by the Addressee (for instance a "wiggle" to indicate a shape's orientation: Plate 10.1B), and on the Addressee inferring the Communicator's intentions. Participants turn out to be remarkably successful communicators under these constrained conditions (de Ruiter *et al.*, 2010). Given that they do not have access to pre-existing conventions, the participant pairs need to take into account the presumed beliefs and knowledge of their interlocutors when selecting and interpreting novel symbols as Communicators and Addressees respectively. Manipulation of the task structure shows that game performance (i.e. number of spatial configurations successfully re-created by the two players) improves when Communicators are able to see the Addressees' behaviors (event 5 in Plate 10.1B), suggesting that they take into account how Addressees interpreted their messages (de Ruiter *et al.*, 2010). This interpretation is reinforced by another study (Blokpoel *et al.*, 2012) showing that changes in the Communicators' movement characteristics after a misinterpretation of the Addressees are dependent on the nature of the error made by the Addressee. If an Addressee had placed her shape in an incorrect location, but with correct orientation, the Communicator tended to pause relatively longer on the Addressee's goal location. Such change in behavior is intended to indicate that a long pause should be interpreted as being dissociated from the rest of the movement, making it in effect less ambiguous for the Addressee which of the locations on the board was marked by the Communicator as the Addressee's goal location. This behavior cannot be explained by an appeal to a simple heuristic "if location in error then pause longer," because Communicators did not pause longer when both location and orientation were in error. Rather, in those cases, Communicators understood the error was produced by a different type of misunderstanding on the part of the Addressee, leading Communicators to adjust their movement differently.

In sum, the communication game induces the generation of symbols that pertain to the inferred knowledge of the communicative partner. Within this task, communicative difficulty is easy to manipulate, using different combinations of shapes (for examples see Blokpoel *et al.*, 2012). Furthermore, it allows manipulating common ground knowledge across communicators, by having pairs encounter problems for which they previously had jointly established a solution. In this chapter, we discuss empirical findings and computational hypotheses in the context of this interactive task that throw light on the fundamental properties of human referential communication. We start by giving an overview of evidence from patient studies which show how neurological lesions may lead to alterations of communicative abilities.

Neurological alterations of communicative interactions

Clinical and experimental observations have clearly indicated that patients with severe damage to the language system can retain their communicative abilities (Goodwin, 2006; Willems *et al.*, 2011). In contrast, patients with right-hemisphere damage have been reported to have difficulties with conversational components of language (Sabbagh, 1999). The latter difficulties pertain to language use that requires an appreciation of non-literal speaker's intentions, as in the cases of sarcasm, indirect requests, metaphors, and humor interpretation (thus outside the domains of standard syntactical, phonological, or semantical levels of linguistic processing).

Another source of information on neural structures supporting our social interactive abilities comes from patients suffering frontotemporal dementia (FTD), a deterioration of the ventral base of the frontal lobe progressing towards the anterior temporal lobes (Snowden, Neary, & Mann, 2002). The analyses of the neurobiology of these patients reveal that intrinsically motivated social relationships are affected when the frontal lobe and right temporal pole degenerate (Fiske, 2010). The behavioral variant of FTD (bvFTD), also referred to as frontal variant FTD (fvFTD), is associated with a lack of insight, as when patients fail to recognize that anything is wrong with their behaviors (Avineri, 2010). The patient is able to reason about social rules even though the same patient has difficulty putting these rules into action (Mikesell, 2010). In a similar vein, patients can understand that others can have different beliefs but perform badly when asked about the emotional state of another person (Mates, 2010). Social deficits may be seen during conversational exchanges where a patient is unable to keep track of events occurring during the interaction, and thus is unable to hold a coherent conversation. Semantic dementia, also referred to as temporal variant FTD (tvFTD), is associated with predominantly temporal lobe atrophy, typically greater in the left than in the right hemisphere (Weder *et al.*, 2007). Studies involving semantic dementia patients show that the anterior temporal lobes are important for accessing knowledge of coherent concepts (Lambon Ralph *et al.*, 2010). When these patients are shown a picture of a cat and are asked to point out other related items from a list, they point to photos of animals sharing superficial features with the cat, rather than conceptual similarities. For instance, the patients might include furry and long-tailed animals, and exclude tigers and lions. Taken together, these observations might suggest a degree of specialization between temporal and frontal contributions to human communication. The anterior temporal lobes might be particularly relevant for processing coherent concepts, whereas the frontal cortex might be involved in putting this conceptual knowledge into action as when social behaviors are guided by mental models of other agents. This suggestion fits with evidence obtained in patients with lesions in the ventromedial prefrontal cortex (vmPFC), a brain region consistently found more activated in functional imaging studies by tasks that rely on theory of mind than tasks that do not (Amodio & Frith, 2006). Evidence from lesion studies corroborates these findings, indicating that the vmPFC is a critical part of a network of neural structures important for taking into account the mental states of other people during decision-making (Bechara *et al.*, 1994; Kalbe *et al.*, 2010; Shamay-Tsoory, Aharon-Peretz, & Perry, 2009; Shamay-Tsoory *et al.*, 2003; Stone, Baron-Cohen, & Knight, 1998). Similarly to the consequences of frontal lobe atrophy in FTD, brain injury in the vmPFC is associated with a constellation of symptoms which include impulsivity, perseveration, and compulsive behaviors (Damasio, 1994), and vmPFC patients also seem unaware of their socially inappropriate behavior. Yet, the same patients are able to recognize that their behavior is inappropriate when they view their own behavior on video (Beer *et al.*, 2006). A related finding comes from another study in which participants needed to press a left or right key for discriminating between male/female names and strong/weak words. Healthy participants typically become slower in the incongruent condition in which the same key is mapped to stereotypically incompatible stimuli, e.g. male names and weak words, or female names and strong words. Patients with vmPFC lesion do not show this response bias on this implicit task, but their performance is matched to controls when making explicit judgments regarding gender-related stereotypical attributes, suggesting that their stereotypical knowledge is still intact (Milne & Grafman, 2001).

These and other studies have led to the suggestions that the vmPFC serves a unitary underlying function, namely to access and mediate model-based representations of the (social) environment to infer meaning, which might be used by other brain regions involved in processes related to decision-making (Euston, Gruber, & McNaughton, 2012; Jones *et al.*, 2012; Krueger, Barbey, & Grafman, 2009; Roy, Shohamy, & Wager, 2012; Schoenbaum *et al.*, 2009). Accordingly, damage to the vmPFC region interferes with patients' avoidance of unsavory others (e.g. using the scarf of a busker – requiring stereotype representations), but not of contaminating objects (Ciaramelli *et al.*, 2013). The moral judgments of patients with vmPFC lesions also seem particularly sensitive to a harmful outcome of a social interaction, rather than to the underlying intention of the agent (Ciaramelli, Braghittoni, & di Pellegrino, 2012). This observation also fits with the notion that the vmPFC is crucial for incorporating model-based representations of the agent into the decision process. Accordingly, it might be expected that the vmPFC is crucially involved in adjusting behaviors to a mental model of an interlocutor during interaction. Using a version of the communication game outlined in the previous section, we tested whether vmPFC patients spontaneously adjust their behavior according to their beliefs of an Addressee's cognitive abilities. Healthy and lesion control participants spent longer on communicatively relevant locations of the game board when they believed to be interacting with a child, as compared to an adult Addressee. The vmPFC patients were able to communicate as effectively as the control groups, but they did not adjust their communicative behavior to the characteristics of the presumed Addressee (A. Stolk, D. D'Imperio, G. di Pellegrino, & I. Toni, unpublished data). Furthermore, although patients clearly detected communicative errors and adjusted to those errors by moving slower in the subsequent trial, they did not adjust their communicative behavior to the cause of the error. For instance, they failed to make the communicatively relevant location more discriminable from other visited locations of the game board to the Addressee. These findings suggest that patients are still able to produce communicative actions, but they are not able to take into account the inferred knowledge and beliefs of their interlocutor when doing so. In contrast, testing verbal communication in patients with vmPFC lesions did not reveal differences from healthy controls. Namely, there were similar reductions in time and words used for verbal referential descriptions during a collaborative referencing task (Gupta, Tranel, & Duff, 2012). Taken together, these findings suggest that the vmPFC is necessary for using a mental model of an interlocutor. In contrast, interactions based on verbal material might bypass those models and rely on purely linguistic phenomena, e.g. an increased accessibility of syntactic and semantic nets sharpened by their recent use in the communicative interactions (Sass *et al.*, 2009; Segaert *et al.*, 2012).

Neural mechanisms of communicative interactions

Evidence from patient studies indicates an important role for the frontal and temporal lobes in supporting our communicative abilities. Functional imaging studies probing human theory-of-mind abilities corroborate these findings, showing consistent involvement of brain regions in the frontal and temporal lobes, including the superior temporal sulcus, the temporo-parietal junction, the temporal poles, and the medial prefrontal cortex (Amodio & Frith, 2006; Frith & Frith, 1999, 2006; Grezes *et al.*, 2004; Saxe *et al.*, 2004; Vogeley *et al.*, 2001; Walter *et al.*, 2004). As mentioned earlier, the majority of imaging studies that aimed to probe this theory-of-mind network has been conducted in non-interactive settings in which participants read or view story scenarios that trigger the participant to reason about the story character's belief (e.g. Saxe *et al.*, 2004). To date, the exact roles of the distinct brain regions involved in the theory-of-mind network during genuine communicative interaction remain unknown. Similar to sensorimotor simulation theory (Rizzolatti & Craighero, 2004), the theory-of-mind framework remains silent on how we organize our behavior for conveying intentions. For instance, it is still unknown whether, and if so how, these brain regions even support the human ability to generate novel shared symbols, a fundamental property of human referential communication. In this section, we discuss recent findings that may throw light on these issues.

To investigate whether the mechanisms supporting the human ability to share novel symbols are involved both when generating and understanding novel symbols, Noordzij and colleagues (Noordzij *et al.*, 2009) recorded brain activity with fMRI from one subject of each pair interacting within the communication game. As indicated in a previous section, in this interactive task pairs have to solve communicative problems involving the joint re-creation of a spatial configuration of two geometric shapes, shown to one of the players only. In a first experiment, participants either generated novel symbols to convey to Addressees where and how to position their shapes (as Communicators, event 2 in Plate 10.1B), or they generated identical symbols but with no communicative necessity (non-communicative control). Namely, in this experimental condition it was made explicit to them that their Addressees also saw the spatial goal configuration so there was no need for them to consider their interlocutors when generating those symbols. In a second experiment, participants observed novel symbols generated by their Communicators to infer their meanings (as Addressees, event 3 in Plate 10.1B), or to keep track of the location where the Communicators last moved their shape twice (non-communicative control). Contrasting neural activation in each communicative condition with that evoked during their respective controls, they found that generating (by Communicators) and understanding novel symbols (by Addressees) relied on spatially overlapping portions of their brains (the right posterior superior temporal sulcus – pSTS). Furthermore, the hemodynamic response of this region was strongly modulated by the ambiguity in meaning of the communicative acts, but not by the sensorimotor complexity of those acts. This finding does not fit with the suggestion that our communicative abilities are supported by automatic sensorimotor resonances between a sender of a message and its receiver (Keysers & Perrett, 2004; Rizzolatti & Craighero, 2004). Instead, this study provides a first indication for a computational overlap between generating and understanding novel shared symbols, involving processes that fall outside the sensorimotor and linguistic domain.

To implement a more stringent and informative test of the computational overlap hypothesis, we used magnetoencephalography (MEG), a technique that allows one to characterize temporal and spectral dimensions of neural activity, besides the spatial distribution of that activity. Studying the neural dynamics of the predicted overlap between generating and understanding novel shared symbols also gives rise to the possibility of exploring whether these processes rely on a cognitive set implemented through tonic neural activity, or on phasic processes related to low-level features of the stimulus material. We therefore had pairs of participants engage in live communicative interactions. Communicative difficulty increased over the course of the experiment, in order to have the pairs continuously (re)negotiate meanings of symbols, a core element of daily dialogue. Neural activity was measured from one participant of each communicative pair, alternating between the role of Communicator and Addressee on a trial-by-trial basis, and distinguished from activity evoked during another interactive game that involved the same stimuli, responses, attention, and between-participant dependencies but no communicative necessities (Stolk, Verhagen *et al.*, 2013). Namely, in this non-communicative control interaction, the same participants solved their individual problems following learned rules. During communicative interactions, two brain regions exhibited significantly stronger signal power, most pronounced around 55–85 Hz (gamma band). This effect emerged from a broadband spectral change in neural activity over vmPFC and right temporal cortex, and it was present when participants were generating as well as understanding novel shared symbols (Plate 10.2 in color plate section).

Further characterization of the overlap, using an absolute index of neural activity (i.e. source-reconstructed time-resolved estimates of gamma-band activity: Gross *et al.*, 2001), revealed three important features of the underlying neural dynamics. First, sharing the meaning of novel symbols relies on processes with a surprisingly matched phasic temporal dynamics as during non-communicative control interactions (cf. color and gray traces in Plate 10.2). This finding argues against computational modules that are exclusively and sufficiently dedicated to social cognition (Adolphs, 2009). Second, the tonic upregulation of neural activity across Communicator and Addressee was present well before the occurrence of a specific communicative problem (during baseline epochs), with baseline neural activity in the right temporal lobe (TL in Plate 10.2) predicting task performance in an upcoming event (see Figure 4 of Stolk, Verhagen *et al.*, 2013). This finding supports the notion that crucial cognitive elements of human communication are not stimulus-locked. Rather, conceptual knowledge abstracted from the history of communicative interactions needs to be continuously aligned to the current conversational context (Clark, 1996). Third, there were distinct temporal profiles of neural activity in those regions with overlapping increases in gamma-band activity during generation and comprehension of novel shared symbols. A ventrolateral portion of the right temporal lobe (TL, Plate 10.2) showed a tonic upregulation of neural activity, but without clear transient responses time-locked to the sensorimotor events occurring during those epochs. The ventromedial prefrontal cortex (vmPFC, Plate 10.2) showed decreases in neural activity when participants observed actions in both the communicative and non-communicative tasks and increases when participants started planning their actions. This pattern fits with the recent observation that this region is crucial for guiding our (communicative) decisions with inferred knowledge and beliefs of a communicative partner (A. Stolk, D. D'Imperio, G. di Pellegrino, & I. Toni, unpublished data). The right posterior superior temporal sulcus (pSTS, Plate 10.2) is sensitive to computational demands that occur early in planning and that rise during action observation, i.e. with presentation of new stimulus material.

Previous work has highlighted the right pSTS as an important element of the cerebral system supporting human referential communication, both for Communicators generating novel symbols as well as for Addressees trying to understand those symbols (de Langavant *et al.*, 2011; Gao, Scholl, & McCarthy, 2012; Mashal *et al.*, 2007; Noordzij *et al.*, 2009,

2010). However, the exact contributions of this region, let alone the necessity, to human communicative interaction remain unknown. Namely, the involvement of the right pSTS in establishing shared symbols is one among several contributions associated with this region, including the perception of biological motion and goal-directed actions, moral judgments, and mental state attribution (Arfeller *et al.*, 2013; Bahnemann *et al.*, 2010; Grossman, Battelli, & Pascual-Leone, 2005; Schultz *et al.*, 2005; Shultz *et al.*, 2011). Presumably, this heterogeneity might reflect superficial differences of an underlying unitary function. The neural dynamics indicate that right pSTS is also upregulated as a function of the cognitive set (already before the occurrence of stimulus material), but with clear transient responses to incoming visual information (see Plate 10.2), suggesting that this region might be involved in the integration of stimulus material with priors (Jakobs *et al.*, 2012). Accordingly, we reasoned that these priors could capture (1) statistical regularities of the sensory stimuli experienced by the participants (Iacoboni, 2005; Schippers *et al.*, 2010; Tognoli *et al.*, 2007; Turesson & Ghazanfar, 2011); (2) conceptual predictions based on semantic conventions (Schultz *et al.*, 2005; Wyk *et al.*, 2009; Young *et al.*, 2010); or (3) conceptual predictions based on a dynamic conversational context shared among communicators (Menenti, Pickering, & Garrod, 2012). To test these hypotheses, we used low-frequency repetitive transcranial magnetic stimulation (rTMS) to perturb functioning of this region while participants observed novel symbols generated by their communicators to infer their meanings (Boroojerdi *et al.*, 2000; Mottaghy *et al.*, 2002). We found that general task performance was not affected by rTMS, whereas task-learning was disrupted according to TMS site and task combinations. Namely, rTMS over pSTS led to a diminished ability to improve understanding of those novel symbols on the basis of the recent communicative history, while rTMS over MT+, a contiguous homotopic control region involved in integrating position information when viewing moving objects, perturbed improvement over trials in visual tracking (non-communicative control) of exactly the same time series of stimuli used in the communicative setting (Stolk, Noordzij, Volman *et al.*, 2013). This finding increases our understanding of the neural mechanisms of human communication by showing that the right pSTS, in contrast to MT+, is necessary for continuously adjusting conceptual predictions (hypothesis #3) according to the recent history of interactions of the communicators, over and above the statistical regularities of the sensory stimuli experienced by the participants (that are also present in the control task). The task-, region-, and learning-specific effect observed in this study suggests that human communicative abilities operate on conceptual inferences, rather than sensorimotor brain-to-brain couplings (Hasson *et al.*, 2012), and that those conceptual inferences are continuously updated. It remains to be seen whether the right pSTS supports the dynamic updating of communicative inferences also when communication relies on linguistic material with strongly established semantic conventions (Mitchell *et al.*, 2009; van Ackeren *et al.*, 2012; Willems *et al.*, 2010).

The neural evidence reviewed thus far points to mechanisms that are shared by interlocutors of the communicative exchange, and that involve flexible conceptual priors based on the shared history of interactions of communicators rather than statistical regularities in the stimulus material. However, it remains unclear how this conceptual knowledge is shared among communicators in the first place. The neuronal computations supporting this ability might be synchronized across interlocutors by the symbols used during a communicative interaction (Hari *et al.*, 2013; Hasson *et al.*, 2012; Rizzolatti & Craighero, 2004). Alternatively, the conversational meta-knowledge shared across a pair of interlocutors might be neuronally implemented over temporal scales independent from individual communicative events (Stolk, Verhagen *et al.*, 2013). We addressed this issue in another study, using fMRI to simultaneously record brain activation in pairs of participants building a pair-specific conversational context across multiple communicative interactions (Stolk, Noordzij, Verhagen *et al.*, 2013). During these interactions, participants solved communicative problems for which the pairs already had established common ground and communicative problems in which common ground yet had to be established. We observed that as common ground emerged within a pair of interlocutors, activity in the right superior temporal gyrus (STG) also increased, during both production and comprehension of a communicative action. To investigate whether the emergence of common ground, neuroanatomically supported by right STG, was specific to the context and participants of the interaction, we applied a methodology originally refined in electrophysiology, spectral coherence analysis, to the fMRI time series and contrasted the joint neural dynamics evoked within pairs with those evoked in participants from different pairs. This analysis showed a significantly stronger within-than between-pair coherence at frequencies lower than the dominant experimental frequency and with zero phase-lag, indicating a temporal synchronization of blood-oxygen-level dependent (BOLD) changes in right STG that was specific for elements of a communicative pair, and over a timescale spanning several communicative interactions (25–100 seconds, whereas one interaction lasted ~20 seconds). These findings indicate that sharing conceptual knowledge among communicators relies on conceptual operations shared across participants of a communicative pair, and superseding individual communicative symbols.

In sum, the work outlined thus far shows that participants can successfully share novel symbols in the absence of an *a priori* common code (e.g. a common language). This work also shows that the generation of shared symbols upregulates the same neuronal mechanism in the same brain regions across pairs of communicators, and over temporal scales independent from transient sensorimotor events. This finding indicates that the communicative meaning of a symbol arises from the (pair-specific) conversational context rather than from the stimulus material itself. Mechanistically, the meaning of novel shared symbols might be rapidly inferred by embedding those symbols in a conceptual space whose activation predates in time the processing of the symbols themselves (van Berkum *et al.*, 2008). This conceptual knowledge thus needs to be continuously aligned to the conversational context (Clark, 1996). Taken together, the current neural evidence suggests that jointly establishing meaning, a feature crucial for human communication, relies on *knowledge and beliefs knowingly shared and updated* between the communicators during the course of their interactions. Currently, it is still an open question how novel meaning is found, and mapped onto a symbol. In the next section, we elaborate on computational processes that might support our abilities to engage in communicative interaction and to share novel symbols.

Computational features of communicative interactions

The overall ability to generate and interpret novel communicative acts arguably relies on a large number of cognitive functions, ranging from object recognition to theory-of-mind. Thinking of the cognitive operations germane to the generation of novel shared symbols, three functions seem to stand out: *parsing*, *perspective-taking*, and *meaning-mapping*. To grasp a meaning, an Addressee minimally needs to parse a signal into communicative and instrumental parts and then infer the meaning of the communicative parts. To convey a meaning, a Communicator needs to reason about how the Addressee will parse and interpret a signal, through some form of perspective-taking (Blokpoel *et al.*, 2012; van Rooij *et al.*, 2011). These functions, parsing and perspective-taking, are arguably also involved in communicative interactions that rely on pre-existing conventions. The same holds for meaning-mapping, but this process seems to be more heavily taxed during communicative exchanges in which novel symbols have to be created and understood. In this section we will focus on this meaning-mapping process.

A characterizing feature of meaning-mapping, both in everyday conversation as well as in the communication game used in our neuroscientific research, is that addressees can often infer the intended meaning of a new symbol on first encounter or otherwise within a few trials (de Ruiter *et al.*, 2010; Volman, Noordzij, & Toni, 2012). This phenomenon cannot be easily accommodated by traditional reinforcement learning theories (Kaelbling, Littman, & Moore, 1996), game theories (Osborne, 2004), fast and frugal heuristics (Gigerenzer, 2008), or Bayesian models (Tenenbaum, Griffiths, & Kemp, 2006). Those models require either *a priori* internal models of all possible novel signals (i.e. the models have meanings of symbols built in as conventions), or an unrealistically large number of training trials (Steels, 2003). An alternative account that does not seem to suffer from these problems can be found in structure mapping theory, or analogical reasoning (Gentner, 1983; Gentner, 2003). In analogical reasoning, one uses representations of the relational structure of concepts to find *analogical matches* between different concepts (e.g. "the atom is like a solar system, with electrons circling the nucleus in much the same way as planets circle the sun"). Based on such matches, one can then *transfer knowledge* from a base concept to a target, generating new concepts (e.g. "perhaps the revolving of electrons is caused by the attraction of the nucleus like the revolving of the planets is caused by attraction of the sun"). This kind of reasoning seems to meet the computational requirements for fast, even one-trial, learning. Using a case study from the communication game, we will illustrate how analogical reasoning can, in principle, explain how Communicators can generate novel symbols whose meaning can be correctly inferred by Addressees on first encounter.

To be able to explain how movements made by Communicators in the communication game can take on novel meanings that Addressees can understand quickly, we will make the plausible assumption that players share considerable amounts of general world knowledge, i.e. everyday knowledge that the players have both acquired outside the context of the communication game. For instance, in our case study we will assume that players have basic geometric knowledge (e.g. concepts of "circle," "triangle," "frame of reference," "line," "point," etc.) as well as basic concepts of motion such as "direction," "speed," etc. To use this knowledge to infer the meaning of the movement depicted in Plate 10.3 (see color plate section) (bottom; what we refer to as a "wiggle"), multiple inferential steps are necessary. Each step in this inferential process gradually builds more sophisticated, abstract (and potentially novel) representations of the observed movements such that at some point the meaning becomes evident. The inferential steps involve what we call *analogical augmentations*: by finding analogies between specific observations and non-game-specific knowledge, one can augment the raw observations into more and more abstract representations of location and orientation. For instance, we can represent the transition between two consecutive positions of the circle as "like (drawing) a line" (Plate 10.3, top). This analogy may seem quite trivial. In fact, it involves representing the positions of the circle and the relations between these positions, e.g. the circle is now "right_of" its previous position. Furthermore, this analogy requires the knowledge that a line is a relation between two positions that have a spatial relationship (e.g. "right_of"). Only then can an analogical match be found, viz. between the positions and relationships, to transfer the relation "line" onto the observed circle positions. Those abstract representations of location and orientation can eventually analogically match to the representation of the triangle, allowing the Addressee to infer its location and orientation. Note that, given different representations and knowledge, widely different meaning mappings become possible. This is consistent with the diversity of strategies observed in players of the communication game (Blokpoel *et al.*, 2012; de Ruiter *et al.*, 2010).

The computational account of meaning-mapping that we roughly outlined above and in Plate 10.3 illustrates that there are computationally sufficient mechanisms for generating and understanding novel symbols. Unlike most standard learning models, these mechanisms involve various forms of analogical reasoning. That is, to generate novel meaningful symbolic representations one needs to be able to systematically augment one's representations such that these representations support cross-domain analogical mappings. In the case of the communication game we illustrated that this involves analogical mappings between the domains of geometry and motion. Given that for any given pair of representations there may exist augmentation paths that lead to analogical matches, the model outlined here may best be seen as a meaning *hypothesizer*. That is, it defines the set of candidate meanings for a given signal, without specifying how people select the most plausible or probable meaning from the set of candidate meanings. Combining an analogy-based model with rational, probabilistic, or coherentist models might offer a more complete picture (Thagard, 1989; van Rooij *et al.*, 2011).

Conclusions

This chapter elaborates on neurobiological and computational mechanisms supporting the generation of novel shared symbols. Functional imaging data, supported by the observation of consequences of brain injury and transient interference with brain function, highlight a fundamental role for right temporal and ventromedial prefrontal brain regions in the coordination among interlocutors during referential communication. Empirical evidence obtained in an interactive communicative setting shows that generating and comprehending novel shared symbols upregulates the same neuronal mechanisms in cortical regions known to be crucial for processing conceptual knowledge, across pairs of communicators, and over temporal scales independent from transient sensorimotor events (Stolk, Verhagen *et al.*, 2013). In fact, the neural dynamics observed in the right superior temporal gyrus suggest that those conceptual operations may span multiple communicative exchanges, temporally synchronized within a communicating pair, and modulated when novel knowledge is generated among the interlocutors (Stolk, Noordzij, Verhagen *et al.*, 2013). We suggest that the right posterior superior temporal sulcus supports our ability to benefit from recent communicative experiences with a communicative partner (Stolk, Noordzij, Volman *et al.*, 2013). The ventromedial prefrontal cortex seems crucial for taking into account inferred knowledge and beliefs of the interlocutor when choosing from a set of possible communicative options (A. Stolk, D. D'Imperio, G. di Pellegrino, & I. Toni, unpublished data). Taken together, the empirical findings and computational considerations suggest that the meaning of a novel symbol arises from a conceptual space dynamically defined by the ongoing interaction, rather than from the stimulus material itself. Plate 10.4 (see color plate section) summarizes these considerations and the main issues addressed in this review.

This review raises a number of outstanding issues that deserve further investigations. The ability to quickly converge on a common ground of knowledge and beliefs across communicators, efficiently building new and reconfiguring existing semiotic conventions, emerges at different levels of human communication, from infants learning a language without access to the local communicative conventions, to adults with purportedly limited communicative means (shape movements on a game board) as in the studies outlined above. The present work indicates that the meaning of novel shared symbols might be rapidly inferred by embedding those symbols in a conceptual space whose activation predates in time the processing of the symbols themselves (van Berkum *et al.*, 2008). Even during a simple conversation, we continuously update and sharpen our (conceptual) priors according to the recent history of the communicative interaction. We present a draft of a computational model that taps directly into the mystery of how the human mind constrains the inferential process that leads to action selection and understanding within communicative interaction. Future studies might shed light on the mechanisms of how representations are constructed from, and integrated with, incoming stimulus material.

Currently, there is a debate as to whether our theory-of-mind abilities can be subdivided in a cognitive component, supporting our abilities to take into account knowledge and beliefs of another agent, and an affective component, supporting our abilities to take into account the feelings of another agent (Gupta *et al.*, 2012; Shamay-Tsoory *et al.*, 2009). Recent investigations from our lab seem to initially support such a dissociation, as when measures of fluid intelligence and systemizing abilities, but not empathy and reward-related tendencies, have been shown to account for significant portions of inter-subject variability in the ability to quickly grasp novel communicative meanings according to recent communicative interactions (Stolk, Noordzij, Volman *et al.*, 2013; Volman *et al.*, 2012). In contrast, empathy scores appear to be more closely related to audience design abilities (Newman-Norlund *et al.*, 2009). Taken together, we suggest that while pro-social attitudes (approximately indexed by empathy) might provide the motivational drive necessary for adjusting communicative behavior to a given agent (Tomasello, 2008), other general-purpose cognitive abilities (approximately indexed by fluid intelligence) might provide the computational tools necessary to cope with the complexity of human referential communication (van Rooij *et al.*, 2011). Studying human development might provide a relevant handle for understanding how those motivational drives and cognitive abilities are implemented and coordinated (Stolk, Hunnius *et al.*, 2013). In a first attempt to address these issues, we have investigated children's ability to influence the mental state of others, and whether these abilities are influenced by the extent and nature of children's social interactions (Carpendale & Lewis, 2004; de Rosnay & Hughes, 2006; Dunn & Shatz, 1989; Hrdy, 2009; Lewis *et al.*, 1996; Perner, Ruffman, & Leekam, 1994). The rationale and focus of this study is quite different from a large body of existing developmental work that has focused on our ability to attribute mental states to others (Baron-Cohen, Leslie, & Frith, 1985; Wellman, Cross, & Watson, 2001). In a nutshell, our work suggested that referential communicative abilities might be bootstrapped within social interaction itself: 5-year-olds' internally generated communicative adjustments to their mental model of an addressee were shaped by their early social experience with other cognitive agents (Stolk, Hunnius *et al.*, 2013). Those findings open the way for systematic and sensitive investigations into the contribution of early social experiences towards children's communicative abilities, raising the possibility to chart the developmental trajectories generated by different sources of social interaction through longitudinal studies with objective measures of the time spent on those interactions. It is known that, in adults, social network size has a positive impact on neural circuits deemed relevant for social cognition, e.g. vmPFC, pSTS, anterior cingulate cortex, and amygdala (Bickart *et al.*, 2011; Kanai *et al.*, 2012; Lewis *et al.*, 2011; Sallet *et al.*, 2011). Accordingly, it appears relevant to explore how brain development is influenced by early social experiences that have an impact on our communicative abilities, and whether such effects are long-lasting.

Finally, it should be emphasized that this review has largely focused on empirical observations obtained in the context of a highly controlled experimental setup, designed to capture one crucial element of communicative interaction, namely sharing meanings of novel symbols extended over several seconds. It remains open for discussion whether this approach is adequate for understanding the theoretical components and the cerebral mechanisms supporting human communication in more naturalistic settings. Certainly, it will be important to test how the present findings generalize to other communicative materials (e.g. linguistic and/or gestural), and to interactive situations where communicative roles can be frequently exchanged, as during natural dialogue.

References

Adolphs, R. (2009). The social brain: neural basis of social knowledge. *Annu Rev Psychol*, *60*, 693–716.

Amodio, D. M., & Frith, C. D. (2006). Meeting of minds: the medial frontal cortex and social cognition. *Nat Rev Neurosci*, *7*(4), 268–277.

Arfeller, C., Schwarzbach, J., Ubaldi, S., Ferrari, P., Barchiesi, G., & Cattaneo, L. (2013). Whole-brain haemodynamic after-effects of 1-Hz magnetic stimulation of the posterior superior temporal cortex during action observation. *Brain Topogr*, *26*(2), 278–291.

Avineri, N. (2010). The interactive organization of "insight": clinical interviews with frontotemporal dementia patients. In A. W. Mates, L. Mikesell, & M. S. Smith (eds.), *Language, Interaction and Frontotemporal Dementia: Reverse Engineering the Social Mind* (pp. 115–138). London: Equinox.

Bahnemann, M., Dziobek, I., Prehn, K., Wolf, I., & Heekeren, H. R. (2010). Sociotopy in the temporoparietal cortex: common versus distinct processes. *Soc Cogni Affect Neurosci*, *5*(1), 48–58.

Baron-Cohen, S., Leslie, A. M., & Frith, U. (1985). Does the autistic child have a "theory of mind"? *Cognition*, *21*(1), 37–46.

Barr, D. J. (2004). Establishing conventional communication systems: is common knowledge necessary? *Cogn Sci*, *28*(6), 937–962.

Bechara, A., Damasio, A. R., Damasio, H., & Anderson, S. W. (1994). Insensitivity to future consequences following damage to human prefrontal cortex. *Cognition*, *50*(1–3), 7–15.

Beer, J. S., John, O. P., Scabini, D., & Knight, R. T. (2006). Orbitofrontal cortex and social behavior: integrating self-monitoring and emotion–cognition interactions. *J Cogn Neurosci*, *18*(6), 871–879.

Behrens, T. E., Hunt, L. T., & Rushworth, M. F. (2009). The computation of social behavior. *Science*, *324*(5931), 1160–1164.
Bickart, K. C., Wright, C. I., Dautoff, R. J., Dickerson, B. C., & Barrett, L. F. (2011). Amygdala volume and social network size in humans. *Nat Neurosci*, *14*(2), 163–164.
Blokpoel, M., Kwisthout, J., Wareham, T., Haselager, P., Toni, I., & Van Rooij, I. (2011). The computational costs of recipient design and intention recognition in communication. Paper presented at the Proceedings of the 33rd Annual Conference of the Cognitive Science Society, Austin, TX.
Blokpoel, M., van Kesteren, M., Stolk, A., Haselager, P., Toni, I., & van Rooij, I. (2012). Recipient design in human communication: simple heuristics or perspective taking? *Frontiers Hum Neurosci*, *6*.
Boroojerdi, B., Prager, A., Muellbacher, W., & Cohen, L. G. (2000). Reduction of human visual cortex excitability using 1-Hz transcranial magnetic stimulation. *Neurology*, *54*(7), A400.
Brennan, S. E., Galati, A., & Kuhlen, A. (2010). Two minds, one dialog: coordinating speaking and understanding. In B. Ross (ed.), *Psychology of Learning and Motivation* (Vol. 53, pp. 301–344). Burlington, MA: Academic Press.
Camerer, C. F. (2003). Behavioural studies of strategic thinking in games. *Trends Cogn Sci*, *7*(5), 225–231.
Carpendale, J. I., & Lewis, C. (2004). Constructing an understanding of mind: the development of children's social understanding within social interaction. *Behav Brain Sci*, *27*(1), 79–96; discussion 96–151.
Carruthers, P. (1996). Simulation and self-knowledge: a defence of theory-theory. In P. Carruthers & P. K. Smith (eds.), *Theories of Theories of Mind* (pp. 22–38). Cambridge: Cambridge University Press.
Chomsky, N. (1995). *The Minimalist Program*. Cambridge, MA: MIT Press.
Ciaramelli, E., Braghittoni, D., & di Pellegrino, G. (2012). It is the outcome that counts! Damage to the ventromedial prefrontal cortex disrupts the integration of outcome and belief information for moral judgment. *J Int Neuropsychol Soc*, *18*(6), 962–971.
Ciaramelli, E., Sperotto, R. G., Mattioli, F., & di Pellegrino, G. (2013). Damage to the ventromedial prefrontal cortex reduces interpersonal disgust. *Soc Cogn Affect Neurosci*, *8*(2), 171–180.
Clark, H. H. (1996). *Using Language*. Cambridge: Cambridge University Press.
Damasio, A. R. (1994). *Descartes' Error*. New York: Putnam.
Danchin, E., Giraldeau, L. A., Valone, T. J., & Wagner, R. H. (2004). Public information: from nosy neighbors to cultural evolution. *Science*, *305*(5683), 487–491.
Dawkins, R., & Krebs, J. (1978). Animals signals: information or manipulation. In J. R. Krebs & N. B. Davies (eds.), *Behavioural Ecology: An Evolutionary Approach* (pp. 282–309). Oxford: Blackwell.
de Langavant, L. C., Remy, P., Trinkler, I., McIntyre, J., Dupoux, E., Berthoz, A., & Bachoud-Levi, A. C. (2011). Behavioral and neural correlates of communication via pointing. *PLoS ONE*, *6*(3).
de Rosnay, M., & Hughes, C. (2006). Conversation and theory of mind: do children talk their way to socio-cognitive understanding? *Br J Devel Psychol*, *24*, 7–37.

de Ruiter, J. P., Noordzij, M. L., Newman-Norlund, S., Newman-Norlund, R., Hagoort, P., Levinson, S. C., & Toni, I. (2010). Exploring the cognitive infrastructure of communication. *Interaction Stud*, *11*(1), 51–77.
de Saussure, F. (1910–1911). *Cours de linguistique générale* [Course in General Linguistics]. Paris: Payot.
Dunn, J., & Shatz, M. (1989). Becoming a conversationalist despite (or because of) having an older ibling. *Child Devel*, *60*(2), 399–410.
Euston, D. R., Gruber, A. J., & McNaughton, B. L. (2012). The role of medial prefrontal cortex in memory and decision making. *Neuron*, *76*(6), 1057–1070.
Feiler, L., & Camerer, C. F. (2010). Code creation in endogenous merger experiments. *Econ Inquiry*, *48*(2), 337–352.
Fiske, A. P. (2010). Dispassionate heuristic rationality fails to sustain social relationships. In A. W. Mates, L. Mikesell, & M. S. Smith (eds.), *Language, Interaction, and Frontotemporal Dementia: Reverse Engineering the Social Mind* (pp. 199–242). London: Equinox.
Fodor, J. A. (2000). *The Mind Doesn't Work That Way*. Cambridge, MA: MIT Press.
Frith, C. D., & Frith, U. (1999). Interacting minds: a biological basis. *Science*, *286*(5445), 1692–1695.
Frith, C. D., & Frith, U. (2006). The neural basis of mentalizing. *Neuron*, *50*(4), 531–534.
Frith, C. D., & Frith, U. (2012). Mechanisms of social cognition. *Annu Rev Psychol*, *63*, 287–313.
Galantucci, B. (2005). An experimental study of the emergence of human communication systems. *Cogn Sci*, *29*(5), 737–767.
Galantucci, B., & Garrod, S. (2011). Experimental semiotics: a review. *Frontiers Hum Neurosci*, *5*, 11.
Gao, T., Scholl, B. J., & McCarthy, G. (2012). Dissociating the detection of intentionality from animacy in the right posterior superior temporal sulcus. *J Neurosci*, *32*(41), 14 276–14 280.
Garrod, S., & Pickering, M. J. (2004). Why is conversation so easy? *Trends Cogn Sci*, *8*(1), 8–11.
Gentner, D. (1983). Structure-mapping: a theoretical framework for analogy. *Cogn Sci*, *7*(2), 155–170.
Gentner, D. (2003). Why we're so smart. In D. Gentner & S. Goldin-Meadow (eds.), *Language in Mind: Advances in the Study of Language and Thought* (pp. 195–235). Cambridge, MA: MIT Press.
Giese, M. A., & Poggio, T. (2003). Neural mechanisms for the recognition of biological movements. *Nat Rev Neurosci*, *4*(3), 179–192.
Gigerenzer, G. (2008). Why heuristics work. *Perspect Psychol Sci*, *3*(1), 20–29.
Goodwin, C. (2006). Human sociality as mutual orientation in a rich interactive environment: multimodal utterances and pointing in aphasia. In N. J. Enfield & S. C. Levinson (eds.), *Roots of Human Sociality* (pp. 97–125). New York: Berg.
Grezes, J., Frith, C. D., & Passingham, R. E. (2004). Inferring false beliefs from the actions of oneself and others: an fMRI study. *NeuroImage*, *21*(2), 744–750.

Gross, J., Kujala, J., Hamalainen, M., Timmermann, L., Schnitzler, A., & Salmelin, R. (2001). Dynamic imaging of coherent sources: studying neural interactions in the human brain. *Proc Natl Acad Sci USA*, *98*(2), 694–699.
Grossman, E. D., Battelli, L., & Pascual-Leone, A. (2005). Repetitive TMS over posterior STS disrupts perception of biological motion. *Vision Res*, *45*(22), 2847–2853.
Gupta, R., Tranel, D., & Duff, M. C. (2012). Ventromedial prefrontal cortex damage does not impair the development and use of common ground in social interaction: implications for cognitive theory of mind. *Neuropsychologia*, *50*(1), 145–152.
Hari, R., Himberg, T., Nummenmaa, L., Hamalainen, M., & Parkkonen, L. (2013). Synchrony of brains and bodies during implicit interpersonal interaction. *Trends Cogn Sci*, *17*(3), 105–106.
Hasson, U., Ghazanfar, A. A., Galantucci, B., Garrod, S., & Keysers, C. (2012). Brain-to-brain coupling: a mechanism for creating and sharing a social world. *Trends Cogn Sci*, *16*(2), 114–121.
Hauser, M. D., Chomsky, N., & Fitch, W. T. (2002). The faculty of language: what is it, who has it, and how did it evolve? *Science*, *298*(5598), 1569–1579.
Hofstadter, D., & Sander, E. (2013). *Surfaces and Essences: Analogy as the Fuel and Fire of Thinking*. New York: Basic Books.
Horton, W. S., & Keysar, B. (1996). When do speakers take into account common ground? *Cognition*, *59*(1), 91–117.
Hrdy, S. B. (2009). *Mothers and Others: The Evolutionary Origins of Mutual Understanding*. Cambridge, MA: Belknap Press of Harvard University Press.
Iacoboni, M. (2005). Neural mechanisms of imitation. *Curr Opin Neurobiol*, *15*(6), 632–637.
Jackendoff, R. (2002). *Foundations of Language: Brain, Meaning, Grammar, Evolution*. Oxford: Oxford University Press.
Jakobs, O., Langner, R., Caspers, S., Roski, C., Cieslik, E. C., Zilles, K., . . . , Eickhoff, S. B. (2012). Across-study and within-subject functional connectivity of a right temporo-parietal junction subregion involved in stimulus-context integration. *NeuroImage*, *60*(4), 2389–2398.
Jones, J. L., Esber, G. R., McDannald, M. A., Gruber, A. J., Hernandez, A., Mirenzi, A., & Schoenbaum, G. (2012). Orbitofrontal cortex supports behavior and learning using inferred but not cached values. *Science*, *338*(6109), 953–956.
Kaelbling, L. P., Littman, M. L., & Moore, A. W. (1996). Reinforcement learning: a survey. *J Artific Intell Res*, *4*, 237–285.
Kalbe, E., Schlegel, M., Sack, A. T., Nowak, D. A., Dafotakis, M., Bangard, C., . . . , Kessler, J. (2010). Dissociating cognitive from affective theory of mind: a TMS study. *Cortex*, *46*(6), 769–780.
Kanai, R., Bahrami, B., Roylance, R., & Rees, G. (2012). Online social network size is reflected in human brain structure. *Proc R SocLond B*, *279*(1732), 1327–1334.
Keysar, B., & Horton, W. S. (1998). Speaking with common ground: from principles to processes in pragmatics: a reply to Polichak and Gerrig. *Cognition*, *66*(2), 191–198.
Keysers, C., & Perrett, D. I. (2004). Demystifying social cognition: a Hebbian perspective. *Trends Cogn Sci*, *8*(11), 501–507.

Kirby, S., & Hurford, J. (2002). The emergence of linguistic structure: an overview of the iterated learning model. In A. Cangelosi & D. Parisi (eds.), *Simulating the Evolution of Language* (pp. 121–148). London: Springer.

Krueger, F., Barbey, A. K., & Grafman, J. (2009). The medial prefrontal cortex mediates social event knowledge. *Trends Cogn Sci*, *13*(3), 103–109.

Lambon Ralph, M. A., Sage, K., Jones, R. W., & Mayberry, E. J. (2010). Coherent concepts are computed in the anterior temporal lobes. *Proc Natl Acad Sci USA*, *107*(6), 2717–2722.

Leslie, A. M., Friedman, O., & German, T. P. (2004). Core mechanisms in "theory of mind." *Trends Cogn Sci*, *8*(12), 528–533.

Levinson, S. C. (2006). On the human interactional engine. In N. Enfield & S. Levinson (eds.), *Roots of Human Sociality* (pp. 39–69). Oxford: Berg.

Lewis, C., Freeman, N. H., Kyriakidou, C., Maridaki-Kassotaki, K., & Berridge, D. M. (1996). Social influences on false belief access: specific sibling influences or general apprenticeship? *Child Devel*, *67*(6), 2930–2947.

Lewis, P. A., Rezaie, R., Brown, R., Roberts, N., & Dunbar, R. I. (2011). Ventromedial prefrontal volume predicts understanding of others and social network size. *NeuroImage*, *57*(4), 1624–1629.

Mashal, N., Faust, M., Hendler, T., & Jung-Beeman, M. (2007). An fMRI investigation of the neural correlates underlying the processing of novel metaphoric expressions. *Brain Lang*, *100*(2), 115–126.

Mates, A. W. (2010). Using social deficits in frontotemporal dementia to develop a neurobiology of person reference. In A. W. Mates, L. Mikesell, & M. S. Smith (eds.), *Language, Interaction and Frontotemporal Dementia: Reverse Engineering the Social Mind* (pp. 139–166). London: Equinox.

Menenti, L., Pickering, M. J., & Garrod, S. C. (2012). Toward a neural basis of interactive alignment in conversation. *Frontiers Hum Neurosci*, *6*, 185.

Mikesell, L. (2010). Examining perservative behaviors of a frontotemporal dementia patient and caregiver responses: the benefits of observing ordinary interactions and reflections on caregiver stress. In A. W. Mates, L. Mikesell, & M. S. Smith (eds.), *Language, Interaction and Frontotemporal Dementia: Reverse Engineering the Social Mind* (pp. 85–114). London: Equinox.

Milne, E., & Grafman, J. (2001). Ventromedial prefrontal cortex lesions in humans eliminate implicit gender stereotyping. *J Neurosci*, *21*(12), RC150.

Mitchell, J. P., Ames, D. L., Jenkins, A. C., & Banaji, M. R. (2009). Neural correlates of stereotype application. *J Cogn Neurosci*, *21*(3), 594–604.

Mottaghy, F. M., Keller, C. E., Gangitano, M., Ly, J., Thall, M., Parker, J. A., & Pascual-Leone, A. (2002). Correlation of cerebral blood flow and treatment effects of repetitive transcranial magnetic stimulation in depressed patients. *Psychiat Res Neuroimaging*, *115*(1–2), 1–147.

Newman-Norlund, S. E., Noordzij, M. L., Newman-Norlund, R. D., Volman, I. A., Ruiter, J. P., Hagoort, P., & Toni, I. (2009). Recipient design in tacit communication. *Cognition*, *111*(1), 46–54.

Nichols, S., & Stich, S. P. (2003). *Mindreading: An Integrated Account of Pretence, Self-Awareness, and Understanding Other Minds*. Oxford: Clarendon Press.

Noordzij, M. L., Newman-Norlund, S. E., de Ruiter, J. P., Hagoort, P., Levinson, S. C., & Toni, I. (2009). Brain mechanisms underlying human communication. *Frontiers Hum Neurosci*, *3*, 14.

Noordzij, M. L., Newman-Norlund, S. E., de Ruiter, J. P., Hagoort, P., Levinson, S. C., & Toni, I. (2010). Neural correlates of intentional communication. *Frontiers Hum Neurosci*, *4*, 188.
Osborne, M. J. (2004). *An Introduction to Game Theory*. New York: Oxford University Press.
Owings, D., & Morton, E. (1998). *Animal Vocal Communication: A New Approach*. New York: Cambridge University Press.
Peelen, M. V., Fei-Fei, L., & Kastner, S. (2009). Neural mechanisms of rapid *natural* scene categorization in human visual cortex. *Nature*, *460*(7251), 94–97.
Perner, J., Ruffman, T., & Leekam, S. R. (1994). Theory of mind is contagious: you catch it from your sibs. *Child Devel*, *65*(4), 1228–1238.
Premack, D., & Woodruff, G. (1978). Does the chimpanzee have a theory of mind? *Behav Brain Sci*, *1*(4), 515–526.
Puglisi, A., Baronchelli, A., & Loreto, V. (2008). Cultural route to the emergence of linguistic categories. *Proc Natl Acad Sci USA*, *105*(23), 7936–7940.
Rizzolatti, G., & Craighero, L. (2004). The mirror-neuron system. *Annu Rev Neurosci*, *27*, 169–192.
Roy, M., Shohamy, D., & Wager, T. D. (2012). Ventromedial prefrontal-subcortical systems and the generation of affective meaning. *Trends Cogn Sci*, *16*(3), 147–156.
Sabbagh, M. A. (1999). Communicative intentions and language: evidence from right-hemisphere damage and autism. *Brain Lang*, *70*(1), 29–69.
Sallet, J., Mars, R. B., Noonan, M. P., Andersson, J. L., O'Reilly, J. X., Jbabdi, S., . . . , Rushworth, M. F. (2011). Social network size affects neural circuits in macaques. *Science*, *334*(6056), 697–700.
Sass, K., Krach, S., Sachs, O., & Kircher, T. (2009). Lion – tiger – stripes: neural correlates of indirect semantic priming across processing modalities. *NeuroImage*, *45*(1), 224–236.
Saxe, R., Xiao, D. K., Kovacs, G., Perrett, D. I., & Kanwisher, N. (2004). A region of right posterior superior temporal sulcus responds to observed intentional actions. *Neuropsychologia*, *42*(11), 1435–1446.
Schilbach, L., Timmermans, B., Reddy, V., Costall, A., Bente, G., Schlicht, T., & Vogeley, K. (2013). Toward a second-person neuroscience. *BehavBrain Sci*, *36*(4), 393–414.
Schippers, M. B., Roebroeck, A., Renken, R., Nanetti, L., & Keysers, C. (2010). Mapping the information flow from one brain to another during gestural communication. *Proc Natl Acad Sci USA*, *107*(20), 9388–9393.
Schoenbaum, G., Roesch, M. R., Stalnaker, T. A., & Takahashi, Y. K. (2009). A new perspective on the role of the orbitofrontal cortex in adaptive behaviour. *Nat Rev Neurosci*, *10*(12), 885–892.
Schultz, J., Friston, K. J., O'Doherty, J., Wolpert, D. M., & Frith, C. D. (2005). Activation in posterior superior temporal sulcus parallels parameter inducing the percept of animacy. *Neuron*, *45*(4), 625–635.
Scott-Phillips, T. C., Kirby, S., & Ritchie, G. R. (2009). Signalling signalhood and the emergence of communication. *Cognition*, *113*(2), 226–233.
Segaert, K., Menenti, L., Weber, K., Petersson, K. M., & Hagoort, P. (2012). Shared syntax in language production and language comprehension:n FMRI study. *Cereb Cortex*, *22*(7), 1662–1670.

Selten, R., & Warglien, M. (2007). The emergence of simple languages in an experimental coordination game. *Proc Natl Acad Sci USA*, *104*(18), 7361–7366.

Shamay-Tsoory, S. G., Aharon-Peretz, J., & Perry, D. (2009). Two systems for empathy: a double dissociation between emotional and cognitive empathy in inferior frontal gyrus versus ventromedial prefrontal lesions. *Brain*, *132*(3), 617–627.

Shamay-Tsoory, S. G., Tomer, R., Berger, B. D., & Aharon-Peretz, J. (2003). Characterization of empathy deficits following prefrontal brain damage: the role of the right ventromedial prefrontal cortex. *J Cogn Neurosci*, *15*(3), 324–337.

Shannon, C. (1948). A mathematical theory of communication. *The Bell System Technical Journal*, *27*, 379–423.

Shultz, S., Lee, S. M., Pelphrey, K., & McCarthy, G. (2011). The posterior superior temporal sulcus is sensitive to the outcome of human and non-human goal-directed actions. *Soc Cogn Affect Neurosci*, *6*(5), 602–611.

Snowden, J. S., Neary, D., & Mann, D. M. (2002). Frontotemporal dementia. *Br J Psychiatry*, *180*, 140–143.

Sperber, D., & Wilson, D. (2001). *Relevance: Communication and Cognition*. Oxford: Blackwell.

Steels, L. (2003). Evolving grounded communication for robots. *Trends Cogn Sci*, *7*(7), 308–312.

Stolk, A., Hunnius, S., Bekkering, H., & Toni, I. (2013). Early social experience predicts referential communicative adjustments in five-year-old children. *PLoS ONE*, *8*(8), e72667.

Stolk, A., Noordzij, M. L., Verhagen, L., Volman, I., Schoffelen, J.-M., Oostenveld, O., . . . , Toni, I. (2013). Cerebral coherence between communicators marks the emergence of meaning. Paper presented at the 43rd annual meeting of the Society for Neuroscience, San Diego.

Stolk, A., Noordzij, M. L., Volman, I., Verhagen, L., Overeem, S., van Elswijk, G., . . . , Toni, I. (2013). Understanding communicative actions: a repetitive TMS study. *Cortex*, *51*, 25–34.

Stolk, A., Verhagen, L., Schoffelen, J. M., Oostenveld, R., Blokpoel, M., Hagoort, P., . . . , Toni, I. (2013). Neural mechanisms of communicative innovation. *Proc Natl Acad Sci USA*, *110*(36), 14 574–14 579.

Stone, V. E., Baron-Cohen, S., & Knight, R. T. (1998). Frontal lobe contributions to theory of mind. *J Cogn Neurosci*, *10*(5), 640–656.

Tenenbaum, J. B., Griffiths, T. L., & Kemp, C. (2006). Theory-based Bayesian models of inductive learning and reasoning. *Trends Cogn Sci*, *10*(7), 309–318.

Thagard, P. (1989). Explanatory coherence. *Behav Brain Sci*, *12*(3), 435–467.

Tognoli, E., Lagarde, J., DeGuzman, G. C., & Kelso, J. A. (2007). The phi complex as a neuromarker of human social coordination. *Proc Natl Acad Sci USA*, *104*(19), 8190–8195.

Tomasello, M. (2008). *Origins of Human Communication*. Cambridge, MA: MIT Press.

Turesson, H. K., & Ghazanfar, A. A. (2011). Statistical learning of social signals and its implications for the social brain hypothesis. *Interaction Stud*, *12*(3), 397–417.

van Ackeren, M. J., Casasanto, D., Bekkering, H., Hagoort, P., & Rueschemeyer, S. A. (2012). Pragmatics in action: indirect requests engage theory of mind areas and the cortical motor network. *J Cogn Neurosci*, *24*(11), 2237–2247.

van Berkum, J. J., van den Brink, D., Tesink, C. M., Kos, M., & Hagoort, P. (2008). The neural integration of speaker and message. *J Cogn Neurosci*, *20*(4), 580–591.

van Rooij, I., Kwisthout, J., Blokpoel, M., Szymanik, J., Wareham, T., & Toni, I. (2011). Intentional communication: computationally easy or difficult? *Frontiers Hum Neurosci*, *5*, 52.

Vogeley, K., Bussfeld, P., Newen, A., Herrmann, S., Happe, F., Falkai, P., . . . , Zilles, K. (2001). Mind reading: neural mechanisms of theory of mind and self-perspective. *NeuroImage*, *14*(1), 170–181.

Volman, I., Noordzij, M. L., & Toni, I. (2012). Sources of variability in human communicative skills. *Frontiers Hum Neurosci*, *6*, 310.

Walter, H., Adenzato, M., Ciaramidaro, A., Enrici, I., Pia, L., & Bara, B. G. (2004). Understanding intentions in social interaction: the role of the anterior paracingulate cortex. *J Cogn Neurosci*, *16*(10), 1854–1863.

Weder, N. D., Aziz, R., Wilkins, K., & Tampi, R. R. (2007). Frontotemporal dementias: a review. *Ann Gen Psychiatry*, *6*, 15.

Wellman, H. M., Cross, D., & Watson, J. (2001). Meta-analysis of theory-of-mind development: the truth about false belief. *Child Devel*, *72*(3), 655–684.

Willems, R. M., de Boer, M., de Ruiter, J. P., Noordzij, M. L., Hagoort, P., & Toni, I. (2010). A dissociation between linguistic and communicative abilities in the human brain. *Psychol Sci*, *21*(1), 8–14.

Willems, R. M., Benn, Y., Hagoort, P., Toni, I., & Varley, R. (2011). Communicating without a functioning language system: implications for the role of language in mentalizing. *Neuropsychologia*, *49*(11), 3130–3135.

Wittgenstein, L. (1953/2001). *Philosophical Investigations*. Oxford: Blackwell.

Wyk, B. C., Hudac, C. M., Carter, E. J., Sobel, D. M., & Pelphrey, K. A. (2009). Action understanding in the superior temporal sulcus region. *Psychol Sci*, *20*(6), 771–777.

Young, L., Camprodon, J. A., Hauser, M., Pascual-Leone, A., & Saxe, R. (2010). Disruption of the right temporoparietal junction with transcranial magnetic stimulation reduces the role of beliefs in moral judgments. *Proc Natl Acad Sci USA*, *107*(15), 6753–6758.

11 What are naturalistic comprehension paradigms teaching us about language?

Uri Hasson & Giovanna Egidi

Abstract Naturalistic paradigms of language comprehension offer a potential wealth of information for understanding how language processing occurs in everyday use. This information, however, is not immediately apparent and can only be interpreted when considering (1) basic processes that underlie language comprehension (e.g., memory encoding, memory retrieval, integration, prediction of incoming content), (2) processes that modulate or accompany comprehension (e.g., mood effects, attentional biases, emotional responses), and (3) the relation between language-induced activity and pre-existing, semantically rich baseline processes in the brain. Considering these issues conjointly, we outline a general interpretive framework for naturalistic studies of language. We argue that ignoring such issues can lead to serious misinterpretations of neurobiological data.

Introduction

The study of natural language has been a topic of increasing interest in recent years. As outlined in other chapters in this collection, two central aspects of this line of research have been the departure from studying processes strictly limited to the scope of single words or sentences and a strong interest in characterizing the neurobiology of language processing as it occurs in natural circumstances. Our focus in this chapter will mostly be on the contribution of functional magnetic resonance imaging (fMRI) to this enterprise.

Indeed, a principal strength of studying natural language with fMRI is that the method offers a window into the comprehension process without asking participants to engage in either strategic analysis of the input (a typical demand in psychology studies) or any sort of overt behavior. The naturalistic approach to language comprehension with fMRI has been successful on two fronts. The first is testing hypotheses developed from research using non-naturalistic paradigms (e.g., identifying regions involved in action verb processing: Wallentin *et al.*, 2011b). The second, more important one is obtaining new insights on issues that can only be studied within extended discourse, such as processing of narrative-scale event boundaries (Speer, Zacks, & Reynolds, 2007), identification of temporal integration scales in language processing (Lerner *et al.*, 2011) or distinguishing between networks involved in monotonic accumulation of information vs. processing of inconsistencies (Egidi & Caramazza, 2013).

Other strengths and features of the naturalistic approach to the study of language are reviewed in detail in this volume. Our goal in this chapter is to foreground interpretive difficulties that may emerge within naturalistic paradigms. We point to two specific ones: first, what we call the *keyhole error*, which is the tendency to interpret the function of areas tracking a language manipulation as being involved in language processing, and second, what we call the *semantic baseline problem*, which refers to the fact that quantifying brain activity during natural language comprehension in reference to an implicit and not-well-understood baseline may result in theoretical misinterpretations. While these concerns apply, to some extent, to more traditional language studies as well, the lower level of control that characterizes natural language studies means that results obtained within these paradigms are particularly susceptible to these potential confounds.

Defining the keyhole error: are we looking at linguistic processes?

The keyhole error is the tendency to interpret findings identified in natural language paradigms as indicators of language processing, which is akin to looking at the world through a keyhole and concluding that the world is structured very similarly to the keyhole (see Plate 11.1 in color plate section). As such, areas sensitive to inconsistencies may be interpreted as mediating integration of propositions (Hasson, Nusbaum, & Small, 2007), networks showing synchronized activity during processing of a narrative may be interpreted as sensitive to narrative content (Hasson *et al.*, 2008; Wilson, Molnar-Szakacs, & Iacoboni, 2008), and regions discriminating scrambled from coherent narratives may be taken to be linked in a meaningful way to linguistic computations (e.g., Xu *et al.*, 2005).

These interpretations may miss the mark because they do not distinguish processes that are considered core for language comprehension from two other types of processes that take place during comprehension. The first type are processes that accompany semantic and syntactic computations but do not reflect language processing. These can be thought of as *affiliated processes*, as they occur simultaneously with the computations that are considered core aspects of language comprehension. The second type are *basic processes* that serve information processing most generally in both linguistic and non-linguistic domains. This means that the same functions identified for language processing may be performed in other domains as well.

Affiliated processes The areas mediating affiliated process are those where activity fluctuations track discourse features not because of these areas' involvement in linguistic computations, but because of their involvement in processes that usually accompany language processing. These processes can manifest in the recruitment of additional regions (or networks) in support of linguistic functions or in the modulation of activity in regions that process language. The additional areas may be parts of systems associated with attention, emotion, or memory encoding or retrieval.

These processes likely interact with language comprehension in subtle ways; they may be a consequence of linguistic processing or accompany it from early stages. For example, emotional responses accompany the linguistic processing of a narrative and can influence comprehension of subsequent text (e.g., Allbritton & Gerrig, 1991; Egidi & Gerrig, 2009). Similarly, increased relevance of a portion of a linguistic stream due to a semantic factor can determine the amount of influence of prior context on integration (Egidi & Gerrig, 2006). While the distinction between affiliated and core language processes is not clear-cut, it is yet an important distinction between two response profiles that may be found during language comprehension. Progress in neurobiology of language will allow researchers to make these distinctions more clearly.

Basic processes A second manifestation of the keyhole error is that activation patterns in regions typically associated with language comprehension can reflect non-linguistic processes as well. The same brain regions involved in language processing may perform similar computations in other domains. Potential basic processes include those mediating the monotonic accumulation of information (Egidi & Caramazza, 2013, 2014; Humphries *et al.*, 2001), which occurs in discourse comprehension but also might occur in other domains that require integration of input streams. These processes also include the construction of a hierarchical narrative structure, which is a general process that underlies the comprehension of narratives communicated via language, vignettes, non-verbal cartoons, or movies as well as interpretation of short non-verbal communications that could rely on similar networks to those used in language (Xu *et al.*, 2009). In addition, the construction, representation, and use of statistical information, thought to be a fundamental linguistic competence underlying grammar use and statistical learning, is a process that takes place with inputs that are less complex and familiar to people than language (e.g., tones and bird calls: Tremblay, Baroni, & Hasson, 2013). The construction and evaluation of predictions at lexical and sub-lexical levels may be mediated by systems that play a general role in predictive processes.

Basic processes differ from affiliated processes in the type of computations they support: affiliated processes modulate comprehension but are not necessary for it. Basic processes, however, are indispensable to the computations that underlie language-related competence. Hypothetically, suspension of affiliated processes would only modify or partially impair linguistic processing, whereas suspension of basic processes would essentially disable linguistic processing.

Nuisance factors A final cause of the keyhole error originates in the unique nature of the blood-oxygen-level dependent (BOLD) signal used in fMRI. Variations in the BOLD signal may, in some cases, be caused solely by physiological processes. For instance, brain regions where BOLD varies with fluctuations in autonomic nervous system activity (Birn, 2012) or eye movements (Ramot *et al.*, 2011) overlap with regions involved in semantic processing. However, from the perspective of language theories of brain function these BOLD fluctuations may be considered epiphenomenal as they arise as a result of the same circumstances in which language is comprehended, but it is unclear whether they can affect the comprehension process itself.

In the following sections we overview the situations in which the keyhole error can more likely occur. We discuss how this error can be avoided by adopting a broad perspective of the neuroscientific and behavioral literature. Our discussion of the keyhole error is structured into the following sections. We first substantiate the proposition that language understanding can be thought of as engaging many of the systems involved in encoding real-world percepts. We then discuss the role of the following processes during language comprehension: the role of internally generated emotional responses, attention, memory encoding and memory reinstatement, general processes of semantic compositionality, the representation of statistical relations, and predictions. Finally, we outline the mediating role of autonomic effects.

The experience of narrative: from language to the social world

A host of processes extensively studied in the context of social cognition are likely engaged during the comprehension of discourse: these involve empathy, perspective-taking, or more generally theory of mind.

According to some theoretical positions, mostly based on behavioral evidence, the process of understanding discourse, in particular in the form of narratives, is similar in many respects to the experience of everyday life (Gerrig, 1993). On this view, narratives can achieve a sort of transportation. Comprehenders are shifted into a narrative reality, which to some extent substitutes real life as the frame of reference (Gerrig, 1993; Green & Brock, 2000). To illustrate, propositions that only make sense in a narrative world (e.g., an elephant flying) are processed easily even though they are clearly false in the real world. Indeed some neuroimaging work supports this position (Menenti *et al.*, 2009). The use of narratives in neurobiological studies of language can therefore engage a host of social-cognitive functions beyond elaboration of the linguistic stimuli. According to Mar and Oatley (2008), narratives simulate the interpersonal relationships in the story and induce affective empathy for the characters. For this reason, narratives are intuitively ascribed a crucial value as an outlet for empathic development and growth in literary and philosophical studies (Keen, 2007; Mar & Oatley, 2008).

We further note that for this reason, narratives are often used as media to convey a scenario, even when language processing is not the focus of the research. For example, the literature on theory of mind often utilizes narratives to study people's ability to ascribe to others beliefs, emotions, and motivations, and there is a certain overlap between the core network involved in theory of mind and the regions associated with narrative comprehension (which also include areas of the default-mode network: Mar, 2011), thus demonstrating a certain overlap between basic social functions and language comprehension. Consequently, regions theoretically linked to language operations may be involved not in the semantic/syntactic operations that are at the core interest of linguistic theories, but in processes that are more limited in scope and deal with the *contents* used in extended narratives, which oftentimes refer to social interactions. We note that the effects of specific contents have been investigated in several prior works, such as those investigating comprehension of language describing biological motion (Deen & McCarthy, 2010), inconsistencies in emotional or temporal content (Ferstl, Rinck, & von Cramon, 2005), comprehension of action-related information (e.g., Desai *et al.*, 2010), or processing of linguistically conveyed descriptions of visually vivid, emotional, or action-related content (Chow *et al.*, 2013).

Emotions and language processing

One difficulty in interpreting brain activity patterns evoked by naturalistic stimuli is that they have the power to invoke comprehenders' emotional responses perhaps more than controlled stimuli. As such, neurobiological systems implicated in the generation of emotions or the interface between emotion and information processing may be strongly linked to language processing, with emotion being a major affiliated process. There is work showing that narrative-induced fluctuations in emotion may be related to activity in language processing networks (Wallentin *et al.*, 2011a), and that generally, processing emotional content is associated with different activation profiles in lateral temporal cortex, and with particular connectivity modes of left inferior frontal gyrus (IFG) and middle temporal gyrus (MTG) (Chow *et al.*, 2013). For example, in the study by Wallentin and colleagues (Wallentin *et al.*, 2011a), an independent group of participants rated each sentence of a children's story for arousal (on a scale from extreme boredom to extreme arousal) and valence (on a scale from strong negative emotions to strong positive emotions). This resulted in time series of fluctuations on these two dimensions. These time series were then used as explanatory variables in regression models that accounted for BOLD activity while a different group of participants listened to the story. The results showed that increased arousal was associated with stronger BOLD activity in a network of bilateral frontal and temporal regions that are usually associated with language processing, thus demonstrating an overlap between regions involved in linguistic and emotional processing (Plate 11.2 in color plate section). In addition, the study also found that positive valence was associated with increased activation in inferior parietal and medial regions, which are part of the default-mode network and whose activity is associated with mind wandering, which is a state clearly linked to manipulation of contents (see Mason *et al.*, 2007).

These findings are consistent with cognitive theories of comprehension, which have highlighted the sensitivity of comprehenders (in particular readers) to emotional aspects of a narrative. Because of people's ability to be transported into a narrative (Gerrig, 1993; Green & Brock, 2000), they experience emotional responses to the content of a narrative, develop preferences for certain outcomes, or empathize with characters. Behavioral work has shown that these forms of engagement can impact the comprehension process itself so that information that does not accord with comprehenders' preferences can be more difficult to integrate with prior context. For example, when a story protagonist is depicted as honest and deserving, readers have a preference for a narrative outcome with a positive implication for the protagonist, but when a protagonist is depicted as dishonest, readers show the opposite preference. This preference is seen in that endings that mismatch these preferences are read slower than matching endings (Allbritton & Gerrig, 1991; Rapp & Gerrig, 2006).

Narratives are also considered powerful devices for inducing people to experience moods. Indeed for this reason narratives are often used in experimental psychological studies to place participants in different moods, and have been shown to be one of the most effective methods of affect induction (e.g., Gerrards-Hesse, Spies, & Hesse, 1994; Westermann *et al.*, 1996). The narratives generally used in these studies are in the form of humorous or gloomy written texts (Egidi & Gerrig, 2009; Forgas, 1998) or movies (Egidi & Nusbaum, 2012), or are self-generated (e.g., Bless *et al.*, 1996). Being in a happy or a sad mood after such mood induction has been shown to affect several aspects of language processing. For example, it can affect how consistency is built in discourse processing. When comprehenders placed in a happy or sad mood read stories that can end with a positive or a negative ending (both of which are logically consistent with prior context and equally likely to occur) they judge as more surprising those endings that do not match their mood's valence (i.e., happy endings are judged as more surprising by sad participants and sad endings by happy participants: Egidi & Gerrig, 2009). Moods also elicit a rapid neural response that signals difficulty of integration: a greater event-related potential (ERP) N400 component is found for positive or negative story endings that mismatch listeners' moods, even though these endings are linguistically consistent with prior context and equally likely to occur (Egidi & Nusbaum, 2012). Finally, mood strongly modifies the configuration of brain networks involved in processing consistency (Egidi & Caramazza, 2014).

Emotional processes that emerge during discourse processing, particularly within narratives, can therefore affect subsequent linguistic processing and should be considered within neurobiological theories of language. These findings also suggest that a strict dichotomy between "cold" and "hot" linguistic processing should be reconsidered. The networks engaged in the generation of emotions triggered by content and the networks in which these emotions subsequently moderate operations related to language comprehension may overlap with those linked to lower-level language processing, or may interface with them sporadically in a non-stationary manner. Understanding brain mechanisms implicated in the continuous fluctuation of arousal levels and internal emotional states would be a natural way of partitioning between the two processes. In the meantime, the interpretation of activity patterns that track linguistic content should be done while keeping in mind that such activity may reflect the waxing and waning of internal emotional states.

Attention and language processing

An interesting property of naturalistic stimuli is that their richness allows comprehenders relative freedom in selecting what discourse topics are of interest or deserve greater attention. Thus, activity observed during comprehension can reflect an interaction between the semantic, syntactic, or discourse-level features of the stimulus on the one hand, and comprehenders' own motivations on the other. Such covert shifts in attention are an affiliated process that is worthy of examination in the context of language comprehension. Interestingly, differences in attention orientation can induce changes in activation in regions strongly linked to language comprehension. For example, Cooper *et al.* (2011) presented participants with narratives and asked them to focus either on the temporal aspects of the events (i.e., when events occur), on spatial aspects (i.e., where events occur), or on action aspects (which events occur). The stories presented were identical, yet the results documented significant differences in lateral regions involved in language comprehension: the superior temporal gyrus (STG), superior temporal sulcus (STS), and supratemporal plane (STP) between the three conditions, with stronger activity for the action-tracking and space-tracking conditions than for the time-tracking condition. The attentional manipulation affected not only the magnitude of activity but also the distribution of regional activity patterns as documented by a multivariate analysis. Specifically, when quantifying the activation pattern across all voxels in left inferior frontal gyrus (IFG)–pars triangularis (observing all voxels in region as unit of analysis) the results showed a relatively strong similarity in activity patterns for the space- and action-monitoring conditions only, whereas the time-monitoring condition was associated with different pattern of distributed activity. Thus, even core language regions such as IFG are sensitive to strategic modulations of attention that comprehenders adopt. This suggests a strong top-down influence of other neural systems over basic integrative linguistic functions.

General attention systems in parietal cortex have been linked to semantic and pragmatic aspects of language processing. Kristensen and colleagues (Kristensen *et al.*, 2012) manipulated speech prosody for a set of sentences so as to place specific words in focus. When the activation associated with listening to these sentences was compared to that associated with listening to prosodically unmarked texts, a set of regions including the inferior and posterior parietal cortex was found. Independently, these same areas were identified for this participant group in an auditory spatial attention task. The authors took these findings to indicate that the processing of pitch accent utilized, at least in part, a general-attention network, concluding that, "linguistic attention is not separate from nonlinguistic attention" (Kristensen *et al.*, 2012, p. 8).

Other evidence of the role of attention in language processing is provided by work investigating the neural substrates of local and global integration during narrative comprehension (Egidi & Caramazza, 2013). The study found that integration of a sentence with distal context involves systems implicated in working memory load (Wager & Smith, 2003) or top-down attention (Cabeza *et al.*, 2008; Corbetta & Shulman, 2002). The former system accesses the distal information that is relevant at the time of integration, and therefore shows more activity when more contextual information needs to be available. This process is similar to what occurs in task-cueing paradigms (Phillips *et al.*, 2009). The latter system uses context in a top-down preparatory manner for the most sensible information, similarly to what happens in visual top-down attention (Cabeza *et al.*, 2008; Corbetta & Shulman, 2002). These results show that even basic linguistic functions such as accessing relevant contextual linguistic information and integrating it with incoming input are fundamentally attentional functions.

The link between attention and language is not limited to the discourse or sentence level, but is also found at lower levels of language processing. At a sub-lexical level, attention to auditory stimuli increases activity in the STG (Petkov *et al.*, 2004). One concern therefore is that factors that affect attention to auditory stimuli could manifest themselves in STG activity changes.

Memory encoding is part of language processing

Memory processes form a core element of language comprehension. As people understand what is said, they encode the content to memory, and maintain it so that it is accessible when later content is introduced. Thus, continuous encoding to memory constitutes a basic process that underlies language comprehension, narrative comprehension and a multitude of additional cognitive domains. Traditionally, however, neurobiological studies have treated comprehension and memory as separate functions, consistent with the view that they are subserved by at least partially non-overlapping networks. However, the few language studies that have investigated the relationship between comprehension and memory encoding suggest a different picture.

Hasson *et al.* (2007) examined the relation between the network implicated in a semantic contrast between inconsistent and consistent story endings and the network implicated in a memory-related contrast between remembered and forgotten story endings. The study found a striking overlap between the two functional networks thus defined, indicating a shared cortical topology between inconsistency detection and encoding to memory. These data indicate that it is a categorical error to conceive of semantic integration and memory encoding as two distinct cognitive processes. Instead, it appears that the memory encoding is achieved, at least in some networks, as a direct outcome of information processing in the region. Work by Hasson *et al.* (2008) also showed a similar pattern using movies and a different analysis method. In this study, inter-subject synchronization of BOLD time series during movie viewing was associated with better memory for movie content, in regions including the right anterior temporal cortex and STG. In addition, greater activity in bilateral IFG was related to memory in this manner as well (though in absence of changes in synchrony).

The work by Egidi and Caramazza (2013) mentioned above suggests that not one but several non-overlapping networks subserve the encoding of language content to memory, and these depend on the nature of language computations performed. For texts where the meaning of a final sentence was determined only by the most recent context, there was a relatively weak relation between brain activity during ending comprehension and subsequent memory for this ending. In contrast, when the meaning of the final sentence depended on integration with a broader context, activity in a bilateral frontotemporal semantic network was related to subsequent memory. Thus, the amount of information considered during integration and the ease with which a sentence is integrated with recent or more distal context is related to the networks that encode content to memory.

Accessing context: more on the role of memory processes

An account of mechanisms underlying contextual integration is lacking in naturalistic studies of language. The dominant paradigm for studying contextual effects consists of placing target sentences against the backdrop of different sorts of contexts. To date, however, the actual mechanisms involved in integration have not been specified. In general, it is accepted that incoming content is integrated or evaluated in relation to the cognitive representations of the prior context. The questions that remain, however, are how much context is made available at any given point, and how it is accessed online. Naturalistic studies seem to hold the implicit assumption that integration takes place against a representation of the context where contextual elements are equally accessible, and indeed context is modeled as "holistic gestalt." This is perhaps most evident in theories arguing that discourse is represented via simulation-like mental models, where the resulting representation is dependent not on the order in which information arrives, but the overall situation it describes. This assumption props the view that from a neurobiological and cognitive perspective, shorter and longer narratives are essentially processed via the same systems.

Recent work (Egidi & Caramazza, 2013), however, suggests that the online construction of meaning during language comprehension does not follow this simple process model. Instead, separate systems appear to be invoked depending on whether incoming information is integrated against recent or distal context, and whether the incoming information is coherent with more or less recently introduced content. Specifically, the study identified a set of regions that showed greater activity when a final sentence in a story was consistent with local context (mostly parietal, insular, and medial regions). It also identified regions sensitive to attentional load, including the supramarginal gyrus (SMG), superior parietal lobule (SPL), and anterior intraparietal sulcus (aIPS), which showed greater activity when global context was relevant for the comprehension of this final sentence. Finally, the study identified regions associated with top-down attention processes (SPL, IPS) that reflected readiness to the most sensible incoming information once the global context had been taken into account. Thus, the length of a text may in and of itself induce activity in different systems. Minimal texts that can be understood by relying on local textual relations may utilize one system, whereas those that require integration over a larger context may utilize other systems. The implication for naturalistic paradigms is that one cannot assume that comprehending different types of texts fundamentally involves the same brain networks. Thus, just as word and sentence processing are usually considered as regulated by different mechanisms, we argue that there are different levels of processing within discourse comprehension itself, as the integration process is highly sensitive to the amount of prior context that is potentially related to incoming information.

An important determinant of discourse processing are mechanisms by which prior context (linguistic and extralinguistic) is brought to bear on the integration of incoming information. Psychological theories of discourse comprehension have proposed memory-based mechanisms, mostly automatic, that allow re-accessing prior context via memory cues present in working memory. These cues trigger a resonance process that selectively increases the activation of relevant prior information (Gerrig & O'Brien, 2005). This work has shown that context is not maintained active so that all information is equally accessible at all times. Instead, the relative accessibility of prior information waxes and wanes as function of its relation to incoming information (Gerrig & McKoon, 2001). This resonance process appears to be automatic and non-strategic in that it can bring to mind even prior information that is irrelevant to the sentence being understood. From this perspective, continuous and automatic memory retrieval is a core aspect of online comprehension (Gerrig & O'Brien, 2005). Other information tracking mechanisms, mostly strategic, have also been proposed. According to this latter view, comprehenders keep track of relevant information contained in a narrative (e.g., time, place, characters' goals) and continuously update their situation model of the text each time they encounter a modification of these parameters (van den Broek, Rapp, & Kendeou, 2005). However, despite the demonstrated importance of both memory-access mechanisms for discourse comprehension, the neurobiological bases of reinstatement of discourse contexts have not been examined to date.

Interestingly, the study of the neural correlates of reinstatement has been gaining significant prominence in studies of memory, though with yet little impact on neurobiological theories of language comprehension. Examining this work may shed light on how information is continuously re-accessed and re-elaborated in relation to incoming information. Particularly relevant work (Johnson *et al.*, 2009) evaluated whether the subjective experiences of having previously encountered an item or being familiar with it rely on similar neural networks. They presented participants with words to memorize under three different encoding contexts. Using multi-voxel pattern analysis, they showed that activation patterns during a recognition task could discriminate in which of the three contexts the word was encoded. Classification was accurate for both recollection (when participants explicitly remembered having seen the word in the list) and familiarity (participants were sure it was old). The areas that could discriminate the encoding context based on recall activity were regions highly involved in language processing: left IFG, left superior frontal gyrus (SFG) and posterior STS and middle temporal gyrus (MTG). Thus, this study shows that regions associated with core language functions are involved in fundamental memory-based processes.

It is important to note that contextual reinstatement is detailed and can therefore be a good basis for accessing prior context during language comprehension. Activation patterns during recognition of a target word can signal whether the word was encoded in the context of negative or positive emotional information, in an auditory or visual modality, or even whether it was encoded in relation to visual spatial information or visual object information (Danker & Anderson, 2010). This may explain how incoming contents encountered during language comprehension prompt retrieval of prior context.

Thus, both behavioral and neurobiological work on contextual reintegration suggest that an important aspect of activity evident in natural language paradigms may coincide with the reactivation of prior information and the context in which it was introduced. Separating the networks mediating this core memory process in linguistic contexts is an open question for future research.

General compositional processes shared by linguistic and non-linguistic domains

Whether semantic integration processes identified with natural language paradigms are language-specific or are shared by other domains is a fundamental question that has not been extensively examined in the literature. The emerging picture is that there are neurobiological systems mediating general compositional processes for both linguistic and non-linguistic domains. For example, Humphries *et al.* (2001) presented two types of stimuli to participants in an fMRI study: either sentence pairs or sequences of environmental sounds that described the same events (e.g., either the sentences *there was a gunshot and then someone ran away* or the sound of a gun and the sound of footsteps fading into the distance). Both types of stimuli evoked neural activity in bilateral temporal regions associated with semantic processing, including posterior superior temporal gyrus and sulcus, thus showing a common neural substrate for the semantic processing necessary for sentence and sound-sequence comprehension.

Visual and language-conveyed narratives may also rely on the same cognitive systems. It has been shown that visually presented narratives containing an unexpected element evoke an ERP response similar to the N400 found in language comprehension (Sitnikova *et al.*, 2008). This study by Sitnikova *et al.* (2008) showed that actions inconsistent with a narrative goal additionally evoked a P600 effect often associated with syntactic repair. Such findings confirm the reasonable expectation that high-level integration processes underlying linguistically conveyed narratives do subserve comprehension of narratives in general. Analogously, semantic processing of verbal stimuli and environmental sounds has been found to elicit similar neural responses (e.g., Cummings *et al.*, 2006; Saygin *et al.*, 2003).

The comprehension of narratives, whether read or presented in forms of movies, may rely on systems that code for the hierarchical organization of events. This hypothesis has been extensively investigated by Zacks and colleagues (e.g., Zacks *et al.*, 2001; Zacks & Swallow, 2007; see Chapter 4 in this volume). Beyond identifying networks whose activity tracks event boundaries for narrative text (Speer *et al.*, 2007) and action sequences (Zacks *et al.*, 2001), this group's research has also examined movie perception. In one study (Zacks *et al.*, 2001), participants were scanned while watching a movie. They then watched it again while segmenting it to coarse- or fine-grained events. Regions that tracked event boundaries included mainly posterior regions – both medial and lateral (cuneus, precuneus, SPL, posterior cingulate, right parieto-temporal regions), with smaller involvement of frontal cortex. Whitney *et al.* (2009) coded narrative shifts in auditory stories by identifying changes in basic narrative building-blocks, such as character, time, location, and action. By using random sentence boundaries as a control condition, the authors identified brain regions where activity tracked such changes. They documented sensitivity to narrative shifts in the right precuneus and posterior cingulate cortex, as well as the middle aspect of cingulate gyrus on the left. The role of this network in responding to event boundaries was also identified in several other studies based on verbal materials (e.g., Speer *et al.*, 2007) thus showing a common neural architecture underlying comprehension of events in narratives conveyed by several media and real-life experiences as well.

Do these findings indicate language processing or a more general semantic integration process? Work by Hasson and colleagues, inspired in part by methods developed by Zacks and his group, suggests that the brain systems implicated in event segmentation may actually be mediating an even lower-level function that is not related to semantic schema-based knowledge but to more general changes in environmental structure. In one study (Tobia *et al.*, 2012a) participants listened to long series of rapidly presented tones (rate = 3.3Hz) in which four tones were presented repeatedly. Some sections of the series were highly ordered as determined by their transition constraints (e.g., 123441233412334) whereas others were random; over timescales of about 10 seconds, shifts of regularity occurred so that participants had several opportunities for noticing changes in regularity. Participants indicated when they noticed a change in regularity in the auditory sequence. On the basis of these ratings, it was possible to quantify points in the auditory stream where there was consensus regarding regularity changes, thus allowing the identification of brain systems where activity prior to the key press was associated with the perception of a change. This analysis identified a network of regions whose topography strongly resembled that found in the studies by Zacks and colleagues.

Another approach (Tobia *et al.*, 2012b) examined if there are neural systems sensitive to changes in the degree of input regularity over time, in particular whether these regions overlap with language processing areas. Participants passively listened to the same type of stimuli used in Tobia *et al.* (2012a). The relative degree of disorder in 10-second sliding windows (consisting of 32 transitions between four tones) was manipulated to change slowly over time, so that it was possible to formally calculate the rate in which regularity changed over time and identify regions sensitive to the *degree of change in regularity*. The analysis revealed a set of midline regions including the lingual gyrus and cuneus bilaterally, as well as the central aspect of the cingulate gyrus, the pre-supplementary motor area (SMA), the left insula and left ventral premotor cortex (vPMC).

In summary, examining the neurobiological basis of the segmentation of inputs into units is a promising framework for future work. It seems that this system, consisting mainly of posterior midline regions in occipital cortex and central midline regions of the anterior cingulate, mediates both schema-based segmentation of narratives as well as purely statistical-based parsing of non-narrative inputs. It is possible that the ability to segment narratives into units developed from the simpler coding of statistics in the context of perceptual learning.

Core systems for the representation of statistical relationships

The domain of prediction and statistical learning has been repeatedly linked to that of language processing (on both the lexical and sub-lexical level), but the relation between the two is still a new domain of research. Predictions depend on a statistical knowledge base, but research identifying the systems that support such predictions has not arrived at clear-cut conclusions. Some have proposed that there is a basic (hippocampally centered) system with the capacity to represent statistical relationships between elements. On the micro-scale of individual tokens, this system supports associative learning, for example that item *B* tends to appear after item *A* (Turk-Browne *et al.*, 2010). Furthermore, it has also been suggested that the same system encodes macro-scale statistical features of the input so that it tracks the overall regularity (entropy) of input streams (Strange *et al.*, 2005). Such a system may play an important role in language processing, as there are multiple levels of regularity at different stages of linguistic processing: phonemic, syllabic, morphological, and sentential. Theoretical positions and behavioral research have argued for the existence of such a basic system. The auditory scaffolding hypothesis (Conway, Pisoni, & Kronenberger, 2009) exemplifies this approach in arguing that people's intense experience with sound patterns provides a supporting structure, or scaffold, for the capacity to track sequential structure in multiple domains, including non-linguistic ones.

There is evidence that brain regions that are considered to perform core language functions also mediate statistical processes. For example, Petersson and colleagues (Petersson, Folia, & Hagoort, 2012) have shown that the left IFG is sensitive to violations of a previously learned artificial grammar. This result supports the notion that the involvement of this region in syntactic processing may be due to its more basic involvement in representing abstract grammatical structure. The authors suggest that the left IFG is not involved in specific language-related computations such as the evaluation of long-range dependencies (syntactic movement) or representation of nested structure but "is a generic on-line structured sequence processor" (Petersson *et al.*, 2012, p. 89). It has also been suggested that left IFG is sensitive to the complexity of structured inputs. In one study (Bahlmann *et al.*, 2009), artificial grammars based on a simple associative transition structure (modeled via first-order Markov process) were contrasted with more complicated grammars that consisted of a hierarchical dependency rule of the form (e.g., A^n B^n) where A and B were visual stimuli with different feature types. A region-of-interest (ROI) analysis of posterior left IFG (BA 44) showed greater activity for the hierarchical condition. The authors interpret the findings as supporting the hypothesis that the region is "engaged in domain-general processing of hierarchical sequences" (p. 166). In addition, the hierarchical grammar evoked greater activity in right pre-SMA and the left precentral gyrus (PCG) and sulcus, which are areas extensively involved in both general auditory sequence learning (Brown *et al.*, 2013) and explicit prediction of future stimuli (Schubotz, 2007). The involvement of these regions in predictive processes may indicate that differences in activity are not due to differences in complexity, but to the fact that naturally occurring predictive mechanisms were more heavily utilized in one condition. We note, however, that Bahlmann *et al.*'s study, conducted in a non-naturalistic paradigm, required grammaticality judgments after each stimulus, and these could have been more difficult for the hierarchical stimuli, thus biasing some of the mentioned BOLD difference patterns.

The study by Tobia *et al.* (2012b, presented above) further found that structure-tracking may take quite nuanced forms, with immediate applications to language research, as this tracking is mediated by lateral temporal and ventral premotor regions. One design feature of that study was that when computed over 10-second sliding windows, two distinct features of the stimuli would change continuously: the *relative diversity* of tokens (the extent to which the proportion of different tokens were similar), and the *strength of contingencies* between them (the degree to which each token predicted the subsequent one). The results indicated sensitivity to both relative diversity and strength of contingencies in areas typically linked to language comprehension. Sensitivity to diversity was found bilaterally in the posterior aspect of supratemporal plane, SMG, and insula. Sensitivity to the strength of transition constraints was found in several regions including the ventral premotor cortex and lateral temporal cortex. Thus, when a context (even an overly simplified one) licenses predictions via frequency- or transition-based constraints, different networks are invoked. They may be implicated in tracking the regularity of the context or even in making predictions. Given the involvement of both premotor and temporal cortex and sub-lexical and lexical processing, it is important to consider whether these regions may be more generally implicated in prediction per se.

Neurobiological studies of responses to musical structure reveal similar systems (Seger *et al.*, 2013). Seger *et al.* presented participants with classical music pieces that could end with an expected resolution, or three types of resolutions that varied in their degree of expectancy violation. They found sensitivity to the degree of musical surprise in left anterior STG, posterior aspect of left IFG, and SMA. All these regions showed increased activity with greater surprise.

Despite such findings, overlaps in activation patterns as seen for music, language, and artificial grammars do not necessarily constitute evidence of similar computations in these domains. Rogalsky *et al.* (2011) targeted this issue in a study comparing activation patterns to jabberwocky sentences, scrambled jabberwocky sentences, and musical progressions. In regions where activity overlapped for music and sentences, a multi-voxel pattern analysis (MVPA) classifier still successfully discriminated speech from music. In addition, regions associated with syntactic well-formedness (sentences as compared to scrambled sentences) were not associated with musical processing. Thus, although these regions track structure and regularity in several domains, they are still sensitive to the type of input being processed.

To conclude, while there is some evidence that temporal, inferior frontal, and premotor regions associated with language comprehension may mediate lower-level prediction based processes, more work needs to be done on whether similar computations are carried out when processing environmental inputs, music, or language itself.

Autonomic effects

We have already introduced the interpretive difficulties that may arise as a consequence of emotional responses to discourse content in naturalistic language paradigms. It is reasonable to expect that such responses will be manifested in particular activation patterns, e.g., in the mesolimbic system as these regions may invoke the emotional response itself. A similar, but fundamentally different effect of cognition/emotion/attention on BOLD activity is introduced when the autonomic nervous system (ANS) affects BOLD fluctuation patterns via a purely physiological (non-functional) pathway (see Iacovella & Hasson, 2011, for a recent discussion). In this pathway, cardiac and respiratory fluctuations affect BOLD patterns due to variations in cerebral blood flow, vasodilation, concentration of carbon dioxide, and even respiration-induced motion. Somewhat alarmingly, regions where the BOLD signal is affected in this way overlap with the distribution of regions identified as the default-mode network (DMN), a network involved in semantic processing (Binder *et al.*, 2009).

The aforementioned effects are considered purely physiological. However, there are brain systems that monitor ANS activity, perhaps as a source of additional (visceral) information. For instance, the insula has been implicated in monitoring of arousal, and particularly cardiac rate (Pollatos *et al.*, 2007). Relatedly, the somatic marker hypothesis (Bechara, Damasio, & Damasio, 2000) suggests that regions involved in decision-making may monitor visceral, though more emotional, responses and integrate those in decision contexts.

The study of Wallentin and colleagues (Wallentin *et al.*, 2011a) described before, in which brain activity during listening to a children's story was correlated with arousal and valence ratings for each sentence, also calculated the correlation between the arousal ratings and an ANS measure collected during story listening. This measure reflected heart-rate variability (HRV) and was quantified as the ratio of low- to high-frequency power in the cardiac response profile. The study found a correlation between the arousal ratings and this ANS measure. As discussed earlier, the results also showed that increased arousal was associated with stronger BOLD activity in frontal and temporal regions usually associated with language processing. The HRV measure may therefore have also contributed to the BOLD pattern of results, thus showing a common neural substrate not only to language and emotion, but to autonomic responses as well.

Metz-Lutz and colleagues (2010) also documented an impact of narrative events on ANS indices. They presented participants with a dramatic play in an MRI scanner, and later asked those participants to provide a report of their thoughts and feelings for every unit of the play. They could thus identify events associated with participants' *adhesion* to the narrative, that is, moments in which they experienced the narrative as real. They also identified a more objectively defined set of events based on the director's instructions. The findings brought out an interesting relation between event structure and the ANS index. Both objectively defined and subjectively defined narrative events were linked to changes in heart-rate patterns (as quantified via a HRV measure). Specifically, both events were associated with a reduction in the HRV autocorrelation function, i.e., reduced power in the lower frequency of the HRV. This pattern indicates vagal influence on heart rate activity, i.e., involvement of the parasympathetic system which mediates more temporally extended physiological processes. In addition, subjectively defined events were also associated with invoking a more rapid heart rate. Here too then the literature points to systematic relations between narrative structure and changes in autonomic function, which can easily lead to BOLD changes in and of themselves via the pathways discussed above.

To summarize, the existing literature suggests that contents that evoke emotional responses cause concomitant changes in BOLD fluctuations via different pathways, some of which are related to functional activation, and some which are due purely to nuisance factors and can be treated as epiphenomenal. Simply partialling out the effect of simultaneously recorded physiological responses from the BOLD signal is a poor solution to the problem, since, as mentioned, these changes can be meaningfully related to the cognitive and emotional states introduced by the content.

The semantic baseline problem: are we looking at qualitatively meaningful evoked changes or induced changes to ongoing activity patterns?

The final point we address is that quantifying activity relative to baseline may result in misinterpretation of the role of brain regions or networks. This is because the baseline state itself may constitute a cognitive state similar to the one in place during semantic processing of language content. What we call the *semantic baseline problem* thus refers to the difficulty in determining whether the observed activity fluctuations reflect a qualitatively important perturbation to an otherwise impoverished baseline state, or alternatively, a relatively subtle modulation of baseline activity that is inherently rich in semantic processing.

On the interpretive level, the above-mentioned concerns are similar in nature to the distinction between evoked and induced activity as raised in the fields of electroencephalography (EEG) and magnetoencephalography (MEG) research. In those, evoked activity refers to activation patterns that are phase locked to a stimulus; i.e., these reflect activity in a system that was inactive prior to stimulus presentation. In contrast, induced activity refers to a change in ongoing brain activity profiles that are in place prior to stimulus presentation, e.g., changes in the power or phase of a particular frequency band that exhibited oscillation prior to stimulus presentation. As such, evoked changes are identified by averaging activity time-locked to appearance of particular stimuli, whereas induced activity can only be identified when averaging time-frequency snapshots of power profiles after stimulus appearance.

If what we observe during studies conducted with natural language paradigms is only a minor shaping of the baseline state, then the background can and should be treated as a dominant cognitive element, with language serving as a subtle but systematic modulator of that state. For this reason, understanding the relation between baseline processes and activity patterns in natural language paradigms is a core issue for a correct interpretation of experimental findings. While it may appear more intuitive to interpret findings under the assumption that language processing induces fundamental changes, there is a body of work suggesting that brain networks implicated in particular cognitive processes may maintain structured connectivity outside the context of those cognitive functions.

The principle has been demonstrated in a number of studies. For instance, Simmons and Martin (2012) showed that regions associated with tool use or social cognition (i.e., regions activated by tool- or social-related contents) maintain their differential connectivity patterns during the resting state. Networks sensitive to action observation also show coherent fluctuations during rest (Molinari *et al.*, 2013).

With respect to language, several studies suggest that regions known to mediate language comprehension form functional networks during the resting state; that is, they do not organize ad hoc when language input is experienced, but maintain functional connectivity outside a language processing context. One study (Hampson *et al.*, 2002) examined whole-brain resting-state correlations of IFG regions (BA 44, 45) and documented strong connectivity with bilateral STG and MTG. A more specific analysis examined correlation between left IFG and left BA 39 (including also the angular gyrus). The correlation between these two regions was significant, and the strength of correlation varied with scores on a reading comprehension subtest.

Expanding on this work, Koyama *et al.* (2010) examined the resting-state functional connectivity of six different left-hemisphere seed regions that have been specifically linked to reading and spoken language comprehension (i.e., fusiform gyrus (FFG), IFG, PCG). Some of the networks demonstrated topography typically found during word reading, for example, connectivity between FFG and IFG. Most interesting, when examining the overlap of these six networks, common overlaps for five of the six were found in left posterior MTG and the posterior aspect of left IFG. The authors suggested that these resting-state connectivity patterns may be the consequence of people's intensive experience with reading, which results in continued maintenance of the networks offline. Whether these networks maintain some type of endogenously driven semantic processing is an interesting question for future work.

The aforementioned findings lead to the question of whether synchronized activity that constitutes resting-state networks is maintained during comprehension, and whether language comprehension at all instantiates ad hoc connectivity networks. Keeping in mind that BOLD synchronized activity is typically dominated by power in lower frequencies (<0.1 Hz), it is important to know if this synchronized activity is actually perturbed during processing of exogenous stimuli. Lohmann *et al.* (2010) examined this particular issue. They analyzed data from four studies of language processing and two studies not involving language processing in a way that enabled tracking low-frequency BOLD fluctuations independent of the experimental paradigm per se. They partialled out variance that could be attributed to the experimental design, low-pass filtered the data to focus on the low-frequency range (<0.1 Hz), and examined connectivity patterns in the signal. This approach could determine whether language processing specifically induces patterns of functional connectivity that are independent of the experimental timing per se (given the low-frequency filter). Seed regions were defined in BA 44 and frontal operculum, and the authors documented strong connectivity to contralateral right hemisphere areas as well as left STS. Importantly, this connectivity with left STS was not found in the two non-language studies. Taken together, these studies show that some semantic-processing networks are maintained during rest, but that language processing may be further associated with instantiation of particular functional-connectivity patterns in the low-frequency range. Thus, extended language inputs may either make use of pre-existing connectivity networks or instantiate specific networks during comprehension.

Speaking in favor of the idea that language processing may reflect modulations of activity in pre-existing networks are several studies that have specifically targeted the nature of resting-state activity and its susceptibility to the specific thoughts experienced during rest. Doucet *et al.* (2012) examined how resting state activity within five networks depended on the nature of endogenous thoughts reported by participants. They derived a representative time series from each network, and determined whether connectivity between these networks varied with participants' (self-reported) engagement in imagery or inner language. They found that increased engagement in internal language was associated with reduced activity in the default-mode network and a frontoparietal network. A similar study (Preminger, Harmelech, & Malach, 2011) showed that specific types of guided internal deliberations (near future planning vs. episodic retrieval) can systematically alter activity in areas implicated in mind wandering. They documented a number of regions that showed higher activity during near-future planning, and interestingly, these included the lateral temporal cortex bilaterally, IPL bilaterally, and the left IFG/IFS. Thus, internal deliberation in absence of language processing can result in systematic activity changes in areas implicated in semantic access (the so-called DMN: Binder *et al.*, 2009) as well as regions associated with sentential semantic and syntactic processing (IFG, temporal cortex).

Finally, we consider the possibility that natural language paradigms can induce changes in what are naturally occurring fluctuation dynamics in a given region. To illustrate: Skipper *et al.* (2009) showed that meaningful gestures are associated with an interesting activation pattern in the ventral and dorsal premotor cortex: when a movie contained meaningful gestures, activity peaks in these regions were associated with gestures. In contrast, when a movie contained non-meaningful gestures, these were equally associated with peaks and pits in the time series. Interestingly, peaks in the BOLD signal occurred quite frequently in both conditions, with a mean interval of ~7 seconds. The findings suggest that the premotor cortex, which is involved in action production, is sensitive to the meaningfulness of gestures in the context of language comprehension. It is possible however that gesture-based content does not directly evoke these often-occurring peak/pit patterns, but serves to simply adjust an existing intrinsic (baseline) activity mode of the region. Recent work on intrinsic profiles of rapid fluctuations during rest (Davis *et al.*, 2013) demonstrates that the premotor cortex shows a spontaneous, non-random pattern of activity fluctuations during rest, with a very similar peak-to-peak interval to that documented by Skipper *et al.* (6 seconds). Given this endogenous pattern, one possibility is that the presence of meaningful stimuli serves to align the internal activity generators in the region. On this explanation, the premotor cortex is predisposed to react quickly to frequently changing stimuli (during rest) and this capacity is utilized also in the presence of meaningful stimuli to allow rapid reactions to those.

Conclusion

Our goal in this chapter was to outline an interpretive framework for addressing data obtained with fMRI naturalistic paradigms. We began the chapter by asking what naturalistic paradigms tell us about language, and we hope to have convinced the reader that while these paradigms hold a potential wealth of information for understanding how language processing occurs "in the wild," this information is not readily apparent but can only be deciphered by considering a set of processes that either underlie language comprehension or accompany it.

We have attempted to show that interpretations of data collected within naturalistic paradigms will benefit from being informed by at least two separate domains of study. On the one hand, there is much theoretical research (supported by neurobiological findings) pushing the boundaries of language comprehension to consider more farther-afield issues such as (i) access to particular contents (e.g., emotional, temporal, action-based),

(ii) the role of attention in language, and (iii) social-cognition elements such as empathy and theory of mind. On the other hand, various processes take place during language comprehension and may co-vary with it, thus making it more difficult to separate brain areas or activity patterns mediating linguistic information processing from areas mediating other co-occurring processes.

To alleviate interpretive difficulties and to ground neurobiological theories in a broader context of cognitive processing, future research could collect a large body of covariate information, including physiological measures, as well as resting-state information from individual participants. This covariate information would allow modeling the changes to endogenous activity that are introduced by language processing per se. Information about systems mediating affiliated processes such as auditory attention, emotional responses, or recollection processes for the same participants could also help dissociate core linguistic processes from affiliated ones.

References

Allbritton, D. W., & Gerrig, R. J. (1991). Participatory responses in text understanding. *J Memory Lang*, *30*(5), 603–626. doi:http://dx.doi.org/10.1016/0749-596X(91)90028-I

Bahlmann, J., Schubotz, R. I., Mueller, J. L., Koester, D., & Friederici, A. D. (2009). Neural circuits of hierarchical visuo-spatial sequence processing. *Brain Res*, *1298*, 161–170. doi:10.1016/j.brainres.2009.08.017

Bechara, A., Damasio, H., & Damasio, A. R. (2000). Emotion, decision making and the orbitofrontal cortex. *Cereb Cortex*, *10*(3), 295–307.

Binder, J. R., Desai, R. H., Graves, W. W., & Conant, L. L. (2009). Where is the semantic system? A critical review and meta-analysis of 120 functional neuroimaging studies. *Cereb Cortex*, *19*(12), 2767–2796. doi:10.1093/cercor/bhp055

Birn, R. M. (2012). The role of physiological noise in resting-state functional connectivity. *NeuroImage*, *62*(2), 864–870. doi:10.1016/j.neuroimage.2012.01.016

Bless, H., Clore, G. L., Schwarz, N., Golisano, V., Rabe, C., & Woelk, M. (1996). Mood and the use of scripts: does a happy mood really lead to mindlessness. *J Pers Soc Psychol*, *71*, 665–679.

Brown, R. M., Chen, J. L., Hollinger, A., Penhune, V. B., Palmer, C., & Zatorre, R. J. (2013). Repetition suppression in auditory-motor regions to pitch and temporal structure in music. *J Cogn Neurosci*, *25*(2), 313–328. doi:10.1162/jocn_a_00322

Cabeza, R., Ciaramelli, E., Olson, I. R., & Moscovitch, M. (2008). The parietal cortex and episodic memory: an attentional account. *Nat Rev Neurosci*, *9*(8), 613–625. doi:10.1038/nrn2459

Chow, H. M., Mar, R. A., Xu, Y., Liu, S., Wagage, S., & Braun, A. R. (2013). Embodied comprehension of stories: interactions between language regions and modality-specific neural systems. *J Cogn Neurosci.* doi:10.1162/jocn_a_00487

Conway, C. M., Pisoni, D. B., & Kronenberger, W. G. (2009). The importance of sound for cognitive sequencing abilities: the auditory scaffolding hypothesis. *Curr Dir Psychol Sci, 18*(5), 275–279. doi:10.1111/j.1467–8721.2009.01651.x

Cooper, E. A., Hasson, U., & Small, S. L. (2011). Interpretation-mediated changes in neural activity during language comprehension. *NeuroImage, 55*(3), 1314–1323. doi:10.1016/j.neuroimage.2011.01.003

Corbetta, M., & Shulman, G. L. (2002). Control of goal-directed and stimulus-driven attention in the brain. *Nat Rev Neurosci, 3*(3), 201–215. doi:10.1038/nrn755

Cummings, A., Ceponiene, R., Koyama, A., Saygin, A. P., Townsend, J., & Dick, F. (2006). Auditory semantic networks for words and natural sounds. *Brain Res, 1115*(1), 92–107. doi:10.1016/j.brainres.2006.07.050

Danker, J. F., & Anderson, J. R. (2010). The ghosts of brain states past: remembering reactivates the brain regions engaged during encoding. *Psychol Bull, 136*(1), 87–102. doi:10.1037/a0017937

Davis, B., Jovicich, J., Iacovella, V., & Hasson, U. (2014). Functional and developmental significance of amplitude variance asymmetry in the BOLD resting-state signal. *Cereb Cortex, 24*(5), 1332–1350. doi:10.1093/cercor/bhs416

Deen, B., & McCarthy, G. (2010). Reading about the actions of others: biological motion imagery and action congruency influence brain activity. *Neuropsychologia, 48*(6), 1607–1615. doi:10.1016/j.neuropsychologia.2010.01.028

Desai, R. H., Binder, J. R., Conant, L. L., & Seidenberg, M. S. (2010). Activation of sensory-motor areas in sentence comprehension. *Cereb Cortex, 20*(2), 468–478. doi:10.1093/cercor/bhp115

Doucet, G., Naveau, M., Petit, L., Zago, L., Crivello, F., Jobard, G., . . ., Joliot, M. (2012). Patterns of hemodynamic low-frequency oscillations in the brain are modulated by the nature of free thought during rest. *NeuroImage, 59*(4), 3194–3200. doi:10.1016/j.neuroimage.2011.11.059

Egidi, G., & Caramazza, A. (2013). Cortical systems for local and global integration in discourse comprehension. *NeuroImage, 71*, 59–74. doi:10.1016/j.neuroimage.2013.01.003

Egidi, G., & Caramazza, A. (2014). Mood-dependent integration in discourse comprehension: happy and sad moods affect consistency processing via different brain networks. *Neuroimage, 103*, 20–32.

Egidi, G., & Gerrig, R. J. (2009). How valence affects language processing: negativity bias and mood congruence in narrative comprehension. *Mem Cognit, 37*(5), 547–555. doi:10.3758/MC.37.5.547

Egidi, G., & Gerrig, R. J. (2006). Readers' experiences of characters' goals and actions. *J Exp Psychol: Learning, Memory, and Cognition, 32*, 1322–1329.

Egidi, G., & Nusbaum, H. C. (2012). Emotional language processing: how mood affects integration processes during discourse comprehension. *Brain Lang, 122*(3), 199–210. doi:10.1016/j.bandl.2011.12.008

Ferstl, E. C., Rinck, M., & von Cramon, D. Y. (2005). Emotional and temporal aspects of situation model processing during text comprehension: an event-related fMRI study. *J Cogn Neurosci, 17*(5), 724–739. doi:10.1162/0898929053747658

Forgas, J. P. (1998). Asking nicely? The effects of mood on responding to more or less polite requests. *Person Soc Psychol Bull, 24,* 173–185.

Gerrards-Hesse, A., Spies, K., & Hesse, F. W. (1994). Experimental inductions of emotional states and their effectiveness: a review. *Br J Psychol, 85,* 55–78.

Gerrig, R. J. (1993). *Experiencing Narrative Worlds: On the Psychological Activities of Reading.* New Haven, CT: Yale University Press.

Gerrig, R. J., & McKoon, G. (2001). Memory processes and experiential continuity. *Psychol Sci, 12*(1), 81–85. doi:10.1111/1467–9280.00314

Gerrig, R. J., & O'Brien, E. J. (2005). The scope of memory-based processing. *Discourse Proc, 39*(2–3), 225–242.

Green, M. C., & Brock, T. C. (2000). The role of transportation in the persuasiveness of public narratives. *J Pers Soc Psychol, 79*(5), 701–721.

Hampson, M., Peterson, B. S., Skudlarski, P., Gatenby, J. C., & Gore, J. C. (2002). Detection of functional connectivity using temporal correlations in MR images. *Hum Brain Mapp, 15*(4), 247–262.

Hasson, U., Furman, O., Clark, D., Dudai, Y., & Davachi, L. (2008). Enhanced intersubject correlations during movie viewing correlate with successful episodic encoding. *Neuron, 57*(3), 452–462. doi:10.1016/j.neuron.2007.12.009

Hasson, U., Nusbaum, H. C., & Small, S. L. (2007). Brain networks subserving the extraction of sentence information and its encoding to memory. *Cereb Cortex, 17*(12), 2899–2913. doi:10.1093/cercor/bhm016

Humphries, C., Willard, K., Buchsbaum, B., & Hickok, G. (2001). Role of anterior temporal cortex in auditory sentence comprehension: an fMRI study. *NeuroReport, 12*(8), 1749–1752.

Iacovella, V., & Hasson, U. (2011). The relationship between BOLD signal and autonomic nervous system functions: implications for processing of "physiological noise." *Magn Reson Imaging, 29*(10), 1338–1345. doi:10.1016/j.mri.2011.03.006

Johnson, J. D., McDuff, S. G., Rugg, M. D., & Norman, K. A. (2009). Recollection, familiarity, and cortical reinstatement: a multivoxel pattern analysis. *Neuron, 63*(5), 697–708. doi:10.1016/j.neuron.2009.08.011

Keen, S. (2007). *Empathy and the Novel.* New York: Oxford University Press.

Koyama, M. S., Kelly, C., Shehzad, Z., Penesetti, D., Castellanos, F. X., & Milham, M. P. (2010). Reading networks at rest. *Cereb Cortex, 20*(11), 2549–2559. doi:10.1093/cercor/bhq005

Kristensen, L. B., Wang, L., Petersson, K. M., & Hagoort, P. (2012). The interface between language and attention: prosodic focus marking recruits a general attention network in spoken language comprehension. *Cereb Cortex.* doi:10.1093/cercor/bhs164

Lerner, Y., Honey, C. J., Silbert, L. J., & Hasson, U. (2011). Topographic mapping of a hierarchy of temporal receptive windows using a narrated story. *J Neurosci, 31*(8), 2906–2915. doi:10.1523/JNEUROSCI.3684–10.2011

Lohmann, G., Hoehl, S., Brauer, J., Danielmeier, C., Bornkessel-Schlesewsky, I., Bahlmann, J., . . . , Friederici, A. (2010). Setting the frame: the human brain activates a basic low-frequency network for language processing. *Cereb Cortex, 20*(6), 1286–1292. doi:10.1093/cercor/bhp190

Mar, R. A. (2011). The neural bases of social cognition and story comprehension. *Annu Rev Psychol*, *62*, 103–134. doi:10.1146/annurev-psych-120709-145406

Mar, R. A., & Oatley, K. (2008). The function of fiction is the abstraction and simulation of social experience. *Perspect Psychol Sci*, *3*, 173–192.

Mason, M. F., Norton, M. I., Van Horn, J. D., Wegner, D. M., Grafton, S. T., & Macrae, C. N. (2007). Wandering minds: the default network and stimulus-independent thought. *Science*, *315*(5810), 393–395. doi:10.1126/science.1131295

Menenti, L., Petersson, K. M., Scheeringa, R., & Hagoort, P. (2009). When elephants fly: differential sensitivity of right and left inferior frontal gyri to discourse and world knowledge. *J Cogn Neurosci*, *21*(12), 2358–2368. doi:10.1162/jocn.2008.21163

Metz-Lutz, M. N., Bressan, Y., Heider, N., & Otzenberger, H. (2010). What physiological changes and cerebral traces tell us about adhesion to fiction during theater-watching? *Frontiers Hum Neurosci*, *4*. doi:10.3389/fnhum.2010.00059

Molinari, E., Baraldi, P., Campanella, M., Duzzi, D., Nocetti, L., Pagnoni, G., & Porro, C. A. (2013). Human parietofrontal networks related to action observation detected at rest. *Cereb Cortex*, *23*(1), 178–186. doi:10.1093/cercor/bhr393

Petersson, K. M., Folia, V., & Hagoort, P. (2012). What artificial grammar learning reveals about the neurobiology of syntax. *Brain Lang*, *120*(2), 83–95. doi:10.1016/j.bandl.2010.08.003

Petkov, C. I., Kang, X., Alho, K., Bertrand, O., Yund, E. W., & Woods, D. L. (2004). Attentional modulation of human auditory cortex. *Nat Neurosci*, *7*(6), 658–663. doi:10.1038/nn1256

Phillips, J. S., Velanova, K., Wolk, D. A., & Wheeler, M. E. (2009). Left posterior parietal cortex participates in both task preparation and episodic retrieval. *NeuroImage*, *46*, 1209–1221.

Pollatos, O., Schandry, R., Auer, D. P., & Kaufmann, C. (2007). Brain structures mediating cardiovascular arousal and interoceptive awareness. *Brain Res*, *1141*, 178–187. doi:10.1016/j.brainres.2007.01.026

Preminger, S., Harmelech, T., & Malach, R. (2011). Stimulus-free thoughts induce differential activation in the human default network. *NeuroImage*, *54*(2), 1692–1702. doi:10.1016/j.neuroimage.2010.08.036

Ramot, M., Wilf, M., Goldberg, H., Weiss, T., Deouell, L. Y., & Malach, R. (2011). Coupling between spontaneous (resting state) fMRI fluctuations and human oculo-motor activity. *NeuroImage*, *58*(1), 213–225. doi:10.1016/j.neuroimage.2011.06.015

Rapp, D. N., & Gerrig, R. J. (2006). Predilections for narrative outcomes: the impact of story contexts and reader preferences. *J Memory Lang*, *54*, 54–67.

Rogalsky, C., Rong, F., Saberi, K., & Hickok, G. (2011). Functional anatomy of language and music perception: temporal and structural factors investigated using functional magnetic resonance imaging. *J Neurosci*, *31*(10), 3843–3852. doi:10.1523/JNEUROSCI.4515-10.2011

Saygin, A. P., Dick, F., Wilson, S. M., Dronkers, N. F., & Bates, E. (2003). Neural resources for processing language and environmental sounds: evidence from aphasia. *Brain*, *126*(Pt 4), 928–945.

Schubotz, R. I. (2007). Prediction of external events with our motor system: towards a new framework. *Trends Cogn Sci, 11*, 211–218.

Seger, C. A., Spiering, B. J., Sares, A. G., Quraini, S. I., Alpeter, C., David, J., & Thaut, M. H. (2013). Corticostriatal contributions to musical expectancy perception. *J Cogn Neurosci.* doi:10.1162/jocn_a_00371

Simmons, W. K., & Martin, A. (2012). Spontaneous resting-state BOLD fluctuations reveal persistent domain-specific neural networks. *Soc Cogn Affect Neurosci, 7*(4), 467–475. doi:10.1093/scan/nsr018

Sitnikova, T., Holcomb, P. J., Kiyonaga, K. A., & Kuperberg, G. R. (2008). Two neurocognitive mechanisms of semantic integration during the comprehension of visual real-world events. *J Cogn Neurosci, 20*(11), 2037–2057. doi:10.1162/jocn.2008.20143

Skipper, J. I., Goldin-Meadow, S., Nusbaum, H. C., & Small, S. L. (2009). Gestures orchestrate brain networks for language understanding. *Curr Biol, 19*(8), 661–667. doi:10.1016/j.cub.2009.02.051

Speer, N. K., Zacks, J. M., & Reynolds, J. R. (2007). Human brain activity time-locked to narrative event boundaries. *Psychol Sci, 18*(5), 449–455. doi:10.1111/j.1467–9280.2007.01920.x

Strange, B. A., Duggins, A., Penny, W., Dolan, R. J., & Friston, K. J. (2005). Information theory, novelty and hippocampal responses: unpredicted or unpredictable? *Neur Networks, 18*(3), 225–230.

Tobia, M. J., Iacovella, V., Davis, B., & Hasson, U. (2012a). Neural systems mediating recognition of changes in statistical regularities. *NeuroImage, 63*(3), 1730–1742. doi:10.1016/j.neuroimage.2012.08.017

Tobia, M. J., Iacovella, V., & Hasson, U. (2012b). Multiple sensitivity profiles to diversity and transition structure in non-stationary input. *NeuroImage, 60*(2), 991–1005. doi:10.1016/j.neuroimage.2012.01.041

Tremblay, P., Baroni, M., & Hasson, U. (2012). Processing of speech and non-speech sounds in the supratemporal plane: auditory input preference does not predict sensitivity to statistical structure. *NeuroImage, 66C*, 318–332. doi:10.1016/j.neuroimage.2012.10.055

Turk-Browne, N. B., Scholl, B. J., Johnson, M. K., & Chun, M. M. (2010). Implicit perceptual anticipation triggered by statistical learning. *J Neurosci, 30*(33), 11177–11187. doi:10.1523/JNEUROSCI.0858–10.2010

van den Broek, P., Rapp, D. N., & Kendeou, P. (2005). Integrating memory-based and constructionist processes in accounts of reading comprehension. *Discourse Processes, 39*, 299–316.

Wager, T. D., & Smith, E. E. (2003). Neuroimaging studies of working memory: a meta-analysis. *Cogn Affect Behav Neurosci, 3*(4), 255–274.

Wallentin, M., Nielsen, A. H., Vuust, P., Dohn, A., Roepstorff, A., & Lund, T. E. (2011a). Amygdala and heart rate variability responses from listening to emotionally intense parts of a story. *NeuroImage, 58*(3), 963–973. doi:10.1016/j.neuroimage.2011.06.077

Wallentin, M., Nielsen, A. H., Vuust, P., Dohn, A., Roepstorff, A., & Lund, T. E. (2011b). BOLD response to motion verbs in left posterior middle temporal gyrus during story comprehension. *Brain Lang, 119*(3), 221–225. doi:10.1016/j.bandl.2011.04.006

Westermann, R., Spies, K., Stahl, G., & Hesse, F. W. (1996). Relative effectiveness and validity of mood induction procedures: a meta-analysis. *Eur J Soc Psychol*, *26*, 557–580.

Whitney, C., Huber, W., Klann, J., Weis, S., Krach, S., & Kircher, T. (2009). Neural correlates of narrative shifts during auditory story comprehension. *NeuroImage*, *47*(1), 360–366. doi:10.1016/j.neuroimage.2009.04.037

Wilson, S. M., Molnar-Szakacs, I., & Iacoboni, M. (2008). Beyond superior temporal cortex: intersubject correlations in narrative speech comprehension. *Cereb Cortex*, *18*(1), 230–242. doi:10.1093/cercor/bhm049

Xu, J., Gannon, P. J., Emmorey, K., Smith, J. F., & Braun, A. R. (2009). Symbolic gestures and spoken language are processed by a common neural system. *Proc Natl Acad Sci USA*, *106*(49), 20 664–20 669. doi:10.1073/pnas.0909197106

Xu, J., Kemeny, S., Park, G., Frattali, C., & Braun, A. (2005). Language in context: emergent features of word, sentence, and narrative comprehension. *NeuroImage*, *25*(3), 1002–1015. doi:10.1016/j.neuroimage.2004.12.013

Zacks, J. M., Braver, T. S., Sheridan, M. A., Donaldson, D. I., Snyder, A. Z., Ollinger, J. M., . . . , Raichle, M. E. (2001). Human brain activity time-locked to perceptual event boundaries. *Nat Neurosci*, *4*(6), 651–655. doi:10.1038/88486

Zacks, J. M., & Swallow, K. M. (2007). Event segmentation. *Curr Dir Psychol Sci*, *16*(2), 80–84. doi:10.1111/j.1467-8721.2007.00480.x

Index

Locators in **bold** refer to figures/tables/plates

Abbreviations in sub-headings
BOLD = blood-oxygen-level dependent signal
NOLB = natural organization of language and the brain